Dear Anne

MOI

THE MAKING OF AN AFRICAN STATESMAN

I hope your memories of Kenya are as fond as mine.

Andrew Morton

Lots of love

Andrew Morton

5th february 1999

Michael O'Mara Books Limited

First published in Great Britain in 1998 by
Michael O'Mara Books Limited
9 Lion Yard
Tremadoc Road
London SW4 7NQ

A CIP catalogue record for this book is available from the British Library

ISBN 1-85479-253-9

1 3 5 7 9 10 8 6 4 2

Plate section designed by Martin Bristow

Designed and typeset by Keystroke, Jacaranda Lodge, Wolverhampton

Printed and bound by Clays Ltd, St Ives plc

Picture Acknowledgements

The publishers are grateful to the following sources for permission to reproduce
photographs in the plate section: The Government of Kenya; Camerapix, Nairobi;
Popperfoto; Reuben Cheshire; Dr David Silverstein.

Whilst every effort has been made to acknowledge all photographs, the publishers
apologise if the name of any contributor has been omitted.

'My brother told me. "Never turn your back on Europe. The deal makers. The contract makers. The map drawers. Never trust Europeans," he said. "Never shake hands with them." But we, oh, we were easily impressed — by speeches and medals and your ceremonies. What have I been doing these last few years? Cutting away, defusing limbs of evil. For what? For this to happen?'

Michael Ondaatje, *The English Patient*

Acknowledgements

I would like to thank His Excellency Daniel T. arap Moi for giving me access to his family, friends and political colleagues, past and present, for the hospitality he showed to me and my family and for sparing the time for me to gain insights into his character and political philosophy.

I would also like to thank Ambrose Adongo, the late Mohamed Amin, Soseter Arassa, Peter Barclay, the Reverend Paul Barnett, Colin Blane, Eric Bomett, Joel Bultut, Henry Cheboiwo, Philemon Chelagat, James and Rebecca Chelimo, Paul Chemirmir, Micah Cheserem, Elizabeth and Reuben Chesire, Bernice Dalziel, Richard Dowden, Arthur Garbutt, Tony Groag, Yusuf Haji, former Chief Justice Robin Hancox EGH, CBE, Sir John Johnson, Geoffrey Kariithi, G. G. Kariuki, James Karugu, John Keen, Dr Julius Kiano, Donald Kimutai, Ben Kipkulei, Bethwell Kiplagat, Raphael Korir, Sally Kosgei, Joshua Kulei, the late Roger and Gill Lambert, Philip Leakey, Dr John Lonsdale, Kenneth Matiba, Reuben Matiso, Professor Philip Mbithi, Peter Mboya, Anna Mudavadi, Alfonse Mullame, Njenga Mungai, Stephen Kalonzo Musyoka, Sheila Murumbi, Shariff Nassir, Geoff and Cathy Nightingale, Lee Njiru, Charles Njonjo, Reverend Danny Njuguna, William ole Ntimama, Jeremiah Nyagah, Philip Ochieng, Raila Odinga, Isaac Omolo Okero, Dr Perez Olindo, William (Bill) Omamo, Patrick Orr, Dr James Sambili, Justice J. F. Shields, Dr David Silverstein, Harbans Singh, Bromley Keables Smith, Gedion Tarus, Louise Tonbridge, Taitta Toweet, John Troon, John Ward, Dr David Western, Bob Whitford and Duncan Willetts.
In particular I would like to thank John Lokorio, Deputy State House Comptroller, for his considerable assistance and insights.
There are other valuable contributions from civil servants, politicians and others who have asked to remain in the background. To them I owe a debt of gratitude.

I would also like to thank my researchers Kate Ricketts, James Cook and Nicky Plummer, my publisher Michael O'Mara for helping me navigate the tricky Kenyan political scene and, of course, my wife Lynne and children Alexandra and Lydia who endured the English winter while I was poolside in Nairobi.

Andrew Morton
August 1998

Contents

Foreword   vi

Introduction   The Naming of Parts   1

Part I   The Making of a Nation

Chapter one   Welcome Home the Cattle   24
Chapter two   By the Banks of the Jordan   33
Chapter three   Conversion at Midnight   43
Chapter four   In the Lions' Den   53
Chapter five   The Road to Independence   60
Chapter six   Struggle for the Soul of Kenya   75

Part II   The Making of a President

Chapter seven   The Man Behind the Mask   90
Chapter eight   The Great Survivor   100
Chapter nine   The Passing Cloud   115
Chapter ten   Pistols at Dawn   133
Chapter eleven   Man in a Hurry   144

Part III   New World, New Order

Chapter twelve   The Strange Death of Bob Ouko   154
Chapter thirteen   High Noon   163
Chapter fourteen   Stop This Nonsense   174
Chapter fifteen   The President and the Showman   189
Chapter sixteen   A Question of Succession   197

Chronology   208

Select Bibliography   211

Index   213

Foreword

The instructions were effective enough, but hardly Ordnance Survey. 'Turn right at Voi, head down a dirt road for seventy kilometres, watch out for a rusty roadsign and then turn into the bush. Follow the dried-up stream for eight kilometres and turn right at a baobab tree. You will find my tented camp two kilometres down the track.'

As a result I spent a fascinating weekend with Philip Leakey, a member of the fractious but formidable family whose work into the birth of mankind revolutionised palaeontology. As we sipped our Tusker beer watching the moon rise over Mount Kilamanjaro, the talk ranged from the murky world of the American Secret Service, his brother Richard, a wildlife warrior turned politician, and then to the personality of President Daniel T. arap Moi. In what was to become a three-year odyssey, I criss-crossed Kenya in a quest for insights into and answers about this enigmatic character. Enigmatic because even though Moi has been in the public spotlight for most of his adult life, little is known of his background or his persona, either in private or in public.

It was a journey that began in May 1995 when I first met the President at State House in Nairobi in a 'get-to-know-you' meeting. I had heard little but ill of him, and he nothing of me. He agreed, albeit reluctantly, to give the project a fair wind. Ironically, while he was perfectly happy to address head-on all the many concerns the West had about Kenya, notably corruption, human rights and tribal violence, he was, after so many years of disguising his character, less willing to reveal the inner recesses of his psyche to a white man with little knowledge of the country's history and less of its politics. The building of trust was a slow and painstaking process, an unlikely relationship between an author known for writing about the intrigues at Buckingham Palace, and a President with a tarnished international reputation. Cynics suggested that I had taken the Kenya shilling simply to burnish his image. The truth was more simple; I wanted a fresh challenge after writing about the British royal family for thirteen years, and Moi was an eminently suitable, even if not an obvious, case for a biography. As for the President, he had hesitatingly agreed with some in his intimate circle that his life should be put on record, so that present and future generations might gain an insight into both the man and the times through which he has lived.

So, how was I to begin? It soon became clear that Moi's life – indeed Kenya's history – is not contained in books and university archives but in the hearts and minds of his people. In a land where the storyteller is revered and folk memory powerful, Kenya is fertile terrain for the exposition of oral history. Moreover, there are still a number of Kenyans alive who were present at the birth of the nation and who witnessed Moi's development from a mission boy to a teacher, a local leader and a national and international politician. They remembered the coming of the colonialist and the missionary, the days of the Mau Mau and the struggle for Independence. Here then was a unique opportunity to visit the well of Kenyan history, to speak to those actually involved with the momentous events which shaped the nation, many of whom had never been interviewed before. So, rather than rely on the interpretations of others, be they academics or journalists, I preferred where possible to listen directly to the nation's living source material, the men and women who had shaped modern Kenya. While this approach yielded a wealth of fascinating material, the constant danger was that I would be drawn into writing a history of Kenya rather than a biography of one of the country's central figures.

Along the way I conducted interviews in rough huts with chickens scratching around my feet, or lying in hot springs by Lake Bogoria, or by the glow of a campfire, the sound of bullfrogs drowning out the voices on my tape recorder. Many interviews were accompanied by a ritual of prayer and the consumption of milky, peppery *chai* that Kenyans insist is infinitely superior to English tea.

For a writer, wearily familiar with the evasions and equivocations of the British ruling elite, it was a refreshing change to interview people who spoke with a disarming frankness and surprising honesty about their President. Indeed, the saccharine of the sycophants was matched in equal measure by the acid of those who had either lost their place in the sun or had always lived in the shadow of power. Most startling was the openness shown by State House officials, the kind of candour which most Whitehall mandarins would shrink from. They were adamant that I should speak to everyone, from Moi's staunchest foes to his most stalwart allies, confident that their man would stand up to the most searching scrutiny. This policy was underlined when I came to formally interview the President at the end of the project. He was at pains to make clear that he had not interfered so as to encourage me to form my own views about him, his career and his country. Indeed in a nation where nothing is as it seems I also spoke to Western journalists who disliked Kenyans, had never been outside Nairobi and had no contacts in the government, human rights lobbyists who admitted they focussed on Kenya because it was relatively free and open and Western academics with little knowledge of KANU. Yet these were the self-same intelligentsia whose opinions and reports form the basis for the world's perspective on Moi and Kenya.

At the same time, one of the first things you learn about Kenyan society, particularly in Nairobi, is that wildfire rumour forms the currency of everyday life, presumably because the bush telegraph, rather than the mass media, has always been the preferred method of communication. Tracking down rumours, particularly about the President, formed an essential core of my work, much of which inevitably led to a series of dead ends. So, for example, I spent much time with John Ward, the indefatigable father of Julie, who was brutally murdered in the Maasai Mara game park in 1988. One of the more lurid stories surrounding her unsolved murder was that a number of those close to the President had been involved, something which therefore implied a degree of presidential connivance in her death. After much pushing at creaking doors to find the facts of the case it could be proved beyond reasonable doubt that the story, seized on with undisguised relish by the international media, was a well-constructed fiction.

This became a familiar conclusion; that the most graphic stories concerning the President were simply grisly inventions, promoted by his political enemies and amplified by the Western media which, with few means of verifying the authenticity of claims, simply rehashed these fabrications. As Moi's biographer I was left with a problem. By publishing a detailed rebuttal of every rumour swirling around the President, be they stories of the dreaded Romanian Securitate training the Kenyan intelligence service, or of Moi suffering from AIDS, the book would cross the boundary from biography into public relations. The Julie Ward story, for instance, which took up much time, was a dead end, shedding more light on the workings of Kenyan society and of the international media than on the President. Instead, I focused on those major stories, such as the murder of Foreign Minister Bob Ouko, the coming of multi-partyism, and the Rift Valley clashes, which had made a direct impact on the President, and attempted to explore his thoughts and feelings about these events, as well as his reactions to them.

Given the fallibility of memory, as far as possible I cross-checked accounts with other interviews and any documentary evidence that was available. The reports and observations of colonial District Commissioners, held in the vaults at the National Archives in Nairobi, were particularly useful in painting a portrait of life in the Rift Valley during the early part of the century, as were the accounts of the early missionaries. Similarly, the papers of former Chief Justice Robin Hancox gave a vivid insight into the difficulties of administering justice in a developing nation.

As the work progressed it became clear that the body of evidence, both oral and written, rather contradicted what might be called the Kikuyu and the colonial theories of Kenyan history. The former hold that the colony was liberated thanks only to the endeavours of the Mau Mau fighters, that the period under Jomo Kenyatta was a golden era and that, thanks to Moi, everything since then has been a slide into corruption and incompetence. This view is complemented by the colonial view of history which regards Kenya as a Garden of Eden handed over by a benevolent, even charitable, British government at Independence, and subsequently ruined by the natives. It is a belief manifested in the 'Nanny-knows-best' attitude of the donor nations towards not only Kenya, but other developing nations as well, using these countries as templates for drastic experiments in social and economic engineering. Not surprisingly, my own interpretation of the place of President Moi in Kenyan history, based on the plethora of evidence accumulated over three years, is somewhat at variance with conventional analysis.

When I first approached this task, I attempted to be as open-minded as possible about the President, his country and its history. It is my sincere wish that those reading this volume will approach this book in the same spirit.

Introduction

The Naming of Parts

The key to the conundrum that is modern Kenya, and to the enigma of the character of the country's second president, lies in the simplicity of a name – Daniel Toroitich arap Moi. It is a name that betrays the tensions at the heart of the man and the nation. His first name, Daniel, speaks of his own stern upbringing in mission schools and reflects the profound impact the arrival of Christianity had not only on his own tiny clan, the Tugen from the remote hills of the mighty Rift Valley, but on the spiritual culture of the forty-odd disparate tribes which make up Kenya. At the beginning of the century the Christian and the British colonialist walked side by side. As a growing boy Moi, like the country he would one day rule, was imbued with the language, the values and the culture of an alien nation from a distant continent, a country whose rule lasted less than a century but whose influences moulded modern Kenya. The President, almost in spite of himself, is an Anglophile to his fingertips.

When he wakes shortly before dawn, Moi switches on the radio to listen to the BBC's World Service; every week videos of BBC TV's Sunday religious programme, *Songs of Praise*, are flown out to him in the diplomatic bag; he buys his suits from Savile Row; while he named two of his children, Doris Elizabeth and Philip, after the Queen and the Duke of Edinburgh. On his private visits to London he becomes downcast at seeing so many churches neglected, once remarking with sorrow during a trip to Westminster Abbey that he and his entourage were the only worshippers in this bastion of British Christianity.

His second name, Toroitich, meaning 'bring home the cattle,' is rich in tribal resonance, reflecting the rural, semi-pastoral traditions of his Tugen clan – part of the larger Kalenjin tribal grouping – and the deeply rooted role of cattle in his culture. It is a name that echoes the days, not so long ago, when animals mattered much more than money, land or crops, and when manliness, conflict and status were defined by the cattle which featured so prominently in a tribe's time-honoured ceremonies and rituals. The name is symbolic of the tensions and tussles engendered by the clash of a colonial, Christian, capitalist culture with a traditional tribal society, tensions which continue to be played out in the hearts and minds of most Kenyans, and which are a key to the understanding of the character of the President.

His last names refer to his family, arap Moi meaning 'son of Moi' – and it is to family, clan and tribe, rather than to the state, that many Kenyans still owe their ultimate loyalty. From birth, most, particularly rural Africans of Moi's age group, learned to place the collective good of the tribe above their own needs; to defer instinctively to the will of the chief or the elders' councils; to respect and value the wisdom of patriarchs; to arrive at decisions by consensus and compromise whilst implacably, and even violently, treating with those who opposed the wishes of the tribe. This morality is being inexorably and rapidly eroded by the continual onslaught of Western values, which place personal happiness above the well-being of the group, and individual rights over the needs of the many. This philosophical struggle is central to any understanding both of Moi's political thinking and of the history of Kenya since Independence.

In the President's name, then, lie many of the unresolved conflicts, tensions and stresses of modern Kenya, emblematic of the continual shifting balance in Moi's heart and mind between his tribal roots, his Christian doctrine, his colonial background and his African heritage. He was born when British authority in Kenya was at its height, was one of the pioneer students of the Christian mission movement, and was among the first generation of African teachers. Politically, he is the longest serving Member of Parliament, having acted as one of the squabbling Kenyan midwives to the birth of a nation, and later having helped, first as Vice-President and then as President, the bawling, needy infant to progress and mature. It is no exaggeration to say that the history of the nation flows through the veins of the tall, commanding figure of Daniel Toroitich arap Moi. He is the personification of Kenya in the twentieth century.

For Moi, once described as a 'giraffe' because of his far-sightedness, the modern and colonial are inextricably linked in his personal experience and his political apprenticeship. He has lived through the time when the word of the location chief was law, and when the colonial District Commissioner was a distant but ever-present threat; the years of Mau Mau fighting; the struggle to release Jomo Kenyatta, Kenya's first President; the striving to overthrow British rule and the formation of the Kenya African National Union (KANU) which he now leads. Moi's experience is unique, especially as the overwhelming majority of Kenyans were not even born when the Union Jack last flew over State House in Nairobi. The country has only been independent for thirty-five years, since the Beatles topped the charts with 'She Loves You', less than half the President's lifetime.

While the settlers, colloquially known as the 'Kenya cowboys,' may nowadays have retreated to their suburban watering holes in Karen and the Ngong Hills, the days when the white man reigned supreme are so close one can still touch and smell them. At State House in Nairobi it is easy to drift back forty years or so to the days of colonial rule. Afternoon tea is still served by bow-tied waiters from ageing silver teapots engraved with the initials of King George VI, English hunting prints decorate the walls, the plumbing might still be described as sturdy, colonial and functional. The red plush-lined balcony from which the Governor gave his annual address to leading members of the settler community remains, as does an elderly and out-of-tune grand piano, another relic from the colonial era. 'I really must get round to Africanising this place,' says the President, slightly embarrassed. A large wooden giraffe in the entrance hall, David Shepherd elephant prints in cheap warped frames, silver-capped ivory tusks set either side of the ubiquitous red carpet, pastel drawings by Joy Adamson of tribesmen in traditional dress and, strangely, in one waiting room, an odd display of plastic African dolls, some with arms and legs missing – all give the sense that the house has a new owner who has never really got around to sorting out the clutter left behind. That sense is symbolic, for while the black, red and green stripes of the Kenyan flag may flutter outside, or the odd portrait of the President decorate the walls, the smell of the past lingers on.

As a one-time connoisseur of palaces – the Gulf State potentates certainly have a gilt complex – I was surprised when I first wandered around State House at the confusion of periods and the threadbare, down at heel decoration. This lack of ostentation was perplexing, given published reports of the cult of personality surrounding Moi, and that, as one of Africa's remaining 'Big Men', he has allegedly salted much of the content of his country's treasury into personal offshore accounts. One expected the kind of conspicuous consumption and extravagance consonant with such an image. Yet the rather faded feeling one encounters in Nairobi is mirrored up-country. Both State Lodge, Eldoret, and State House, Nakuru, have the air of public buildings gone slightly to seed, places where the roses need pruning and the furnishings have seen much better days. Indeed, for many years the President's home on his private estate at Kabarak, just outside Nakuru, was a similiarly modest establishment, a wood and stone one-bedroom farmhouse with a corrugated-tin roof which he had built himself. In the late 1980s a number of close friends, feeling that the building was inappropriate for the nation's leader – especially as the roof leaked – organised a private subscription to finance a more fitting presidential home. Its solid, unfussy but imposing style is characteristic of many of the red-tiled schools and Nyayo hospital wards which Moi has had a hand in building.

Inside it is decorated as though it were an official residence; miniature national flags of many countries, silver-capped ivory tusks, ostrich eggs, all feature in the porticoed entrance hall, while other presents given to him during his numerous official trips around the world decorate some of the rooms. Just as the strong, masculine lines, solid construction, large comfortable rooms, and ascetic decoration of the house indicate an owner who eschews fussy and ostentatious display, so the formality of the interior is further evidence of a man who has little time either for self-aggrandisement or for the materialism of modern living.

At the same time, the plethora of official presents gives few clues as the private taste or personality of the President. The character of the man, rather than his official persona, is elusive. Only in his library is a little of the individual uncovered. While there are biographies, mainly presentation copies, of international figures, the most striking feature is the number of well-thumbed bibles that fill the shelves. Before he retires each evening Moi reads from the Holy Scriptures, particularly favouring the New Testament.

Thus first impressions are of a serious, even austere, man, not much given to the fripperies and diversions of life, a man dedicated to his Christian faith, and having few material needs or ambitions; a country-lover of simple tastes and demands who enjoys nothing more than to sit under the trees on his estate at Kabarak, drinking tea and chatting with farmworkers or anyone else who happens to be around. It is noticeable that at times of stress or political turmoil it is to the rural constituency, his natural home, that Moi retreats. There is also a guileless, almost other-worldly quality, akin to the lifestyle of a studious man of the cloth, about his private life. As an example, when a combine harvester on his 3,000-acre farm broke down he and his farm manager spent an agitated day ringing around to find a spare part – it never occurred to the President to use his authority to solve the problem more quickly. This unworldly diffidence – he has often been described as a humble man, although he can also be quite vain in a very male,

African way – comes across on first meeting. Many who have enjoyed an audience with him have described their conversation as like talking to one's father.

Yet there is no disguising his authority. He is a tall man, a strapping six-footer, with the healthy build of a man who was a keen sportsman in his youth. When he speaks – his gravelly bass voice reminiscent of Louis Armstrong – he uses his arms to make great arching gestures to illustrate a point. On public occasions he is immaculately dressed, a trademark rose in his buttonhole (a trait copied from the early Scottish missionaries); off duty, however, he will generally wear a blazer and grey slacks. Meeting him in private, the talk is invariably of politics: for example, the situation in the Middle East; the West's hypocritical approach to democracy in oil-free Africa and in the oil-rich Middle East; the conflagration in central Africa.

Amidst these stern preoccupations there is a place for laughter, particularly among those of his Kalenjin age group. Every few days his old schoolfriend Paul Chemirmir, a jovial character who favours pork-pie hats and loud checked jackets, drops in to see the President at State House in Nairobi, tells him a few jokes, swaps a couple of stories and then wanders off. 'Moi has a great sense of humour,' observes Philip Leakey, a member of the famous Kenyan settler family, and once a minister in Moi's Cabinet. 'When he is in the company of men, particularly his own tribe, he will really let rip. I've seen him laughing until his ribs ached. This is a side of him never seen in public.'

The side that is on show, particularly on state occasions, is that of the African chief, stiff, unsmiling, proudly aware of his position. His personal physician, the Chicago-born heart surgeon David Silverstein, describes the transformation:

> When you are travelling overseas you will see the change in Moi before your eyes. Just before the plane lands the casual man who's been in rolled-up shirtsleeves, chatting to everyone, will suddenly smarten up. He brushes his hair, puts on a smart jacket and pins the presidential rose to his buttonhole. His bearing will stiffen and he becomes the President and head of state, exuding power and authority.

Just as Kenyatta carried a fly whisk as a sign of his authority, so Moi clasps a silver-topped ivory stick, known as a *rungu*, as a mark of leadership. Like the Queen's handbag, it is an essential prop. During a visit to the Commonwealth Summit in Melbourne, Australia, in 1981, he accidentally dropped and broke the ivory *rungu* as he walked down the steps of his aircraft during a stopover in Los Angeles. He was so disconcerted to lose this essential prop that a replacement had to be specially flown out.

The upright carriage, seemingly immobile features and stern countenance contribute to an image, certainly in the West, of President Moi as one of the last of the old-style African tyrants, a dictator as corrupt as he is malevolent. In the world of the sound-bite and the photo-call, Moi's bearing as a traditional African chief fares badly, especially when compared to the affable style of leadership evinced by South Africa's President, Nelson Mandela. So often his physical inflexibility is translated as political obduracy, the body language of the man seeming to signify an unbending and rigid leadership. His hesitant spoken

English underscores in the minds of his critical Western audience that this is a man clinging to power by means other than intellectual ability. While his unwillingness to explain his actions and those of his government to the media, unlike his articulate neighbour, Uganda's President Yoweri Museveni, merely add to a damning picture.

Just as Moi's public image is unfashionable, so too his political style and philosophy have fallen out of vogue, especially since the collapse of Communism. But while it is easy to dismiss him as a corrupt dictator the core of argument in this biography, is that precisely because he does not conform to this easy cliché of an African leader, his life and character beg more difficult but ultimately rewarding questions: about the nature of the relationship of the Western world to Africa, and to Kenya in particular; about the peculiar problems of ruling an emerging nation; about the hybrid nature of Kenya's elite; above all, about the retiring character, public and private, of Daniel Toroitich arap Moi.

In order to appreciate any portrait of Kenya's President it is worth looking at the canvas on which it is painted. The current Western view of Moi is coloured by a background dominated by the prevailing global political and economic orthodoxy, that of the 'New World Order.' The ending of the bipolar world, and with it the triumph of capitalism over Communism, has radically altered the stance adopted by the developed nations toward the developing world. No longer does America shore up corrupt regimes simply because they had been bulwarks against Communist Russia. Instead, there is now a strictly applied link between the introduction of multi-party democracy, civic rights, and economic liberalisation in a given developing country, and the continuation of donor aid and 'soft' loans to that country. So far, so noble.

The fact that democratic capitalism is now effectively the only workable ideology in the developed world has, however, led to the fallacy that it is the perfect model for all countries, all societies, at whatever stage of political and economic development. It is a continuation of the Whig theory of history, that the democratic capitalist nation state is the ultimate goal of government, rather than a makeshift Eurocentric system that has fostered suffering and war as much as it has promoted individual freedoms. In the years following the victory of the West over Marxism the obvious defects in free-market economics – for example, that capitalism magnifies existing inequalities in society – have simply been ignored, while the opening up of markets in Kenya, and Africa as a whole, have resulted in savage social consequences. Like the colonialists of a century ago, the donor countries have insisted that the natives keep swallowing the bitter economic medicine.

At the same time, the coming of the New World Order has seen two competing models of democratic capitalism, the American and the Japanese. While both are highly successful economically, they have achieved that success from differing cultural approaches. The American model instinctively insists on individual rights at the expense of collective responsibility, and short-term personal happiness above the long-term common good, as well as manifesting a reliance on market-orientated economics and a suspicion of government intervention.

By contrast, the Japanese place greater emphasis on deference to authority, on communal success at the expense of individual gratification, and on the significance of education and family values as sources of social unity. At the same time a substantial contribution to Japanese economic success has been strategic government intervention, the protection of domestic industries through high tariffs and other measures. This support for local industrial saplings has enabled them to survive the cruel sharp winds of economic competition and grow into some of the most successful multinational corporations in the world.

While it might be effectively argued that the Asian model of democratic capitalism is more appropriate to Africa, it is the American pattern of economic liberalism and democratic individualism which has inevitably dominated policy among Western donor countries. Underpinning the assumption that the American economic and political world view is the model to which all nations should aspire is the firm conviction that it is morally just; truth and justice marching arm in arm with McDonald's and Coca-Cola. Nowadays what is good for General Motors is not just good for the United States but for the rest of the world, a perspective that informs the work of the majority of Western journalists, aid agencies and human-rights groups. Those nations which depart from this perceived norm of preferred behaviour are seen to have transgressed not just economically and politically, but morally. They have sinned against the New World Order. In the new orthodoxy, little account is taken of the impact of untrammelled free-market economics on fledgeling industries in developing countries, nor is there any debate about the competing virtues of human rights or civic rights and economic rights. So, for example, the limits of any discussion about Kenya's stifled economic development are defined in terms of individual corruption, with scant reference to the impact of paying one-third of the country's gross national product – the equivalent to the profits from tourism – in debt relief to overseas banks.

While it would be foolish to ignore the pernicious effects of corruption on Kenya's body politic, it must be acknowledged that corruption was there before Moi, and that it will be there after him. One of the lessons of history is that corruption accompanies the formation of every elite during the birth of a nation. In Kenya, a nation in which every Cabinet member can still recall the day when they could afford to buy their first pair of shoes, there is a fertile administrative and cultural soil in which individual greed can flourish. In the early years after Independence government rather than private enterprise provided the bulk of domestic investment; civil servants are allowed to run their own businesses, which creates a conflict of interest; while the Africanisation programme of the 1960s enriched numerous provincial and district commissioners, as well as politicians, when business concerns were transferred to Kenyan entrepreneurs. Contrary to the prevailing Western view, senior administrators who served under both Kenyatta and Moi agree that corruption in the civil service, and the opportunities for it, have been substantially curtailed under the latter's rule.

While it is corruption that hits the headlines, the question of competence equally vexes the President. All too often he finds that his instructions are not carried out and his plans come to naught. Kenya is now a populous, complex society and he recognises that he cannot do everything, be everywhere. Inevitably, as the years tick by his prodigious energy is waning. He must rely more and more on able, effective lieutenants, men he can trust. So often, however, he is let down. Far too many Cabinet ministers, judges, police officers, generals and others throughout the administrative, legal and military hierarchy are simply not up to their jobs, either through incompetence, inability, lethargy, or drunkenness. It is an issue he continually complains about both publicly and in private.

For example, when in February 1997 he addressed a crowd at Chepkorio in the Rift Valley on the issue of forestry he made Kenya's Forestry Director stand up before the throng while he rebuked him for allowing foresters, whose job is to conserve the environment, quite improperly to own their own sawmills. This inevitably caused a conflict between their personal profit and public duty; Moi threatened to sack those who abused their positions. Here was a classic example of a situation where the line manager – that is to say the Forestry Director – should have been issuing directives, rather than the head of state. Replicate this issue a hundred thousand times and you have some idea of the scope of the difficulties facing any leader attempting to administer a rapidly developing African country. It helps explain why someone like Moi's political confidant Nicholas Biwott, unpopular both inside and outside State House, has kept his place in the sun for so long. In the hard-headed day-to-day business of government, Biwott is a heavy hitter, a man who actually gets things done, enacts directives, sees through policies. Loathed by many, there are others, seeing at first hand the practical problems Moi faces simply in running the country, who appreciate Biwott's continuing presence in government as a miracle of effectiveness in a soporific system.

This complex issue of graft also involves a delicate tribal and cultural equation. When Moi succeeded Kenyatta he decided that rather than prosecute elite members of the majority Kikuyu tribe led by Kenyatta, who had waxed fat on the fruits of independence, he should declare a general unspoken amnesty in the interests of nation-building and reconciliation. Moreover, taking action to snuff out corruption can bring terrifying repercussions. When, in 1996, Moi ordered the removal of the head of Mombasa port, Simon Mkalla, because of an alleged car-import scam, members of Mkalla's coastal tribe rioted in the streets in protest at the humbling of one of their leaders. As Michael Blundell, one of the early settlers and an architect of independence, once observed:

> In the eyes of most Africans, high position enables the holder thereof to benefit first himself, then his family, then his clansmen, his tribe and lastly the people of his country as a whole. Indeed, we must remember that up to 1840, every great house in the United Kingdom was built by an individual who had a major office of profit under the crown or was in the circle of the king's friends.

In the West it is always easier to castigate the transgressions of greedy natives rather than examine the roots, and the morality, of an economic system under which the world's poorest people make the rich richer. As Peter Eigen, chairman of Transparency International, observed in his 1997 report on global corruption: 'I urge people to recognise that a large share of corruption is the explicit product of multinational corporations . . . using bribery to buy contracts in the developing world.' In a continent whose debt is greater than its total economic output, the challenge facing the United Nations and donor countries is to recognise that the debt burden and some of the International Monetary Fund (IMF) and World Bank economic prescriptions are human-rights issues which have a direct impact on the social and economic well-being of millions of Africans. A decade ago Kenya introduced IMF-endorsed 'Structural Adjustment' policies which liberalised the agricultural sector. Now the country is forced to import foodstuffs from the selfsame countries, like America, which imposed that change, while Kenyan farmers who changed from food to cash crops now find themselves subject to the whims of buyers from American multinationals. It is a system which benefits the industrialised world at the expense of the primary producer, and it could be argued that if the West had promoted economic and social issues with the same zeal and commitment with which it supported political pluralism and economic liberalisation, then Kenya might now be in better shape. As Professor Katama Mkangi has pointed out: 'The 1997 famine in Kenya is a good example of implementing foreign-imposed policies without clearly understanding their long-term consequences.' It is now recognised, belatedly, that most countries undergoing West-imposed Structural Adjustment Programmes have suffered devastating effects on the environment, a drastic decline in incomes and dramatically lower spending on education and health. At the same time SAPs degrade national governments by sidelining their responsibility to provide for people's needs.

None the less, the prevailing orthodoxy places the President firmly in the dock, condemned for conflicts with the donor nations over the pace of economic and political reform, for his warnings about the dire consequences of multi-party politics in a country where tribal loyalties often suffocate national allegiance, for his emphasis on conciliation and consensus, which harks back to tribal virtues, but which sits oddly in a world promoting an adversarial legal and political system. He is a sinner still to be redeemed before the altar of the New World Order. In fact, often all Moi is guilty of is defending the uniquely African traditions and values of his people, of guarding the sovereignty of his country, and of attempting, albeit sometimes hesitantly and awkwardly, to define a specific Kenyan approach to the problems and issues facing a new nation.

This defence cuts little ice with his international antagonists, who point to a deafening chorus of articulate and principled domestic criticism, be it from lawyers, church leaders or opposition politicians, to underline the case against Moi. It should be understood, however, that tribal self-interest, and not just a noble belief in wider democracy, has also informed the actions of the domestic opposition to President Moi, particularly in the turbulent embrace of the multi-party state, and that tribalism is a feature of Kenyan political life often overlooked by the West. It is no coincidence that members of the numerous and well-educated Kikuyu tribe, who enjoyed the richest fruits from the tree of independence under Kenyatta, now form the vanguard of Moi's enemies.

That Moi takes so little trouble to state his case or encourage others to speak on his behalf says much about the nature of the man. For much of his life he has survived by disguise, a characteristic that means that he instinctively shies away from self-revelation. As a child he silently submitted to the routine of the mission; as a young man he stoically accepted the insults of white teachers and the injustice of colonial rule; as a Legislative Council representative he kept his composure as racist insults flew; as Vice-President under Jomo Kenyatta he displayed imperturbable sangfroid in the face of physical assault and verbal abuse. This patience brought its own reward, but there was a downside, for even in the early days as President he was dismissed by the ruling Kikuyu elite as 'the passing cloud', a man unfitted to the highest office. 'He never showed his true feelings, his face was always a mask,' recalls a former colleague; another perceptive observer describes this quality differently: 'His strength lies in his apparent weakness.'

While these qualities of fortitude, composure and self-control, which have now become reflexive, have enabled him to endure, the Kenyan President is a biographer's nightmare, happy to let you get near, but not close. Like certain other heads of state he has mastered the art of selective deafness, as well as the skill of ignoring or diverting any question which may trespass into the realms of his personal thoughts and feelings. It is a characteristic ruefully admired by those in his circle. During his presidency he has given fewer than a handful of interviews, while published compilations of his speeches and a book expressing his 'Nyayo' philosophy (which means 'following in Kenyatta's footsteps') of love, peace and unity, reveal little about the man, even though they give a degree of insight into his political thinking.

Perhaps because serving his nation is now second nature, he rarely, if ever, thinks of himself before his country. He has been on public parade for so long, his day-to-day life a rigorous round of meetings and audiences, that Moi the President and politician has subsumed the personality of Moi the man. When he took a short holiday in Israel in 1996, there was a collective sigh of relief from those close to him who witness the gruelling schedule he sets himself. It was his first break in more than forty years of public life.

Decades of self-sacrifice have taken their toll on his personal life. In 1974 he divorced his wife Lena after nearly twenty-five years of marriage. The hectic years spent criss-crossing the country in support of Kenyatta, coupled with Lena Moi's reluctance to immerse herself in the political world, finally became too heavy a burden. Family friends say that the final break-up came after Lena refused to dance with Kenyatta during a social event at the Rift Valley Technical College. As an uncompromising Christian she believed that dancing was sinful, but the insult to the President gravely embarrassed Moi. 'It was for the best that they parted,' says the Reverend Paul Barnett of the African Inland Mission, who has known the couple for fifty years. In accordance with his tribal tradition – the language has no word for divorce – Lena Moi was accommodated in Moi's family home at Kabimoi in Baringo District, his constituency, and has been supported by him ever since. Even today she keeps a room of the house as a shrine to her former husband, believing that when he sets aside the cares of high office he will return to her.

The couple have eight children: Jennifer, the eldest, was born in 1952; followed by Jonathan, well known as a rally driver; Raymond, a director of the troubled Kenya Creameries Corporation; John Mark; Doris Elizabeth and her twin, Philip, a former army officer; and Gideon, a successful polo-playing businessman who, among his other ventures, is a director of the *East African Standard* newspaper. Finally, there is an adopted daughter, June, the adoption of children from poor families being very much a part of Tugen culture.

Since both parents were educated in the tenets of the conservative African Inland Mission, it was natural that the children were brought up in a Christian household, although the boys did undergo traditional Tugen circumcision rituals when they reached puberty. Theirs was a strict upbringing, Moi wanting his children to follow his lead and become straightforward, honest, sober and self-disciplined citizens. While he tried to make time for his growing family it was inevitable that, with politics consuming his life, he saw them less often than he would have liked. This combination of absence and sternness produced the inevitable backlash, and as adolescents the boys rebelled against their father's austere moral code; indeed, on at least one occasion they were disciplined by senior members of the Presidential Guard. Ironically, when Philip Moi visited his father at State House, Nairobi, recently he was talking about the need for the *wananchi* (the people) to be honest and disciplined. While the President did not actually roll his eyes heavenwards, he did tell his son: 'It's good that you have realised this at long last.'

Unlike the Kenyatta clan, there is little sense that Moi is using his position to create a family dynasty or to encourage his offspring to follow him into politics. If anything, believing that his boys do not have the toughness or stamina for the hurly-burly of Kenyan political life, he has done his level best to deter them. Moi believes also, as is customary among the Kalenjin tribe, that a man should prove himself and win the respect of others before he can become a leader.

Just as importantly, he feels that his children should not exploit the family name for their own advantage. During one episode involving his son Philip, the President sent a memo to various government departments saying that they should not give him preferential treatment in the award of business contracts simply because of who he was. It is, however, simply wishful thinking to expect the boys, now all involved in various business projects, not to take advantage of the opportunities which come their way, or to believe that others will not cling to their coat-tails.

There is a sense that, in spite of his high hopes, Moi has had little joy from his family. Those who know the family well observe that, with the possible exception of Gideon and June, the President feels disappointed and rather let down by his children. It is noticeable that, in contrast to the days when Kenyatta was President, his family rarely appear at formal public functions, such as Madaraka Day, to give him support. 'He is quite a lonely man, although he is always surrounded by people,' says a friend who has known him since his days as a teacher. This observation is tempered by the recognition that in recent times he has had great joy from his growing brood of grandchildren.

Others believe that his bachelor lifestyle has enabled him to focus more clearly and with greater dedication on the problems facing the country, rather than being distracted by family concerns. His is a world where men predominate; Moi is naturally more at ease in male company, particularly of his own age, than with women. In the presence of women he is courteous, charming, punctilious, but ultimately uncomfortable. As one female diplomat put it: 'He's a sweetie. The kind of guy you could take home to meet your mother.' However, women's groups who seek audiences with him often feel that while he listens to their concerns with patience and understanding, he puts the issues from his mind as soon as they have left the room.

The dominance of men in Kenyan society strikes many Western commentators as old-fashioned, and Moi and other African leaders are routinely described as behaving like medieval monarchs, their word law, their actions wilful, their every gesture lauded by a sychophantic male court. While this description may enable Westerners, who consistently judge Africa by the standards of their own culture, to understand Moi as he appears to Western eyes, it is ultimately misleading. More accurately and appropriately, Moi's behaviour conforms to that of a traditional African chief, specifically a man whose background and beliefs have been shaped by the culture of his Kalenjin tribal group. In Kalenjin culture the tribal chief did not have absolute authority: decisions were made after consulting, often for days, with other elders, and action taken only after convincing the rest of the clan to follow the plan in question. At the same time generosity and hospitality, especially towards guests, was by time-honoured tradition the expected behaviour of the chief, who would often be given additional cattle or goats to enable him to cope with the burden of leadership. Thus hospitality and accessibility formed part of a political process which, as has been said, placed a high value on conciliation and consensus.

Vibrant echoes of that Kalenjin tribal culture may be seen intertwined with his Christian roots in the President's daily behaviour. Unlike Kenyatta, who rarely ate with others, Moi shares his every meal and virtually every waking moment with his entourage – State House officials, civil servants, loca' politicians and other guests, from farmworkers to diplomats. He routinely eats breakfast at seven in the morning with thirty others, discussing the issues of the day. One morning it will be the cheap price and high quality of South African wheat imports, another the latest antics of the Opposition. By then, though, he will have been working for several hours, formulating or adjusting his views after listening to the BBC World Service and watching CNN, conducting a number of audiences or telephone conversations with senior domestic and international figures such as the British High Commissioner. Throughout the day he will be seeing delegations and individuals in a constant whirl of meetings and audiences. Invariably these engagements, each of which should last around twenty minutes, overrun the time allotted to them. 'Come and greet Mzee,' a member of his entourage will say to a new arrival, and within a matter of moments there is the familiar outstretched hand, a few words of welcome, before the President moves on.

Moi's style is in sharp contrast to that of his predecessor, who preferred watching traditional dancing to glad-handing, keeping audiences brief, brisk and businesslike. Whereas Kenyatta enjoyed the backing of the majority Kikuyu tribe, Moi has no such advantage. By instinct and design, his whirlwind daily round not only tests the social and political temperature, but it also brings many into the embrace of the tribal chief, forging a sense, however superficial, of extended family and of allegiance. During his punishing visits around the country – he will think nothing of driving 1,000 miles a day along tortuous roads on 'meet-the-people' tours – his style is accessible and spontaneous, stopping to address a gaggle of countryfolk, to talk to a score of children, or to buy vegetables from hawkers. His actions are often unplanned, off the cuff, his manner approachable, and this readiness to meet his people contrasts with the strictly timetabled, remote routine of many Western heads of state. Furthermore, when he speaks in his native Kalenjin or Swahili, rather than in English, he becomes a different person:

'I don't write my speeches,' he says, 'they must come from the heart.' He plays his audience like a skilful musician, by turns humorous, then serious; sometimes he will even break into song. 'Unlike some leaders who grow aloof and distant when they have been in power for years he has never disowned his past nor changed his character,' says his lifelong friend Paul Chemirmir. It is one reason why it rankles with Moi so much when he is described as a dictator. 'I can walk down the street among my people. They know me,' he says.

Sometimes during a stopover he will call out from his trademark blue open-topped Mercedes, 'Who is your leader, who is your leader?', before handing out a gift of cash to be dispersed among the *wananchi* (the people) to help pay for school fees. He observes that in rural areas a recognised leader will always step forward, but in the cities there is no such social hierarchy, a sign of the breakdown in traditional groupings. Moi's practice of handing out money has been criticised domestically. KANU politician Peter Okondo complained: 'This bad habit of the President's is a bad example; it undermines rectitude in the minds of children. Free money is a bad concept.'

Such actions are, however, a public expression of the hospitality expected of the chief, as well as of his own Christian charity. Instances of his concern, unbidden and unpublicised, abound; he paid for the South African ANC leader Oliver Tambo to have hospital treatment in Sweden following his release from detention; paid to send the Chief Justice's secretary abroad for cancer tests; and has ensured that dozens of youngsters have continued their education by paying their school fees as well as using his own finances to build many schools and churches all over Kenya. Egerton College lecturer Dr Edward Sambili, whose father, a peasant farmer, died when he was young, would have had to give up his education if Moi had not stepped in. Not only did he pay to send Sambili, who comes from a family of thirteen, and his wife to study abroad, but he made him a gift of land and money to build a house. 'The President is a kind man who helps those trying to achieve success,' says Sambili.

Critical observers say that the President's largesse is simply a partial redistribution of the money he has plundered from *wananchi* during his time in government. Walk into any bar in Nairobi and the stories of Moi's vast wealth are trotted out, focusing mainly on his overseas bank accounts in Austria and Switzerland where, it is said, he has squirrelled away billions of shillings. It is an allegation *The Times* correspondent Sam Kiley was happy to repeat, when he wrote that Moi was 'deeply unpopular having amassed a fortune to rival the $9 billion (£5.6 billion) held by his friend Mr Mobutu' (then the President of Zaire).

In a country which would be rich if rumour were cash, these insinuations are treated with bewildered distress by Joshua Kulei, a senior State House official who administers Moi's business holdings.

I can say categorically that the President has no bank accounts overseas. He lives his life by example and is always encouraging people to leave their money here and invest in this country. As you know, the President has simple needs and lives a simple life, he is not an extravagant man. That is not his character. He has been a businessman for many years. While he has earned money through his businesses his main income comes from his farm at Kabarak.

During the 1950s Moi became one of the first African entrepreneurs, combining trade with teaching. He dealt in animal skins, paraffin and other goods, as well as owning his own *posho* (corn meal) mill and general store. Later he joined Reuben Chesire to start a transport company in the Rift Valley, selling his shares in the late 1970s, and he now has a substantial holding in Siginon, a transport company with more than forty trucks. During the 1970s he obtained a loan to buy his 3,000-acre farm at Kabarak, and over the years he has amassed a decent portfolio of business in the Rift Valley, including a petrol station at Nakuru, a tea and coffee estate in Kericho, and a sisal farm, as well as holding a number of directorships of banks and companies in the Rift Valley.

While he has benefited by being one of the first African businessmen in a land brimming with opportunity, Moi's personal wealth, at least during the 1970s, was relatively modest. At that time he was forced to borrow cash from a fellow MP to make ends meet when the Kikuyu elite, who wanted to oust him from the vice-presidency, tried to bankrupt him, knowing that he had acted as guarantor for many people who were buying land but who did not have the funds to underwrite those loans. Essentially he is a man who sees business opportunities (he is constantly urging his staff to use their talents to invest and so enrich the country), without being a particularly adroit or astute entrepreneur. As far as Moi is concerned, business is as much a public service, bringing jobs and infrastructure to a locality, as it is a means of personal advancement. As he says: 'When you are alive you work hard and exploit the land for your own benefit and the benefit of the people. When you are dead and the earth is piled on top of you, you don't have a second chance.'

This pragmatic nationalism, combined with his Christian morality and the tribal culture surrounding the chief, are key elements in understanding not just the man, but also the politician. Moi's political thinking was forged during his apprenticeship in the 1950s and early 1960s, a time when he, together with Jomo Kenyatta, Tom Mboya, and other leaders, believed that the government's strength came from the masses and that it was only through national unity, in the form of a one-party state, that the immense problems of building a nation could be overcome. Moi says often: 'What is the point of having the vote if you cannot read? What use is democracy to a man with no shoes?' While these sentiments have been interpreted as those of a tyrant riding roughshod over the democratic process, in reality they reflect his awareness of the realities of life in Kenya, balancing economic rights against the more fashionable human or civic rights. As the Attorney-General, Amos Wako, argues: 'There is a linkage between democracy and development that encompasses economic and social rights. Without democracy, there can be no peace . . . Without development there can be no sustainable democracy.'

At the same time, Moi tries to articulate, albeit without much success in the international arena, an African perspective on the issues of governance which beset Kenya. He may admire the West, but he does not believe that its culture is always appropriate for his country. 'Kenya is unique in its own way,' he remarked during an afternoon visit to a school in the Rift Valley. 'We in Kenya live differently from others. We eat ugali [a thick corn-meal porridge] with our hands, something that if we did it in London would be considered a disgraceful thing to do.' As an example the introduction of the queue-voting system, which was to prove so disastrous, was President Moi's attempt to bring to Kenyan politics a democratic procedure which had its roots in the country's history. 'The West think that a size 46 suit will fit all men,' he says. 'But all men, all nations are different.' Yet while wanting to retain the best of African culture, Moi was one of the first Kenyan politicians to acknowledge the need for change and to relinquish some tribal customs. As a Legislative Council member he lectured the backward Pokot tribe about adopting modern lifestyles, and as President he has advocated an end to female circumcision and to the tradition of inheriting wives. 'We must discard values which are incompatible with modern living,' he argues.

While these sentiments have seen him criticised as a 'colonial stooge', at heart Moi is a fervent one-nation nationalist who sincerely believes that education is the only way to produce a homogeneous, stable Kenya, a nation at peace with the world and with itself. He knows that there is little he can do to help the sixty-year-old peasant, and therefore concentrates his energies on the country's youth, vigorously supporting the *harambee* (let's all pull together) self-help programme to build schools, clinics and other facilities for communities. One of his first acts as President was to donate 400 acres of his farm for the Kabarak High School, which draws pupils from all tribes and all regions of Kenya. It was a symbolic gesture to encourage others to look to the future as Kenyans, rather than as members of individual tribes. Similarly, his interest in architecture and his conservation programmes, particularly for forests and wetlands, reflect this belief that Kenya has a long-term future. 'If I don't set an example, who will?' Moi asks visitors when he takes them round his farm, proudly showing the indigenous trees he is growing in a nursery garden. 'We must be able to look fifty years ahead,' he argues. 'If the Europeans can do it, why can't we?' Many recognise that Kenya would be a prairie today if it were not for tree conservation and planning programmes, endeavours that have at least gained him international acclaim.

If President Moi's nationalism is hands-on, practical and muscular – 'He only has time for dreams when they become reality,' says an aide – his politics are informed by a stern Christian morality. His continual strictures on sexual promiscuity, his warning of the threat of AIDS, and his condemnation of homosexuality, all are consonant with the ethos of a country which, in Billy Graham's phrase, is 'notoriously Christian'. From the nightwatchman who carefully paints the phrase 'God is Great' on his bicycle saddle, to Opposition politicians who advocate prayer as a method of civil disobedience, and to the President's entourage who studiously read their Bibles on the presidential jet, Christian worship and standards affect every facet of national life. Educated in the severe disciplines of the African Inland Mission, Moi's upright bearing, abstemious behaviour, plain diet, appetite for work, shining health, verbatim knowledge of the Bible and strict Old Testament morality make him remarkably similiar to many of his mission-school contemporaries, the first generation of Kenyan Christians. Indeed when he retires in 2002 he plans to spend much of his time preaching God's word throughout Kenya.

Central to Christianity, of course, is a belief in love of all men. While Western visitors to State House are taken aback when Moi states that unless you love people it is no use being in politics, this belief is at the core of his Nyayo philosophy of peace, love and unity. During the 1950s his faith forced him, along with many other Christians, to reject Mau Mau violence, while his implacable opposition to Communism owed as much to his Christian morality as it did to his respect for Britain and the West. During one official overseas visit the President gave the maverick Kenyan politician Martin Shikuku a terse ultimatum when he arrived for dinner sporting a hammer-and-sickle badge in his lapel: 'If you want to wear that you can eat elsewhere.' He has, too, spoken privately during Cabinet meetings in order to make clear his abhorrence of violence and bloodshed:

You cannot shed blood. That blood will haunt you to your grave – it is unforgivable in God's eyes. If I ever have to shed blood, I will resign. The Bible tells you, if you are protecting the rights of your people, you can kill and you can defend yourselves. But if you are murdering to solve our political problems, then that is not right.

In the light of the political murders of Pio Pinto (1965), Tom Mboya (1969) and J. M. Kariuki (1975) during Kenyatta's presidency, and the unsolved killing of Foreign Minister Bob Ouko in 1990, Moi's pious sentiments may seem hypocritical. While it is generally agreed both by KANU and Opposition politicians, as well as impartial observers, that the murders during Kenyatta's era were the work of the Kikuyu elite and that Moi himself was singled out for execution to prevent him from attaining the presidency, one killing has considerably dented his image of moral probity, that of the Luo leader Bob Ouko. It will be argued in Chapter Twelve, using new information, that the murder was essentially a Luo affair and that, far from exulting in Ouko's death, Moi was appalled to lose a man who was at once a trusted and valued friend and a staunch defender of his regime both at home and abroad. Moreover, those who might well have suffered the President's wrath, notably former Rift Valley police chief James Mungai, who physically and verbally abused Moi during his tenure as Vice-President, not only escaped punishment but earned his forgiveness. As his personal physician, David Silverstein, says, echoing the views of many of his circle: 'Moi can be politically tough and quite ruthless. But a killer, absolutely not.'

Yet his presidency has been dogged by accusations that, to ensure its survival, his administration has routinely and flagrantly abused human rights, tortured suspects, detained the innocent and promoted ethnic division. These accusations deeply wound Moi, who constantly cites the fact that all detainees were released once he became President, that Kenya is signatory to every human-rights convention, and that it now has a standing commission to investigate allegations of abuse. At the same time there have been numerous instances in Kenya where human rights abuses have taken place, although there is little evidence to suggest any systematic pattern of criminal behaviour which might imply deliberate government policy or involvement. Indeed, an investigation of the so-called 'state-sponsored ethnic cleansing' of the Rift Valley, which is dealt with in detail in Chapter Fourteen, reveals a rather different picture.

In fact, any analysis of the administration of justice or the work of the police in Kenya reveals that the problem is more to do with lack of resources rather than intentional violations of or indifference to human rights. The police and judiciary are poorly paid and equipped, record-keeping is archaic and prison conditions appalling. The private papers and correspondence of the former Chief Justice, Robin Hancox, one of the last expatriate judges, give the impression of a judicial King Canute, battling against the tide of corruption, incompetence and lack of resources which constantly threatens to overwhelm him. He is endlessly begging money from the British High Commission to pay for simple things, such as the binding of volumes containing the judgments of courts of appeal, while on another occasion he notes how he had to organise a human chain of lawyers, police and court staff to clear the filth from the basement of the Kisumu court house. So when the American-based Kennedy Foundation demanded in the early 1990s that Kenya initiate a constitutional court, Hancox's letter to the then British High Commissioner, Sir Roger Tomkys, spelt out his frustration: 'A constitutional court is a luxury which Kenya cannot afford. It will provide a talking shop for lawyers, plush appointments for certain favourites and fantastic fees.'

This divide between the theoretical prescriptions and practical reality of human-rights issues epitomises the philosophical gulf between the developed and the developing world. As far as Hancox is concerned, he can recall few instances of presidential interference in judicial verdicts. 'Even when the judgment was not to his liking Moi accepted it – albeit through gritted teeth,' recalls the former Chief Justice. 'He may be disgruntled but he accepts the decision and always manages to give the impression later that he understands the reasons behind it.' Only rarely does Moi write to the Chief Justice to complain, usually about drunken or corrupt magistrates or obviously wrong-headed decisions, such as the release on bail of armed gunmen. The truest test of Moi's attitude towards the legal system was shown in 1984 when one of his best friends, Michael Kiptanui Tenai, a farmer, was murdered following a scuffle on his land at Moi's Bridge. Four men, including a former Assistant Minister, Simon arap Choge, were arrested and convicted of his killing. On appeal, however, they were released on legal technicalities. Hancox, who as the Appeal Court judge had to take this sensitive decision, recalls: 'Moi went up in smoke and said it was disgraceful. In any other African country, I would have been on the next plane out. However, Moi accepted the decision even though it was his friend who had been killed.'

Moi's punctiliousness in following proper procedures – his election as President was a model of constitutional propriety – and his Christian principles are an integral part of his political life. These values are demonstrated time and again in Kenya's foreign policy, a policy based on the principle of 'good neighbourliness'. Very often the Kenyan Government has done more than was strictly necessary to serve the national interest, simply because of the moral element in its collective thinking; Kenya's involvement in the problems of Mozambique is a case in point. Personally, Moi has always greatly admired the state of Israel, not only because it is the cradle of Christianity, but also because of a widespread belief among the Kalenjin tribe that they are descended from 'wandering Jews' of ancient times. He feels that the Jews, perhaps more than any other race, understand both the black man's burden and the problems of a new nation state in a hostile world. 'The Jews are the most persecuted people on earth while the Africans are the most humiliated,' he is fond of saying. His personal friendship with several Israeli presidents, together with the warm bilateral relations between the two countries, led to Moi being asked to address the Knesset in 1994, a rare honour to be accorded to a visiting head of state.

In recent times, however, Moi's foreign policy of peaceful coexistence and studious neutrality has come under attack, particularly with regard to the crisis in the Great Lakes region. This has seen his neighbour, President Yoweri Kaguta Museveni of Uganda, intervene aggressively in civil wars in Zaire (now the Congo Republic), the Sudan and Rwanda, either by providing a safe haven for rebel armies, or by promoting the cause of rebel leaders, particularly Laurent Kabila, who ousted President Mobutu Sese Seko from power in the former Zaire. While Museveni and other younger African presidents are lauded for their scepticism of the West and their desire to resolve African problems locally, conversely Moi is now portrayed as a relic from the past, a dinosaur clinging to power. Yet it is precisely because he has attempted to draw on Kenyan traditions in order to resolve his country's problems that he has fallen into disfavour with Western nations.

Undoubtedly, however, a new wind of change is sweeping across the sub-Saharan region. There is excited talk of an African renaissance, particularly as the continent's sleeping giant, South Africa, is at last becoming a major player in the region. That a country with a GDP greater than that of the rest of Africa put together has been isolated for so long is the equivalent to the development of post-Second World War Europe without Germany, or the Pan-Pacific basin without Japan. Only now are the repercussions, for other African nations, of South Africa's long quarantine becoming clear.

The reintegration of South Africa into the African family of nations has significantly altered the dynamics of the continent, the country's sheer economic size and authority giving her a muscle which nations like Kenya lack. Hence the heightened importance of the revival of the long-defunct East African Community comprising Kenya, Uganda and Tanzania, re-established as the Secretariat of the Commission for East African Co-operation at Arusha in 1996, in order to give the region a significant voice. The symbolism of this co-operative's new regional flag and passport are not lost on Moi, who has spoken of his 'hope and dream that political federation for East Africa will finally be achieved'.

When he addresses the Organisation of African Unity, or speaks at other international summits, he keeps in his mind's eye a clear vision of just where the greatest impact of policies and decisions will be felt – which is among the voiceless rural majority. His concern in regional conflicts is for the effect on the women and children, the old and the helpless, for it is they who suffer most in civil strife. Similarly, when he takes decisions affecting domestic policy, he considers the ordinary people of his rural constituency first and foremost. They are his security and his strength; he understands them intimately, articulating their fears and concerns. Often, during a conversation or in discussion, his mind will be on issues other than those being debated, invariably relating to rural areas he has visited. He will then unnerve his audience by asking about, say, the state of a tarmac road in Kakamega, or the need for a medical clinic in Eldama Ravine.

Those who try to get between Moi and the *wananchi* soon find themselves out of a job. While he is obliged to deal with the Kenyan elite, the intellectuals and the noisy urban throng, there is little fellow feeling between them. Yet it is they who catch the eye and ear of the international community, and who currently win the lion's share of donor funding, be it for AIDS research or civic education programmes. The days when foreign aid concentrated on providing boreholes and vaccines for the rural poor are fading although it is the people of the rural constituency who still make up the overwhelming majority of Kenyans. Michael Blundell describes the country like this:

> To me there are three Kenyas. First the frothy, unbalanced, greedy, corrupt and often overwhelmingly ambitious political scene. Secondly, the rapidly increasing number of middle-class executives in the commercial sphere, academics in the universities, research workers, skilled technicians in the world of communications; indeed the intelligentsia who are the main components of a small but expanding modern state. Thirdly, outside both these worlds altogether, are the thousands of small farmers in the valleys and hills hundreds of miles from the human whirlpool of Nairobi. The incandescences, the burning indignations, the criticisms of government by lawyers, businessmen, expatriates and workers hurrying along the city roads in the early morning, upon which the visiting journalist feeds, are not found away in these great rural areas. To all these people the politics of Nairobi reflect only a few far-distant hopes; better water supplies, more and better schools, hospitals and roads.

Just as Moi, unfashionably, champions the rural majority, so his way of working echoes their historic way of life. Decision-making at State House bears traces of the traditional *baraza*, during which the community would gather to discuss a local issue and would eventually, often after several days, reach a consensus. So the President will allow issues and problems to brew and develop rather than nip them in the bud. In an increasingly fast-moving and fractious society this time-honoured approach is a source of frustration, especially as so many decisions are funnelled through State House. Indeed, it is only recently that Moi has set up a government think-tank to address long-term problems affecting the country.

At the same time, again in the the spirit of the *baraza*, in which everyone was entitled to a say, Moi takes soundings from all and sundry, whether they always know it or not. His style is to remain silent and listen while others make their case. It is a method he employs in Cabinet, as former Cabinet Secretary Professor Philip Mbithi observes: 'Normally when the ministers are debating hotly, he sits back and listens. He doesn't take notes, just makes marks on the documents all the time. At the end he will summarise what people have said and tell them what he thinks.' Moi undoubtedly likes to act as the silent referee as others thrash out the issues. Bethwell Kiplagat, a former Kenyan diplomat, says: 'Moi has an ability to encourage genuine discussion and debate. In the work I did, we discussed issues in a very free and frank atmosphere. At the same time he has the courage and strength to go back when he has made mistakes. He will amend terms of appointments, reinstate people and review policy statements.'

While those he knows and trusts, such as his former pupil and confidant Nicholas Biwott, have the ear of the President, what is noticeable is that casual visitors are often surprised to discover that their ideas have been incorporated into a presidential speech or edict. An aide remarks: 'People often ask who are his advisers. The real answer is that he takes advice from everyone.'

Just as Moi's Christianity, belief in education and practical nationalism have been the fixed reference points of his political credo, so patience, silent watchfulness and an ability to listen form the basis of his political style. As a shrewd judge of character – 'What do you want?' he will say tersely when someone spends time praising him – and a master tactician, perhaps one of his greatest strengths is patience, an ability to observe the political scene dispassionately and wait for the moment to act. 'I know them all, I know what makes them work,' he says, referring to his political rivals. He rarely strikes when expected, allowing those who have grown too big to have enough leeway so that when the axe falls it seems as if they have themselves been the authors of their own downfall. The ousting of the overmighty power-broker, Charles Njonjo was a classic example of Moi's political style: patient, calculated, unexpected and bloodless. 'He is not a man to play poker against,' says David Silverstein, who knows both Moi and Njonjo well.

One of the President's favourite sayings is: 'You can never tell what is in the back of an African's mind,' and it is a phrase that might apply equally well to him. So it may come about that a Permanent Secretary will have enjoyed lunch with the President, only to find a note of dismissal on his desk when he returns. 'Moi seems as though he is sleeping, but he is slowly but surely building up to a point where he is going to hit you,' remarks one civil servant who suffered that fate. 'His is a more hands-on style than Kenyatta, who behaved like a king keeping himself distant from the day-to-day running of government. Moi takes a keen interest in the mechanics of governance, all the more so after the 1982 coup attempt.'

Indeed, the 1982 coup attempt, as well as a number of significant events during Moi's presidency, including the murder of Bob Ouko, highlight the attributes which transcend all others in Moi's political behaviour, and which are central to an understanding of it – trust and loyalty. Trust is the glue which binds a society together, be it in business, social or political relationships. While a high degree of trust is linked to national success, Kenya, like many other developing countries, is a low-trust society, that quality only truly residing at the level of the family, the clan and the tribe. Only slowly is trust being developed at a national level. As a result, unlike developed nations, there is little cohesiveness among the ruling elite. In Britain, for example, many of the ruling class share similar values and backgrounds, maintaining alliances often formed during their schooldays. This social glue enables the governing class to operate efficiently and successfully, treating outsiders with suspicion.

Conversely, at a time of rapid expansion which has necessarilly forced the President to delegate authority, Kenya only has an embryonic 'locker-room' culture. Such is the country's tribal, linguistic and cultural diversity that the process of achieving consensus – indeed the entire intimate shorthand of command and decision-making – is a great deal more intricate and cumbersome than in more cohesive nations. Because Kenyatta came from the most advanced and numerous tribe, he had the good fortune to be able to rely on the Kikuyu elite for support, often to the exclusion of other tribal groups. In Cabinet, Kikuyu ministers regularly spoke their own language rather than the *lingua franca* of Swahili or indeed English in order to exclude others from confidential affairs of state. Moi, from a small, relatively backward tribe, has no such fortune. He has had to rely on a series of political alliances with other tribes not only in order to stay in office, but also to demonstrate that all Kenyans, all tribes are involved in the great task of nation-building.

In the absence of the social bindings common in Western nations, the traditional vulnerability and isolation of the leader is more acutely felt in Kenya than in other more cohesive countries. As David Western, the Director of the Kenya Wildlife Service who has spent years living amongst rural Kenyans, observes: 'What people from the outside world don't appreciate is that in Africa, especially in Kenya, trust is the basis of all working relationships. Until you have established trust, nothing else will flow.' Moi, by instinct and necessity, is a man who though slow to trust will support his lieutenants to the hilt once they have won his confidence. Yet this unflinching support of those in whom he has faith has produced numerous disasters, from the rigging of the 1988 elections to the Goldenberg Bank scandal. As various political colleagues have commented: 'Moi trusted some people too much and for too long.' Since the 1992 elections, however, it has been a different story, as the President has adopted a far more professional, rather than personal, approach in his dealings with his colleagues.

In the same way, and for the same reasons, the President habitually values loyalty above competence, and he has been criticised – particularly by those who have lost their place in the sun – for his tendency to believe without question those loyal to him. Bethwell Kiplagat comments that 'Moi can be moved to tears when he sees suffering but if information goes to him of disloyalty he will never call you. Once someone has given information about you to him, he doesn't check. He believes it and then he acts on it, whether it's right or wrong.' It is a view shared by the former Attorney-General, Charles Njonjo, who suffered a long trial following accusations of 'traitorous' behaviour. 'Kenyatta would check out things, Moi doesn't. I have said to Moi, verify the information you get. It is one thing that Moi is bad at doing.'

Moi's perceived personal failings are first generated, and then exacerbated, by a society still in a raw state of evolution, of social, political and economic flux. The virtues of trust and loyalty, while important, do not assume the same critical importance in more sophisticated, homogeneous and stable societies. Indeed, in many respects attempting to govern an intrinsically unstable and divided nation like Kenya is far more demanding than in a settled society such as Britain. It is for this reason that Moi believes that the greatest achievement of his career has been the maintenance of peace and stability, giving the country the social soil within which the tender roots of democracy can grow. The longer he can hold the ring, he argues, the more chance the nation has of becoming a homogeneous society in which tribal and regional differences will eventually become secondary to an overriding belief in the country called Kenya. Only with the passage of time and the proper education of the coming generations – he is proud of the fact that, unlike in neighbouring countries, no Kenyan children have lost out on schooling because of civil war – will Kenya save itself from violent, and almost certainly retrograde, change.

The West, and many Kenyans, take the country's peace and stability for granted, assuming that Kenya can absorb any amount of outside pressure and social upheaval. Moi, however, sees the day-to-day reality of a nation where violence lurks just beneath the surface, where tribal frictions, the rapid rise in population, high unemployment and urban poverty make for an explosive cocktail. His job is akin to juggling whilst standing on top of a series of sliding metal plates which are balanced on a tightrope. At any moment this shakily constructed entertainment might plunge into the abyss.

Kenya is a fragile country. Assailed by drought every decade, her economy is sustained by the vagaries of tourism, cash crops and donor aid, while around her borders have raged appalling civil war, famine and disease. This is a land where the ancient tensions between the Cains and Abels, the settled and the pastoral, become ever more acute as the population increases and land hunger intensifies. From colonial times, the rural Kenyans and their urban rivals were artificially bound together in a country whose boundaries were decided by outsiders, and where forty-two different tribes divided by thirteen vernacular languages and by competing or conflicting customs coexisted in a land which its rulers sought to exploit rather than unite. As independence approached the country was ill equipped to survive the ruthless roulette of capitalism, especially as the colonialists departed the country taking with them the chips needed to play the game. These problems were exacerbated by the colonial policy of divide and rule, under which the tribes were separated and suspicious of one another, and as a result of which one tribe, the Kikuyu, better educated and developed, enjoyed the first profits of independence.

But if the foundations of independence were built on shifting sands – a problem by no means unique to Kenya – the rest of the building, too, is badly built and prone to subsidence. Even the cultural and economic mortar which holds the whole edifice together, the stuff that binds a people to a government and a nation, seems to be largely absent. While the political elite is Kenyan, the economic nobility is Asian and white, with a significant smattering of those Kikuyu who made fortunes in the first years of independence. At the first whiff of trouble those who own the country yet are alienated from the political process head for Jomo Kenyatta Airport and their overseas bank accounts – hardly a recipe for economic prosperity, long-term investment or faith in a recently independent government.

Culturally, the focus of allegiance for many Kenyans is the tribe rather than the nation, a tension which is made manifest in the perpetual debate about central government versus 'majimboism', or regionalism, and in the conflict between Westernised urban dwellers and the more traditional, semi-pastoral rural people. This conflict is expressed politically in fragmented, tribal-based political parties, where tribe, not ideology, determines party allegiance. Moi is acutely aware that, because the state was artificially formed, the level of patriotism and national consciousness is low. Since Independence, much of the sense of nationality has had to be created, and then reinforced through such means as the harambee self-help programmes, in order to bind Kenyans to the country. One of the President's arguments for the continuation of the one-party state, centred around KANU, was precisely because it bolstered a sense of nationhood in a divided people. 'The difference between Kenya and Britain,' he says, 'is that if there was no Tory or Labour Party, Britain's culture would remain because the country came into being as a nation state before political parties arose. But in Kenya the country is in part defined by the existence of its political party, especially as KANU is the only national party.'

Structural instability, weak government, a fragile sense of nationhood – and then there enters into this equation the influence of the West. Drive round Nairobi for just a few minutes and it isn't long before you see the familiar white United Nations vehicles with their red number plates, or the four-wheel-drives of aid agencies. Ostensibly benign and beneficial their work may be, but the existence of what is essentially a government in miniature serves to highlight the feebleness of Kenya's sovereign government, and its inability to serve the needs of its people. What relevance has Harambee House, the centre of government, to a rural Kenyan who pays no taxes, sees his children educated thanks to the Save the Children Fund, his boreholes drilled by the United Nations, and a tarmac road built because of a loan from one or more of the donor countries? Only now, however, are the pernicious effects of this dependency culture being recognised. Furthermore, it is a two-way process; donor countries adopt arrogant, patronising postures towards developing nations, while the Africans themselves lose the political will to work out their own solutions to their own problems.

The President of the World Bank, Jim Wolfensohn, was horrified by the colonialist attitude of the donor countries – and of some of his executives – when he visited fifty nations, including Kenya, during a worldwide tour in 1996. He found the donor organisations self-serving, command-driven structures who treated locals with disdain and imposed solutions to local issues without any consultation with the indigenous populations. Since that eye-opening trip, Wolfensohn and his reforming team have instituted a revolution in the way the World Bank does business working in partnership with local communities, finding out their needs and goals before offering loans. This changing attitude was belatedly acknowledged at the 1997 Group of Seven summit who agreed that the way forward for Africa was investment rather than 'aid with strings', and that the issues of debt relief and the pain of economic reform should be more carefully addressed.

The damage has already been done, however. Ever since Kenya's independence, the continual wash of Western values has driven a wedge between the people of the rural areas, whose lives are still governed by immutable and time-honoured tribal customs, and those in the urban centres, invariably better educated, who have embraced Western values and lifestyles. Within an hour's drive of the capital the silicon chip meets the Stone Age. During the 1990s the pressure exerted by the West for Kenya to undergo a simultaneous political and economic revolution, introducing multi-party democracy and liberalising markets, nearly toppled Moi from his precarious tightrope. It was, it seemed, not good enough for the President to reform and modernise the one-party democracy, which had seen elections every five years and vigorous competition for seats, the West wanted a pluralistic democracy irrespective of the tribal tensions this inevitably generated.

As the president observes:

The multi-party system has split the country into tribal groupings. I am surprised that Western countries believe in the balkanisation of Africa. Therefore people will concentrate on their tribal groupings and they will not think about one nation. Tribal roots go much deeper than the shallow flower of democracy. That is something the West failed to understand. I'm not against multi-partyism but I am unsure about the maturity of the country's politics. People don't look ahead, they are so short-term. When we went multi-party I predicted that we would go back to our tribal groupings but the West didn't listen. The West got what they wanted.

While the infamous tribal clashes preceding and following the multi-party elections in 1992 were a bloody manifestation of Moi's concerns, even today some Western governments and aid agencies seem to believe that bloodshed is an inevitable, indeed necessary, component of encouraging a more democratic and accountable political environment. In 1996 a detailed internal document produced by a major aid agency on the state of democratic development in Kenya made clear that violence and even civil war were 'integral' parts of the process of genuine democratisation in Kenya and should be planned for.

This then, at least so far as the West's policy in Kenya goes, is the heart of darkness, an acceptance that death and destruction are the handmaidens of democracy. Clearly this is a prospect the President by instinct and office will resist, a factor in his hostility towards outside agencies. A century after the first wave of colonialists arrived in the country, the Western nations are still playing God with African lives. As one British commentator recently observed of the current international scene: 'No country is at present safe from the restlessness of post Cold War governments, their armies, their agencies and their charity bosses.'

Such a view perhaps explains why Moi has much sympathy with those who argue that Kenya – and other developing countries as well – should throw away the begging bowl and go her own way. But despite his sympathy for the idea, such prescriptions produce a wan smile in the President, who is aware that development aid from donor countries is still vital to his country's well-being. Even so, the thrust of Kenya's policy is to encourage investment rather than aid, so that within a generation the cycle of dependency may finally be broken.

Until that time comes, Moi counsels patience, stoically accepting the humiliations imposed by the donor countries because of the needs of his people. Perhaps, then, Daniel Toroitich arap Moi is well named. Cast unexpectedly into the den of Kenyan politics, he has dealt with the prowling lions of the Opposition and the West whilst guiding his flock in a land assailed by drought and famine often of biblical proportions. Attacked and ridiculed, he has remained steadfast to his vision of Kenya as he leads the nation on a great and dangerous adventure into the next millennium. It is a journey which began in another age, more than seventy years ago, in the remote hills of the Rift Valley.

PART I
The Making of a Nation

Chapter one

Welcome Home the Cattle

They were the demigods of Empire. Tall, rangy, athletic, they arrived on the boat from England to Mombasa filled with high ideals and utter certainties. Educated at Oxford, Cambridge or the Scottish universities, they were the last generation of those who believed Cecil Rhodes' maxim that to be born an Englishman was to draw the winning ticket in the lottery of life. They came as missionaries, soldiers, farmers and administrators, conquering the Dark Continent with a bible in one hand and a gun in the other.

By the time Bernard Francklin, a Colonial Office administrator, arrived in 1916 the pen was rapidly cocooning a country forged by force of arms within a web of rules and regulations. Like all the other settlers, Francklin fervently believed in a monstrous sleight of hand; that the British, in conquering East Africa, were actually doing the indigenous tribes a favour by taking their land and exploiting their resources.

What is more, he would have seen not the slightest irony in the fact that while he arrived midway through the First World War, at that time the most catastrophic war in history, he sincerely believed that his mission was to keep the peace and to civilise the 'noble savage'. He would have agreed with Lord Cranworth's view, expressed in his book *A Colony in the Making*: 'It is generally a benefit we confer when we take over a state. We give peace where war prevailed, justice where injustice ruled, Christianity where paganism ruled.' In reality, British domination of East Africa was a result of the need to protect the 'jewel in the crown of Empire' – India. During the 'Scramble for Africa' that began in the 1880s, European imperial ambitions saw the continent carved up between, principally Germany, France and Britain, with the British focusing on eastern and southern Africa as a means of securing the Suez route to India. This meant controlling Egypt, the Nile Valley and the headwaters of the White Nile in Uganda. Ironically Kenya, initially administered by the Imperial British East Africa Company until it became a protectorate in 1895, was annexed in order to secure communication with Uganda from the coast.

As far as Francklin was concerned, however, the economic imperatives were secondary to the noble ideals of his calling as a colonial officer, defined by Lord Lugard, one of the foremost colonial administrators in Africa, who demanded that the few hundred men who ruled Britain's interests in Africa should have 'an almost passionate conception of fair play, of protecting the weak and of playing the game'. For several years Francklin worked in Nyeri; then, in 1924, the year in which Kenya's second president was born, he was posted for a time to one of the most remote and backward regions in the whole of Kenya, Baringo District, Daniel Toroitich arap Moi's home area.

A few miles north of the Equator, Baringo is a region of swooping valleys, rugged hills, and surprising waterfalls, where climatic variations cause the landscape to change from arid to savannah and then to the semi-tropical almost at will. As you look out from the slopes of the rugged Tugen Hills over the vast Rift Valley 4,000 feet below, surrounded by olive, eucalyptus and cedar trees, the dull chink of the bells tied on goats and brown-haired Lebuson sheep echoing in the distance, it is not hard to be transported back to biblical times.

Such restful rural scenes can be deceptive as Francklin was to discover. Typically, the lush rolling plateau towards Eldoret had been settled by the white man, leaving the native population, overwhelmingly members of Moi's Tugen clan, to scratch a living on the less hospitable slopes, where they mainly grew maize and millet and herded animals. Moreover, after eight years of colonial service, Francklin's early ideals had seemingly been crushed between the voracious hammer of imperial needs and the mute anvil of native indifference and resentment. His official report, written in 1924, is suffused with a weary acknowledgement of native exploitation and colonial greed. Referring to the Tugen tribesmen, who then numbered some 17,000, he states:

> This tribe, though friendly, have a poor opinion of Europeans on the whole and distrust them. Not a few of the older members of the tribe looked forward to the day when they believe that the government will have made enough money out of them and leave them in peace. In the absence of any benefits conferred on them by the government, to which it is possible to point, it is difficult to combat this view.

His report goes on to admit: 'The revenue amounts to Ksh114,687. Expenditure Ksh13,936. The net profit therefore to the government is 100,750 shillings . . . of which no part is devoted to the benefit of the natives or the development of the district.'

Francklin's jaundiced views of his colonial masters were matched by his fatalistic attitude towards the indigenous population. He despaired of their cultivation techniques, their absorption with witchcraft and their lamentable diet and health. In dry, understated tones he wrote: 'The conditions under which the tribe lives are very primitive.' The death rate, particularly among the children, was extremely high, while outbreaks of anthrax among their cattle had spread to Tugen families. Blindness caused by the tsetse fly was endemic.

While he acknowledged that colonialists did little or nothing to help, he had a poor opinion of the Tugen's efforts at self-sufficiency: 'The Touken [*sic*] are very poor cultivators and content themselves with cutting down bush and forest on steep hillsides, firing it, scratching the ground with their ridiculous little hoes and sowing Wimbe seed broadcast. The crops are seldom if ever weeded.' As a result, he observed, 'a large proportion of the tribe exist on the verge of starvation, ekeing out a scanty food supply with wild berries'. These physical hardships resulted in a population decrease of 775 in the year, mainly, Francklin acknowledges, as a result of 'scarcity of food which affects the stamina of the tribe, and to the heavy taxation, which is beyond the means of the tribe, poverty stricken as it is'. It was a combination of the hut and poll taxes which drove more than 900 Tugen tribesmen to seek work as labourers on colonial farms in Eldama Ravine. According to Francklin, 'a considerable number' died on their return to the tribal reserves established by the colonial rulers.

The unvarnished observations of Bernard Francklin in his 1924 report on Baringo District provide a painful snapshot of life under the unyielding colonial yoke, a burden made all the heavier by the unremittingly harsh environment. Naked exploitation, the careless breaking up of families and the destruction of communal life – this was the day-to-day reality of the colonialists' civilising mission. As one elder has recalled of that period in Kenya's history: 'From that time the state of things began to change more and more rapidly, and ceased to be at all like it was in the olden days. The country became like a new country that was unknown to us.'

It was into this hostile world that the man who was to become Kenya's second president was born. He arrived at a time of unprecedented upheaval, the 1920s and 1930s effectively a watershed marking the era when the old tribal values and customs were challenged and fatally compromised by an uncharitable Christian and capitalist culture foisted on the indigenous peoples by their conquerors, in a land where any attempts to challenge the new order – such as the Kenyan nationalist Harry Thuku's party, the Young Kikuyu Association, in the 1920s – were ruthlessly crushed. The effects of that traumatic upheaval reverberate today.

Such concerns were so much distant thunder on an afternoon in September 1924 at Kurieng'wo, an isolated escarpment high in the Tugen Hills in the Sacho Location of Baringo District. It was here that Kimoi arap Chebii had his *chang'ap gotik*, a collection of huts and granaries where he and his two wives, Kabon, the senior, and Tarkok the younger, lived with their family. On that afternoon, as the goats and sheep were being herded into the compound, Kabon gave birth to her fifth child, a boy who would eventually become Kenya's second president. (While the girls from Alliance School always present Moi with a birthday cake on 2 September, there is doubt about the actual month he was born in. The President feels it was September because so many significant events in his life have occurred during that month.)

He was given the name Kapkorios Toroitich, which means 'welcome home the cattle'. Not only did Moi's name pay homage to his ancestors, it was also a recognition of the importance of cattle in Tugen culture. As 'Moi' means calves, 'arap' son of, and 'bii' cowshed, his father's name, Kimoi arap Chebii, indicates that he was born when the family's cattle had given birth to several calves, while his own father, Chebii, had been born in a cowshed.

Cattle were central to the family's very existence and were the reason why their clan, the Soot or Sot, had migrated to the region at some time between the eighteenth and mid-nineteenth centuries. Originally they had herded and farmed on the slopes of Koilege, or Mount Kenya. Like many other tribes, they had fought endless skirmishes with the Maasai, the dominant tribe during this period. The Maasai's belief that all the cattle on earth were owned by them, together with their reputation as warriors, ensured sporadic but bloody battles with rival tribes.

One such clash with the warring Maasai led to the Tugen herdsmen fleeing Mount Kenya in disarray. President Moi's ancestor, another Chebii, with his wife and three sons, Kabaget, Kimagui and Chepkeres, were forced to hide from the enraged Maasai out to avenge the blood of their fallen warriors. The east was blocked by the inhospitable slopes of Mount Kenya and with the Maasai quickly advancing, the family feared that they would be butchered. From their hideout the family, already weakened by fatigue and hunger, planned their escape. As legend has it, a time-honoured but effective plan was hatched. The boys were dressed in girls' clothes, their mother disguised herself as a woman in an advanced state of pregancy, while Chebii made himself look as though he were mentally and physically decrepit. The plan worked and they resumed their journey westwards, eventually reaching the safety of Mochongoi on the Laikipia escarpment, where Chebii and his wife, exhausted by their ordeal, decided to rest for a time.

Eventually his three sons scouted ahead to look for suitable land where they could settle. Their journey took them along the Laikipia escarpment toward the Tugen Hills. Before they reached the hills, the eldest brother, Kabaget, decided that the lowland area, with its warm climate and good pasture, was an ideal place in which to raise livestock. Accordingly he stayed there while the two remaining brothers continued their search. Kimagui, the second brother, decided that that plateau below the Tugen Hills, with its open woodland rich in wild fruits, berries and honey, was suitable, leaving the youngest brother, Chepkeres, to climb the slopes of the Tugen Hills alone. He liked what he saw, for the lush vegetation, the wetter climate and the coolness in the evenings reminded him of the family's previous home on the slopes of Mount Kenya. The place where he settled became the present-day Sacho, and he and his brothers were the forefathers of the Sot clan of the Tugen peoples.

The tribe's history of roaming from place to place because of war, famine or disease has prompted a number of Tugen scholars, including the President himself, to argue that the tribe is descended from the lost Jewish tribes of ancient history. There is an enduring legend that the Tugen and Maasai, to whom they are related, followed the River Nile on their journey south from Misri, modern-day Egypt, although other scholars argue that the tribe originated from southern Ethiopia. This 'lost tribe' theory is further borne out by the similiarities between Tugen social and religious customs and those described in the Bible, particularly elements of the Old Testament, something which provides at least one explanation as to why the African Inland Mission found such fertile soil in Baringo District.

Ironically, while early Christian missionaries to Kenya dismissed indigenous tribes as 'savages' because of what they considered to be their primitive culture and beliefs, closer inspection shows that Tugen culture is sophisticated, humane and practical, its political procedures remarkably similar to those of ancient Greece. During the pre-colonial period the Tugen were one of the smaller clans in what was to become known from the 1950s onwards as 'the Kalenjin' (meaning 'I tell you'), an agglomeration of Nilotic-speaking clans which comprise the Kipsigis and Nandi, far and away the majority, as well as the Keiyo, the Pokot, the Marakwet, the Sabaot, the Terik and the Tugen. During the colonial period, the British deliberately tried to divide the Kalenjin by placing large settler farms between the tribal groupings so as to act as buffer zones. Since Independence rival tribes have tried to divide the various clans within the Kalenjin tribe but without success. For outsiders fail to realise that the Kalenjin are a homogeneous tribe. Besides a common language, the various clans which make up the tribe shared similar cultural values and habits. Ownership of land was communal, the land itself having no particular value. As is shown by the tale of Moi's ancestors, tribespeople moved and settled where they wished within the territory of the tribe. Cattle were the constant preoccupation, defining a man's status and his lifestyle, their importance far beyond their economic value, so that they became part of the tribe's customs, and even assumed a quasi-religious significance. The existence of a rich vocabulary used to describe cattle, the way young men proved their valour by taking animals from rival tribes, the songs, the dreams and the dances – all point to the central role cattle played in the thoughts and feelings, as well as the daily lives, of Kalenjin tribespeople. Indeed, the Tugens' legendary long-distance running prowess is jokingly ascribed to the fact that they were such determined and successful cattle raiders.

Even today, this 'cattle complex' plays an important part in their lives. During the Mau Mau conflict in the 1950s, for example, many Tugen people were horrified and alienated by the way Kikuyu fighters were prepared to hobble or disfigure cattle during skirmishes with the colonial authorities. Among the Kalenjin tribal group, the Tugen and Pokot still place greater importance on cattle than the more settled tribes such as the Nandi and Kipsigis. Indeed, they ridicule other tribes like the Luo and Kikuyu, who till the earth rather than tend their flocks. Naturally, Bantu agriculturalists like the Kikuyu and the Kamba take quite the contrary view, since they believe in the virtue of 'holy sweat', that land is given by God for man to make fruitful by labour. You civilise the land by hoeing it; therefore, if you till the land, it becomes your property.

This conflict between the settled and the semi-pastoral, is as old as history itself. However, the Kalenjin's historic indifference to land compared with the Kikuyu and other settled tribes was to assume a greater significance during the race for property following Independence. It is worth noting, too, that the Tugen, whose values attach to cattle rather than acres, were the one clan who did not take part in the vicious Rift Valley land clashes during the early 1990s. War was primarily a means of collecting cattle for a marriage dowry or to increase the size of one's herd – in other words, raiding operations were not undertaken to devastate the surrounding countryside, to slaughter or capture large numbers of the enemy or to bring fresh lands or people under Tugen control. Some raids were opportunistic adventures lasting a few days, others were more carefully organised. The type of warfare conducted by the Tugen and other Kalenjin clans did not lend itself to excessive cruelty or vindictiveness; women and children were seldom attacked or captured, and victorious forces would often withdraw rather than massacre an enemy tribe.

The arrival of the British in the 1880s brought warfare on an unimagined scale, as the first Commissioner of the Protectorate, Sir Arthur Hardinge, noted cynically: 'These people must learn submission by bullets – it's the only school; after that you may begin more modern and humane methods of education.' In some cases, however, for example, that of the Maasai, the British managed to persuade indigenous tribes to sign treaties; in others, particularly among the

Kalenjin, resistance was fierce. The Kalenjin, especially the dominant Nandi, attacked both the Imperial British East African Company's caravan routes, and the work parties building the railway between Mombasa and Uganda, which passed through their grazing lands in the Nyando Valley. Eventually, in 1906, the Kalenjin were defeated – eleven years after the first of five military expeditions had been deployed against them – although resistance to British rule continued well into this century; the last expedition embarked against the Elgeyo clan in 1919 – just five years before Moi was born.

It is not surprising, therefore, that even after Independence the whole of Baringo District was a closed area, visitors needing a pass to enter the region. As a result of the restrictions, and of the rugged remoteness of the region, the Tugen people are seen by other tribes as isolated, backward and naive in their dealings with the modern world. Even today, the Tugen and the Maasai are the least likely of all Kenya's tribes to move out of their home areas to cities like Mombasa and Nairobi. They have learned self-sufficiency, distrusting outsiders and preferring to remain among their own people.

This isolation has meant that development, particularly in education and commerce, has been slow. Levels of literacy are lower than the national average, while the Tugen people remain wary of the cash economy, frowning especially on moneylenders. At the same time, the majority of Tugen have retained their traditional tribal and religious beliefs for much longer than many other tribes. Perhaps more than most, they have kept a sense of identity in the face of the acquisitive consumer culture imported wholesale from the West.

In traditional Tugen culture generosity was valued, selfishness or stinginess despised. Strangers who passed through the area were fed at the expense of the host's own family. A dignified and quiet bearing was admired. Restraint under all circumstances was the mark of a man. Outbursts of temper and emotion were strongly frowned upon, and the maxim '*Sisinge sikwasta nererkek,*' meaning 'Be silent until your anger has abated,' was followed by Tugen people.

In general, a sense of modesty and equality prevailed in pre-colonial Kalenjin society. The tribe operated open parliaments which were democratic in the classical sense: resolutions were by consensus, and no one individual could force a decision or determine the clan's course of action without full consultation. These communal tribal meetings, or *barazas*, were essentially the community's court and local council, and once an issue had been decided, that was the end to the matter. It was not raised in the future, and least of all simply for the sake of scoring points or creating divisions in the community for factional gain. The adversial legal and political systems which prevail in the West are as alien to Kalenjin culture as was the notion of a formal political opposition – to them, an opponent was an enemy. In essence, the traditional Kalenjin legal process emphasised reconciliation, rather than, as in the West, fixing guilt and exacting punishment, thereby increasing and perpetuating bitterness.

While there were councils of elders, or *kokuet*, headed by a chief, he could not make decisions without the approval of the other members. Everyone could participate at the *baraza*, and those people whose arguments and judgements were consistently sensible would eventually become elders, having demonstrated their worth to the community.

Within the Tugen the Sot family was held in high regard. The men were widely respected as natural leaders, while the women were sought after as good, reliable wives and mothers. Moi's father, Kimoi arap Chebii, was an honoured elder in the community, while Chebii's younger brother, Kiplabat Chepkeitany, who lived close by, was chosen by the colonial authorities as the Senior Chief in Sacho Location. During Moi's early childhood the family compound was where villagers congregated for meetings. That meeting place has now moved to the main street in Kabartonjo, where Moi's sister, Rebecca Chelimo, lives with her husband, James, in a modest brick-built dwelling yards from the newly opened African Inland Mission cathedral which Moi helped build.

Rebecca Chelimo remembers her family as respectable, and respected within the community. While by modern standards the family lived in poverty – in times of drought the young Moi and his elder brother, Tuitoek, would search for wild roots to eat – in relation to others at that time they were well-to-do, with a substantial herd of some 30 cattle and 200 goats, which needed two of Chebii's children to graze them. Again, the fact that Moi's father had two wives, Kabon and Tarkok, emphasises Chebii's standing in the community. Each wife had her own place of residence, known as a *boma*, and her own granary; in fact, Kimoi arap Chebii had six granaries in all. Not only was he able to support two wives, but he fathered thirteen children in total, seven by Kabon and six by Tarkok. The first-born, Tuitoek, had already served in the King's African Rifles during the First World War; the young Moi also had three older sisters, including Rebecca, and two younger brothers, Kiprop, who died before fathering a family, and Chesang, who died during a circumcision ceremony. In addition to his immediate family Moi had five half-sisters, all called Sote, and a half-brother, Chesire.

Not only was Moi's father respected in the local community, he was seen as a senior figure in the Sot family. In 1928, however, when Moi was four years old, his father was summoned to attend an important meeting of elders in the lowlands, which was probably convened to discuss serious famine in the region. Upon his return he developed a severe fever, possibly Spanish influenza, which broke out around Eldama Ravine at that time, and after a week's nursing, Kimoi arap Chebii died.

He was given a full and honourable burial by his eldest son, Tuitoek, according to Kalenjin custom, customs which, even today, many members of the tribe follow. The traditional religion of the Kalenjin peoples centred around the worship of a Supreme Being mostly called Asiis, the driving force behind everything, the ultimate arbiter and guarantor of right. As there was a fundamental belief among the Kalenjin that after death the spirit lived on and that there were good and evil spirits, after Kimoi's death, therefore, a number of sacred ceremonies were carried out both to honour Chebii and to ward off profane spirits. While this ritual was taking place, the young Moi would have been kept away. Children were not permitted to witness these ancient rites, for it was felt that they could mimic them in their play and so detract from their importance. The young Moi therefore remained unaware of the tragedy that had befallen his family, and of the fact that his elder brother Tuitoek, who had recently married, was now head of the household.

Despite the death of the father, it was an uncomplicated life. 'Life then was easier,' recalls Moi's sister Rebecca. 'If people lived today like we did then we would all be a lot happier.' The girls rose at dawn and cleared the compound; then, after a simple breakfast of goat's milk and *Wimbi*, a cooked brown millet, the children performed their duties. Three children did the milking while the others went to the *shamba* (cultivated field) to look after the crops.

As a small child, Moi went out with his sisters to herd the animals, graduating by degrees from tending the calves with his sister to joining the men with the cattle, sheep and goats. The rhythm of his training was closely linked with his age, for each boy in Kalenjin society is born into a certain age set of peers, and together they pass through different stages of life, all marked by specific ceremonies. In all, there are seven age sets, each lasting for between twelve and fifteen years, and these form a recurring cycle in Kalenjin history: Kaplelach, to which Kimoi arap Chebii belonged; Kipkoimet; Sawe; Chumo, to which Moi belongs; Maina; Nyongi, to which his elder brother Tuitoek belonged; and Kimnyigei. In each period a boy learns different skills and values; as in many African societies, the emphasis in Kalenjin culture was on an individual's responsibilities as part of the family and village, rather than on personal freedoms. So in his early years he would learn the techniques of herding and protecting the family's animals. Then would come the circumcision ceremony at around fifteen years of age, which marked both puberty and his acceptance into the warrior class. From there he would go on to marry, then to become a father, and eventually a respected elder. Long before then, he would have formed a close bond of trust with others in his age set, a bond which would endure until death.

By all accounts Moi was a dutiful and obedient youngster, his sister Rebecca recalling incidents of squabbling only with difficulty. From a young age Moi was always armed with a *rungu* (a small club), a bow and arrow or occasionally a small sword to ward off attacks from leopards, eagles or baboons – cattle rustling was a rarity – and the children spent hours shooting arrows at targets. They enjoyed high-jumping games, or would play in a swiftly flowing stream which ran down the escarpment near their compound, using makeshift ropes made from vegetation to swing from trees overlooking the brook. Sometimes, if there was a 'good moon' a dance would be held in the compound. At times of celebration – on feast days, or a child's naming ceremony for example – or to welcome a visitor, a goat would be slaughtered.

On reaching a certain age, in the years preceding pubescence, Moi and several other boys in his Chumo age set built their own hut to sleep in. Each evening they sat around the fire, telling stories before falling asleep on the cowhides and sheepskins covering the floor. While his mother still cooked meals, it was unusual in Kalenjin society for women to play anything other than a supporting role in the upbringing of a child. As an example, Moi would have been ridiculed if he had sat with his mother at nightfall, rather than with other boys.

On the surface this was an unruffled rural idyll, a simple yet civilised upbringing in a community concious of its heritage and mindful of its responsibilities. Moi's sister Rebecca has no painful memories of sickness or famine, either in the household or the village. 'If we did have anything like that it was dealt with like anything else,' she says philosophically. Beneath this calm exterior, however, was a Tugen community in turmoil as it attempted to cope with the unremitting demands of its colonial masters and the twin scourges of locusts and drought. District Commissioner Bernard Francklin's extraordinarily frank and revealing report about the Baringo District in 1924 was echoed by other administrators during the years of Moi's childhood in the 1920s and 1930s. By 1927 the 'semi-starving' North Tugen were 'ekeing out a precarious existence on the borderline of starvation', so much so that by 1935 their physical condition was so poor that it took six weeks to feed a man to the point where he could do a reasonable day's work as a labourer on a settler's farm. Conditions became so bad that in 1928, around the time of the death of Moi's father, a *safari* (the word means an overland journey, as well as a hunting expedition) of 1,000 porters was despatched from Eldoret via Tambach carrying food for the starving Tugen. This action by the colonial authorities was not prompted by altruism, however. Aid was conditional on labour service. Gangs of starving Tugen were put to work opening up roads into the area to help the locust campaign, since a great deal of damage had been done to white settlers' crops.

At the same time hundreds of Tugen men were driven out of the area by the iniquitous hut tax – throughout the colonial period Africans paid more in taxes than wealthy Europeans – which was an inevitable result in a society where cattle, not money, constituted the main source of power and currency. This policy had been implemented deliberately by the colonial authorities in order to build a labour market both for the settler farms and the extension of the Ugandan railway. In 1923, for example, more than 1,400 men from Baringo District left their homes to work. By 1942 around four in ten of the able-bodied men of North Baringo were away from the district at any one time, working for wages of Ksh4 a month. It goes without saying that throughout this period revenue raised from the hut tax far exceeded expenditure on the region.

Just as bad as the financial deprivations caused by the hut tax was its method of collection. The authorities used Nubian mercenaries – descendants of this warrior tribe had settled near Eldama Ravine – to ensure that no family escaped the tyranny of taxation. The Nubians worked not just as tax collectors but also as porters and clerks for their colonial masters. The arrival of these armed warriors, who were both hated and feared by the locals, always boded ill. For example, if they were acting as porters for a colonial official they would organise it so that local tribespeople carried their loads from their village to the next, where the local men would be made to take over, and so on throughout the district. If a man seemed tired whilst carrying, the Nubians would kick him from behind – a grave insult in Kalenjin society – or beat him up. On one occasion they came to Moi's village and forced the men to carry the District Commissioner's dogs on their backs. 'They were very hard times,' recalled Moi's elder brother, Tuitoek, in an interview before his death at the age of 104 in 1993.

In 1934, the Nubian scourge was very much in the mind of the village chief, Moi's uncle Kiplabat Chepkeitany, when he convened a *baraza*. It was held to discuss a request from the Christian missionaries who had recently begun working in the Sacho area, to send a number of children to a new school run by the African Inland Church fifty miles away in Kabartonjo.

Naturally, the overwhelming majority of families who gathered at the meeting were hostile. They believed that there was little point or purpose in educating their children – sending a child to school merely took away a much-needed pair of hands. Moi's uncle, however, argued that if the community educated their children then they would be able to take over the jobs of the hated Nubians. In order to reinforce his argument, and to show others a lead, he chose his son, Kibowen, his nephew, Toroitich, and Lachumba, the son of a near neighbour, as the three representatives of Sacho Location who would attend the Kabartonjo mission school. There was open hostility to sending girls, not least because it was felt, by Moi's family, among others, that the girls could work the *shamba* and herd the cattle effectively. Initially Moi's elder brother Tuitoek was undecided about whether to allow Toroitich, as he was still known, to attend school. Like other villagers, he was deeply suspicious of the teachings of the missionaries, who at that time were both 'feared and respected'. Eventually, however, he relented and gave his brother his personal blessing. 'You see how I am suffering, carrying these loads for the white man – all for nothing,' he told Toroitich. 'You go to school. You won't then have to suffer like me. Please go and read what they teach. They might be useful to you and us all.'

When the meeting finally agreed that the boys should go, the elders and the rest of the village blessed them and told them to study well at the mission school so that the rest of the village would be released from the brutality of the Nubians and their colonial masters. For the ten-year-old Moi and his companions there was little sense that they were either sacrificial lambs or willing converts to Christianity, above all, their being sent away was seen by these youngsters as a great adventure. There had been much talk among the local boys of missionaries, schools and the prospect of better things. Now they saw before them an exciting new world beyond the confines and routines of the village.

As they walked proudly along the dirt path on the first stage of their fifty-mile journey, dressed in their traditional goatskins and armed with *rungus* and swords, they had no inkling that they were leaving behind a community whose culture, economy and social structure were rapidly unravelling in an unequal struggle between traditional Kalenjin values and beliefs, and a dominant Christian and capitalist culture.

Ironically, every step on the long march to education, seen by their elders as a way to liberate the community from the body of colonialism, merely drew them further into its embrace.

Chapter two

By the Banks of the Jordan

A small caravan of native bearers and white missionaries snaked its weary way through the bush. As they marched away from their camp at the remote outpost of Rumuruti, they slowly skirted the Laikipia escarpment before heading west. Suddenly their progress was halted by an ominous sight. A short distance away a rhino pawed the ground, preparing to attack these intruders. Then the huge beast charged, and as it picked up speed it seemed to be pounding directly toward a white ark containing baby twins, Erik and Arthur Barnett. With all hope lost, their Australian-born father, the Reverend Albert Edmund Barnett, dropped to his knees and cried out to the Heavens: 'Lord, save us!' At that very moment the rhino veered away and trotted off into the distance, leaving the caravan to continue its journey. That episode, which occurred in 1911, not only confirmed the Reverend Barnett in his mission to expound God's gospel to the indigenous tribes, but was also to prove fortuitous for Daniel arap Moi. The Barnett family were to exert a considerable influence on his life: Erik officiated at his marriage while his younger brother, Paul, built Moi's first house.

Following his arduous journey the Reverend Barnett, one of the first African Inland Mission evangelists, arrived at a place which would eventually be renamed after him, Kabarnet (*kap* means place of). By 1918, however, after a few years spent locked in combat with hostile colonial officials, he and his Swedish wife, Elma, relocated to Eldama Ravine, a former Maasai colony whose name means 'many sunrises'.

Several years later they were joined there by another Australian couple, Ernest and Emmie Dalziel, whose all-consuming passion, according to their daughter Bernice, 'was to win souls to a true knowledge of and love of Jesus Christ'. The Dalziels, learning from the experience of their friends, decided to avoid Kabarnet, in 1926 building a mission station in Kabartonjo.

Besides the Dalziels, Stuart and Elise Bryson, who developed AIM bush schools around Kapsabet, joined the Barnetts for several years, and their numbers were further augmented by Tom Collins, an evangelist who spent most of his life trying to convert the Pokot, and by the Maxwell family. Two native teachers, Stefano Chepkong'a, who started a bush school in Moi's home area at Sacho Location in 1936, and Leah and Reuben Seroney, the parents of Moi's eventual political rival, Jean Marie Seroney, were part of a travelling coterie of AIM teachers. All of them, in their way, made a profound impression on the young Moi.

It was to this new home at Kabartonjo that Moi arrived in 1934. He exchanged his tribal goatskin garments for khaki shorts and singlet, a pile of sheepskins for a bare, wooden-slatted bed in a dormitory, and the gentle rhythm of a world governed by the needs of the herd to a regime ruled by the striking bell. It was a hard, rigorous, disciplined life. Every morning at six o'clock they had prayers before walking downhill to the river to collect water in four-gallon drums. Seven times the pupils made that one-and-a-quarter-mile journey before breakfast. Then, after that meal, the girls went to the *posho* mill to grind flour, while the boys worked in the garden – this routine of hoeing and planting was to be one of Moi's enduring childhood memories. When these chores were done it was time for collecting firewood and grass – the girls the smaller kindling, the boys the large logs. In the afternoon they learnt their letters – Moi was taught the alphabet by Elma Barnett – and had Bible readings and prayers. Once a week one of the boys trudged the twelve miles to Kabarnet in order to pick up the mail and newspapers from the Government Post. The Dalziels were always amazed that these youngsters, Moi included, were able to return from this long journey by five o'clock and then head immediately for a game of football. It wasn't as though the mission diet was particularly sustaining. They ate *ugali* or *Wimbi*, together with a mélange of boiled weeds and wild flowers.

Whatever the day-to-day austerity of this life, it quite failed to quench the excitement of Moi's elder sister, Rebecca, at the prospect of joining them. She was not alone. Word had spread like wildfire among the Tugen teenagers, who were exhilarated and enthused by the chance to make a new start in the mission station. 'My generation was now at school and I would have felt left out if I hadn't gone,' she recalls. 'It was an exciting place to go, a place to be educated, explore Christianity and achieve our goals in life.' Her memories contrast vividly with the hindsight of historians. As one academic put it: 'Colonial schooling was education for subordination, exploitation, the creation of mental confusion and the development of underdevelopment.'

Rebecca had already tried to sneak out of the family compound to make the fifty-mile trip to Kabartonjo once before, but had been caught and punished. However, when her younger brother arrived home and described his life there she was even more resolved to leave. Moi agreed to help and together they carefully planned her escape.

She crept out of the compound in the dead of the night and made her way to the mission station in Sacho, where Stefano Chepkong'a was waiting for her. Guided only by his lantern, they walked through the night, arriving in the vicinity of Kabartonjo by daylight. Once at the school, she was greeted by scenes of real commotion as shouting, bellowing and sobbing parents of children who had also run away from home stood outside the stout wooden fence of the mission compound, calling the names of their loved ones. Some tried to cajole their off-spring to leave, others brandished whips and threatened to punish them severely if they did not return.

Rebecca Chelimo was spared this emotional tussle. First of all, her home village was a long way away, and secondly the village chief, her uncle Kiplabat Chepkeitany, had decreed that if children managed to escape and walk further than Kapropita their parents were to leave them in peace. Today Rebecca and James Chelimo, who met his wife at mission school, chuckle as they recall those turbulent scenes, in the mid-1930s, when families were literally torn apart as the children fell under the spell of the first Pied Pipers of Christianity. They acknowledge, though, that there would be an international outcry if the same were to happen today. The episode also serves to illustrate vividly the fear and hostility which greeted the first missionaries, and, among the Africans, the growing gap between the generations, between those who eventually accepted the Christian faith and those who adhered to traditional Tugen culture.

Those who embraced the African Inland Church adopted a particular brand of fundamentalist Christianity as austere as it was conservative. The African Inland Mission, which had been founded in Pennsylvania, America, in 1895, depended almost entirely on the energy of the missionaries and the support of their congregations. Unlike the Roman Catholic Church, it was repelled both by native customs and by the policies of the colonial government, a feeling which was reciprocated. The views of the AIM missionary Stuart Bryson, whose daughter

Margaret is married to the former Attorney-General, Charles Njonjo, about the indigenous population were typical: 'In cases of illness, misfortune or death, debased and devilish practices of divination and revenge take place . . . there was all the time the dark background of heathenism with its fear, cruelty and malevolence. To bring men and women out of that darkness and deliver the prey of the Terrible One [Satan] was the reason we were there.'

This revulsion against traditional rituals and practices was not lost on the first Vice-President of Kenya, Jaramogi Oginga Odinga, another mission boy, who wrote in his biography, *Not Yet Uhuru*:

> Over the years it had dawned on me that I had listened to many preachers and they seemed to preach one thing in common: the suppression of African customs. They were not satisfied to concentrate on the word of the Bible: they tried to use the word of God to judge African traditions. An African who followed his people's customs was condemned as heathen and anti-Christian.

As a consequence both of their Tugen culture and the rigid AIC beliefs which they assimilated from a young age, the pioneering native AIC Christians have qualities which clearly mark them out from other native believers. They have an inner spiritual toughness complemented by a physical robustness; when Kenyans describe followers of the African Inland Church – or the President, for that matter – they hold the palm of one hand vertically to signify a sternly upright bearing and manner. During my research I spoke to a number of the early AIC converts, many of them now in their eighties. Similar qualities shone from all of them: a strong sense of purpose; rigorous self-discipline; high standards of morality and decency; strict sobriety; a devout Christian faith, as well as an ability to quote the Old Testament at will. Humility and acceptance in the face of adversity were balanced by a puritanical disdain for rival creeds, particularly Roman Catholicism. They all shared, too, robust good health. (Moi was only ever ill in 1939 when he caught malaria.) This was due in part to the plain and frugal diet of their early years at mission school. Even today Moi is happiest when eating simple traditional fare like *ugali*, *Wimbi* and goat's meat.

The young Moi adapted well to this sternly invigorating climate. His fellow pupils called him Kapkorios – 'Big Head' – not because he was conceited but because his head was indeed large. His sister Rebecca remembers a little boy who had changed considerably since he had left home. Africans were banned from wearing shoes, a privilege only whites enjoyed – and his demeanour seemed quieter and more studious. 'He was a humble boy,' she recalls, using a word which recurs often in descriptions of Moi. The Reverend Dalziel's daughter Bernice, who now lives in Western Australia, remembers a child who 'showed an eagerness to learn all he could . . . He had an amazingly strong determination for one so young to succeed in all he did.'

His perceptive intelligence was also evident from early on. When a teacher asked the class where God was, the pupils were puzzled. Moi piped up: 'He's every-where,' a reply which made a deep impression on Elizabeth Chesire, among others. She had gone to study at the mission school in 1933 but had left two years later to marry. In that same year, 1935, the school was closed for a time due to widespread famine. The older boys were sent home but the younger ones, including 'Big Head', were billeted with Christian families who lived near by. Elizabeth and Isaiah Chesire, her husband, took him in to their modest hut in the first-ever native Christian settlement at Kapropita. These were difficult days, scratching an existence by rooting for wild vegetables and ekeing out meagre supplies of *ugali*.

The hardships he willingly endured, coupled with the time he spent in a Christian household, seem to have strengthened Moi's resolve to convert to the Christian faith. Elizabeth Chesire believes that the spiritual blessings of Christianity over the Kalenjin faith often tipped the balance as potential converts considered their options. 'Under Kalenjin culture we were taught to fear a Supreme Being,' she says. 'There was no way of touching or feeling it or even being close to the Creator. So when the missionaries came and said that you can meet the Creator and promised eternal life and salvation, that had an allure which the Kalenjin faith could not match.'

On 20 October 1936, in a leafy clearing known locally as Jordan on the banks of the River Bebyemit (which means olive trees), a modest stream running near the mission station, Kapkorios Toroitich arap Moi was baptised by the Reverend Dalziel. He was only the fifteenth person to have been baptised in the locality, a poor return after so many years of endeavour. Like many other converts, he chose Daniel from the Old Testament, although the name also featured in a song popular in the mission at that time: 'Dare to be a Daniel, dare to stand alone . . .' There is a certain aptness to it, as Bernice Dalziel observes: 'I wonder how often Moi has felt like the Daniel of biblical times, alone in the lions' den?'

It was a turning point. Once Moi converted to Christianity he no longer mixed with other villagers as freely or as easily as before, tending to prefer the company of other Christians. While he still visited his home in Sacho Location, much of his free time was taken up helping his fellow Christians to preach the gospel in nearby villages.

Certainly the Reverend Dalziel needed all the help he could muster from his flock to keep alive the evangelical flame of the African Inland Mission. It did not go unnoticed that the standard of AIM education fell below that of other faiths, let alone the government schools, as the AIM leaders had, in 1922, refused government funding for schools, with the inevitable result that standards drastically declined.

The mission school at Kabartonjo did not escape this decline, so that by 1938, with falling pupil rolls and Ernest Dalziel's failing health, it was decided to allow pupils to move to other schools. As Bernice Dalziel recalls: 'Very reluctantly, and with a sad sense of loss, my father let young Moi and a couple of other lads go.' So that year Moi moved to Kapsabet mission school in the heart of Nandi country, more than 100 miles from his home village. Whatever he might have hoped, however, life in his new school replicated Kabartonjo in that it was equally strict and rigorous. It also enjoyed a similarly dismal educational reputation.

Moi earned his keep by working in the garden of the school's missionaries, Stuart and Elise Bryson and Reg and Zan Reynolds. For his toil he was given an allowance of *posho* and salt, but he had to hunt for his own wild vegetables. These were boiled in water rather than cooked in oil and then eaten with *ugali*. 'It was,' noted his best friend at the school, Gedion Tarus, with masterly understatement, 'a very plain diet.' Only on Christmas Day, after they had listened to the radio in Mr Bryson's home, were they allowed a piece of meat and a bowl of rice.

Every day began at dawn with an hour of prayers and hymns followed by breakfast of *ugali* and salt. Then the girls, who were strictly segregated from the boys, went to collect firewood and water. They would then mill the maize for *posho* while the boys worked in the garden and fields. In the afternoon there were two hours of lessons, the bell sounding every half-hour so that they could change subjects.

They studied Swahili, English, the Bible, nature, maths and agriculture under the tutelage of the missionary families, as well as other teachers who included Jean Baxter, Jeremiah Birra and Francis Leftley (Moi remembers the latter with affection and gratitude for the help she gave him). As Gedion Tarus recalls, however: 'The missionaries were not interested in academic achievement but to change the individual who would go back and convert others. I was the first one in our family to break away, and saw the mission as a kind of rebirth.'

When lessons were over the girls played netball or high jump while the boys enjoyed endless games of football. As Kalenjin people are individualistic rather than team players, these usually degenerated into games of kick and rush. Moi was a defender who earned the nickname 'Wheelbarrow' because of his wide arcing tackles – if he didn't make contact with the ball, he certainly did with his opponents.

At dusk there were prayers before supper and then the girls and boys retired to their separate huts built of mud with grass thatch, dormitories where they slept on beds made of sacks filled with wet grass – a constant source of complaint. Such was the segregation between the sexes that if a boy was caught even talking to a girl he was punished with a long session digging in the garden under the hot midday sun. Moreover, even when the young men and women were at an age for marriage, the missionary took total control. The girls lined up, a potential suitor picked out his fancy and then asked the missionary for permission to talk to her. If she agreed, the missionary sat behind the couple to listen to what was being said.

While the missionaries watched boys with hawk-like suspicion when it came to the opposite sex, Moi was an exception. He was seen as honest and trustworthy, the only male pupil allowed to accompany and supervise the girls when they went to collect mud and sand for repairs to mission buildings. In what was to be his first teaching position, he was asked to take the younger classes for Bible study. It was an indication both of his deeply held Christian faith and of his responsible character. As well as regularly teaching at Sunday school, he had the job of collecting tithes during church services, a sign of his growing maturity. As fellow pupil Paul Boit recalls: 'He wasn't an ambitious boy, but a trusted and responsible young man who behaved like an elder even though he was quite young.'

Although the memories of Moi's contemporaries may be coloured by time, and perhaps by the high office he eventually attained, two events in his teenage years underwrite his Christian commitment as well as his quiet determination. In 1939, when Moi was fifteen, Stefano Chepkong'a fell ill, and was taken to a mission hospital, leaving the Sacho school with its twelve pupils unattended. When Moi came to hear of this, he wrote to the Provincial Education Officer in Eldoret saying that he would like to take over the running of the school until Stefano recovered. He was granted his wish and temporarily discharged from his studies at Kapsabet. In spite of his efforts, however, the Sacho school eventually closed, and the remaining pupils were transferred to Kapropita mission school.

Moi returned to his Kapsabet mission school later in 1939 to find the Christian community buzzing with excitement over the arrival of the first ever Nandi Bible. It had taken Stuart Bryson and the evangelist teacher Samuel Kimnyige, who became the first ordained Nandi pastor and later a bishop, eight years of pains-taking effort to translate the Old and New Testament into Kimnyige's native tongue. Moi made it clear that it was his burning ambition to own a copy, but without funds it was an almost impossible desire. His mission teacher and pastor, the Reverend Reg Reynolds, learned of Moi's dream, and as a result hired him to drive two cows from the mission school to a Dr Ashton who lived at the African Inland Mission in Kapsowar, some seventy-five miles away. It was a difficult three-day trek across tough unyielding country, and he took his friend Gedion Tarus along for company. The distance did not particularly trouble them for each weekend they regularly ran the twenty-odd miles to Gedion's home in Kipsigak in the Nandi Hills. Gedion, who went on to represent Kenya in distance races, recalls: 'It was a hard journey, we slept by the road and lived off the milk from the cows we were herding.' On the first night they stopped at Eldoret, spending the second in Karuna before arriving at their destination. For his trouble Moi was given two shillings and, true to his word, used it to buy a copy of the new Nandi Bible.

The following year, 1940, he and his friend Gedion Tarus passed their Common Entrance exam and were transferred to the nearby Government African School in Kapsabet. Moi's school number was 503, Gedion's 506 – a stark numerical indicator of how few children had been educated in the district since the school had been founded.

The main difference between his old and new schools was that for the first time in his school life Moi was in a distinct minority, for of the 120 boys, only 20 or so were committed Christians. There were several Catholics but the overwhelming majority obeyed traditional Kalenjin teachings, and the Christian boys became a target for abuse and occasional beatings. Fights regularly broke out although, by all accounts, Moi never became involved. They were called either 'kipsukulin', meaning boys from the mission school, or 'chebisaas', a word derived from the sound of a Tilley lamp being slowly extinguished, a noise linked to the early missionaries when they camped in the bush. Effectively it was a term of insult, implying that these pioneer Christians had betrayed their tribal origins.

'We were not really liked, other boys spited us,' recalls Gedion Tarus. 'It taught us humility and to turn away from trouble. All of us, including Moi, had abandoned the traditional life and there was no turning back. For that he paid a big price.' Perhaps the most anguishing dilemma these young Christian boys faced was whether to take part in the ritual Kalenjin circumcision ceremony, a traditional rite of passage which marked the transition from boyhood to manhood. At Kapsabet Government School Moi knew, as did everyone else, that his Chumo age set had undertaken that coming-of-age ceremony, and he faced cruel taunts from boys, some younger than himself, that he was not yet a man.

His predicament, and that of hundreds of other Christian teenagers, lay in the fact that the AIM, in concert with other missions, had long taught against anything which did not conform to Christian traditions.

This was the heart of the matter, for while the Christian and Kalenjin religions, with their worship of a single deity, were not altogether dissimiliar, the attendant cultural trappings of faith were entirely alien. So while many native Christians felt instinctively that their tribal customs and their Christian belief were not mutually exclusive, the missionaries held quite the opposite view, confusing the external manifestations of faith with faith itself. Herein lay the conflict.

This missionaries' antipathy towards the practice focused on the physical act of circumcision rather than the cultural factors that lay behind it. In fact, the coming of age, or *keeba tuum*, was considered to be the most important event in the life of the Kalenjin. Initiation rites for both males and females extended over a period of months and included not only the rite of circumcision but also induction into the secret rituals of the tribe and the teaching of tribal history and customs. The months the initiate spent in camp amounted to nothing less than schooling for adulthood.

Following the ritual of circumcision the boys were taken to a camp where they learned about morality, and about how to dress, good manners, generosity towards strangers, self-discipline, and the need to behave with dignity and humility. In short, they were taught how to become responsible citizens who honoured their families, defended their communities and respected their customs.

For the teenage Moi, enthused by and grateful toward the Christian missionaries who had become his surrogate family, the circumcision ceremony presented him with the most testing challenge of his young life. He was not alone in his torment. Many Christian boys simply left the mission school for their initiation ceremonies, returning after several months.

Moi himself took a middle course. In 1944 he and a schoolfriend, Benjamin Cherono, went to Kabarnet hospital to be circumcised.

It is noticeable that like Kenyatta, also a mission boy who missed some indoctrination rites of his Kikuyu tribe, and who became a stickler for tradition in later years, so Moi has ensured that his own children have undergone the full Kalenjin rituals.

The cultural significance of the circumcision ceremony, and the controversy surrounding it, merely served to underline the sense of isolation felt by Moi and other Christian boys during their days at Kapsabet Government School. During weekdays they walked to their former mission school for prayers, while on Wednesday, the usual day for hymns and prayers at their new school, Moi would take the place of the missionary if the latter was otherwise engaged. On Sunday mornings he and Gedion Tarus trekked twenty-five miles to preach at Koyo church; 'We found the walk easy because we were walking for God,' recalls Gedion.

Their rigorous spiritual life was matched by the spartan existence at the school. They were plagued with bedbugs in their dormitory and were only allowed to wash themselves and their clothes in the river once a week. Inevitably illness was rife – once every three months the principal, A.S. Walford, took the whole school to the hospital to be wormed. It was very much a self-help community. At weekends they cut firewood – women's work in Tugen culture – or learned carpentry. What they slept on, ate from or sat on, the boys made themselves. 'Great keenness is shown by the boys in workshops where they tackle their jobs with speed and zeal,' reported Walford. During the 1940s Gill Lambert, the wife of the then District Commissioner, Roger Lambert, taught the boys how to spin and weave so that they would be able to make their own blankets and pullovers. Now in her nineties and living in a nursing home in Britain, she remembers Moi – 'dear Daniel,' as she calls him – as 'very polite and well-mannered'. 'He was a strong character and I knew he would go far,' she says.

At times of ease, one of Moi's greatest pleasures was taking part in singing sessions with his teacher Japetha Abugwi Luseno, who also taught him his impeccable copperplate script. Moi's booming bass voice was perfectly suited to the negro spirituals which Luseno taught the choir. (At a recent Nakuru Agricultural Show the President delighted the audience by singing the chorus of 'Nobody Knows The Trouble I've Seen'.) It was during choir practice that Moi struck up a friendship with Paul Chemirmir, known affectionately by one and all as 'the Joker'. The son of a chief, he had been educated by Paul Barnett at his mission school in Eldama Ravine, and at weekends he and Moi would return there to sing in accompaniment to the organ at the African Inland Church. On one occasion the District Commissioner gave them the princely sum of 1 Kenya shilling because he had been so impressed with their rendition of Christmas carols.

When Chemirmir arrived at Kapsabet in 1941 Moi, now seventeen, had just been made a prefect. He now slept at the end of the dormitory by the door to make sure the other boys in his charge could not sneak out at night. 'He didn't beat anybody, unlike other prefects,' recalls Paul. 'He was quiet and if you did something wrong he would talk to you like a father.' A perk of Moi's position was that he was allowed to stay up later than the other boys listening to the war news from the BBC on a crackly valve wireless.

In the eyes of his contemporaries, he displayed the qualities of a muscular Christian, naturally obedient and peaceable but ready to intervene in a crisis. 'He was a very likeable character and would never pick a fight,' recalls Joel Bultut, now the Chairman of Kabarnet County Council. 'During meals boys had a tendency to fight over food but Moi would wait for things to settle down and wait his turn.' On one occasion he rushed to break up a vicious fight between several boys, on another he sat stoically while a boy tried to strangle him because he had beaten him at draughts. 'If you quarrelled with him or tried to pick a fight, he didn't answer,' remembers Gedion Tarus.

It came as no surprise when, in 1942, he was appointed school captain. Just as his demeanour displayed maturity and quiet leadership, he also demonstrated a reliable academic proficiency. Records show that he averaged 75 per cent in his classwork and his teachers noted in his reports that: 'Daniel Kapkorios arap Moi is a promising young boy. He has a promising character and has a bright future.'

A member of the Library Committee and an enthusiastic defender in the football First XI – he eventually played for the Parliamentary team – Moi took an active part in every aspect of school life. Naturally there were rivalries and jealousies – his schoolfriend Jean Marie Seroney, later a leading politician, never forgot that in the school Debating Society Moi was the Chairman while he was just the Secretary. That schoolboy competitiveness continued into their political careers.

Moi's qualities of leadership were tested when a colonial officer arrived at the school asking for volunteers to help take a Nandi tribesman to hospital. Stricken with smallpox, he had been left to die by his community, who were terrified of catching the disease. Moi, Gedion Tarus and two others agreed to help and drove with the officer in his Land Rover to Kamoiywa in Chemundu Location. There they found the village deserted except for a native of the Terik clan, considered to be low-class people, who was quietly nursing the sick villager. They took him to hospital where he eventually recovered.

A challenge demanding different qualities presented itself later in the year. The school Principal, A. S. Walford – known by the boys as 'Chepsungulgei', 'the one who fidgets' – had slaughtered a cow and for weeks the boys had to eat meat from the gradually rotting carcass. There was already resentment in the area about the way the military, under wartime regulations, had requisitioned the best cattle for themselves. After three weeks the boys rebelled, marching through Kapsabet to make their protest to the District Commissioner, Roger Lambert. As they walked along the road Moi, who was at the head of the striking boys, was angrily upbraided by Reverend Reynolds, who came out of his mission school to see what the commotion was about.

Finally they reached the office of the DC, who allowed two boys – Moi and Tarus – to explain their case. As Moi was school captain, and might therefore have faced retribution for this protest, his friend Gedion outlined the position. The local doctor was called for, inspected the meat and, with typical British understatement, commented: 'It does not look like a cow that has been slaughtered today.' The boys won their case. There was nearly another strike when they were forced to wear uncomfortable khaki shorts which had no seams, flies or pockets because of wartime savings on labour and materials.

All this happened at a time of drought, disease and pestilence as the country faced the greatest agrarian crisis of the war. 'Famine conditions were avoided, but only by a narrow margin,' noted Roger Lambert in his annual report. The scarcity was exacerbated by the haemorrhage of men conscripted to the war effort, and by the gradual transition in Kenyan agriculture from basic foods like maize to cash-crop cultivation. In fact by 1945, according to an official government report, native Kenyans were less well fed than they had been before the arrival of the white man.

Whatever their tribulations, of Moi's generation of schoolboys, no doubt the Principal would have picked out J. M. Seroney, Shadrak Kimalel (later an Ambassador), Gedion Tarus and Daniel Moi as standing out from the rest of his pupils. All passed the Nyanza Competitive Examination, which gave them the opportunity to attend Alliance High School, then the most academically advanced African school in Kenya. While Seroney and Kimalel did transfer, Tarus and Moi were convinced by their teachers and by missionary friends that their destiny lay in teaching, especially as Kapsabet had just started its first teacher-training programme.

It was a near-run thing, however. Others in the local Christian community, including the Reverend Paul Barnett, believed that Moi had the makings of a first-class preacher. Instead, he took his blankets to the aptly named Moi dormitory (each was named after a Nandi clan) to undergo a year-long course of teacher training. 'I liked teaching,' he has said. 'It was a worthwhile profession. It made me feel that I was helping my people.'

Just as his life as a pioneer Christian had taken him away from his people, now his new career as a teacher seemed destined to draw him back to his roots.

Chapter three
Conversion at Midnight

For Reuben Bomett it was his longest day. At five in the morning he and a group of Nandi warriors, including his father, had gone into battle against the British invaders during what would be remembered as the third of the Nandi wars of resistance. By noon his father lay dead and Reuben, then a boy of twelve, found himself upside-down deep in a large cavity, his head held fast in the rocks. As the heat of the afternoon sun took its toll Reuben, bleeding and parched with thirst, cried out, pleading with his assailants to pull him free.

Instead, a Nubian fighter repeatedly prodded his spear down the hole in an attempt to kill Reuben. He was so far down that the spear just pierced his flesh but no more, and although he was in intense pain he managed to remain silent. After a while, however, the torment was such that he cried out again for help and the Nubians, hearing him, fired a shot into the cavity. While the noise of the blast rendered him unconcious, the bullet failed to hit him. In the evening the Nandi warriors returned to the field of battle and, hearing a weak shout, pulled him from his painful prison.

As Reuben recovered from his ordeal, his now widowed mother made the decision to leave their home at Kaptumo in Nandi country and settle in Eldama Ravine. So in 1900 the Bomett family, including Reuben and his brothers Paul and David, headed for their new home. From these inauspicious beginnings, the Bometts were to become the most influential and well-to-do family in Eldama Ravine, as well as the first family to convert to Christianity in the district, the men enthusiastic elders of the African Inland Mission church founded by Albert Barnett.

When Barnett's son Paul arrived in the township in 1941 following years of schooling and missionary training in America, one of his first acts was to baptise Paul Bomett's third daughter, Helena, who was born in 1926. A devout Christian, Helena, her brother William and sister Dina formed a gospel trio; later, after finishing her schooling at the Tenwek Mission, Helena went on to become a primary-school teacher. 'She was an iron lady but with a great sense of humour,' recalls Paul Chemirmir, who regularly visited the church with his friend Daniel arap Moi.

Over the years Moi was to become a regular visitor to Eldama Ravine, where he often stayed with either the Bometts or the Barnetts; indeed, it was from the Bomett family that he was to choose his wife. By now he had graduated from his year-long teacher-training course at Kapsabet Government School and in 1944 was transferred to Tambach African School on the slopes of the Kerio Valley as a P3-grade teacher on a salary of Ksh47 a month. Besides teaching Swahili and mathematics, the twenty-year-old Moi supervised sports. 'He showed us how to play the strange football,' recalls John Chebii, one of his first pupils. At the same time the young Moi was becoming a familiar face in the district because of his endless visits to churches, either to preach the gospel or to take part in services.

Moi's own peregrinations coincided with a renewal of energy in the African Inland Mission, Paul Barnett building a number of churches and mission schools. From time to time Moi, himself an enthusiastic carpenter, pitched in to help or gave Barnett food and shelter when he was passing through Tambach. In 1945 the American built a small mission school at Tenges, and there was talk of asking Moi to become the first teacher. Even in those days the missionary was deeply affected by Moi's character. 'He had a good outspoken Christian testimony. There is no doubt about his Christianity which is to the bone,' he says. 'He was a man of integrity and just as honest as could he be, and he has impressed me more and more as I have got to know him these last forty years.'

Before the Tenges school got off the ground, Moi discovered that he was wanted elsewhere. In 1943 a number of Italian prisoners of war were employed to build a new government African school at Kabarnet, Moi's home district, and shortly after it opened Moi, together with two other Tugens, were taken on as the first Kenyan teachers under the supervision of C. A. Berridge.

As the most junior member of staff, Moi taught the Class One intake, concentrating on agriculture, carpentry, Swahili and sport. When he took his class of twenty boys for agriculture lessons they occasionally went to the *shamba* of Isaiah and Elizabeth Chesire to work on their land. Indeed, their son Reuben's first memory of Moi is when he taught him how to hoe and to climb trees.

The same energy which he had expended on expounding the gospel he now applied to his new school. Thanks to the efforts of Principal Berridge, Moi and his two colleagues the school soon achieved first-class results. Even the District Commissioner, R. Hickson Mahony, was enthusiastic about the school's success. In his 1947 report he wrote. 'Six candidates who sat the primary school examination, all passed, three with sufficiently high marks to allow them to proceed to the Alliance High School for secondary education. Great credit is due to Mr C. A. Berridge, the principal for this 100% success.'

For Moi, who had not been given a permanent position, Kabarnet was only a short sojourn before he returned to Tambach, where he graduated from teaching children to teacher training. He both taught at the Government African School and was trained, and eventually became an instructor, at the Kagumo teacher-training college. The latter, which had 160 or so trainees, was run on quasi-military lines by a cadre of white principals, mostly demobbed officers. Their behaviour reminded him of the other side of the colonial coin – the

British attitude, characterised by patronising superiority and calm aloofness towards native Kenyans which rankled with so many. This attitude was codified in pay and conditions for teachers, which were based on skin colour rather than seniority or ability. So while Moi maintained his friendship with the missionaries and other white teachers from his own schooldays, a number of incidents increased his awareness of the basic injustices of the colonial regime.

One of his abiding memories during his time as a trainee teacher at Tambach was the uncompromising hostility of the white staff towards independent thought and endeavour. During one classroom discussion he prefaced an observation with the words 'I think'. This was too much for his white principal, who responded with the damning retort: 'It's not for you to think or question us. It's your job to do as you're told. You Kenyans are like animals.'

President Moi still talks about that episode today, as he does about other behaviour by the *mzungus* (white men) which was deliberately intended to demean and degrade native Kenyans. As he now recalls:

> We were more than aggrieved to see our products being turned into tools for furthering colonialism and white settlerism. The system of racial segregation and discrimination in employment and other fields of social development was cleverly worked out so that the African always found himself working as a *karani* (clerk) for the foreigner or being kept away from towns to work as a teacher in the so-called Native Reserve. Those from higher institutions of learning could only be given jobs as assistants, mostly to work under less well-educated, inexperienced whites. The situation could not be bettered without personal sacrifices from the *wananchi* so most of us decided to leave teaching for politics to help improve the situation.

On one occasion during his travels round the district he hitched a ride from a settler in his pick-up truck. Rather than let him sit in the front, the settler made Moi stand at the back of the open-truck bed, clinging on to the sides as best he could as the pick-up lurched along dust roads. He was actually lucky to get a lift; in those days most Kenyans would run and hide if they saw a white man's car coming down the road. Even when he became a member of the Legislative Council this discrimination did not ease. After he and fellow MP Masinde Muliro were unceremoniously thrown out of a downtown Nairobi hotel they introduced a motion to end racial discrimination in bars, hotels and other public places. Grudgingly the settler majority approved the motion although they insisted that everyone had to wear a tie to be allowed entry. 'Those were the kinds of things that we faced at that time,' he says.

Indeed such behaviour was merely an assertion of the system of, effectively, apartheid which existed not just in Baringo District but throughout Kenya. In the Rift Valley native Kenyans were banned from hotels, bars and social clubs, and the settlers viewed the wearing of shoes or hats like the white man with open hostility. For many years they were prevented from growing cash crops, while any attempt to start a business met with official opposition. Their place was firmly at the base of the Kenyan social, political and economic hierarchy. The primitive education system was specifically designed only to allow natives on to the very bottom rung of colonial society, and no further. Yet by gaining admittance even at this lowest level, educated Kenyans like teachers, clerks and other government officials, inevitably trained in mission schools, were then able to test how far up the ladder they could climb. These 'progressive natives' were thus collectively the incubus within the colonial system, at once supporting its structures whilst simultaneously working towards its eventual demolition.

Progress towards independence – indeed, just the idea that Kenyans could be free of their colonial masters – was a flower that bloomed more readily in some regions than others. In Baringo, a closed and backward district without radios, newspapers or independent native organisations, the very idea that Kenya could one day be an independent nation was but a whisper in the wind. None the less, voices were being heard, albeit *sotto voce*. For a time Argwings Kodhek, one of Kenya's founding fathers, was a teacher at Tambach before going to Britain to study law. 'I had great admiration for Kodhek,' says Moi. 'He was a brilliant man and very good teacher.' Ironically, another voice was that of a white man, Mr Hammond, a supporter of the British Labour Party who came to Tambach as one of the teachers. During informal discussions he talked about the need for change, and of how colonial rule was essentially wrong, sentiments which coincided with the Labour Party's landslide victory in Britain at the general election of 1945, and the end of imperial rule in India. Indeed, the granting of independence to India in 1947 had a profound effect not just on Kenyans but on all Africans, since it demonstrated that colonial government – which behaved like a collective *laibon* (sorcerer), unpredictable, malevolent, yet necessary, could be overthrown.

The ending of the Second World War in 1945 had also brought something of a sea change, with the return of many young men who had been drafted into the King's African Rifles; their experiences had opened their eyes as to how oppressed they were in their own country. Those who had witnessed the whirring mechanism of empire at closer quarters now more clearly understood its bogus mystery. A Kenyan farmer, Rhoderick Macleod, the brother of the future Colonial Secretary, Iain Macleod, observed that the returning African soldier 'didn't take kindly to removing his hat in his own country in the District Commissioner's office in order to ask for a pass to visit a cousin in the next village'.

This shifting mood coincided with the return to Kenya of Jomo Kenyatta. He had lived in London, in the heart of the imperial darkness, since 1931 and on his return was able to tell his countrymen that Britain was a hypocritical society, whose idea of democracy ended at the white cliffs of Dover. During his years in London Kenyatta earned a reputation as an anthropologist as well as a political leader; his book, *Facing Mount Kenya*, had been published in 1938. When he returned to Kenya in 1946 his election as leader of the Kenya Africa Union (KAU), a group started by Harry Thuku when the Kikuyu Central Association was banned, sparked a nationalist flame which slowly fanned out from its centre in the Kikuyu reserve and the slums of Nairobi.

Naturally the colonial authorities were quick to stamp out any nationalistic sparks. The Governor, Sir Philip Mitchell, rejected African nationalism as an 'emotional movement rather than a rational policy'. He supported a slow evolution towards multi-racialism, with the British acting as trustees of the

Africans for generations to come. Africans, he believed, were not ready to participate in national politics and should limit themselves to local activities.

In the face of such obduracy and the increasing moderation of the KAU, the burgeoning independence movement, fuelled by a hunger for land, split in two – those 'progressive natives' who favoured change by evolution, and radicals who sought it by revolution.

During those days of mounting unrest, Moi's dreams were more prosaic – to find a permanent job and eventually a wife. He taught at Tambach Government School during the day and in his spare time studied for the London Matriculation Examination, which he duly passed. In January 1948 the Senior Education Officer for the Rift Valley recommended him for the award of an education certificate, adding in his letter to the Director of Education in Nairobi: 'I know him to be quite outstanding both in ability and character.' Just eighteen months later, in August 1949, Moi was granted a permanent appointment. 'He is efficient, reliable and has a sense of responsibility,' wrote his principal. 'In fact he is one of the best teachers on the staff. I do not hesitate to recommend him.'

During holidays he spent time at Eldama Ravine, staying with either the Bometts or the Barnetts. As the Bometts were the leading Christian family in the area, it was both natural and inevitable that Moi would look to one of their number as a future wife. Even though they were both deeply committed Christians, his courtship of nursery-school teacher Helena Bomett conformed to traditional custom. In obedience to Kalenjin lore, under which a potential suitor must ask the brother of the bride's father for permission to marry, Moi spoke privately to Reuben Bomett. Following this discussion, Reuben called a meeting of his brothers, Paul, Helena's father, and David, as well as village elders. During the pre-nuptial *baraza* Moi was allowed to sit inside the meeting hut, but near the door, a sign that he could linger but not take part in any decisions. He was asked questions about his family history, his clan, and so on in order to make sure that the couple's bloodlines were suitably distant. However, since those at the meeting knew a good deal about him because of their Christian links, the questioning did not last long. The bride price, which was reasonably substantial, was two heifers, one ox and four sheep.

The couple were duly married in 1950 at the now sadly dilapidated African Inland Mission church in Eldama Ravine, the wedding attended by 500 guests, including many teachers and former pupils from Tambach and Kabarnet. Moi's friend Francis Cherogony, by then the town council clerk in Kabarnet, was best man, while the Reverend Erik Barnett officiated.

Daniel arap Moi and his wife seemed destined for a quiet life of local respect and local renown. His work as a teacher at Tambach Government School, where the couple lived in a house in the grounds, continued to earn plaudits from his superiors; 'He is man of outstanding ability and integrity,' ran an education report of April 1951. The following year, 1952, Jennifer, their first child, was born, followed a year later by Jonathan Kipkemboi. Both were christened by their parents' old friend, the Reverend Paul Barnett.

Whatever the Mois' domestic calm, however, in the country as a whole storm clouds of unrest were gathering. While white agriculture prospered, over-population and overgrazing in the tribal reserves set up by the colonial authorities meant that many of the landless went to work on farms in the Rift Valley or moved to the slums of Nairobi. Postwar unemployment reached 20 per cent, with 22,000 homeless Kenyans roaming the streets of Nairobi. Low wages, rapidly rising prices, the return of 75,000 Kenyan soldiers, land and business restrictions as well as political impotence served to fuel discontent both in the towns and countryside. For many Kenyans, the *kipande*, a tin box containing a pass and an identification card which they had to wear slung from a cord around their necks, symbolised British oppression.

By the late 1940s Kenyatta's moderate KAU policies, which promoted self-improvement and gradual peaceful reform, were rapidly overtaken by a new mood of rebellion, with radical trade unionists such as Bildad Kaggia and Fred Kubai challenging Kenyatta's ascendancy. At the 1951 KAU Conference the radicals staged a successful coup against the moderates, isolating Kenyatta, who was now effectively held hostage by the militant nationalists. While KAU radicals organised underground resistance to the colonial authorities in a secret Kikuyu movement which came to be known as Mau Mau, whose members were bound together by blood oaths, they faced increasing opposition from Kenyatta and Kikuyu chiefs loyal to him. During 1951 and 1952 he held a series of rallies throughout Kenya where he strongly denounced Mau Mau militancy, and it was rumoured that this made him the object of assassination plots hatched by his political rivals.

In July 1952 Kenyatta travelled to Eldama Ravine, where he addressed a large KAU rally. Among his audience were the Bomett family, who acted as his hosts throughout his stay in the district. (He made an impact of sorts – a local schoolboy's answer to the exam question 'Who is Jomo Kenyatta?' stated: 'He is the Minister for Community Development'.) His speech at Eldama Ravine was a repetition of the message he had delivered to a huge rally in Nyeri, where he had called for national unity rather than subversion, and had proclaimed that violence and thuggery would only delay Kenya's independence.

In October 1952 the new Governor of Kenya, Sir Evelyn Baring, alarmed by the rise of Kenyan militancy and urged on by fearful white settlers, declared a State of Emergency. This followed the assassination of Senior Chief Waruhiu, a leader loyal to the government and a prominent Christian. As British armed forces swung into action, thousands of young men and women who had taken the Mau Mau 'warrior oath' fled to the Aberdare and Mount Kenya forests from where, under the leadership of Dedan Kimathi, they conducted a guerrilla war against the authorities and loyalist Kenyans.

As the forest fighters prepared for insurrection, police arrested the six leaders they believed to be responsible for directing Mau Mau operations: Jomo Kenyatta, Paul Ngei, Achieng Oneko, Bildad Kaggia, Kungu Karumba and Fred Kubai. Following a five-month trial at Kapenguria the six men were convicted, mainly on the evidence of paid informants, some of whom were later proved to have lied on oath. John Lonsdale, a Cambridge academic who has extensively investigated the evidence leading to Kenyatta's conviction, believes that the latter would have been acquitted of the majority of charges if he had been given a fair hearing. Such an acquittal did not square with the temper of the times, however. When Kenyatta and his co-defendants were given the maximum legal sentence of seven years' hard labour and exiled to northern Kenya, the novelist Elspeth Huxley expressed the mood of the settler community, describing the nationalist leader as an 'African Hitler'. The settlers saw their way of life coming under violent threat from the Mau Mau, whom they universally regarded as ruthless and bloodthirsty killers, and not men and women fighting to free their tribe from the yoke of colonialism.

The feeling was rather different among the native teaching fraternity at Moi's school in Tambach. His brother-in-law, Eric Bomett, who was then an education officer, remembers that the sole topic of conversation was the unfair detention of Kenyatta. Indignant staff sent money they raised to Nairobi to help pay for Kenyatta's defence lawyer, Dingle Foot. 'The teachers, including Moi, believed that Kenyatta was trying to liberate the country by peaceful means,' recalls Eric Bomett. 'They were totally against the British on this issue.'

While they supported Kenyatta's peaceful protests, they were firmly opposed to the Mau Mau cult of violence, particularly their intimidation and murder of Christian Kenyans. At the same time, given that their bloody struggle was as much about land grievances as nationalist aspirations, the overwhelming fear was that if the Kikuyu fighters triumphed they would take Kalenjin land. The Kalenjin believed that the Kikuyu were wrapping tribal self-interest in the cloak of nationalism. As they did not share the Kikuyu's language or their culture, their calls to pledge allegiance to the House of Mumbi fell on deaf ears.

Furthermore, many Kalenjin, particularly Nandi elders, remembered the Nandi wars of resistance. They argued that as the Kikuyu had not come to their aid during their struggle against the colonialists, there was no reason for them to ally themselves to the Kikuyu during this present conflict, which the Kalenjin saw as merely the latest in a century-long series of skirmishes, rather than a turning point in Kenya's history. At the same time, the brutality of the Mau Mau, especially their deliberate mutilation of cattle and the horrifyingly sudden and indiscriminate night attacks on men, women and children, offended both Kalenjin cattle culture and their warrior code.

Given this antipathy, it was no surprise that Kalenjin tribes worked hand in glove with the colonial authorities, loyally reporting the presence of Mau Mau groups, helping the police and army to kill or detain others and joining the police and prison service. Indeed, leafing through reports for the Baringo District during what came to be called 'the Emergency' is rather like reading a hunting card. 'The Tugen did extremely well . . . in liquidating Mau Mau gangsters who come in looking for food. The total score of the year was over 30,' said one summary, while another report stated: 'The Tugen deserve high praise for reporting these [Mau Mau] gangs quickly and for their initiative and whole hearted co-operation with security forces.'

As a Christian and a pacifist, Moi found Mau Mau violence deeply repugnant. Moreover, his faith singled him out as a particular target, since his beliefs made it impossible for him to swear the Mau Mau oath of loyalty. Many Christian Africans, particularly in Central Province, met gruesome deaths, and even in loyalist Kalenjin districts it was very dangerous for Christians to travel. Moi's friend Erik Barnett, now the AIM Field Director, had the misfortune to own a car with the registration number 1, which inevitably led to a warning that he was first on the Mau Mau list of those to be executed.

While Moi was hostile towards Mau Mau violence, in reality the Emergency was essentially tangential to his life. Now in his late twenties, he had become a local luminary, as well as something of a high-flyer. Pragmatic, practical and energetic, he was the mainstay of the local Sunday school, and regularly organised sports and other social events in the Tambach community. At school he was promoted to T2 status, which meant that he was involved in teacher training. A further sign of the respect in which he was held came with his election to the Western Region Education Board. Recommending a further incremental rise in Moi's salary, his principal wrote: 'I have a high regard for his integrity and for the growing responsibilities he carries ably in teacher training and the general life of the school.'

Shortly afterwards Moi was promoted once more, becoming the headmaster of the Kabarnet Intermediate School, although Berridge was still overall principal. He taught maths, English history and English in a style which, after years of teaching future teachers, his young charges found rather sophisticated. 'He used a lot of notes and would write from one end of the blackboard to the other in a straight line,' recalls Reuben Chesire. 'He kept us busy so that when we went to play games he would be writing on the blackboard ready for the next lesson.' For the majority of his pupils, however, the most striking memory of their new headmaster was his European style – he arrived in class wearing a trademark blue shirt, grey shorts, long canary yellow socks, and shoes.

Although Moi had a house in the school grounds, he had now saved enough from his salary to build his own home. This was a long, low, timbered structure, which still stands today, in Timboiwo, near to his Sacho birthplace in the Tugen Hills. A sign of his growing affluence and his business instincts was the *posho* mill he had built near by – rented to locals to grind their maize – and his ample herd of sheep, goats and cattle. Even today, Timboiwo is only a scattering of shops and houses linked by a narrow tarmac road; then it consisted of just a dirt track and a couple of wooden shacks nestling in a heavily wooded hillside.

As the coming man, it came as no surprise to his colleagues when, in 1953, he was chosen to attend a special civics course at Jeans College, Kabete. The thirty-odd young men, who included the future Minister for Agriculture, Jeremiah Nyagah, had been hand-picked by the authorities as possible future moderate leaders of Kenyan society. During their training they were given a broad overview of the British Empire, as well as of their responsibilities as citizens in a developing colony like Kenya. Obviously the thinking behind the course was to weld those with influence and prestige at a local level to the existing mechanisms of authority.

Indeed, the attention focused on the history of violent political protest in Kenya, particularly Mau Mau, has inevitably overshadowed the separate peaceful developments in the local political framework of the colony after the Second World War. As the Kikuyu tribe formed the backbone of the Mau Mau fighters and Kenyatta became the first president, then inevitably historians have traced the country's independence movement to the struggles of the majority tribe. However other Kenyan tribes and academics argue that the Mau Mau conflict may indeed have delayed rather than accelerated independence. What is undeniable is that after Uhuru, it was those nationalists who were nurtured in the non-violent tradition who took over the reins of power, few former Mau Mau fighters ever attaining high office. Limited local political developments were encouraged by the colonial authorities, who saw Kenya's future as being that of a multi-racial society dominated by the settlers. Yet it was fledgeling civic groups like the Local Native Councils, made up of chiefs and other worthies, which were a training ground for many future political figures. More importantly, the local committees and the Local Native Councils were the only available means for nominating the handful of indigenous Kenyans to the Legislative Council, at that time the sole national political forum, albeit a settler-dominated one, in the colony.

It is worth noting that election to these bodies was conducted by the time-honoured tribal system of queue-voting, a method which was to prove so controversial during the 1980s. As the District Commissioner J. A. Cumber explained:

> The method adopted for these elections was simple. Candidates stood in line several yards apart with their supporters formed up behind them. All but the two longest files were then dissolved and told to fall in behind one of the two remaining files. After this was done and measures taken to ensure that no foreigners [i.e. outsiders] were present, both files were counted and the candidate having the greatest number of supporters was declared the councillor for the location.

Since the Emergency limited all political activity by native Kenyans the issues discussed were small beer – the issue of bicycle licences, or borehole fees, for example. None the less, this did not stop personality conflicts. 'Councillors have a lot to learn about the conduct of a District Council,' reported the District Officer for Baringo in 1953. 'There was far too much personal animosity and spite and personal advantage came into things too much. Councillors are far too ready to believe rumours and listen to young schoolboys.'

It was these councillors who gathered at Kabarnet in 1952 to nominate the candidate to represent the Rift Valley in the Legislative Council. At that meeting it was decided to nominate John ole Tameno, a Maasai veterinary officer. His three-year tenure proved something of a disappointment, however, as his fond-ness for the bars and clubs of Nairobi did not go down well. In September 1955 he was forced to resign. The search was now on for a new candidate, a man who could pass the necessary test of fluency in English and who, above all, was sober. Inevitably the focus fell on the educational community, one of the few professions employing literate Kenyans.

The Rift Valley Provincial Commissioner first approached Moses Mudavadi, a schools inspector who was the only Kenyan in the region with his own Land Rover. He declined to be selected, however, arguing that as a Luhya it would not be appropriate for him to represent the Kalenjin-dominated region. As a result the search widened. Each of the ten District Councils for the Rift Valley administrative region was asked to nominate a candidate, the Provincial Commis-sioner emphasising that he would prefer it if all councils could agree on a single individual. At Kabarnet the elders of Baringo District Council, who included Chief Joel Chemirmir, Joel Bultut and Moi's brother-in-law, James Chelimo, gathered in the presence of the District Commissioner, H. J. Simpson.

Daniel arap Moi, as the headmaster of the Kabarnet Intermediate School, was the obvious frontrunner. Since he had spent the last few years in Tambach, however, the elders decided to approach Enoch Kiprotich Ngulat, who had been at the Kabarnet school since it opened. When he was invited to the meeting and offered the candidature he turned it down flat, leaving the way open for the councillors to ask the new headmaster.

Moi, who was proposed and seconded by Chief Daudi and Chief Tibi, two councillors from Sacho, was then invited to attend the meeting. Again the council were faced with another refusal, Moi arguing that he had only just started as the headmaster at Kabarnet, that he was committed to his career in education and, no doubt with his recent experience of the Mau Mau still uppermost in his mind, that he was not at all keen on politics. His brother-in-law pleaded with him to reconsider, while the District Commissioner assured him that his pay and pension prospects would not be affected if he decided to return to teaching. After an hour-long discussion the meeting broke up in disarray without any firm decision having been taken.

That evening a four-strong delegation consisting of friends and teachers came to Moi's home at Tambach and tried to convince him to change his mind. They were joined by one of his next-door neighbours, Moses Mudavadi, whose influence had earned him promotion to Kabarnet in the first place. As the hours ticked by Moi began to waver, until Mudavadi finally clinched the argument by adding his personal assurance to the DC's that Moi would not lose any benefits if he returned to teaching. At midnight, Daniel arap Moi reluctantly accepted the nomination as a candidate for the Legislative Council. As he now recalls:

> I had not expected this at all and I was very hesistant to accept as my name had been put forward for the post of secretary to the Baringo African District Council. I was not a politician, I was a teacher and I liked teaching very much. After discussing the matter with a a few friends I decided to accept. I said to myself: 'Let me go for a short period. If I don't like it, I can come back to teaching.'

His election to the Legislative Council was by no means certain, however. As other district councils had also nominated candidates, the Provincial Commissioner convened an electoral college – that is, a body of electors chosen from among those with votes, whose task it was formally to select the candidate. Each District Council therefore sent three representatives to Menengai Primary School in Nakuru for the meeting to decide who should represent the Rift Valley. The Baringo delegation, which included Joel Bultut, now the Chairman of Kabarnet County Council, arrived a day early and began lobbying other districts. It was as well they did, for they soon realised that Nandi District also had a strong candidate. Bultut recalls: 'We argued that the main reason for choosing Moi was that he wasn't a drunkard, he was a Christian and a humble man. The issue of drink was uppermost because of behaviour of the previous incumbent.'

On 16 October 1955 the electoral college gathered to choose their new representative from a list of ten nominated candidates. In a secret ballot Moi received twenty-seven votes while the Nandi candidate got three. After he was formally proposed by Baringo District Council and seconded by Marakwet Council, the Provincial Commissioner telephoned the Governor, Sir Evelyn Baring, to confirm the choice of representative for the Rift Valley.

There was little time for celebration, for in two days' time Moi had to be at the Legislative Council in Nairobi to be sworn in. Together with Councillors Joel Bultut and Joseph Sadalla, he set off for Nakuru railway station. It was a new experience as none of them had ever travelled on a train before. As the first-class carriages were for whites only, the second-class compartments for Indians, they travelled third class. Moi paid the Ksh4.50 fare himself and stood all the way to Nairobi, surrounded in his carriage by the heady sights and smells of Luo country folk carrying fish from Lake Victoria or clutching live chickens to sell at market in Nairobi. All the while they chewed sugar cane, which they then raucously spat on to the wooden floor.

It was not, perhaps, the most auspicious beginning for the new Legislative Council member for the Rift Valley.

Chapter four

In the Lions' Den

Nairobi in 1955 was a city under siege. Rolls of barbed wire littered street corners; Europeans chatted on hotel verandahs, a beer in one hand, the other hovering near the leather holster containing a loaded pistol. On the rooftops British soldiers, Bren guns at the ready, stood guard as groups of Africans were processed prior to detention, resettlement or release. The tension was palpable, and each morning the famous Nairobi rumour mill went into overdrive as news of the previous night's activity was garnered and embellished; tidings of a murder in the morning soon became a massacre by mid-afternoon.

None the less Operation Anvil, launched in April 1954, had been accorded a success. During this draconian measure Nairobi had been ringed by 25,000 troops and systematically searched for guns, ammunition and Mau Mau supporters. Around 30,000 Kikuyu, Embu and Meru were detained and sent to camps which were to become known worldwide for their brutality and torture. Another 20,000 Kenyans were expelled from the city. This awesome display of military might, coupled with the capture of Mau Mau leaders General China and Dedan Kimathi and the introduction of an amnesty which resulted in 1,000 forest fighters giving up the struggle, had broken the back of resistance. It was estimated that from 16,000 fighters in 1954, there were only 2,500 active by October 1955.

This success was achieved at a high price in lives and money. According to official figures, during the Emergency at least 11,000 Mau Mau as well as nearly 2,000 Kikuyu loyal to the government were killed, as opposed to 95 Europeans and 29 Asians. It has led more than one commentator to observe that Mau Mau was as much a civil war between the militant and the loyalist Kikuyu as it was a reaction to colonial oppression, a factor which defined the vicious political infighting with the ruling KANU party in the 1960s.

At the same time, with more than half the annual budget spent on prisons and police, Kenya teetered on the brink of bankruptcy and the capital, scoured of its Kikuyu labour force, faced ruin. When the tired, dusty and rather overawed Legislative Council member for the Rift Valley arrived in this unhappy place he suffered something of a culture shock. From the quiet loyalist backwater of Kabarnet, dominated by a single tribe, to the busy streets of Nairobi, a city which, though multi-tribal, was clearly racially divided, was a distance measured not just in miles. Indeed, the colour bar was so well defined that in some main streets, for example, one pavement was reserved for whites only.

Weary though he may have been, Moi had business to attend to. He and his two travelling companions went to Parliament for a meeting with Eliud Mathu, who was then the leader of the six African representatives in the Legislative Council. His was the first friendly face they met – when Mathu was first elected to the Legislative Council he had stayed with Moi at Tambach during a nationwide tour intended to introduce himself to the people.

Accommodation was organised with a fellow Christian, Ronald Ngala, a member of the Church Missionary Society who was then working as a schools supervisor. The two shared a tiny room in Pumwani, the only district in racially segregated Nairobi where indigenous Kenyans were allowed to live. It was from here that, on 18 October 1955, Moi set off for the Legislative Council to swear the oath of allegiance and to hear the Governor's state-of-Kenya address.

The following week, when the Governor's address was formally debated by the Council, Moi felt sufficiently confident to make his maiden speech. He rose to a smattering of applause and, after welcoming the Governor's report, went on to take up the issue of education in the Rift Valley, a subject to which he was to return on numerous occasions during the remaining lifetime of the Legislative Council. Whilst admitting that the Rift Valley was educationally backward he asked what development plans the Minister of Education had in mind for primary and intermediate schools and wondered why the Governor did not mention the need for a teacher-training centre for African Land Units. As well as paying tribute to farm guards and asking that they be compensated for their loyalty during the Emergency, he also urged the Minister for Agriculture to investigate the planting of date palms in East and West Suk, among the most backward regions of the Rift.

It was a solid, if undramatic, beginning to his parliamentary career. At the time he admitted to feeling a little unsure of himself although as he recalls: 'I had been placed in a position of responsibility by my people and that carried me through. Also my own dignity and my way of life as a Christian.' He was thankful too, that Eliud Mathu, who was to become State House Comptroller following Independence, took him under his wing. Mathu remembered Moi as 'straight-forward and honest'. 'When I saw him for the first time I quickly realised there was good material for leadership. Although he was very religious he did not shout about it,' he added.

At Christmas 1955, as the first Legislative Council session drew to a close, Moi travelled to Eldama Ravine, getting a lift home to Kabarnet in the lorry of a local Asian businessman, a journey that took twelve hours. It graphically brought home to him that he had to have transport if he was to have any chance at all of effectively representing his 40,000-square-mile constituency – an area the size of England. Now that his salary had risen to the dizzy heights of Ksh833 a month – more than three times his headmaster's pay – Moi felt sufficiently affluent to buy his first Land Rover. There was, however, a problem – he did not know how to drive. When he arrived back in Nairobi, he contacted his old schoolfriend Paul Chemirmir, who came to his rescue. When Paul arrived he discovered his friend behind the wheel of his new purchase, wearing a look of perplexity on his face. Paul took over, drove him to Naivasha and then found a quiet stretch of road where Moi practised. After that Moi drove to Eldama Ravine and since that day has never had a lesson or passed a formal test. Within two years he had clocked up 240,000 miles in his beloved Land Rover with its KFF 82 registration, using the vehicle to help him build a relationship with the numerous tribes in his vast constituency. But while his energy was prodigious, not everyone was struck by his simple message of unity and his urging of people to learn to live together. Maasai activist John Keen, who was to become an outspoken KANU MP, remembers an occasion in 1956 when he invited Moi to meet Maasai elders at the Narok Government School to discuss their long-held grievances about land issues, and to ask his help in advancing their cause in the Legislative Council. Keen was not impressed. 'I didn't think very much of him – he wasn't articulate. He was only a young man, very quiet, sober.' Keen, who helped run guns for the Mau Mau during the early 1950s, later watched Moi's performances in the Legislative Council. 'He was never very impressive, not forceful. Moi certainly contributed but as I was an angry young man, I wanted someone who was far more aggressive. He wasn't.'

As well as visiting constituents, during those early days Moi used the Land Rover to help build up a small general store he had opened at his home at Timboiwo – he moved out of the school compound when he was elected to the Legislative Council. He bought sugar, salt and paraffin in exchange for animal skins from Asian merchants in Nakuru to sell in the district, becoming one of the first Kenyans to take advantage of the relaxing of regulations controlling African commerce.

When he returned from Nairobi after his first session in the Legislative Council, his friends noticed the changes in Moi. He now dressed in suits and ties rather than the shorts and long socks which had been his trademark as a teacher. In fact he encouraged teachers and others to become more Westernised in their dress and manners. He and his family were better fed – eating a richer diet than they had ever had before.

Overall, Moi seemed more confident, more aware of and alive to possibilities not just for himself, but for Kenya. On returning to his home district he first called on Moses Mudavadi. He confessed to his friend that initially he had felt anxious because he was new to the game of politics and did not know how to play the rules. Yet he was determined to continue, of that there was no doubt. Furthermore, in spite of his misgivings, there was an air of excitement and celebration, as well as pride, as Baringo's most famous son arrived back in the fold. To mark the occasion community leaders organised a fund-raising, *harambee*, which raised Ksh800, to help pay his expenses.

While the local colonial officers expressed their satisfaction with the new man – 'reasonable and moderate' was the description in one report – Moi and his followers soon realised that the tolerance of the British was only skin deep. Each time he arrived back in the district from Nairobi he was watched or followed by tribal police, who reported his movements to the District Officer. Then as now, if he wanted to hold a meeting he had to obtain a licence which specified the place and time of the meeting and the names of permitted speakers. Any motions to be put had to be submitted beforehand for censorship. Inevitably the authorities used the licence as a weapon with which to shape or limit political debate. Working in a closed district further lengthened the odds against his initiating any worthwhile political activity, as Moi himself explained to members of the Legislative Council: 'Usually I have to write letters to those District Commissioners to let them know that I am visiting these districts. At the same time there are police barrier posts which if I did not have any letter from the District Commissioner or I did not have a licence I would not be allowed to pass through.' The fact that he was able to hold meetings at all was only due to a slight thaw in colonial policy, however. In 1955, when Moi entered politics, for the first time the authorities allowed Africans to organise political parties at district level. This move stemmed from the theory that indigenous Kenyans should be introduced to the political process very gradually, and from the ground level upwards. Such a policy would, it was believed encourage 'a simple and orderly development of African political life' and political opinion.

This concession, which was designed to encourage the moderates in African society, resulted in renewed activity in the towns which already had long experience of trade unions and other associations. Moi's former teacher Argwings Kodhek set up the Nairobi African District Congress while Tom Mboya, a Luo trade unionist, who founded the Nairobi People's Convention Party, used it as a springboard to become one of the first eight African-elected members of the Legislative Council in 1957.

In the Rift Valley, the very existence – or even any experience – of independent native societies was virtually unheard of. In 1949 a branch of the Kalenjin Union was founded in Kabarnet with members drawn from the ranks of government and African District Council employees. Their aims were prosaic: to abolish prostitution among Tugen women, and to prevent children from migrating towards the towns, and therefore trouble. It was in this unpromising ground that the seeds of democracy and nationalism were sown. Inevitably, and unsurprisingly, for many years the Rift Valley showed few signs of blossoming political life.

However, a visit to the region in 1955 by the Coutts Committee to inquire into the best method of electing African members to the Legislative Council seemed promising. 'A good deal of interest was shown,' noted the District Commissioner; 'everyone wanted to go the whole hog of universal suffrage by secret ballot.' Yet very quickly a wave of apathy enveloped this embryonic political scene; 'Little interest was shown,' noted one official in 1956. Even two years later, as

Above: A rare photograph of Daniel arap Moi, his wife Lena, and their children enjoying time off with friends.

Below: New Legislative Council member for Rift Valley Daniel arap Moi chats to the Queen Mother at the Kamariny Show in Elgeyo, Marakwet in the 1950s.

President Moi in the State House gardens with his three sons, from left to right, Gideon, Jonathan and Philip.

above: As Rift Valley Legislative Council member, Moi was the first African politician to be allowed by the colonial authorities to see Jomo Kenyatta and his fellow detainees, who were held at Lodwar in northern Kenya. This picture, taken in October 1959 by a colonial district officer, shows, from left to right, Bildad Kaggia, Kungu Karumba, Henry Cheboiwo, who accompanied Moi on the gruelling journey, Jomo Kenyatta, Daniel arap Moi, Paul Ngei and Fred Kubai.

below: Members of the KADU delegation at the Lancaster House Conference in 1960 which met to decide Kenya's constitutional future. Pictured, from left to right, are Masinde Muliro, Justus ole Tipis, Daniel arap Moi (in Colobus monkey skins worn as a sign of leadership), and Wafula Wabuge.

Above: After the absorption of KADU into the ruling party, KANU, Moi was given the post of Minister for Home Affairs. It was in this capacity he attended a political meeting in Kabarnet in 1965. Seated to his left are J.M. Seroney, his former schoolfriend and political rival, and three other MPs, Daniel Yego, Edward Tanui and Henry Cheboiwo.

Right: Moi laughing at a comment made by Joe Murumbi, Kenya's second Vice-President. To his left is Dr Njoroge Mungai, who had presidential aspirations, while on his right is C.M.G. Argwings-Kodhek, one of Moi's tutors and former Foreign Minister.

Left: A photograph of Daniel arap Moi taken in Nairobi in June 1963.

Above: Three giants of Kenyan politics: President Jomo Kenyatta, Tom Mboya and Daniel arap Moi discussing tactics during a break in the infamous Limuru Conference in 1966 which saw the ousting as Vice-President of Jaramogi Oginga Odinga.

Right: Moi addresses a public rally in Sabor shortly after his appointment as Vice-President in 1967.

Above: Vice-President Moi and his wife Lena admire miniature models of the Empire State Building in New York during a visit to America in 1969.

Below: President Jomo Kenyatta and his Vice-President, Daniel arap Moi. Moi always says that Kenyatta taught him the virtue of patience, an essential quality during the 1970s when Moi was, as he says, 'humiliated, insulted, harassed and manhandled' by powerful politicians close to Mzee.

Kenya's progression towards Uhuru gathered momentum, the local tribes remained indifferent. 'In general the Tugen people have paid little attention to politics and the Njemps and Suk have shown no interest whatsoever,' reported the District Commissioner. Such was local ignorance of wider political developments that on the eve of Independence a rumour went round the Suk tribe that 'Uhuru' was the new nickname of the District Officer for Marigat. Hewing such stony ground would have tested the most astute political organiser, let alone an inexperienced, if energetic, former headmaster thrown into the lions' den of politics.

Undaunted, Moi continued with his stolid support for and defence of the African majority in his unwieldy constituency. On his return to the Legislative Council in 1956 he voiced his opposition to the recommendations of the Coutts Report, which argued for a limited franchise for African electors based on education, property and ability to speak English, and instead advocated universal franchise. By contrast, the Coutts criteria effectively saw the enfranchisement of conservative, middle-aged and wealthy elders of 'proven reliability', who if they met those criteria received up to three votes each.

While welcoming the bill as opening the way to 'a healthier political destiny of the African people in Kenya,' Moi cautioned against the qualitative franchise envisaged by the Coutts Report. He compared it to the 1832 Reform Act in Britain which gave only a limited franchise based on property. 'Mr Coutts's recommendations do not represent a new growing spirit in the minds of the Kenya Africans. The multiple vote . . . was brought in from somewhere outside Kenya and was never advocated by any Kenyan. This multiple vote should cease immediately before the 1960 election and this would reflect the needs of the Africans as they are now.' As he was soon to discover, Moi was in a distinct and isolated minority in the Legislative Council as the bill sailed through; he was soon to realise that the successful passage of a pro-African measure, however limited, was rare.

Behind the elaborate courtesies and formalities of the Legislative Council chamber, the hard fact remained that no matter how moderate, reasonable and convincing the arguments of African members, they were for the most part ignored. After the defeat of a modest motion to appoint an African as the Chairman of an African District Council, Eliud Mathu voiced his exasperation: 'We are so used to disappointment and frustration that we are almost immune now because the constructive suggestions coming from the Africans are turned down by Government.'

While Mathu was a veteran climber at the Legislative Council rockface, Moi was still a novice. But as the months went by this reasonable, fair-minded man, with his enormous respect, amounting almost to reverence, for the British and their democracy, found himself increasingly angered and thwarted, by the stubborn realities of a settler-dominated government which either ignored or discounted his proposals or his warnings about Kenya's future. His cause was not helped by the fact that his speaking style, certainly in his early career, was hesitant and long-winded, and his arguments often rather woolly. Once he had come to enjoy the support of other African colleagues following the crucial 1957 election, however, he became markedly more self-assured and aggressive.

Time and again, Moi's belief in education as the only way truly to empower and enlighten his fellow Kenyans came shining through. It was, and remains, the central plank of his personal and political philosophy. During various debates in 1956 he returned consistently to the part education must play in the peaceful birth of the Kenyan nation. He warned that the government was storing up trouble by failing to educate children to a reasonable standard, so that when they left school they were of use neither to their parents nor to employers. Only extensive education could 'facilitate the growth of a stable, progressive and well-informed society,' he said.

His finest moment during his political apprenticeship came in December 1956, when he introduced a motion proposing the formation of an African Teachers' Association. Teaching, he argued, was 'a profession which will bring up the future leaders of this country, the children of whom are brought up under Western culture and they need to be brought up properly'. He contended that a professional association would maintain discipline and standards as well as allow the airing of grievances about pay and conditions. Following the successful passage of this motion Samuel Ayany, Stephen Kioni, Ignatius Mkok and others founded the Kenyan National Union of Teachers in 1957, and it was formally registered in December 1958.

While Moi's achievements in education earned lasting approval from the teaching profession, his constituents remained far more concerned about local issues. The thorny problem of 'destocking' – reducing cattle holdings – had vexed colonial authorities and local native leaders throughout the 1950s. On the one hand, numerous District Officers believed that only by reducing the number of cattle could overgrazing, and thus the consequent soil erosion, be prevented in the region. On the other, tribal chiefs argued that the colonial government ignored the high cultural and economic value placed by Kalenjin natives on their cattle. Because serious soil erosion, particularly in Central Province, had only become a problem during the colonial period after natives had been driven off their land, non-cooperation with soil-erosion schemes was one of the first acts of protest against the government.

In the Rift Valley feelings were running high, the tribesmen fearing that the government was going to grab their cattle and slaughter them at a recently built abbatoir. Moi took up their cause with a will, a vigorous speech, lasting for 15 minutes, resulting in a softening of official attitudes towards destocking and cattle trespassing on to settlers' farms (which were confiscated). Such was the local impact that even today when Moi visits the Pokot tribe they sing him a song composed during that time.

While his interventions on the cattle issue pleased the pastoralists, he garnered similar praise from forest-dwelling tribes for tackling government policy on wood-lands, particularly the Lembus Forest, about which he harassed the government for five years. Since the arrival of the settlers, the Lembus tribe, who had lived in the forest since time immemorial, had been left in the position of squatters, neither allowed to build permanent structures nor given any kind of facilities such as schools or shops. Yet they were expected to pay taxes. This unjust arrangement had been a cause for complaint since the 1930s, but it was not until the late 1950s that the government agreed in principle to return the forest to its rightful owners.

While Moi gained the political credit for a campaign which had been running for generations, he had in fact demonstrated his 'green' credentials early on, complaining in a speech in May 1956 that government forestry policy was rapidly turning productive land into desert. During several debates he voiced his fear that unless Africans were actively involved in conservation and exploitation of the forests they would be 'progressively alienated' from this natural resource. He urged the government to set up a forestry school for Africans, and to send Africans overseas to learn more about forestry work.

Significantly, during that same speech in which he voiced his concern about the natural environment, he gave his view about the eternal debate concerning the balance of wildlife and people living in the national parks. 'The National Parks – the area allocated to wild game is so much that human beings take second place. I do not see why wild animals are given preference to human beings,' he complained, adding that the government had taken no notice of protests from the Maasai regarding lions and other predators from the national parks attacking and eating herd boys and their animals.

In March 1957 Moi was focused on another struggle was to win the first ever election designed to send eight African members, elected rather than nominated, to the Legislative Council. There was a sense of naivety and amicable cooperation about the whole exercise; the era of political infighting, personal vendettas and public violence would come soon enough. Even so, there was a little skulduggery. As an Education Officer, Moi's friend Moses Mudavadi was one of the admin-istration team responsible for registering native voters. When he went to enrol voters in East Baringo many of them asked why he was writing their names down and giving them cards. He told them: 'You keep the card and vote for Toroitich.' Most accepted his advice.

Moi's election rivals were two Maasai elders, Justus ole Tipis, and Moi's predecessor in the Legislative Council, John ole Tameno. The candidates were each represented by a symbol, the lion, the cow or the elephant, which they drew from a basket. Since virtually all the population was illiterate these simple symbols were essential. Moi drew the lion, Tipis the cow and Tameno the elephant. Given the Kalenjin cattle culture and the common view that lions were a dangerous nuisance, Tipis had a distinct advantage.

Before polling day, however, the candidates actually had to try and meet as many of the potential voters as humanly possible. It was no easy task in a vast region with few serviceable roads and no public transport. As Tameno had no vehicle, and Tipis only a ramshackle car, Moi insisted – against the advice of his campaign manager, Joel Bultut – that they should all travel in his Land Rover. This was the usual arrangement adopted by white Kenyan candidates, but it was a novel approach for Africans. The arrival of the three potential African leaders, each clutching his animal placard, in the villages to canvass support inspired excitement and not a little good-natured banter. Such was the gentle-manly procedure in these friendly elections that the candidates even worked out a speaking rota so that they all had a fair chance to address the electorate.

Moi himself took the whole campaign very seriously. One night during the election he slept on the rush-matting floor in the house of his old schoolfriend Gedion Tarus, who retains a vivid memory of the candidate tapping out an election speech on a battered typewriter until well into the night. His diligence paid off. In spite of heavy rains there was an 80 per cent turnout in Kenya's first democratic election with an overwhelming vote for Moi who polled 4,000 votes as opposed to 1,500 for Tipis and 750 for Tameno. In keeping with the tone of the campaign, after the result was announced by the Provincial Commissioner to a large crowd outside his office in Nakuru, the three rivals and their supporters went to a nearby hotel to celebrate.

This age of political innocence was short lived, for the subsequent extension of the franchise was to expose the factions and fissures that existed in African society. Uhuru would come at a high price.

Chapter five

The Road to Independence

The din of shouting rose to a crescendo. Foul abuse and the odd missile rained down on the African Legislative Council members who sat at the front of the hall in central Nairobi where they had assembled for a political meeting. Daniel arap Moi was so shocked by the violent language that he cupped his head in his hands and put his fingers in his ears. Finally he and other African-Elected Members hurriedly left the meeting, which was rapidly turning into a bear garden. As they made their way out they ran a gauntlet of insults from the mob who had arrived with the sole intention of disrupting the peaceful gathering – it was suspected that they were in the pay of European settlers. Nor was Moi's ordeal over yet. Such was the crush of the crowd surging round his Land Rover that he had to put it into four-wheel drive to push his way through.

It was clear that now Kenyans themselves had the chance to elect African members to the Legislative Council the political temperature was hotting up, particularly as Ghana, under Kwame Nkrumah, had gained independence three days before polling in Kenya began. The first eight African-Elected Members – Oginga Odinga, Ronald Ngala, Bernard Mate, Jawi Muimi, Lawrence Oguda, Masinde Muliro, Tom Mboya and Daniel arap Moi – were to be among the midwives at the protracted birth of a nation. At their first meeting in 1957, held in Tom Mboya's trade union offices in Nairobi, they agreed to work as a loose-knit caucus – the African-Elected Members' Organisation – with the main objective of achieving independence within five years. As part of this aim they felt it was vital that the existing Lyttelton Constitution, which had been introduced in 1954 to maintain a multi-racial but European-dominated government, should be vigorously opposed. Universal suffrage, the abolition of the exclusive reservation of the White Highlands – Kenya's best farmland for whites – and desegregation in schools were other planks in their policy. Jaramogi Oginga Odinga, the fiery, impetuous Nyanza leader, was elected Chairman of the AEMO; as Secretary they chose Tom Mboya, the cool, calculating, Nairobi-born Luo trade union organiser. During the next decade, the personal and political tensions between these two giants of the Kenyan political landscape came to symbolise the ideological battle for the hearts and minds of the Kenyan people.

While the embryonic organisation bedded down, Moi, in his usual way, quietly listened and watched as his new colleagues shaped up for the fight. His still patience, which many have misjudged over the years as indecision or non-comprehension, was a quality recognised but not appreciated by Oginga Odinga, the quintessential man in a hurry. After the first session of the Legislative Council following the historic 1957 election, Odinga described Moi as 'a giraffe with a long neck that saw from afar', implying that he took the long view. In his book *Not Yet Uhuru* he was less kind, however, depicting Moi, Muimi and Ngala as 'influenced by the missions, overawed by settler power and making a slow adjustment to political trends and the need to make independent judgements'. Written in 1967 after his demise as Vice-President, a fall in part engineered by Moi, there is a hint of sour grapes about this opinion, although it is shared by other radical Kenyan politicians.

It is, though, a view that contrasts sharply with the speeches Moi made in the Legislative Council after the March 1957 election. These are markedly more assured in tone, more vigorous in delivery, and wider in political scope than in his early days. This is not altogether surprising, since the watershed election meant that African-Elected Members were now able to argue that their views were sanctioned by a substantial electorate. They were about to flex their political muscles. During one tetchy debate Moi calmly detailed the examples of racial discrimination shown towards him, in another he described how government-appointed chiefs had lost the respect of local people, while in the Budget debate he attacked plans to build a military base, calling instead for the money to be used for African education. He supported Tom Mboya's motion for national political organisations, warning: 'Twenty years ago the African community was regarded as a sleeping giant. It is now awakening from its sleep.'

The need to respect African integrity and aspirations, a desire that all races should live in harmony (and a willingness to work for that end), and an overriding concern for progress through peace and education, were the strands of Moi's developing political philosophy. It was a conciliatory, essentially Christian approach which contrasted with Odinga's conviction that change in the current climate could only be achieved by confrontation. That confrontation was inevitable, however, not least because every move made by the AEMO, particularly their demand to increase to fifteen the number of seats in the Legislative Council, was blocked by the settler majority. As a result, the group decided on a different tactic – to recognise the political realities and take their case to Britain.

While the declaration of the Emergency in 1952 had appeased the 93,000-strong settler community, it had ultimately taken their destiny out of their hands, moving the fulcrum of power north, from Nairobi to London. In the summer of 1957 Tom Mboya and Ronald Ngala travelled to Britain and met the Colonial Secretary, Alan Lennox-Boyd, and other interested MPs, to whom they stated their case for 'undiluted democracy'.

That meeting and other political developments resulted, in October 1957, in a visit to Nairobi by the Colonial Secretary, where he negotiated with the various racial groups, although there was a marked emphasis on placating settler rather than African opinion. In November Lennox-Boyd announced his decision, giving the Africans an extra six seats in the Council, as well as an extra ministry, making two in all. At the same time he decreed that the European-dominated Legislative Council should choose twelve 'Specially Elected Members', four each for Africans, Europeans and Asians.

While the settlers liked the new constitution as it maintained their ascendancy, it was rejected by the AEMO, although they did, after much heart-searching, accept the six new members, who took their seats in March 1958. However, eight Africans who came forward as candidates for the Special Seats, were denounced by Mboya and his colleagues as 'stooges, quislings and black Europeans . . . traitors to the African cause'.

In an act of political folly, the government decided to prosecute seven of the African-Elected Members, including Moi, for endorsing these remarks, charging them with conspiracy and criminal libel. For two weeks in July 1958, Nairobi was gripped by the trial, huge crowds gathering outside the courtroom displaying banners reading: 'To hell with the Lennox-Boyd Constitution' and 'Freedom and Justice for Kenya'. While the defendants were acquitted of conspiracy they were convicted of defamation and fined Ksh1,500 each – almost two months' salary. Constituents in Moi's home district clubbed together to pay the fine. 'The group was steadfast,' he recalls, 'although the colonialists tried to divide us on tribal lines. We wanted to be sent to jail for championing the African cause.'

While the trial captured the public's imagination, other equally significant developments were taking place which would transform Kenyan politics. As African political parties were still only allowed on a district basis, it was up to AEMO members both to form their own local parties and to co-ordinate their local activities with those of other African Legislative Council members. In 1958 Moi formed the Baringo District Independent Party in Kabartonjo, with Joel Bultut as Vice-Chairman. It was the first of four independent district parties – Baringo, Kericho, Nandi and Elgeyo-Marakwet – which Moi helped to pioneer.

That year, Moi held the first of four rallies of the fledgeling party in Marigat. In 1959, however, with the prospect of a round-table constitutional conference – between the British Government on one hand, and the settlers, Africans and Asians on the other – on the agenda, his Baringo party was much more active, Moi addressing some thirteen meetings, although he was not always accorded a warm welcome. When he and his supporters arrived at the Soy Social Club – a European society whose buildings and grounds mirror 1920s Home Counties architecture – he was told firmly to leave by angry settlers. While local grievances, particularly the issue of destocking – the deliberate reduction of the number of grazing cattle – dominated meetings, the party was successful in raising the level of debate. As one District Commissioner reported: 'The average man's political horizon is becoming wider than that covering purely parochial matters.'

The party's work was helped by Moi's new circumstances. In 1957 his great friend Paul Barnett built the family a three-bedroomed house on 40 acres of land at Kabimoi, just outside Eldama Ravine, the plot having been given by the African District Council in recognition of Moi's services to the community.

Inevitably, Moi's new residence, which was officially opened by the Governor, Sir Evelyn Baring, when he visited the district in July 1959, was a magnet for constituents with grievances and concerns. In his first few months as a Legislative Council member he had even been visited by Mau Mau warriors. Brigadier Danny Njuguna, now a clergyman, and a couple of supporters secretly saw Moi to discuss the political situation. While he now shrugs off the dangers of such a meeting, at the time Moi could have faced detention for consorting with Mau Mau fighters. While his open door policy posed personal risks, for Moi the Rift Valley constituent who caused the greatest heart-searching was not able to visit his home. During 1958 international outrage had been expressed at the harsh conditions endured by Jomo Kenyatta and his fellow detainees held in Lokitaung prison, at the northern tip of the Rift Valley. In London, the House of Commons debated the Kenyatta case, while in Kenya Oginga Odinga caused uproar in the Legislative Council by calling for Kenyatta's release and described those detained as Kenya's political leaders. While his emotional outburst initially embarrassed his colleagues, the issue of Kenyatta's confinement came to dominate all political issues, to such an extent that several months after Odinga first raised Kenyatta's plight the full AEMO group issued a statement, which read: 'The arrest and confinement of Kenyatta left a big wound in African hearts, which will only be cured by his return to normal life among the African people of Kenya. Jomo Kenyatta and others in Lokitaung are still the real political leaders of the African people.'

While the forgotten figure of Kenyan politics was once more taking centre stage, he was no longer the man he had been. Years of captivity had taken their toll; he was gaunt, walked with a stoop and seemed quite frail. Even though in April 1959 he was moved to Lodwar, close to Lake Turkana, and later joined by his wife, Ngina, and their two daughters, there was concern about his deteriorating health, as well as endless rumours about his drinking and growing senility (although he was only in his early sixties). As much out of humanitarian as political considerations, Daniel arap Moi decided to see his most famous Rift Valley constituent and find out for himself the conditions under which he was held. It proved to be no easy task. He faced considerable opposition from colonial officials, who believed such a visit would serve little purpose. 'You do not want to be associated with Kenyatta,' they told him.

In November 1959 Moi was granted permission to make the arduous twelve-hour journey to Kenyatta's new place of confinement. He travelled with Henry Cheboiwo, the Secretary-General of the Baringo Independent Party, bringing with them gifts of farm produce and 200 shillings raised from AEMO members and other detainees. Moi spoke privately to Kenyatta for more than six hours, discussing the state of the nation and tactics for the future. Kenyatta's message, which was to become a constant theme in later meetings with Kenya's political leaders, was that only by remaining united would the Africans be able to overcome European hegemony and achieve eventual independence.

Moi, who found Kenyatta in reasonable health and quite well informed about the political scene, returned to Nairobi to brief his AEMO colleagues. If the settler authorities had hoped that the member for the Rift Valley, who was by now seen as the moderate face of African nationalism, would accede to Kenyatta's continued detention, they were proved badly wrong. First at the AEMO meeting, and then in the Legislative Council chamber, Moi argued forcefully for Kenyatta's immediate release. Even as he spoke about his meeting with the imprisoned leader several European Legislative Council members angrily threatened him with jail. Steadfastly, he replied: 'Even if I join him [in jail], it does not matter. He is a leader of the African people and those who do not agree with me will one day agree that he is. He can even help to lessen the tension in this country.' In the face of noisy settler opposition Moi recommended that Kenyatta should participate in the constitutional conference, that he should have a meeting with the Governor, and that his views about the White Highlands should be heard. 'He is not as hostile as you think,' Moi argued. 'Some of you may be thinking that he is extreme. But the Africans know him and although he was implicated with the Mau Mau I sincerely believe that if he is released today this country will be in a better position.'

While the colony's Governor warned against the growing cult of 'Jomo', Moi's visit to Kenyatta came soon after revelations of appalling brutality and murder at the notorious Hola detention camp. On hearing this shocking news Moi quickly requested meetings with Kikuyu inmates at detention camps in Navaisha to check on conditions. The Hola camp scandal, coming within three years of the Suez *débâcle*, and following hard on the heels of disturbances and widespread arrests in Nyasaland (now Malawi), meant that Britain's moral authority – the cornerstone of its imperial policy – was now being challenged as it had never been before. This in turn forced a sea change in British policy, as was evidenced by Prime Minister Harold Macmillan's famous 'wind of change' speech to the South African Parliament in Cape Town made whilst the first Lancaster House Conference, which began in February 1960, was sitting.

Yet before that, even as the morality of Britain's colonial policy came under global scrutiny, the authorities in Kenya continued to turn the screw on African political agitation and debate. The colonial government was actively hostile to the faintest manifestations of countrywide political organisation, refusing licences to hold meetings, banning fundraising and African newspapers, and preventing political activity by members of the majority Kikuyu tribe unless they held 'loyalty' certificates.

While these actions proved to be the last fling of the conservative clique in the colonial administration, at the time it did not seem that the sun was slowly setting on colonialism in Kenya. At the beginning of 1959 the prognosis for independence seemed gloomy indeed. The AEMO was making little if any headway with its twofold demands for an African majority in the Legislative Council and a full-scale constitutional conference.

Indeed, Sir Evelyn Baring had just returned from Britain, where he had attended a conference at Chequers chaired by the Colonial Secretary, Lennox-Boyd, at which it had been provisionally agreed that Tanganyika might achieve independence by 1970, Uganda a little later, and Kenya in 1975. While they were not aware of the details of this meeting, the AEMO members certainly heard the sounds of colonial doors being locked, bolted and barred against further progress.

Frustrated by this intransigence, the AEMO group adopted a new tactic. In the spring of 1959, for the first time in Kenyan history, a multi-racial group of Legislative Council members was formed to lobby the Colonial Secretary for a constitutional conference. This delegation, comprising one European member, the Irish-born Shirley V. Cooke, three Asian members and Moi, Muliro, Dr Julius Kiano and Odinga from the African members, flew to London to state the case for independence on behalf of the newly formed Constituency-Elected Members Organisation (CEMO). After hours of argument Lennox-Boyd finally agreed to a conference to be held in London in 1960, although he refused to be committed to a relaxation of the emergency regulations still in force since Mau Mau, the release of Kenyatta, or the formation of national African political organisations.

This period before the first Lancaster House Conference, held in January 1960, was critical in Kenya's history not just because it exposed the rifts between the emerging political groupings, but also because of the opportunity it gave to these young African politicians – it is worth remembering that most of these nation-builders were only in their early thirties – to define and refine their personal political philosophies. They wanted an independent Kenya, certainly, but what kind of country did these young men envisage?

Cutting through the nationalist rhetoric, the underlying sentiments in Moi's speeches at this time reveal him to be a 'one-nation' Kenyan, his belief in a multi-racial approach to Kenya's problems stemming from conviction, rather than political opportunism. At the same time, this view was tempered by a realistic appreciation of the inequality of life for Africans, and by his constant demands that they be given equality of opportunity in education, health, farming and business.

He stressed the need for universal suffrage for Africans, pointing out that they did not enjoy equal citizenship with other racial groups, and he compared the government's paternalistic attitude towards African democracy with that of the eighteenth-century English statesman William Pitt the Elder, who treated the American colonists before the War of Independence as 'boys'. Again and again Moi returned to the need for full democracy in Kenya: 'It is essential that we adopt a democratic frame of mind, not as a duty but as a habit of mind, a pattern of behaviour.'

At the same time he frequently talked of the need for 'harmony' in racial relations, although he did not neglect to point out the obduracy of the settlers or the advantages enjoyed by the Asian community. 'There is still room for reconciliation,' he said, 'There is still room for people who think that this country is for all. We want them [Europeans and Asians] to live with us, to work together as people who aim at one objective and that is that everybody who lives in Kenya should live happily without fear or suspicion. But at present fear and suspicion prevail.'

This 'one-nation' philosophy was a recurrent theme, Moi asserting that all races must live together in peace, and that separate racial organisations and structures merely divided communities and created suspicions. 'This country is going to be an integrated nation if it is going to be a harmonious one,' he argued, urging the establishment of multi-racial schools. 'If you educate your children in separate schools they will have biased minds and in the long run you will not have such communities sitting together or agreeing on matters of interest to the country.'

The success of Kenya's first multi-racial political group, the CEMO, in securing a constitutional conference served to confirm Moi in his pragmatic 'one-nation' nationalism. As the London conference approached, however, personal differences amongst the African politicians developed into fundamental political rifts. Since there was a ban on colony-wide political parties unless they were multi-racial, the more moderate AEMO members, including Moi, pledged themselves to working within this multi-racial framework, and as a result set up the Kenya National Party (KNP), composed of African and Asian members, and one European member, of the Legislative Council. While this was a logical political extension after the success of the CEMO, the first multi-racial political group, they were opposed by Odinga, Mboya, Kiano and Oguda, who set up the rival and exclusively African, Kenya Independence Movement (KIM), insisting that the rights of Africans to organise nationally should be recognised before there could be co-operation with the Europeans or Asians. Inevitably, it was banned. These two parties foreshadowed the eventual formation of the Kenya African Democratic Union (KADU), the mainly rural party whose supporters were the smaller tribes who had initially joined the KNP, and the Kenya African National Union (KANU), dominated by urban Luo and Kikuyu members, whose most prominent officials had founded the KIM.

While personality clashes and differences over tactics were the outward reasons for the split, the issues of land and tribe, which form the mighty rivers of the Kenyan political landscape, truly separated the African Legislative Council members. Indeed, on the surface both parties shared the same aim: independence; the release of Kenyatta; the ending of the Emergency; the formation of colony-wide political parties for Africans; universal franchise. Moi's speeches, for example, were often virtually interchangeable with those of Mboya and Odinga. In July 1959, with tension at its highest between warring AEMO members, Moi spoke vigorously in support of Mboya's motion for the formation of colony-wide African organisations. 'I urge the Government to allow our people to organise their nationhood by forming Colony-wide political organisations irrespective of colour, race or creed,' he said. 'Most of us have no real freedom to organise our people, to co-ordinate opinion, to see that people express their ideas genuinely through the right channels.'

But at the heart of the split between the two fledgeling political parties was a hidden agenda – the issue of tribal lands. Behind the thinking of Moi and his colleagues and their supporters lay the unspoken fear that the more numerous and advanced settled urban tribes, particularly the Kikuyu, would overwhelm the weaker pastoral tribes, like the Maasai and Kalenjin, and confiscate their traditional tribal lands. The leaders of rural nationalism watched the rise of urban nationalism anxiously, they and their people fearing the spread of Kikuyu influence, a deeply rooted anxiety that had been amply demonstrated by Kalenjin hostility towards the Mau Mau.

While these developments in Kenyan African politics anticipated the future political landscape, at the time they were almost incidental to the principal power struggle amongst the ruling European elite, whose views enjoyed an importance in Westminster out of all proportion to their numbers. Thus a decision in January 1959 by the AEMO members to boycott the Legislative Council in order to advance their demands for a constitutional conference only started to become effective when Michael Blundell, then Kenya's Agriculture Minister, conceded that the rejection of a constitutional conference was 'unwise'. His subsequent resignation as Minister of Agriculture to lead the multi-racial New Kenya Party served to reveal the split between liberal and reactionary settler wings, Europeans determined to resist change joining the United Party, led by Group Captain Briggs.

It was little wonder, therefore, that when the new Colonial Secretary, Iain Macleod, flew to Nairobi to assess the mood of the colony prior to the January 1960 constitutional conference at Lancaster House, he discovered that 'everybody was certain that the Kenya conference was doomed to failure'. He was soon aware of the disunity of the African political group, noting that there were 'many personal antagonisms clearly to be seen within it'. Yet Macleod's analysis ended on an optimistic note, telling the Prime Minister that the conference has 'a true chance of success'.

This sense of optimism, coupled with a dawning realisation of the genuine opportunity which the London conference opened up for the African majority, galvanised the two warring factions into action. As Oginga Odinga wrote: 'The nearer the round table talks came, the more important it was to try to put a divided African house in order . . . by a miracle of effort we achieved a joint conference of leaders in Kiambu.' At that meeting in the autumn of 1959 it was agreed that they would take a joint delegation to London consisting of all the African-Elected Members led by Ngala and with Mboya as Secretary.

This decision showed a recognition that, while they had profound personal and political differences, they all faced a common enemy, the colonial government. Moi voiced his own exasperation with the 'obstinacy' of the existing *ancien régime* in the very last speech to Legislative Council before the conference. Characteristically, the debate was about education policy. 'Everybody in this country is fed up with the Government; fed up with its plans and with its blindness and lack of foresight and only seeing things which are not of interest to our people,' he said. With these words ringing in their ears, business was suspended and the entire Legislative Council set off for London.

Moi's speech was fighting talk much appreciated by his Kalenjin constituents, who had earlier presented him with colobus monkey headgear and skins, sacred raiment traditionally worn by warriors before they went into battle. When he and fellow African delegates paraded through the dismal winter streets of London, their colourful tribal clothing contrasted vividly with their grey surroundings. It was a graphic symbol that this conference marked not just a clash of political ideas and personalities, but of cultures as well.

The point was not lost on the Colonial Secretary, Macleod, who soon felt that the prospects of the conference's success looked as dank and drear as the mists of his native Scotland. Where Kenya was concerned, he had inherited a colony where 90,000 people were held in detention without trial, a primitive infrastructure of roads, education and health, almost universal illiteracy and only a handful of Africans in any positions of consequence inside the colonial administration. As Michael Blundell observed:

Kenya was singularly unfitted for independent African rule. There was only one African District Officer; in the Agricultural Department no African occupied a post higher than the lower grade of Assistant Agricultural Officer, no reservoir of African engineers, lawyers, judges, architects and trained railway and postal communications officers existed and the economy was mainly sustained by immigrant communities.

Macleod had to perform a brilliant juggling act, balancing vociferous nationalist demands against negligible African administrative experience, whilst matching the possibility of African frustration spilling over into violence against the real threat of an intransigent settler minority uniting with Europeans in Rhodesia and South Africa and taking up arms against the British. A civil war which drew in British troops whilst bleeding the Kenyan economy dry was a very real prospect.

In fact, the sting was taken out of this crisis by Macleod's opening speech, in which he stated quite clearly that the time had come for majority rule in Kenya, and for responsible self-government based on Westminster-style parliamentary institutions. This theme was taken up by Ngala and Mboya, who argued that the Africans wished to break with the limited-franchise elections of the past and go forward to universal adult suffrage on the basis of 'one man, one vote'. After the leaders had made their proposals all but one of the forty-seven delegates spoke, most reflecting the views of their delegation leaders. This wearying ritual had a hidden purpose, as Macleod later explained: 'Every delegate comes to London with at least one speech boiling inside him and if you can get all these over in a stream of speeches, which I may say begin to bore the conference after the first day or two, then it is possible to get down to hard conference negotiation when that is over.' The process also helped to generate a certain communal clubbiness among the delegates, in spite of their many differences. When a member of the settler United Party stood up and told the delegates that he refused to be ruled by people who had just come down from the trees, the Africans, far from showing anger, rocked with mirth. Besides Mboya and Ngala, the other principal spokesmen for the African group were Odinga, Moi and Muliro. Another delegate, Jeremiah Nyagah, recalls the difference in tone adopted by his colleagues: 'Muliro was bitterly outspoken. He was very heated after what he had seen when he lived in South Africa. Moi was more experienced both as an elected member and as a teacher. He was a cool man in discussions. Dr Kiano was the youngest delegate and very quiet.'

In the end, a month after the conference first met, Macleod produced a final plan: a Legislative Council of sixty-five members with an effective African majority, the first in Kenya's history, and with a franchise widened to ensure that the electorate were mainly African. At the same time, there were twenty seats for minority elements, whose candidates first had to undergo a primary election to ensure that they enjoyed the support of their communities. It was a compromise which pleased no one, falling short of the African demands for universal franchise, yet at the same time ending settler hegemony. Once again, though, Macleod showed his tactical cleverness by presenting his plan separately to each delegation on a take-it-or-leave-it basis.

As Mboya recalled, when the African delegation expressed their reservations, the Colonial Secretary 'looked firmly at them' and said that he had not asked for their views on the details, but whether they rejected or accepted them. Macleod, a master of brinksmanship, then told the Africans that as they had rejected the proposals he intended to withdraw them and in about six months time send a commission to Kenya. 'It will report to me maybe in a year's time, if that's what you would like ... Thank you very much.' The ploy worked brilliantly. 'No sir, you misunderstand us!' cried almost everyone in the delegation. As Mboya ruefully remarked: 'He used these tactics to shock us and certainly succeeded.'

After this meeting, the African delegation went into a committee room to discuss the proposals further, and to work out how to present the plan to their supporters in the best possible light. Delegate Dr Kiano recalls that meeting:

Odinga was very bitter and wanted to reject the plan whilst Moi was one of the calm voices. He was saying that it was 'a major step forward'. Moi was of those who tried to convince rather than confront – Odinga was the opposite. A man of conviction but a great confrontationalist. Moi always felt that discussion and persuasion was better than confrontation.

In the end, the African delegation accepted the plan, and decided to sell it to the voters by promoting the image that when they had arrived in London, the policy had been Europeans first, then the Asians, and finally the Africans. By their efforts they had caused an about-turn, so that the African was now first. Mboya, Muliro and Mate arrived back in Kenya first, and used this imagery successfully at a huge open-air rally in Nairobi. Blundell and his New Kenya Party, the moderate voice of settler interests, were not so fortunate, however. He was greeted with the cries of 'Judas' by angry settlers, and East African simunis – pieces of silver – were hurled at his feet.

Amidst this mood of bitterness and recrimination, there came a glimmer of hope that the African politicians could settle their differences. Moi, Ngala and Odinga had shared the same hotel in London, and over the passing weeks had hatched a plan to start a new party that would unite the two factions, the KIM and KNP. 'We started a political party at the Morton Hotel,' says Moi. 'Divisions began to emerge among us but were more on personal lines than in purpose. We were nevertheless unanimous on the immediate release of Mzee [Kenyatta]'.

In fact, when they proposed the new party to the rest of the delegation all agreed except Mboya, Muliro and Onyango Ayodo, who said that they would only consider signing the document which outlined the new party once they had returned to Kenya. It was strongly suspected that the reluctance of Mboya, who, though feted by the West, was seen as an arrogant dictator by his colleagues, was due to the fact that he had his eyes on the ultimate prize of leadership of the Kenyan Africans, using his own trade union to build a personal power base. Back in Kenya, with Mboya staying in the wings, the Legislative Council members, including Moi, who had signed the document proposing a united African political movement, met at Dr Kiano's house in Riruta to agree on a public declaration to launch the new party. Also present at the meeting was James

Gichuru, the former President of the KAU who had stood down when Kenyatta arrived home in 1946, who was invited to be the leader of the new party, the idea being that he would symbolise Kenyatta's presence. It was, too, at this caucus meeting that it was agreed to call the new grouping the Kenya African National Union.

The first KANU leaders' conference was held in March 1960 in Kiambu, away from the hotbed of Nairobi politics. In spite of opposition Mboya, together with Odinga, Kiano, Ngala, Argwings Kodhek and three others were appointed to a nine-man committee, chaired by Gichuru, which was deputed to draft KANU's constitution. This was to be ratified at a full conference in Kiambu in May, when the party's national officers would also be elected.

In the interim Moi and fellow parliamentarian Taitta Toweet had fused the four Kalenjin independent district parties into the Kalenjin Political Alliance (KPA), which, its leaders claimed, represented around 900,000 Kalenjin-speaking people. Its main policy was to provide determined and effective representation for their rural interests, and also made clear its claim upon the control of land in western Kenya, an argument based on the historical precedent that the Kalenjin had used this land long before the Europeans arrived. At the same time, the KPA stated that they had no desire to interfere with European agriculture in the White Highlands. At the party's inaugural meeting, held at Kapkatet, the Kipsigis' trading centre, Moi, who was joined by Luhya leader Masinde Muliro and Justus ole Tipis, representing the Maasai, told an 8,000-strong crowd that 'it was the wishes of the people' which would determine the length of the new Lancaster House Constitution, rather than those who wanted it to run to a fixed time limit.

Mboya had also been hard at work, organising his People's Congress Party into a well-disciplined phalanx that would support him at the Kiambu conference. According to Odinga, Moi and Ngala had threatened to boycott the KANU elections if Mboya attended, and the fact that they were both away when the conference was held – Ngala visiting the United States, Moi on a Commonwealth Parliamentary Association course in Britain – was seen by their colleagues as indicating that their hearts were not truly in the new party. Muliro, an implacable opponent of Mboya, had gone further than either Moi or Ngala by saying that he would not co-operate in organising a single mass African party if Mboya was involved. The absence of these three leading African politicians, together with the formidable political grouping they had assembled beforehand, served to heighten the atmosphere of suspicion and mistrust at the conference in May.

With Moi away, it was left to Toweet to lead the Kalenjin Political Alliance delegates through the day of high drama and low insults which saw the birth of KANU, the first colony-wide African political party. Lobbying started early. The Rift Valley delegates, already believing that the whole affair was a carve-up between Kikuyu and Luo activists, had their worst fears confirmed when their leader, Toweet, newly appointed as Assistant Minister for Agriculture, was howled down by other delegates. The Kalenjin faction, who were formally linked to the Kenya National Party, now refused to vote for anybody because they could see that the elections were effectively a putsch by the supporters of KIM aimed at putting their leaders, Odinga and Mboya, in senior positions. In the end the absent Ngala, who had led the successful Lancaster House delegation, was given the modest post of Treasurer while Moi, the senior elected African member of the Legislative Council, was appointed Assistant Treasurer.

Following the meeting, Toweet issued a statement saying that even though the Kenya National Party representatives had been at Kiambu they did not endorse the result because they had refused to vote on realising that the meeting was 'tribally organised and sectionalised'. Toweet waited for Moi and Ngala to return before briefing them on the implications of the conference result. Events were now moving swiftly. In tandem with the formation of the Kalenjin Political Alliance had come the emergence of the Maasai United Front, who were equally concerned about the future of their lands and incursions by the Kikuyu and Luo. The leader of the Coast tribes, Ronald Ngala, who had declined the post of Treasurer, forged the Coast African People's Union, while Muliro had mobilised his Luhya supporters to form the Kenya African People's Party. Their fears of domination by the larger tribes seemed justified following an imprudent comment by Mboya, who had said, after the official formation of KANU at the conference, that there was going to be a new Kenya which would be Kikuyu and Luo. 'This statement was the one that precipitated the formation of KADU,' recalls Toweet.

On 25 June, just six weeks after the formation of KANU, the leaders of these four provincial political alliances, as well as of the Somali National Association, met at Ngong and merged to form the Kenya African Democratic Union (KADU). Ngala was elected leader with Muliro his deputy, while Moi was elected Chairman of KADU's All-Union Conference, with John Keen as Party Secretary.

The scene seemed set – urban versus rural nationalism, as in the days of KIM and KNP, the Rift Valley and Coast tribes pitted against those of western Kenya and the Central Province. At stake were ancient tribal lands, particularly in the Rift Valley. Yet there was a ghost at this banquet of bickering which assumed a shape more substantial than the guests at the feast. Like Nelson Mandela in the 1980s, the name Kenyatta was now invested with a mystique which was inextricably bound up with the cry of freedom and nationhood. Just four days before the Kiambu conference the new Governor, Sir Patrick Renison, made a statement as clumsy as it was futile, when he announced: 'Jomo Kenyatta was the recognised leader of the non-cooperation movement which organised Mau Mau. Here was an African leader to darkness and death . . . From the security viewpoint I think that Jomo Kenyatta's return to political life in Kenya would be a disaster.' If anything could have united the factions in African politics then it would have been this crass outburst. That it did not do so shows how deep the rifts were.

While the name Kenyatta became a rallying call for the nationalist movement in general, inside KANU his haunting presence actually caused disunity. With the various leaders and their followers at each other's throats, and with the only court of appeal a powerless Kenyatta, KANU never approached the ideal of becoming a homogeneous mass party. Instead, what emerged was a loose-knit, ill-disciplined and fundamentally parochial organisation riven by personality conflicts. As Ronald Ngala observed when he refused the post of treasurer in a party without proper accounts: 'KANU had too many leaders and there were signs that they could be pulled one against the other.'

On the surface, KANU and KADU – Luo and Kikuyu tribes versus the smaller tribes – represented the fundamental fault line in Kenyan African society. This is, however, only a partial snapshot of the political scene. The continuing crisis in KANU was not caused by the threat from KADU but by the divisions within it: the ancient suspicion between Luo and Kikuyu; the tensions, often violent, between the dispossessed Kikuyu nationalists who had supported Mau Mau and the well-to-do Kikuyu loyalists who had done well out of the Emergency. The first of these antagonisms had existed long before KANU, or the colonialists for that matter, and now merely surfaced in another guise. The political murders of Pio Pinto, Tom Mboya and J. M. Kariuki following Independence were the result of the enmities and power struggles that had fermented within KANU during the colonial period. Apart from Moi, the political personalities who eventually joined KANU from KADU were always on the sidelines of power.

With the Kikuyu political weal still emerging from the cocoon of the Emergency, during this period of political shadow boxing other tribal groupings were able to exercise an influence out of all proportion to their size and economic importance. As a tribal umbrella organisation, KADU took full advantage of this hiatus. In the first free Kenyan election it proved to be more disciplined, moderate and pragmatic than KANU, its political philosophy much more in tune with Moi's instincts and aims.

In spite of the divide between the two African nationalist parties, there was a growing awareness that all their vying for position would be to no avail if the country were not able to hurdle the fence that would loom before it in February 1961 – Kenya's first general election held on a common-roll basis. Lancaster House had resulted in the introduction of a complex and untested voting system in a colony with a largely illiterate electorate, at a time when economic chaos threatened to drive the country to civil unrest and ruin.

Given the personal acrimony between African Legislative Council members and their supporters, the factional conflict inside KANU, and the tribal orientation of the two African parties, what is remarkable is that the elections passed off relatively peacefully. Certainly in Kikuyu-dominated districts KADU was largely irrelevant, KANU politicians like Dr Kiano reserving most of their energies for attempts to heal the divisions between the loyalists and former Mau Mau supporters.

Indeed, independent observers were surprised by the uncommon congruity of the two election manifestos. A rapid transition to independence, the Africanisation of the administration, the acceleration of African agricultural development and speedy industrialisation were the main policies offered by both parties, which also agreed on maintaining a mixed capitalist society whilst establishing a welfare state. The KADU programme placed a high emphasis on human rights and pledged legislation to guarantee normal freedoms enjoyed in democracies, a pledge which caused the *Daily Nation* to comment that the manifesto reflected 'the decent, honest Christian views of the party's two main leaders, Mr Ronald Ngala and Mr Masinde Muliro.'

The main difference between the parties was the place Kenyatta assumed in their campaigns. For KANU, the 'release Kenyatta' theme dominated the election, but it did not assume the same significance for KADU; indeed, on one occasion Toweet attacked the 'deification' of Kenyatta. Furthermore, within KANU the 'Kenyatta na Uhuru' ('No independence without Kenyatta') strategy was not so much a noble crusade as a tactic which Odinga and senior Kikuyu politicians used in a vain attempt to diminish the power and influence of Mboya and Gichuru. With one side accusing Odinga of being a tool of the Eastern Bloc, and the other claiming that Mboya was nothing more than a puppet of the CIA, it seemed that KANU was on the brink of utter self-destruction.

While the Kenyatta issue drove KANU to the edge of the abyss, his continued detention was a minor concern in Moi's Baringo constituency. Land-settlement schemes, education, the destocking programme, and the drought (which later that year would necessitate famine relief for 5,000 people) occupied the minds of his Tugen voters. Moi campaigned hard for the seat. In this he was driven by a sense of betrayal from within his own family, for his brother-in-law, Eric Bomett, had decided to stand against him, ostensibly as an independent candidate but in reality as a KANU supporter. 'Moi is a man who is slow to anger,' says Joel Bultut, his one-time campaign manager, 'but he was angry with Eric.'

Bomett admits that his decision was the start of a cool period between him and Moi, but argues, with a chuckle of remembrance: 'It was not personal, it was a matter of principle. Naturally he wasn't pleased that his brother-in-law was standing against him.' Whatever his reasons, it was an ill-judged move. Moi had consolidated his support since entering the Legislative Council, appealing to both the conservative tastes of the local elders for his work in the constituency, particularly with regard to the Lembus Forest and the destocking programme, while his numerous speeches in the Council championing the rights of Africans, as well as his previous work as a teacher in the district, struck a chord with the emerging educated groups. Polling was impressively high with 86.1 per cent of those eligible recording their votes. Equally striking was the size of Moi's majority. He polled 5,225, with Eric Bomett attracting just 503 and suffering the ignominy of losing his deposit.

While Bomett backed the wrong horse in his home district, he did pick the eventual election winner. At end of the 9-day polling period for the 44 contested open seats it emerged that KANU was easily the dominant party. It captured 19 seats and attracted 67.4 per cent of all votes cast as opposed to 16.4 per cent for KADU, which nevertheless gained eleven seats. Other successful candidates for the seats reserved for minority racial groups included four for Michael Blundell's liberal New Kenya Party, three for the Kenya Coalition Party, three for the Kenya Indian Congress, one for the Kenya Freedom Party, and sixteen independents. With African support thrown behind those who had won who seemed willing to work together to achieve racial harmony and integration, there was a sense of optimism, a feeling that great things could be achieved quickly.

That mood of quiet euphoria was quickly punctured by the Governor, Sir Patrick Renison, who, in a broadcast on 1 March, announced that Kenyatta would not be released until a government was formed and proved to be workable. He did say that the exiled political leader was to be moved from Lodwar to Maralal, somewhat nearer to Nairobi, adding that after a government had been formed politicians, church leaders and journalists would be permitted to visit him.

The Governor also agreed that KADU leaders Ngala and Muliro as well as Gichuru and Mboya of KANU could visit Kenyatta. This decision threw KANU into turmoil, for Odinga and others on the Governing Council suspected that Gichuru and Mboya would try to convince Kenyatta that they should co-operate in forming a government pending his release. If this ruse succeeded, they could use their governmental positions to consolidate their authority at the expense of Kenyatta and Odinga. After a stormy six-hour meeting KANU's parliamentary group flatly refused the Governor's offer, saying that they would not co-operate in the formation of a government unless and until Kenyatta was freed.

KANU's decision did not impress Kenyatta. When Ngala and Muliro visited Kenyatta on 8 March, the exiled leader regretted that KANU had not taken part in the visit. His message was much the same as it had been when Moi saw him in 1959 – he urged African leaders to show a united front, saw the Lancaster House agreement as a basis for a further move towards independence, and made it clear that he did not feel bitter towards other races.

Eventually, a joint KANU-KADU delegation was chosen to visit Kenyatta and other exiled nationalist leaders at Lodwar. This historic meeting in the turbulent summer of 1961 turned into something of a political beauty contest as the two rival parties, both hoping that Kenyatta would side with them, vied to impress him and his fellow detainees. After KANU officials had given their version of political events, Kenyatta made it clear that he was not for either side, but 'for all the people'. He made it plain that as there were no policy differences between the two parties, disunity was caused by personality conflicts, and made a plea for the two political parties to work together.

In response to Kenyatta's appeal for unity, it was left to Moi, who lead the KADU delegation, to make the formal reply. He argued that, given the prevailing climate of acrimony within KANU, his party would only consider merging with its rival when the latter displayed a degree of discipline and ended the personal squabbling. None the less the joint delegation agreed a resolution to work more closely together, particularly on two major issues – the immediate and unconditional release of Kenyatta, and full independence by the end of 1961.

Following the meeting, Moi travelled to his Rift Valley constituency to give KADU's official reaction to the momentous events at Lodwar. Crucially, he told his people: 'Our hands are not tied at all. The issue of the release of Jomo Kenyatta is a separate issue from that of forming a government. We cannot take the two together.' The difference between KADU's pragmatism and KANU's principle was summed up by Taitta Toweet, who recalls: 'KADU said that they would form the government and then release Kenyatta. However, KANU said that they wouldn't form the government until Kenyatta was released. This seemed stupid to KADU people because if you're in government, you can do what you like and release Kenyatta. We thought we were approaching it the sensible way round.'

With the Legislative Council suspended and KANU refusing to co-operate in any government, a dangerous stalemate prevailed. The KADU leaders were, however, determined to find a way out of this constitutional morass. Ngala, one of the unsung heroes of Kenyan politics, went to London for talks with Colonial

Secretary Macleod and various Members of Parliament, but in spite of his best endeavours, he could find no way through the impasse of securing Kenyatta's immediate release. Before Ngala left, however, the Colonial Secretary urged him to see the Governor on his return to Kenya, as Macleod hoped to agree a revised constitution formula by the time Ngala arrived back in Nairobi. The deal was that Kenyatta would be released from detention 'in due course', but in the meantime the government would build a house for him and his family in his home district of Kiambu. While this seemed like another of Macleod's 'wet' compromises, it was actually a part of his careful strategy for reintegrating Kenyatta into national life without causing alarm and revolt among the European community.

It was a decisive breakthrough. In discussions with the Governor, leaders from KADU, Blundell's New Kenya Party and the Kenyan Asian Party decided that this formula was enough to allow them to form a minority coalition government. On 18 April 1961 it was announced that KADU would participate in the formation of a government with the proviso that the party would be given effective control of the colony's affairs.

As Ronald Ngala, who became the Leader of Government Business, unequivocally stated: 'We are not going into government; we are the government. We are not just co-operating with a colonial administration. We took this decision in the interests of Kenya.' With these words he ushered in a new era in Kenya's political history – and yet another crisis for the strife-torn KANU.

Chapter six
Struggle for the Soul of Kenya

As Ronald Ngala, Daniel arap Moi and the other KADU leaders who formed Kenya's first African government in April 1961 tried to peacefully resolve the country's difficulties, others took a different view. Brigadier Danny Njuguna, the Mau Mau leader who secretly met Moi during the 1950s, left his Nairobi home to return to his old hunting ground in the Rift Valley where he marshalled his men to prepare for a second war of independence. He was just one of many disaffected radicals or former Mau Mau who decided that the pace of constitutional reform was too slow, the re-emergence of the underground armed struggle coinciding with the renewal of oathing in Central Province.

With Njuguna and others massing in the forests, KADU leaders were well aware of the personal risks. It was a tense time. The security forces had high-grade information that Ngala, Moi, Muliro and Toweet were on an assassination hit list. Arrests were made, precautions taken – sometimes to little effect.

However the threat posed by the army in the forest was as nothing compared to the open warfare within KANU once KADU had officially formed the new government. KANU, although dominant numerically, saw the prospect of power slipping from its grasp, something which served to exacerbate existing tensions and divisions within the party. All at once KADU, dismissed as stooges of the colonialists, seemed to hold the whip hand. Shortly after KADU took power Ronald Ngala, the first African Leader of Government Business, was able to announce a number of advances which demonstrated the value of co-operation rather than confrontation; all the men who had been detained with Kenyatta were to be allowed to return to their home areas, while the British Government agreed a financial aid package for Kenya of more than £18 million. Ngala later explained: 'We took this decision [to form a coalition government] in the interests of Kenya. The alternative, with KANU refusing to participate in the government and the Governor refusing to release Kenyatta, was government by decree. This would have done untold damage to our economy. We decided also that our participation in government was the quickest way to get Kenyatta released.'

In those early days Ngala, Moi, Muliro and other KADU leaders entertained genuine hopes that their government would smoothly take Kenya into independence and beyond. Their ambition was not without substance. With KANU in disarray, KADU politicians believed that moderate politicians from the other party would join them. Moi, who was made Parliamentary Secretary – the modern equivalent is Assistant Minister – in the Ministry of Education, and later Minister for Education, was quietly satisfied when Bernard Mate, who had been a regular visitor at his Pumwani lodgings, crossed the floor. There were fears within KANU that two more of Moi's moderate friends, Jeremiah Nyagah and Dr Kiano, were seriously considering defecting – and they might not be the only ones.

While Odinga and others accused KADU of being party to the continued restrictions on Kenyatta, the KADU-led government quietly organised the building of a new home for him and his family. Moi held fund-raising sessions for Kenyatta in his Rift Valley constituency, as did other KADU politicians elsewhere. Given Kenyatta's ambivalence about his political inclinations, this was a further exercise in wooing the most substantial figure in Kenyan politics. In a matter of months the man about whom no one might speak any good – if they could speak anything at all – had been transformed into a man of whom no one dared speak any ill.

It was a sign of his authority that the pivot of political debate was centred on the court of Kenyatta, rather than on the unstable minority government in Nairobi. He continued to play the role of concerned neutral, caring more about the fate of the nation than the advantage of either of the main political parties. Then, on 14 August 1961, Kenyatta was finally freed. The myth was about to become man. With the release of Kenyatta and fellow detainees came the ending of the phoney political war. For the first time the full spectrum of African political thinking was on view, from the moderate shades of KADU to the more radical hues of those in KANU who supported the forest fighters. All eyes were on Kenyatta to see where in the political rainbow he now stood. In the weeks following his release he ceaselessly addressed the question of national unity, attempting to allay settlers' fears as to his radicalism while also trying to stand above the party-political fray. At a mass rally in Nairobi in early September he said: 'If we are going to have unity . . . then I see no reason for having two parties.'

In this spirit of unity one of his first political acts was to call a meeting in Nairobi of all elected Africans to discuss further constitutional advances. In the afterglow of his release there was a degree of harmony between KADU and KANU, both parties agreeing to demand a constitutional conference in September 1961, and independence by February 1962. This brittle alliance soon collapsed over an issue which was to dog Kenyan politics to the present day as majimboism or regional government was to become the centrepiece of KADU's constitutional strategy. By contrast, KANU argued forcefully for unitary government, believing that regional administrations were unwieldy and tribalistic. This substantial policy difference cut to the heart of Kenya's constitution, and its resolution was to define the country's political topography for generations. In essence, majimboism was a system of checks and balances designed to safeguard the integrity of smaller tribes which were in danger of being overwhelmed by the larger, better-organised and more educated tribes, particularly the Kikuyu. It was also a recognition of the primacy of the tribe, large or small, compared to the nation state.

In 1961 Kenya was an artificial entity created by colonialists who had welded together more than forty different tribes, numerous languages and cultures in a country whose very existence was based not on serving the will of the indigenous population, but on benefiting a transient and alien minority, and a rich and powerful Western nation thousands of miles away. It was, therefore, little wonder that, among Kenyan Africans, ultimate allegiance was owed to ancient tribal groupings rather than a repressive and exploitative nation state. This sentiment was particularly true of rural and coastal peoples – the backbone of KADU's support – who tended to view Nairobi and all 'up-country' politicians with suspicion and fear.

On the other hand, KANU, its membership mainly drawn from the larger more urbanised tribes, was more acceptant of the existing centralised system of government. The party viewed majimboism as yet another colonialist-inspired plot to divide and rule the African by pitting region against region, tribe against tribe, though there was also an unspoken acknowledgement that Kikuyu ambitions to expand west into the Rift Valley would be hampered under a majimbo constitution. Paradoxically, it was KANU, ostensibly the more radical party, which accepted, lock, stock and barrel, the unitary colonial structure in all its arbitrary, artificial and British glory. As the Kenyan historian Wunyabari Maloba has noted:

> The singular aim of the political elite by 1963 was to inherit the state. But they failed to realise that the state . . . was oppressive, ruthless and a vehicle through which settlers and Britain exploited the Africans. To inherit the state intact was unfortunately to advance the aims for which it was so uniquely suited and created.

This policy schism between KANU and KADU finally forced Kenyatta's hand. After weeks of watching the fight – on one occasion he threatened to form his own party – he finally entered the lists, and in October 1961 took his place as President of KANU. His previous guise as the neutral statesman was quickly discarded as he began to trade insults with KADU. In a thinly disguised attack on

KADU at a Labour Day rally he pointedly referred to 'traitors' who 'were delaying our independence'. Moi, as Chairman of KADU, pointed out that these remarks had reduced their author to his 'proportionate size' politically. 'Kenyatta should not have denounced KADU's regionalist policy before discussing it with us,' he said. 'I appeal to Mr Kenyatta, as an old man, in the interest of this country to reconsider his present stand and come to his senses as a nationalist.'

Moi's colleagues were less charitable, Masinde Muliro accusing the KANU president of single-handedly delaying independence because of his links with 'the thug element' within the Kenya African Union which had caused the Emergency. He made clear why KADU had supported Kenyatta's release: as he had finished his gaol sentence he was entitled to be a free man, but that did not mean he should automatically lead Kenya. At a 20,000-strong rally in Kimilili in the Rift Valley, KADU leaders blamed the failure of the Nairobi conference on their political rivals and spoke of their fears of Kikuyu incursions into the region. 'Her Majesty's Government must sanction regionalism before handing over power to the African if there is to be peace in Kenya,' Moi told his supporters. He also denounced Kenyatta's leadership, because 'he advocates the one-party system as a means to achieve tribal domination'.

If KADU's gloves were off, Kenyatta found, now that he had entered the political arena, that his fellow gladiators in KANU were reluctant to help him out, those KANU elected members who had each pledged to stand down so that Kenyatta could take a seat in the Legislative Council now sat on their hands. After horse-trading within KANU, in January 1962 he was returned unopposed for the Fort Hall constituency, enabling him to lead the KANU delegation to London that same month for the second Lancaster House Conference on the constitution of Kenya.

At the first Lancaster House Conference the African delegates had at least tried to hide their differences behind the fig leaf of unity. On the second occasion, in January 1962, their bitterness, rancour and naked ambition were exposed to the world. The Colonial Secretary, Reginald Maudling (who had succeeded Macleod in 1961), spoke in vain when, in his opening statement, he stressed the need for a quick solution to the constitutional problems if the drain on Kenya's economy was to be arrested. In fact, the conference dragged on for nearly two months.

Much of that time was taken up with the debate about regional versus unitary government. Once again KADU demonstrated that its discipline and resolve enabled its delegates to outflank those from its larger rival. Ngala, whose opening speech stressed the need for a constitution that would safeguard individual rights and thus prevent the growth of dictatorship or communism, consistently hammered away at the need for a sound regional structure. The events in post-independence Ghana, where power had quickly devolved to the President, produced the constant conference refrain: 'We are not going to have an Nkrumah done on us.' (On Ghana's independence in 1960, Kwame Nkrumah had become President, his rule swiftly becoming increasingly dictatorial.)

Outside the conference hall there was a degree of easy camaraderie and fellow feeling among the KADU group. After hours their main concern was to put J. M. Seroney to bed because of his tendency to fall asleep at the hotel bar, while Michael Blundell remembers: 'Ronald Ngala sitting quietly in the evenings in our hotel in London after the day sessions at Lancaster House with a mug of beer and sandwiches, gossiping with students and friends from Kenya in that multi-tudinous city.' In fact, Moi was so impressed by the mother country that he named his twins, who were born that year, Philip and Doris Elizabeth in honour of the Queen and the Duke of Edinburgh.

No such fellow feeling affected the rival party's camp. As Ngala and his colleagues consistently forced KANU on to the defensive, Kenyatta, the man described as 'the father of Kenya's nationalism', tried hard to keep his squabbling brood in order. A report in the *New York Times* suggesting that Mboya and fifteen others were planning to leave KANU and ally themselves with KADU highlighted Kenyatta's difficulties. At the same time, Odinga's links with the Communist world made him an object of suspicion within his own party, fellow delegates privately accusing him of planning a revolution. In this fetid atmosphere Kenyatta, his leadership already under question, found it difficult to hold the ring in his own party, let alone to mount attacks against his opponents.

With the conference reaching deadlock over the fundamental issue of central or regional government, the Colonial Secretary asked the rival delegations to form working parties to concentrate on resolving other points of disagreement, namely the powers and functions of the police and the Central Land Board to arbitrate in the vexed question of land allocation regarding tribal reserves and land left by departing settlers. While a compromise was reached on the issue of the police, it was the land question that inevitably created the greatest heat. Michael Blundell remembers the reaction of the KADU delegates when, during the course of a speech, Kenyatta said that the Kikuyu must be allowed to take up land in the Rift Valley. 'Immediately there was a long-drawn-out "Aaah" from the Kalenjin and Maasai representatives, and Willie Murgor from Eldoret produced a whistle and blew a long note of alarm on it.'

A powerful speech by Moi, in which he stated that the Kalenjin would never give up their land, made a deep impression on Blundell as much for its style as its content. 'Africans are astute negotiators and also great judges as to whether they can squeeze anything more out of the other side,' he recalled. 'On this occasion Daniel arap Moi stood up and spoke to the relevant points, introducing them with an immense snap of his fingers. Indeed, I have never known anyone else who can make such a formidable sound which penetrated the large room like the crack of a whip.'

Moi, who was responding to Kiano's argument that land should be held by the central government, told the conference: 'As regards Dr Kiano's remark that, unless KANU's policy on land was accepted, there would be a breakdown and bloodshed, his [Moi's] people of Kalenjin were prepared to fight and die for their land, which after all in Kenya belonged to the people of the various tribes and not to the Kenya government.' This clash showed the gulf between national aspirations and territorial nationalism; the administrative centre which should have been the cradle for the new nation was viewed with grave suspicion and mistrust. Eventually a policy of 'willing seller, willing buyer', which implied a commercial rather than a tribal prerogative, and the establishment of Land Control Boards to regulate and approve sales of land, were the formal mechanisms adopted in an attempt to address this vexatious issue.

While this wrangle was not truly resolved by the end of the conference, many of the issues which were agreed went in KADU's favour – for example, Moi's argument that federal government should be responsible for teacher training was accepted. Under the majimbo framework it was recognised that there would be a parliament of two chambers – a House of Representatives and a Senate – with six regional assemblies and one for Nairobi, their boundaries to be established by an independent commission. Elections were scheduled for May 1963.

Although both parties returned to Nairobi claiming success, in fact neither group triumphed. The regional authorities did not have the powers which KADU wanted, while central government was hobbled by a constitution which ran to 223 pages. What was achieved was a coalition government led jointly by Ngala and Kenyatta, with each of the two main parties given seven ministries. Moi was moved from Education to Local Government, where he was involved in endless meetings and discussions in order to hammer out details of the regional assemblies. He led a delegation of Kalenjin tribesmen to Nakuru, where they gave evidence to the independent Regional Boundaries Commission. Like other Rift Valley districts, the members of the delegation expressed in strong terms their desire to be associated in one region with the Maasai and other Kalenjin groups.

When he was away from his Rift Valley constituency, Moi now shared a house in Nairobi with Justus ole Tipis and J. M. Seroney (who had the annoying habit of cooking steak and strong-smelling chillies every night), and it became a meeting place for KADU leaders. While Moi and his political colleagues tried to put flesh on the bare bones of the framework constitution produced by the Lancaster House Conference, the rising tension in the country, particularly the threat posed by the fighters from the Land Freedom Army underscored the need to work rapidly towards independence.

This uncertain mood was not helped by rival politicians who made warlike noises at weekend political rallies in their constituencies. Kalenjin leader William Murgor in Eldoret told his people that if KADU's regional plan were not accepted he would 'sound a whistle to my people declaring civil war'. Muliro made similar dark promises, while the Kamba politician and recently released detainee, Paul Ngei, violently denounced the European settlers.

In such a charged atmosphere clashes were inevitable. Of the Kalenjin clans, the Kipsigis were particularly aggressive towards Luo and Kikuyu incursion, sounding the war cry across the valleys on the slightest provocation. Similar bellicose threats were made by the Kikuyu, who embarked on large-scale oathing in their Rift Valley strongholds of Molo and Elburgon in support of the formation of a Kikuyu government which would distribute land to their landless fellow tribesmen. Alarmed colonial officers in the Rift Valley noted in one official report: 'African smiths were inundated with orders for spears. Bows and arrows were manufactured and stockpiled; poison was traded for goats or grain and on a number of occasions the war alarm was shouted from hill to hill, leading to the rapid mobilisation of hundreds or even thousands of excited warriors.' Indeed, when the Colonial Secretary, Reginald Maudling, visited Kenya in November 1961 he saw at once that the country was a tinderbox waiting to catch fire. As he commented: 'I think tribalism is more immediately explosive than racialism . . . I am quite certain that there is a danger of serious tribal clashes in this country unless a solution is found.'

In this charged atmosphere Moi had personally to intervene to prevent bloodshed in his home area. The local activities of the Land Freedom Army led to very definite anti-Kikuyu feeling and on one occasion in South Baringo warriors were actually preparing to march on hearing that a Tugen had been abducted by Kikuyu. On another, in November 1962, the Tugen and Njemps prepared to fight each other after the latter had ejected Tugen graziers and their cattle which had encroached illegally on Njemps land. Moi called a *baraza* and spoke to the warring parties, beseeching them to work together for the common good. As the District Commissioner reported: 'Had it not been for the fortuitous presence of Mr D.T. Moi bloodshed might well have resulted.'

The release of Kenyatta and the other detainees seemed, if anything, to make matters worse, as old political animosities were rekindled. It became patently obvious that Kenyatta's grip on his party was tenuous and his personal position weak. Party discipline was virtually non-existent, the selection of KANU candidates for the May 1963 election degenerated into a brutal and disorderly tumult, leading to several deaths. As soon as Kenyatta made one speech, invariably on the theme of conciliation and unity, the defiant language of his colleagues, particularly former detainees like Bildad Kaggia, would give a quite different impression. Whatever the factionalism among his party, however, like Ngala, Kenyatta was careful to woo the settlers. Within days of his release he had emphasised that he did not intend to form a 'gangster government', and had reassured settlers that what they owned they would keep. It was a theme he returned to: 'Those Africans who think that when we have achieved our freedom they can walk into a shop and say "This is my property" or go on to a farm and say "This is my farm" are very much mistaken because that is not our aim.'

No sooner had he spoken, however, than fellow detainees who had been on the radical wing of the old Kenya African Union, of which he had been president, seemed to contradict their leader. Kamba leader Paul Ngei particularly embarrassed the KANU leadership by talking openly of settling the families of freedom fighters on land which would be forcibly taken from the settlers; indeed, he became known as 'Bwana M'shamba' because he consistently promised free land. Ngei nursed old grievances – one of the political characteristics of Kenya in the 1960s was the playing-out of old feuds and enmities inside the pre-Emergency Kenya African Union – and felt that his Kamba tribe were being used as window dressing for KANU to disguise what was essentially a Kikuyu-Luo alliance. The result was the formation in 1963 of the African People's Party, Ngei's rival grouping attracting disenchanted Luo supporters as well as Kamba followers.

With other disillusioned Luo forming the Luo United Movement, which fielded candidates against KANU in the May 1963 elections, and the African People's Party flirting with KADU, once again KANU seemed to be on the brink of breaking up. A repetition of the 1961 election was a definite possibility, and party spokesmen talked openly about the likelihood of electoral defeat. But in truth, things were very different this time. First, KANU had a substantial war chest, whereas KADU, with limited funds, was unable to marshal enough candidates to win a majority, even if all their candidates had won their seats. As the election loomed, KADU, which had survived by its internal discipline, was now itself racked by open dissension, focusing particularly on the territorial ambitions in western Kenya of the Luhya leader, Masinde Muliro.

KADU's weakness was exposed in the results of the election, the first on a one-man, one-vote basis, as had been agreed at the Lancaster House Conference, in which KANU made dramatic gains, especially in the western region. Every major town except Mombasa went to KANU, and it was only on the coast and in the Rift Valley that KADU received solid support. The former's national supremacy was emphasised when it won 83 seats in the House of Representatives as opposed to KADU's 33, while in the regional assemblies KANU's dominance was emphatic, winning 158 seats to KADU's 51.

On 28 May 1963 the new Governor, Malcolm MacDonald, invited Kenyatta to form a government as defeated KADU politicians prepared for opposition. When Prime Minister Kenyatta unveiled his first Cabinet it was clear that the spoils of power were divided between the Luo and Kikuyu, while his inner circle, which included his brother-in-law Mbiyu Koinange, his nephew Dr Njoroge Mungai, and his cousin Charles Njonjo, was very much a family affair. Moreover, he demonstrated that he had learned much from the British, over the next few months using their tried and tested technique of divide and rule to slice away support from his political rivals, both inside his own party and from KADU. (This skill became so effective a feature of his political persona that it was adopted by his eventual successor, Daniel arap Moi.) In his first speech as Prime Minister, he was sharply critical of majimboism which, he said, had delayed independence, while at the same time offering an olive branch to his opponents. 'Only by creating a sense of national unity will it be possible to have the efforts of all the people to make a success of independence,' he said, announcing that 'Harambee' – 'Work Together' – was to be the slogan of the new nation.

Kenyatta's carrot-and-stick approach, attacking majimboism whilst preaching national unity, proved enormously effective, especially as Tom Mboya, acting as his backroom emissary, wheedled and cajoled wavering KADU, APP and independent politicians into the KANU fold. Mboya had no time for majimboism, either: 'The whole concept of nationhood and identification of sovereignty will work to diminish the importance of regionalism,' he wrote. 'If a man is proud of being a Kenyan citizen and being part of an independent Kenya, he will think of his country and not his region. Regions as they are, at present, constitute an irritant and nuisance which cannot survive.'

As KADU leaders fought a valiant rearguard action at the third Lancaster House Conference in September, a trickle of their local politicians switched allegiance. At the conference, meanwhile, KADU leaders felt that they had been sold out by new Colonial Secretary Duncan Sandys who, at KANU's insistence, had agreed to water down majimbo both as a concept and in practice. During an angry meeting with Sandys, a five-strong delegation, led by Ngala, voiced their distress at what they considered to be a betrayal. In spite of their protests, however, KADU was left high and dry, particularly when Kenyatta made it abundantly clear that the majimbo constitution, which was finally ratified at the conference, would have a strictly limited lifetime after independence was declared on 12 December 1963.

For the eleven months of 1964 during which the majimbo constitution existed, KANU, controlling the economy, manpower and central services, worked tirelessly to build the centre at the expense of the regions. The Home Affairs Minister, Oginga Odinga, described with undisguised relish how: 'Regional Assembly presidents, especially from the KADU-controlled regions [Ngala was running the Coast region and Moi the Rift Valley region] were regularly at our ministry protesting that we had usurped the functions of the regional assemblies.' Even when Moi and his deputy, Justus ole Tipis, managed to broker deals involving land allocations, they found themselves overruled by Odinga and his KANU officials.

At the same time as he set about exposing the political and economic impotence of the regional councils, Kenyatta worked hard to bring all sections of the community under their party's umbrella. In a famous meeting with 300 settlers led by Lord Delamere at Kenyatta's Gatundu farm in August 1963, the Prime Minister made a telling speech in which he asked the Europeans to forget past enmities, and assured them that they had a place in Kenya's future. The message to the rest of the world was clear: the shop may be under new management, but the policies remain the same.

As he accepted the constitutional documents from the Duke of Edinburgh at the independence ceremony in Nairobi on 12 December 1963, Kenyatta made a speech developing the ideals underpinning the national slogan, 'Harambee.' Addressing the vast crowd, he told them that they would achieve nothing without hard work and unity. It behoved everyone to work together in a spirit which he asked the audience to 'echo, to shout aloud, to shatter the foundations of the past with the strength of our new purpose . . . HARAMBEE!'

While his words captured the euphoria of the ending of one struggle, the fight for independence, another was only just beginning – the far more difficult task of building from scratch a modern nation state. In the march towards independence Kenyan politicians had papered over their differences in the contest with a common enemy, the colonialists. Now that they had the deeds to the property, the real arguments began about the kind of house they wanted to build.

It was a gloomy gathering at Moi's home in Kabimoi when he, Taitta Toweet and Justus ole Tipis met to discuss the future of KADU. In June 1964 Kenyatta announced the end of majimbo and said that Kenya would soon become a republic. A few days later he left for his first Commonwealth Conference, held in London, where once again he urged all political parties to set aside their differences and act as one. For some wavering KADU supporters, it proved to be the final turn of the screw. At the meeting at Kabimoi, Toweet proposed that they join KANU, saying: 'Gentlemen, we are in a minority party now, should we not work together with Kenyatta?' But while Toweet, who had previously been sounded out by Mboya and Kenyatta, inclined towards crossing the floor, Moi and the others were concerned about their supporters. The Rift Valley had not only demonstrated consistent hostility towards KANU and the Kikuyu, but also enthusiasm for the principles behind KADU. If their leaders simply jumped ship, their supporters would wreak their own revenge by consigning them to political obscurity. As far as Moi was concerned, majimboism was more than just a slogan. Throughout his political career, he had demonstrated his concern for and support of Kenya's smaller tribes. He had embraced the principles of majimbo not only because the system provided a bulwark against domination by the larger tribes, but because it enabled smaller tribes, inevitably more backward, to develop at a pace suitable to them. As the President of the Rift Valley Regional Council he was reluctant to betray his people and his principles.

At the same time, above all else, Moi was and is a pragmatic politician. Over the last few months since Independence it had become clear that the Rift Valley region, like the Coast, was suffering economically because of its support for KADU. Government largesse was showered on loyalist strongholds. After Kenyatta announced in August that Kenya would officially become a republic on 12 December 1964, Moi and other KADU leaders realised that the best they could hope for was to act as a brake on the headlong march towards a unitary state and work for a united nation.

None the less, KADU leaders made a brave show at their last annual conference held in Nairobi in the summer of 1964, at which representatives from seventy constituencies discussed ways of defeating KANU at the next election. During the meeting, only weeks before the party amalgamated with KANU, Moi, once again elected Chairman, remained defiant. He condemned all those who had crossed the floor, demanding that they resign their seats and seek re-election. One of the first to join KANU was J. M. Seroney, the leader of the largest Kalenjin grouping, the Nandi, and this crumbling of Kalenjin unity accelerated the break-up of KADU. Toweet, the Kipsigis' leader, declared himself an independent, but then lost the by-election as his former supporters took their revenge. Toweet's defeat was an ill omen for Moi and the others. Political oblivion beckoned.

At a party meeting in Nairobi, KADU's President, Ngala, spoke to the remaining regional leaders, including Moi, arguing that they should join KANU as a body rather than filtering across in dribs and drabs. In this way they could preserve a degree of effectiveness inside the ruling party. On 10 November 1964 Ngala and Muliro, the President and Vice-President of their party, announced in Parliament that KADU was dead and that they were crossing the floor of the house. Amidst scenes of jubilation, Ngala was carried shoulder high across to the government benches, where he was embraced by Jomo Kenyatta. Ngala explained that the aim of the move was to 'strengthen the national front and speak with one voice on all issues that confront our nation'.

'We are joining the government with no grudge or bitterness,' he said, adding gracefully: 'This is one of the times that we must be prepared to sacrifice our political dignity for the peace and harmony of Kenya.'

While Ngala faced a decidedly unfriendly reception in his Coast constituency when he tried to explain the party's abrupt decision to his followers, Moi had an easier ride, exhibiting in this difficult situation the political adroitness that has served him well during his career. Not for the first time, he worked on the principle of consensus, bringing in local leaders to discuss the political predicament KADU found itself in. He called all the Rift Valley political leaders to a meeting in Nakuru to select a Kalenjin delegation to see Kenyatta at his Gatundu home. While the delegation ostensibly pledged its support for Kenyatta and his government, its mere presence also physically demonstrated Moi's personal standing. The latter assured the President-in-waiting that he could now count upon the allegiance of one and a half million Kalenjin. As one of the Kalenjin delegates, Philemon Chelagat, recalled: 'It was a tactic. Moi often says that if you go as an individual you lose credibility. By going with so many you show that you are the leader of your people.'

This political show of strength was a shrewd move which was to pay handsome dividends when the new President announced the Jamhuri (Independence) Cabinet in December 1964, a year after independence. In the new one-party state, Moi became Minister for Home Affairs, a significant post previously held by Oginga Odinga, who now became the country's Vice-President and Minister without Portfolio. In fact Moi was the only member of KADU's executive to win any kind of ministerial position. While Muliro, whose attempts to suborn the Trans-Nzoia region to his Luhya tribe had alienated Moi and other Kalenjin leaders, was appointed Chairman of the Cotton Seed and Lint Marketing Board, Ngala, Seroney and others were left out in the cold. This particularly rankled with Seroney who, as the leader of the Nandi, the largest Kalenjin clan, and the first Kalenjin member of KADU to cross the floor, felt that one of the glittering prizes should have been his. Educated at Kapsabet with Moi and then at Alliance High School and university in South Africa, the way he used his intellectual superiority and vituperative wit had created many enemies, none more powerful than the 'Grand Vizier' of Kenyan court life, the Attorney-General, Charles Njonjo.

In contrast to Seroney, Moi had remained on friendly terms with many of his opponents, particularly with members of KANU's significant Christian fraternity. Njonjo, who married Margaret Bryson, the daughter of Moi's former mission teacher, was godfather to Moi's sixth child, Gideon, while the Embu MP Jeremiah Nyagah, who became Moi's Assistant Minister at Home Affairs, and Dr Julius Kiano were regular visitors to his Nairobi home. Friendship alone was not enough to explain his meteoric rise, however. As Kenyatta evaluated the tribal equation, it was apparent that Moi's claim to be leader of the Rift Valley could not be ignored. His staunch, not to say chauvinistic, defence of Kalenjin rights during the KANU/KADU days underlined his populist credentials. At the same time, during the early 1960s he had shown himself to be a hard-headed arbitrator in disputes between the Nandi and Kipsigis and, coming from the minority Tugen clan, he found favour with smaller clans like the Elgeyo, Marakwet, Pokot and Njemps, who regarded the larger Kalenjin clans, the Nandi and Kipsigis, with suspicion. His work on their behalf in the Legislative Council had earned lasting respect. With Toweet out of Parliament and Seroney sidelined, Moi was the compromise candidate to represent the Rift Valley in the new government.

Even so, his appointment still came as a surprise, for in the KADU hierarchy Moi ranked below Ngala, Muliro, Shikuku and Toweet. One man who was not surprised was Kenya's last governor, Malcolm MacDonald, who had already spotted Moi's qualities of leadership. In a letter to the Colonial Secretary, Duncan Sandys, in November 1963 he notes:

I have persuaded Kenyatta and Moi (who is easily the most important KADU figure after Ngala and even including Ngala) to get closer together. Moi now goes direct to Kenyatta with most of his regional or tribal troubles instead of coming to me and my having to talk to Kenyatta. Kenyatta has responded in his usual friendly way, with the result that the two of them are now on pretty good terms.

Nonetheless the suspicion remained that Kenyatta had simply chosen an ambitious 'yes man' who would do his bidding, especially as the Rift Valley became the front line in the wholesale redistribution of land. If Moi fitted into Kenyatta's tribal equation, he also entered into his political arithmetic. Moi was an ally at the high table, sharing completely the conservative views espoused by Kenyatta, Gichuru and Mboya. Tribally, Moi's suspicion of Kikuyu and Luo ambitions towards the Rift Valley cemented his adherence to KADU. Ideologically, however, there was little difference between the pragmatic, reformist, pro-capitalist, anti-communist wing of KANU and the new Minister for Home Affairs. Like Kenyatta, Mboya and moderate KANU politicians, Moi looked to the West for political example and economic support, accepting the economic and commercial status quo, property ownership and a multi-racial Kenyan society. By contrast, the Vice-President, Oginga Odinga, and other KANU radicals looked east, viewing the Communist world in a favourable light. Politically Odinga was in the vanguard of those, like former KAU activists and detainees Bildad Kaggia and Fred Kubai, who believed in a fundamental transformation, based on socialist principles of the economy, with particular emphasis on a redistribution of wealth among the masses. Coming at a time when the Cold War was at its height, with Russia, America and China all consolidating client states in Africa, South-East Asia and Latin America, the confrontation in Kenyan politics between pro-West and pro-Communist Bloc factions was an ideological conflict in which the stakes were very high. At his first Cabinet Moi, who, as was his custom, sat quietly watching the personality clashes around him, now saw from the inside the struggle for the soul of Kenya.

On the surface, Oginga Odinga, the undisputed leader of the radicals in KANU, was in his pomp. He had become the new republic's first Vice-President, ahead of Mboya, his deadly rival. With a solid phalanx of support in the Cabinet and the country, for a time his power matched that of Kenyatta. In the first years of independence such was his authority that MPs who did not support him were shouted down in Parliament, his critics regularly threatened with deportation. At the same time he sent army officers to Eastern Bloc countries for training, set up the Russian-funded Lumumba Institute in Nairobi, run by the Goanese-born Pio Pinto, to train KANU activists, teachers and journalists, and tried to organise a pro-Communist parliamentary group. On one occasion he arranged for a delegation of twenty-four Kenyan MPs to visit Russia for the May Day celebrations. Eric Bomett, who was one of the chosen few, recalls that they were well treated, even feted, by their hosts; he even danced with the wife of the Soviet President, Nikita Khrushchev. Of Odinga's pro-Communist activities, Bomett says: 'It was quite clear that here was an attempt to have a nucleus of MPs in Parliament who would champion the Communist cause. We knew what Odinga was doing and we felt influenced by it. Odinga was a nationalist but he was also in the thrall of Communist doctrine and the fear was that he was becoming a puppet of the Kremlin.'

There was a dark side to the cloud of suspicion and rumour, some of it undoubtedly manufactured by Mboya and others, which swirled around Odinga. Guns were discovered in the basement of his offices at Jogoo House, while top secret British and Kenyan intelligence reports claimed that Odinga had planned coups against the government on at least two occasions. The first was allegedly in July 1964 when Kenyatta was attending the Commonwealth Conference in London. Less than a year later, in April 1965, British security chiefs were so concerned that supporters of Oginga Odinga might try to stage a takeover that they alerted President Kenyatta. This information, contained in Chiefs of Staff papers released in Britain in 1996, gave few details of the anticipated rebellion other than to say that 'reports were received that Oginga Odinga and his associates might attempt some kind of armed or other action to seize power during the month of April'. This may help to explain why, a month later, in May 1965, Kenya security forces seized a convoy of eleven lorries carrying Chinese arms and ammunition through Odinga's South Nyanza power base while he was addressing a public rally. Hard on the heels of this incident came news that a Russian ship docked at Mombasa was loaded with tanks and other arms for Kenya, a weapons deal once more linked to Vice-President Odinga, although in the end it fell through.

Just a few weeks earlier, as a violent prelude to the fervid talk of revolts, one of Odinga's closest allies, Pio Pinto, the head of the Lumumba Institute, was murdered in a Nairobi suburb. A charismatic socialist who was adored by the *wananchi*, Pinto's killing on 24 February 1965 truly ended independent Kenya's age of political innocence and idealism. The week before his death Pinto had been warned of the consequences if he stayed in the country. He told friends that he had been approached by Kenyatta's chief bodyguard, who told him that he had a week to leave the country; if he did not he would be killed. Pinto, by turns incredulous and bewildered, spoke to a number of his closest friends to ask their advice. Some said go, some said stay. In the end he decided to flee to Mozambique, but before he could leave he was shot, allegedly by a teenage assassin. His murder stunned Parliament and the nation. 'I had never feared for my life before but now I could see that we were living in a state of fear,' recalls John Keen, then, as now, a noisy backbench MP.

Pinto's murder, and the continuing rumours of plots against Kenyatta, marked the beginning of the end for the Luo politician. Just weeks before Pinto's death a delegation of MPs had visited Kenyatta to warn him that Parliament and key sections of the administration were being systematically taken over by Odinga and his clique. The President listened to what they had to say, then gave them permission to oppose Odinga, promising to organise Cabinet ministers to back them. His overmighty subject was about to be humbled.

This was the start of the so-called 'Corner Bar Group', a body of MPs opposed both to Odinga's strong-arm tactics and his alleged Communist sympathies. While it was some time before Cabinet ministers themselves attended meetings of this ginger group, Moi regularly spoke to them in private, reassuring them that they enjoyed Kenyatta's patronage. Eric Bomett recalls: 'He [Moi] kept assuring everybody that the government supported them, which was very important because some elements in the camp feared Odinga.'

Perhaps the defining moment of this personal and ideological battle was the publication, in May 1965, of the famous Sessional Paper No 10, *African Socialism and its application to planning in Kenya*. Written by Tom Mboya, the Minister for Economic Planning and Development, it rejected both Marxist and *laissez-faire* economics, calling for economic development that recognised the country's unique cultural and social heritage. The paper accepted individual property rights, a mixed economy with limited nationalisation, rapid Africanisation of the commercial and administrative structure, and the retention of the existing colonial legal and economic frameworks. By contemporary standards it is a left-of-centre document. Although in the 1960s it was ridiculed by Kenya's radicals as dangerously right-wing. Odinga, angry at the drip of insinuation and the ceaseless manoeuvring, realised that the battle of ideas was lost and broke cover. He launched a furious broadside against the former KADU leaders who, he felt, were corrupting the ideals behind KANU. Now Moi publicly joined the fray, deploring Odinga's remarks. 'The country will judge who is loyal to the Kenya government', he said ominously.

> I don't see how the Vice-President can call for unity and at the same time bring up the past and suggest that former KADU members are trying to topple the government. When I joined KANU, I did so as a leader and I am behind the President . . . I reject anybody who wants to create confusion and friction.

Reading between the lines of Moi's speech, everyone came to the obvious conclusion; for a senior minister to attack the Vice-President meant that the criticism was authorised by none other than the President himself.

Finally, in February 1966, Kenyatta announced new plans for the party and introduced a new constitution, under which it was intended to abolish the post of national Vice-President and instead establish eight Vice-Presidents, one for each province and one for Nairobi. Moi and Mboya worked behind the scenes to handpick delegates for the landmark KANU conference to discuss these plans, which was to be held at Limuru, outside Nairobi. Unlike Odinga, who was long on rhetoric but short on organisation, Moi proved himself adept at backroom fixing.

Eric Bomett describes his technique: 'As an organiser he was excellent. He would contact MPs individually and when he'd spoken to a few he would get, say, ten or twelve together and speak to them. By finding their views he was able to direct the meeting and reach the conclusion he wanted. Then he'd call another group without the others knowing and the same thing would be repeated.' Moi's consistent ability to build a consensus, which is so critical in a tribally divided nation, is one of the defining characteristics of his political skills.

The atmosphere at the Limuru Conference in March 1966, under the chairmanship of Kenyatta, was electrifying, especially when Odinga lost the crucial vote for national as well as party Vice-President. Instead, the constitution was duly amended and eight regional KANU Vice-Presidents elected, Moi

Moi in mourning for the Father of the Nation, Jomo Kenyatta, who died on 22 August 1978.

On 14 October 1978, Daniel arap Moi was sworn in as the second President of Kenya and Commander-in-Chief of the Armed Forces. Watched by Chief Justice Sir James Wickes, the new President takes the oath of office at a ceremony in Uhuru Park.

Above: Attended by the cameras, President Moi takes his first Cabinet meeting to discuss the funeral arrangements for Jomo Kenyatta. Ironically, he is flanked by two ministers, James Gichuru and Mbiyu Koinange (far right), who were leading members of the Change the Constitution group which aimed to prevent Moi becoming President.

Below: The urbane, pin-striped figure of Attorney-General Charles Njonjo, known as 'the Duke of Kabetshire', was Moi's constant companion during the early years of his presidency. Njonjo's fall was the result of a classic political power struggle.

A joint Army and Police security check was immediately launched by the Kenyan government to round up looters and to prevent further looting of shops in the wake of the abortive Kenya Airforce *coup d'état* attempt on President Moi's government on 1 August, 1982.

Above: In the early years the energy demonstrated by Kenya's second President was in sharp and invigorating contrast to that of his predecessor. Here he leads Cabinet ministers and other dignitaries in erecting gabions along a badly eroded riverbed during a visit to Mwanyani village in Machakos District in 1982.

Below: The Queen and the Duke of Edinburgh visited Nairobi shortly after the 1983 elections. President Moi is such an Anglophile that he named two of his children, twins Doris Elizabeth and Philip, after the Queen and her Consort.

The President and British Prime Minister, Margaret Thatcher, outside State House, Nairobi, during a working visit in 1988. The Prime Minister, who had little time for most African leaders, respected Moi's strength of purpose.

Above: Watched by the then head of the Kenya Wildlife Service, Dr Richard Leakey, President Moi sets light to tons of ivory in Nairobi National Park, a dramatic gesture which showed the world that Kenya was serious about stopping poaching and intent on elephant conservation.

Below: A smiling President with American President George Bush following a prayer breakfast at the White House in January 1990. This rather routine picture gives the lie to allegations made by, among others, the US Ambassador to Kenya at the time, Smith Hempstone, that Moi was furious with his then Foreign Minister, Bob Ouko, for failing to arrange a meeting with the American President and as a result ordered his murder. In fact Moi was delighted with the way Ouko handled the visit.

Above: President Moi and his Foreign Minister, Bob Ouko, whose unexplained murder in February 1990 is a continuing blot on Moi's presidency.

Below: Hand in hand, South African President Nelson Mandela and President Moi walk through the streets of Nairobi watched by Winnie Mandela and Vice-President George Saitoti. The visit, in 1991, came at the height of the multi-party debate.

becoming KANU Vice-President, Rift Valley. After Odinga's downfall, the US Ambassador to Kenya, William Attwood, commented: 'Kenyatta had waited a long time for Odinga and his friends to come out into the open and now the old lion of Kenya had pounced.' At last Kenyatta had consolidated his personal authority within KANU, a party that had existed on the edge of crisis and turmoil since its birth. The ousting of Odinga had finally quieted the unruly infant. While Odinga could have stayed and fought from inside KANU, he resigned, along with some thirty odd ministers, MPs and senators, to form his own party, the Kenya People's Union (KPU). A furious Kenyatta forced them to stand for election. In what came to be known as the 'Little General Election' that May, Odinga's supporters returned to Parliament with only nine seats, mainly in Luoland. Even though the KPU was a tiny tribal party, it represented a return to multi-party politics after a gap of some twenty months.

The parting of the ways between Kenyatta and Odinga was not simply the outcome of a war of ideas; it was also a reflection of the enduring tension that existed between Luo and Kikuyu. As Mboya himself observed, in the colonial days in Nairobi, members of the two tribes would attack each other on sight, and though he managed to keep MPs in his South Nyanza region inside the KANU fold, the existence of Odinga's KPU was a testimony to the age-old suspicion between Kenya's two largest tribes, who share neither a common tongue nor culture. As an example of this lack of common ground, it is often said that a Luo will never be accepted as president because, as a tribe, they are uncircumcised. The return to multi-party politics was less a sign of Kenya's wider embrace of democracy than an indication of increased tribal polarities. Over the next few years, as the Kikuyu elite cemented their ascendancy, the rift grew between the ruling party and the disaffected Luo.

Odinga's downfall also set a precedent in the matter of the position of Vice-President. Never again would Kenyatta appoint someone who could pose a threat to the President's status. Paradoxically, after Odinga's time, the national Vice-President, far from being viewed as the second most powerful man in the country, was seen, rather like the American Vice-President, as a stand-in figure in case of an untoward crisis. It was this perception which contributed to Moi's continued survival in that post during the dark days of Kenyatta's presidency. The appointment, in May 1966, of the Minister for External Affairs, Joe Murumbi, as Odinga's successor fulfilled Kenyatta's criteria. Educated in India, of mixed Goan and Maasai stock and married to an Englishwoman, Murumbi had spent the previous decade in London. As a result, he had neither strong tribal affiliations nor deep domestic roots, so that he commanded little popular support.

Murumbi, who was in any case a reluctant successor to Odinga, was appalled at the way the Kikuyu elite were voraciously lining their own pockets at the expense of the nation. In September 1966 he resigned his post and retired from politics to a farm in his Maasai homeland. What price now the post of Vice-President?

PART II
The Making of a President

Chapter seven

The Man Behind the Mask

Just before Christmas 1966, President Kenyatta and his Attorney-General, Charles Njonjo, sat in the back of the presidential limousine as it travelled from Kisumu to Kericho. Their talk was of finding a replacement for Joe Murumbi, who had abruptly resigned as national Vice-President, and the issue was causing the President some concern. They discussed the obvious list of candidates: members of his family and of the Kikuyu clique from Kiambu District which surrounded him. As each name was mentioned – his powerful brother-in-law Mbiyu Koinange; his nephew, personal physician and Defence Minister, Dr Njoroge Mungai; his nephew Ngengi Muigai; wealthy young businessman Njenga Karume; James Gichuru, the Finance Minister – Kenyatta shook his head in disagreement. He rejected all of them; not one, he said, could win support once they had crossed the Tana River – in other words, outside the Kikuyu heartland. As for Njonjo himself, he says: 'I was a civil servant and not considered for the position.'

The Attorney-General mentioned the Minister for Home Affairs, Daniel arap Moi. Kenyatta considered the suggestion for some moments. Then he stretched out his hand and said: 'That's the man I'm going to appoint.' It was, as it turned out, a shrewd decision. Since his elevation to Kenyatta's Cabinet, Moi had proved himself to be both a loyal government stalwart, and a safe pair of hands as far as the implementation of policy was concerned. The Odinga affair had tested his loyalty to Kenyatta and his backroom skills as a political fixer; he had not been found wanting in either. At the same time he had demonstrated his administrative competence when he successfully headed the National Famine Relief Committee, set up in late 1965 to organise supplies of maize and other famine relief to drought-ravaged villages. Within his ministry he was respected by his civil servants and his junior ministers, Jeremiah Nyagah and Ken Matiba. 'It was a happy team,' recalls Nyagah. The rapid implementation of the Africanisation programme inside his ministry and his steady conservatism in matters of law and order underlined his reliability.

More important, with the fragmenting of the Kikuyu-Luo coalition following the defection of Odinga, Kenyatta needed new tribal allies. By appointing Moi, now the undisputed leader of the Kalenjin, he had secured the firm allegiance of a tribal grouping which had hitherto opposed both him and his tribe, the Kikuyu. This was of even greater significance now that the incursions of Kikuyu families from Central Province were being moved into the Rift Valley in ever-increasing numbers. At the same time, unlike Paul Ngei, the Kamba leader, or Tom Mboya, Moi did not pose a threat either personally or ideologically. 'He was honest, sincere and decent, a Christian gentleman,' says Njonjo. Above all else he was unswervingly loyal, a quality that was to be tested again and again in the eleven years during which he was Vice-President.

Inevitably the appointment of Moi angered the Kikuyu elite. They had little time for Moi, believing him to be lightweight and ineffectual. His very demeanour – sober, quiet and serious, reflecting traditional Tugen characteristics – merely added to that impression. As one senior civil servant who watched Moi closely at numerous Cabinet meetings observes: 'I believe that Moi wore a mask, nobody thought that he would hurt a fly.' His calm demeanour – he rarely gets angry, and when he does erupt it doesn't last long – as well as his ability to listen patiently rather than promote himself and his views, caused many politicians, then as now, to underestimate him. Moi was seen as 'a passing cloud', someone who, lacking true leadership qualities, would eventually drift into the political distance leaving only a fleeting shadow on the social landscape. Certainly that was the consensus among the Kikuyu elite, who treated him by turns with a mixture of irritated contempt and patronising disdain.

Examples of the petty humiliations he suffered are numerous: Kikuyu Cabinet ministers would deliberately speak in their own tongue when they wanted to exclude him; officials at the various State Houses would keep him waiting unnecessarily when he was due to see the President; while Kikuyu ministers, particularly Koinange, would often take his rightful place in the government hierarchy at formal functions. All the while his Kikuyu enemies whispered to the President that Moi was being disloyal, or Moi was trying to undermine the government. From time to time Kenyatta asked Njonjo about Moi's allegiance. The Attorney-General's response never varied: 'I am related to you. Moi is more loyal to you than I am.' And that would end the conversation.

On one occasion Kenyatta summoned Njenga Karume, one of his Cabinet ministers, after he had claimed that Moi was trying to undermine the government. In front of Njonjo and Moi, Karume was asked what he had meant. Njonjo recalls: 'If the ground could have opened up and swallowed Karume, it would have done. He stuttered in reply that he'd lied or was drunk. Kenyatta told him never to tell him lies like that again.'

That said, however, Kenyatta himself regularly treated his Vice-President in an offhand manner merely to test his mettle. Once Moi was summoned to State House in Nakuru to see Mzee but was deliberately kept waiting by the President's aide-de-camp, the Rift Valley Provincial Commissioner Isaiah Mathenge, who allowed numerous groups to call on the President while Moi sat patiently in the waiting room. When Kenyatta rang through to see who was left, Mathenge replied: 'There's only Moi here.' Then Kenyatta came out and started speaking Kikuyu, a language which Moi follows with difficulty. In the end he asked Moi to listen to a choir with him before discussing his business. During the singing, the President dozed off. All the while Moi kept his composure because, as Kenyatta himself had told him, 'patience is a virtue in a leader'. Only after suffering these small indignities was Moi able to discuss his business with the President.

His friend Ngala, among other political allies, could not believe that Moi should accept such consistent humiliation. An impulsive man, the Coast politician, who resigned from the KANU government in 1969, continually urged him to leave the government, maintaining 'It's do or die.' Moi was much more stoical, a characteristic he had exhibited during his youth when he was taunted for his Christian faith. When Ngala said that the latest insult was an indignity too far, Moi usually replied with words to the effect of 'Take it easy, our time will come.'

For, whatever his own feelings, Moi never flinched in his stout, unremitting defence of his President and his policies. Never once did he betray his own ambition, or his concern about the direction of the government. If Kenyatta asked him to jump, Moi simply asked: 'How high?' He would travel anywhere, do anything, see anybody if that was Kenyatta's wish. On one occasion Kenyatta asked him to meet a visiting dignitary and so, because he couldn't find a driver, the Vice-President drove himself – entirely against regulations.

His work rate on behalf of the President was prodigious. One day, for example, he represented Kenyatta at a *harambee* in Central Province. He then drove to Nakuru to open a fund-raising dance, before travelling to Eldoret at nine in the evening to open another charity dance for the Rift Valley Institute of Technology. The glad-handing continued until three in the morning; only then was he able to leave for his home in Kabarak. After less than an hour's sleep he was woken at five by the President, who informed him that he was going to Mombasa from State House, Nakuru. Instead of making an excuse, Moi insisted on accompanying Kenyatta to his coastal retreat before driving back to the Rift Valley – a round trip of some 1,500 miles in less than twenty-four hours.

Such unstinting loyalty was appreciated by Kenyatta. Shortly after Moi became Vice-President, Eric Bomett remembers joining various Kikuyu ministers, including Mwai Kibaki, Mbiyu Koinange and others, at State House, Nairobi. They were chatting convivially with Kenyatta about his new Vice-President. After listening to numerous cutting remarks about his shortcomings, Kenyatta silenced the gathering with the retort: 'You can talk about Moi how you like, but he's the only one who goes round Kenya and knows the people. You people are just around Nairobi.'

Moi became Kenyatta's dependable eyes and ears, not just around the country but also abroad, representing the President on numerous goodwill and diplomatic missions and articulating Kenya's policy of 'positive non-alignment' and 'good neighbourliness'. At home, his energy in promoting the harambee cause was so impressive that he was dubbed 'Mr Harambee'. The aims of the harambee movement, in which local people work together to raise money, or donate services, in order to provide schools, roads, water supplies and other necessities for the community, perfectly suited the political and personal temperament of Moi, a man who is happiest with the rural communities. Harambee was small-scale, local, and benefited mainly farming folk by harnessing their own efforts. Ironically, the harambee movement, so often associated with Kenyatta, was a classic manifestation of KADU policies of district self-help rather than central government interference; as Moi continually repeated at these gatherings: 'We must bridge the gap between the poor and the wealthy.' This gradual redistribution of wealth, a unique feature of Kenya's development in modern Africa, would today be labelled 'trickle-down economics'.

As Vice-President, Moi attended literally thousands of such events all over the country. His presence ensured the success of the harambee and in the process cemented his relationship with the local MP, provincial administrators and other influential members of the community. In this way he quietly and unobtrusively built up his personal constituency in the country. These years of unstinting activity on behalf of the harambee programme have led to numerous schools and hospital wards being named after him, a fact used by his critics as an illustration of the cult of personality that has allegedly been allowed to flourish since he became President.

Yet in spite of his efforts on behalf of Kenyatta and his government, Moi's hold on the Vice-Presidency was always precarious. At first the hostility he endured from the Kiambu elite stemmed initially from what they took to be his perceived weakness, and it was only towards the end of Kenyatta's reign that they came to recognise the strength of his position. At that point he became a potential target for plots to oust him. Furthermore not only was he insecure at the top table of Kenya's politics, but during the 1970s he suffered a serious sag in popularity in his own Rift Valley homeland. As thousands of Kikuyu families moved into the area, virtually doubling the population, the fashionable belief among many Kalenjin was that Moi had sold out his own people in exchange for his new elevated position. He faced criticism from local MPs, particularly J. M. Seroney, William Murgor and John Keen, who felt that he had bent too far to accommodate the Kikuyu. This split in the Kalenjin ranks was eagerly seized upon by Moi's Kikuyu enemies, a cartoon in a Kikuyu newspaper making the most of the breach. This showed a number of Kalenjin milking a cow; a Nandi was holding the horns, a Kipsigis tying the legs, a Maasai doing the milking and the Tugen – that is Moi – drinking the milk. The message, which suggested that the Vice-President had ridden to political success on the backs of his fellow Kalenjin clans, was not one accepted by the Kalenjin themselves.

These rumblings of discontent began just a few weeks after he had assumed the post. Seroney sourly complained to his colleague, Eric Bomett, then the Assistant Minister for Communications, that Moi had only been made Vice-President (and, in 1968, Leader of Government Business) so that he could sell Kalenjin land. Bomett retorted: 'How could he? The land issue is a free-for-all.' Under the principle of 'willing seller, willing buyer', which treated the purchase of land as a commercial rather than a tribal matter, as well as under the law of land tenure and the rules of Land Boards, set up to provide impartial arbitration in disputes, it seemed ostensibly that land could be redistributed fairly.

As Seroney suspected, however, the dice were loaded in favour of the dominant Kikuyu tribe, commercially, legally, politically and historically. Kikuyu culture had traditionally placed a higher premium on land than animals and it was only during the 1940s that the pastoral tribes like the Kalenjin and Maasai began to move away from the time-honoured view that land was a free communal resource.

Compared with other tribes, the Kikuyu were wealthier, better organised, better educated and more business orientated – and comprised one-fifth of the population. The bank managers who made loans, the lawyers who sealed the deals and the businessmen who set up the land-buying collectives were invariably Kikuyu. Legally, the Kikuyu had a further advantage in that most owned title deeds to their existing properties in Central Province, something which enabled them to secure loans on their new land in the Rift Valley. After Independence the Kikuyu were first out of the blocks in the race to buy land from the departing European settlers – half the settlers left the country around the time of Independence – and the commercial logic of 'willing seller, willing buyer' inevitably favoured this economically muscular community. The Kalenjin and, particularly, the Maasai adjusted to the new commercial climate much more slowly.

The undoubted commercial superiority of the Kikuyu, coupled with their political dominance, made them a formidable force. For the first years of Kenyatta's presidency the political imperative was to prevent bloodshed in Central Province between Mau Mau fighters and supporters returning from the forest or detention and Kikuyu loyalists, many of whom had colonised land previously worked by those who had joined the armed struggle. Kenyatta did this by settling a number, although not a sufficient number, of landless Kikuyu on farms purchased under the Million-Acre and other schemes, leaving the more well-to-do Kikuyu loyalists in Central Province.

It is accepted, both by Kenyatta's admirers and his detractors, that the peaceful resolution of the tensions within the Kikuyu community following the end of the Emergency was one of the enduring triumphs of his presidency. His Vice-President appreciated more than most the high stakes the President was playing for, since failure would have probably sparked a tribal civil war. Moi realised that to keep peace in Central Province he had to make concessions in the Rift Valley. At the height of the criticism of his supine behaviour, Moi faced a hostile audience of Kalenjin students who were dismayed by the flood of Kikuyu settlers into their homeland. One student, who later became a Permanent Secretary, remembers Moi's reply to his accusers: 'What I have done, I have done for Kenya. I am looking at fifty years from now and if we don't behave as brothers where will we be? There is enough land to go round.'

While Moi was able to see and accept the wider picture, this did not prevent him from working behind the scenes to secure Kalenjin interests, although he had to exercise extreme caution in order to avoid inflaming simmering tribal resentments. On one occasion in 1967 in Eldoret, the heart of Nandi country, he was approached by a European settler, Roger Latke, who wanted to sell his transport business to the indigenous tribe but could find no takers. The only offer he had had was from the man known as 'the King of the Kikuyu', Dixon Kihika Kimani. Kimani, the son of Rift Valley squatters, had set up the Ngwataniro Muthukanio Farmers' Company to buy land in the region for Kikuyu flooding in from Central Province, was viewed with suspicion bordering on hostility by local Nandi, who saw their birthright being auctioned off to the highest bidder. Latke knew that if he sold his business to Kimani the deal would simply add to the fires of resentment being stoked up in the Rift Valley.

Moi asked the European businessman to name his price, thought for a moment, and then told him: 'Wait and I will try and do something about it.' He contacted a former pupil and KADU activist, Reuben Chesire, the son of Elizabeth and Isaiah Chesire, and outlined his plan. Together they would raise a loan to buy the business and then sell it to the local Nandi when they were sufficiently organised to purchase it themselves. As far as Moi was concerned it was a holding operation, a short-term deal – though in the end it was to last some twenty years. Moi and Chesire raised the Ksh 580,000 asking price from bank loans; even the Ksh 30,000 deposit was borrowed from friends. From such accidental beginnings the Rift Valley Transport Company was born. With sixty employees and twenty-five trucks, it was a decent-sized business which collected milk from local farms; when Moi sold out in the mid-1980s it had virtually doubled in size. The Nandi never did organise themselves to buy him out.

It is a story that not only illustrates his personal impulsiveness and entre-preneurial spirit, but which also demonstrates the balancing act he performed once he joined KANU – fiercely loyal to Kenyatta and his government and party on the one hand, protective and supportive of his Kalenjin community on the other. It was a feat which was to cause him much personal anguish and humiliation in the next fourteen years as all that he and other political leaders had warned about Kikuyu domination came to pass before their eyes. G.G. Kariuki, the Laikipia MP who formed his own co-operative land company, believes that Moi played his hand as well as he could have done given the political climate. 'Even though he had serious opposition from his own people, Moi didn't show it,' recalls Kariuki.

He was able to keep things to himself, to keep self-contained because he knew the repercussions if this policy was not adhered to. The Kalenjin were lucky that Moi was Vice-President because he was able to mobilise them and allocate land to the Kalenjin by talking to Kenyatta. He was the greatest weapon the Kalenjin had. In fact the Kikuyu themselves thought Moi was trying to stop their tribe from buying land and started denouncing him to Kenyatta.

The pressure was remorseless, Koinange complaining on one occasion to the President that Moi had prevented him from buying a large plot outside Nakuru while Moi's numerous and bitter confrontations with the Minister for Land and Settlement, Jackson Angaine, known as 'the King of the Meru', over the allocation of land were legion. On one occasion shortly before the 1974 elections he used fellow Rift Valley MP Taitta Toweet as a stalking horse to acquire a large farm at Molo for local people, rather than see it go to the Kikuyu newcomers favoured by Angaine.

In the end, Kenyatta himself had decreed that he must be informed before this particular farm was sold, and so in order to outflank Angaine and his Kikuyu interests, Moi briefed Toweet and asked him to deal with the matter, but without giving anyone the impression that there might be some kind of problem. As a result, Toweet made innocent inquiries about the property, first with the Land Board and then with Angaine, and was told by each that Kenyatta was the final arbiter of the sale. After a ticklish meeting with the President the sale was agreed, enabling the Kalenjin to settle on land that had been earmarked for Kikuyu newcomers. This had, however, only been achieved by circumventing the State House mafia, rather than by any impartial consideration of purely commercial factors. As Toweet recalls: 'That was a real struggle and it would not have been achieved without Moi helping discreetly in the background.'

The story is an indication of the tact and discretion Moi had to exercise in the face of the overwhelming Kikuyu hegemony at State House. It also illustrates his inherent weakness within the Kenyatta power structure. Besides using fellow Kalenjin MPs as front men, he quietly persuaded banks in the Nandi and Kericho districts to make loans to Kalenjin farmers, and on numerous occasions he acted as a guarantor for Kalenjin land purchase schemes such as Kalenjin Enterprises. Indeed, he gave his name so freely to these projects – acting as guarantor for sixteen Kalenjin farms – that when powerful Kikuyu politicians organised to unseat him during the mid-1970s they considered forcing him into bankruptcy, given that he did not have anything like the funds to underwrite the land schemes to which he had stood surety.

In spite of Moi's work behind the scenes, it was obvious to everyone that the Kikuyu enjoyed more than their fair share of land. The wealth of anecdotal evidence was underlined by an academic study, which showed that by 1971 more than half the acreage under cultivation by individual large-scale farmers in Nakuru District was in the hands of Kikuyu owners. At the same time the World Bank estimated that nearly half the migrants from Central Province and Western Province – approximately 260,000 people – settled in the Rift Valley during the 1960s. This massive influx of different tribes – which virtually doubled the population of the Rift Valley – together with the inequitable distribution of land, were recipes for resentment and friction. Inevitably there were clashes.

As at the time of Independence and again during the 1990s, Molo, the centre of Kikuyu immigration, was the seat of confrontation. At the same time there were skirmishes between the Nandi and Luo in the tea-growing districts of the Nandi Hills, and between the Kalenjin and Kikuyu at the Usher-Jones farms in Kericho, where thousands of Kikuyu squatters took over fertile farmland in defiance of members of the local community who had already purchased the property. The squatters were only evicted after vociferous protests to the government. A similar tactic was more effective around Nakuru, where a number of Kalenjin, Asian and European farmers woke up to find shanty towns of Kikuyu squatters on their property.

In 1969, against this background of rising tension and resentment, J. M. Seroney, the Tinderet MP, issued what was to become known as the 'Nandi Hills Declaration' in which he and Nandi elders complained that the region was being occupied by outsiders, and that the indigenous Nandi were subject to unfair discrimination in jobs, government grants and commerce. As well as being an expression of Nandi chauvinism – for his pains, Seroney was charged with sedition – this declaration was a recognition that local people were losing out, not merely in land, but in every aspect of national progress.

Then, too, there was the growing suspicion that the Kikuyu were using their political dominance to ensure the continued pre-eminence of Central Province. This was confirmed by several reports, notably a 1972 survey by the International Labour Organisation which demonstrated that since independence the Kikuyu had benefited out of all proportion to the tribe's numbers. Kenyatta made his personal priorities clear to non-Kikuyu ministers when he briefed them about their duties. He was given to saying: 'My people have the milk in the morning, your tribes the milk in the afternoon'; in other words, the Kikuyu were to receive first the best and most abundant of whatever was on offer. That Central Province enjoyed the most succulent fruits of independence was not lost on Michael Blundell, who after Independence had become the undisputed leader of the settlers. As he remarked: 'The honey from the economic barrel was largely spread among the Gikuyu people.' (Gikuyu is a term embracing all Kikuyu tribes.) For a time this fact was heavily disguised thanks to Kenyatta's staunchest ally during the early days of his presidency: economic success. The first few years of independence wrought a remarkable change in the country, so that commentators began to talk of the Kenyan miracle. Hundreds of new schools, roads and hospitals were built, while the amount spent per capita on education, seen as the key to self-improvement and social progress, was one of the highest in the world.

Inevitably, economic prosperity underpinned the irresistible rise of the Kikuyu elite, particularly Kenyatta's family and friends. Abuses – particularly those involving the misuse or misappropriation of central or local government funds – multiplied. At one KANU meeting, the Maasai politician John Keen bluntly told Kenyatta: 'It's imperative, Mr President, that if a Kikuyu should be appointed to a position in my home area, it should be an educated Kikuyu.' His remark was a criticism of Kenyatta's habit of appointing his Kikuyu friends and cronies, however inept or corrupt, to parastatal (state-run businesses) and administrative positions in non-Kikuyu districts. As a final retort Keen told the President: 'Mzee, you are practising tribalism of the worst order.' Few were surprised when the Maasai leader was detained shortly afterwards.

With the Kikuyu flooding into the Rift Valley, and the Kikuyu elite exploiting an expanding economy, it seemed that the fears of the small tribes of Kikuyu hegemony following Independence were coming true. Throughout the 1960s Kenyatta moved aggressively towards demolishing the last remnants of the majimbo state, seen by the small tribes as a bulwark against Kikuyu domination. He consolidated power in his own hands whilst establishing a strong central government. A new constitution for Kenya, drafted in 1967, abolished regional government and the Senate, whilst establishing greater governmental control over the civil service and the police. Just as unitary government triumphed over regional rule, so the executive and administration – effectively an alliance between senior ministers and civil servants – became much more significant than either KANU or Parliament. It is not for nothing that Kenyatta has been described as 'the last colonial governor.'

The organisation of the KANU political party was deliberately allowed to fall into decay, so that by the mid-1970s it had become a shadow of the grassroots organisation which had pressed for independence. At the same time the weakness of KANU was matched by the dilution of parliamentary authority, the musings of the National Assembly largely irrelevant to the workings of a government run from State House with powerful Provincial and District Commissioners, invariably Kikuyu, implementing policy. In 1968 one Member of Parliament complained that Kenyan MPs were 'the most underprivileged, demoralized and ignorant in East Africa,' while Cabinet ministers were 'the richest, most arrogant and most miserable people'. The judiciary was the last organ of state to fall under executive control, although Kenyatta came to rue the day he appointed Kitili Mwendwa as the first African Chief Justice.

During the late 1960s, with political detentions frequently used to curb dissent, and with the Kikuyu elite beginning to enjoy untrammelled power, the existence of Oginga Odinga's Kenya People's Union was a continual irritant to the President, who subscribed to Tom Mboya's analysis of the work of government in the aftermath of independence. In his book *Freedom and After*, Mboya wrote: 'The emphasis after independence would be on unity and the magnitude of the problems that they [the government] face will mean that unity will have to take priority over democracy in the sense that the one-party system is the most effective method of overcoming the problems and mobilising the masses.' Crucially, he also argued that the safeguards for democracy lie in the integrity of the leaders and the proper working of the party machinery. As the KANU party fell into disrepair and with (during his later years) an ailing President relying on the Kiambu clique, these checks and balances within the one-party system effectively collapsed.

Just as Moi had helped to bring about the fall of Odinga at the Limuru Conference, so he, together with Mboya and other Cabinet ministers, mounted consistent attacks on Odinga's KPU. Even when 300 KPU members rejoined KANU during August 1968, and the party as a whole withdrew from local elections, Moi publicly emphasised that Odinga's return to KANU had to be unconditional. During a tour of South Nyanza with Tom Mboya, the Vice-President stated that the KPU would not form part of any government, indeed, would be obliterated from the political scene. At various political rallies he welcomed returning KPU politicians into the KANU fold whilst chiding those remaining outside its embrace. In Parliament Moi vigorously defended government policy and police actions against criticism by KPU activists who, on one occasion, accused him, in his capacity as Minister for Home Affairs, of 'malicious insinuations' and of issuing a statement that was 'callous, haughty and supercilious'.

This bruising political battle was brought to an abrupt halt on 5 July 1969, when two shots fired on a busy Nairobi street killed Tom Mboya, Kenya's most brilliant son. His assassination brutally ended the marriage of convenience between the Luo and the Kikuyu, promoted Odinga, whose political star was on the wane, to the position of unchallenged leader of Luo nationalism, and brought the country to the brink of civil war.

As Kenya mourned the loss of a favourite son, Cabinet ministers attempted to absorb the implications of his murder. Moi was in Kituro at the time of the murder, and his brother-in-law Eric Bomett, who saw him minutes after the disturbing announcement came through, recalls him saying: 'This is a great mess. How will the government handle this? I pray to God that he gives us the strength.' Almost immediately, questions began to be asked about who was behind the murder, the finger of suspicion pointing firmly at the government, and in particular at the Kikuyu elite. When Moi visited Tom Mboya's wife Pamela to pay his respects, in common with other government politicians he was stoned and pelted with earth by angry and grief-stricken Luo youths who had surrounded the family compound. Such was the ferocity of the attack that his bodyguard briefly lost his gun in the mêlée. This incident provoked an immediate and equally angry response in Moi's homeland, where Tugen youths threatened to march on

Luoland. The Vice-President had hurriedly to charter a police plane to take him to Baringo, where he soothed an angry meeting.

As tension rose to breaking point, Moi, articulating the government's official position, blamed the murder on a nameless Communist state which had ordered the murder in order to 'divide and seize' the country by removing the man who 'was certainly standing in the way of a form of scientific colonialism'. It was an explanation that did not convince many, particularly the Luo. The suspicion that the Kikuyu elite had orchestrated Mboya's assassination hardened into a certainty with the arrest and ultimate conviction of a Kikuyu, Njenga Njoroge, well known in Nairobi as a KANU member and former Chairman of the party's Central Ward. At his trial in September, Njoroge claimed that he had been set up by 'the big man', someone whose identity has never been revealed. Shortly after his conviction, Njoroge was hanged.

As far as the Luo people were concerned, Mboya's murder was an attack on the whole tribe. There were huge demonstrations and sporadic rioting in Nairobi and elsewhere, while Kenyatta was booed at the requiem mass held for Mboya. For a time Odinga threatened to become the undisputed leader not just of Luoland but of the rest of Kenya, as the *wananchi* united in protest at what they saw as a Kikuyu-orchestrated assassination. In this tinderbox atmosphere, Seroney's Nandi Hills Declaration was seen, in effect, as a statement that his tribe would fight for the land they considered rightfully theirs. These cloaked threats paled into insignificance, however, when news trickled out that the Kikuyu were once again taking an oath of loyalty to the House of Mumbi (Mumbi being the founder of the tribe). It seemed that the largest tribe was not about to give up its ascendancy without a fight. There were skirmishes in Nairobi between Luo and Kikuyu mobs and, as during the Emergency, a number of Christian Kikuyu who refused to take the oath were savagely beaten. What was most worrying was that unlike the Emergency, during which the oathing had been organised by rural tribesmen, on this occasion it was the Kikuyu leadership who arranged the oathing in defence of the interests of their tribe.

During the summer of 1969, as the country came to terms with Mboya's death, a procession of Cabinet ministers, MPs and other leaders visited a fenced-off area of Kenyatta's compound at Gatundu where a Kikuyu elder, assisted by Mbiyu Koinange, administered the oath of allegiance. The Laikipia MP G. G. Kariuki, a one-time confidant of Moi and Njonjo, was one of those involved. He recalls:

Somebody would say: 'Let's go and greet Mzee.' The oathing was very serious – the whole idea was to defend the government. Nobody escaped it. It was a difficult time, a matter of life and death.

As the President himself recalls: 'We took an oath of allegiance to Kenyatta. You must have loyalty in the government and at that time it was right to renew our loyalty.'

In Parliament Moi, while denouncing those who were molesting people and forcibly administering unlawful oaths, urged a greater degree of unity and cooperation among the tribes.

In an effort to placate the Luo and to defuse the growing adulation for Odinga,

Kenyatta agreed to visit Nyanza and Western Province. It was a decision that proved disastrous. In October 1969 he arrived at Kisumu to open a new Ksh 1.2 million hospital donated by the Russians. The atmosphere was ugly, a few youngsters booed the President, and then stones were thrown in the direction of the official party. Kenyatta's bodyguards opened fire on the spot, killing eighteen and wounding twenty-five others. On the following day the KPU was banned, the government blaming the opposition party for organising the disturbance. Odinga and many other KPU activists were placed in detention.

While this gave KANU a walkover in the 1969 elections, the long-term effects have been widespread. A gap was driven between the Luo and the ruling party which it has proved difficult to bridge to this day, mainstream Luo politics were driven underground into the arms of militant revolutionaries, while relations between the Luo and Kikuyu have been characterised by mutual distrust – with the occasional political marriage of convenience breaking this wary cycle of suspicion.

If the killing of Pinto ended the age of innocence in Kenyan politics, the murder of Mboya marked the swansong of tribal unity, or at least the illusion of that unity. With the Kikuyu elite now entrenched in their ambition and their paranoia, few believed that Moi, who had been Vice-President for just a year, could survive for long.

Chapter eight
The Great Survivor

It was hardly the most edifying scene to set before the President. As Kenyatta looked on, his face a picture of thunderstruck amazement, two middle-aged men, yelling at the tops of their voices, punched and kicked at each other, grappling with a ferocity and venom that startled onlookers. At one point Vice-President Moi had to throw himself bodily in front of his leader to prevent him from becoming involved in the vicious mêlée. Kenyatta even drew a ceremonial sword to defend himself as one of the combatants stood in front of him shouting and swearing. Eventually the adversary was dragged away by Moi.

This extraordinary commotion, which took place at State House, Nakuru, 1975, was the culmination of a bitter rivalry between Isaiah Mathenge, the Rift Valley Provincial Commissioner, and the local Police Commissioner, James Mungai. A Nyeri Kikuyu, Mathenge never found favour with the Kiambu Kikuyu clique which surrounded Kenyatta, and which viewed him as an ally of the Vice-President. Mungai was their man, operating particularly for Mbiyu Koinange, Kenyatta's brother-in-law who was the effective power behind the throne. The quarrel itself concerned the arrest of Mathenge's son by Mungai's men following rioting at the University of Nairobi, which had in turn been sparked off by the murder of the charismatic Kikuyu politician J. M. Kariuki. Mathenge saw his son's arrest as yet another insult by an arrogant and overweening policeman who was able to abuse his office and position only by virtue of Koinange's patronage.

This incident, violent, undignified and shaming, symbolised how the well of civic goodwill which had existed since Independence was slowly being poisoned by rancour and self-interest, and the forming of factions and cabals. The murder of Mboya, the detention of Odinga, and the oathing in Central Province had dramatically altered the political landscape of Kenya. Where once power had been shared during the uneasy alliance between the Luo and Kikuyu, the Western tribe was firmly out in the cold. As a result, the 1970s were truly the golden era for the Kikuyu elite who now controlled the engines of government. At the same time, the ruling tribe grew more inward-looking, seeing enemies at the gate and within the compound as political splits and personal ambition tarnished its hegemony.

Several ministers took to carrying sidearms. Bodyguards became the norm. Indeed, as it turned out the fight between Mathenge and Mungai was merely a warm up for the main bout. According to Taitta Toweet, on one memorable occasion there was a furious row between two ministers with shots being fired. State House, Nairobi, came more and more to resemble one of the rowdier saloons in the Wild West. One academic, Dr Scott MacWilliam, describes the political reality rather more drily, arguing that the growth of tribalism in Kenya between 1965 and 1978 was a direct result of the Kikuyu bourgeoisie's ambition to dominate and monopolize Kenya's political and economic life.

The disintegration at the top merely served to fuel the ambitions of others who watched from the wings. During a state reception in honour of President Tito of Yugoslavia in February 1970, a plot was hatched to bring down the government. The Yatta MP Gideon Mutiso was later revealed, self-confessedly, as the 'Chairman of the Revolutionary Council'; his fellow Kamba, the ambitious and ruthless Chief Justice Kitili Mwendwa, had his eyes firmly fixed on the presidency. They encouraged a number of disaffected Luo and Kamba, including Professor Joseph Ouma (now a FORD-Kenya stalwart), to join them as they spread their web of intrigue, which reached into the Kamba-dominated army, the Kikuyu-run Air Force and the police forces of the Western and Coast Provinces. Most important, the Chief of the Defence Staff, Major General Ndolo, was also a party to the plot, of which the aim was to assassinate or capture Kenyatta as he started the East African Safari Rally in April 1971. At the same time, those army officers who were not privy to the conspiracy were to be arrested at Lanet Barracks, to which they had all been invited on the pretext of attending a sports day. The coup, which was backed by Soviet money and by elements of the banned KPU, was discovered only by chance. Just days before the planned rebellion a Kamba army officer who was on detachment in London, having become rather drunk in a bar, revealed the plot to his colleagues. British security services were informed, who in turn quickly informed their Kenyan counterparts and so alerted them to the danger.

Twelve of the plotters, including Mutiso, were convicted and gaoled, although Mwendwa and Ndolo were spared the indignity of a trial; both were subsequently removed from office. The mood of uncertainty and suspicion lingered. At the Madaraka Day celebrations the following year, Kenyatta disclosed 'murmured reports' of subversion, and defiantly castigated conspirators who had threatened his life if he attended the celebrations at Uhuru Park in Nairobi. Moi even called a press conference in order to emphasise the fact that Kenya's security was 'sound and in good hands'. 'There's no reason to panic whatsoever,' he said, a statement which, by its very nature, was bound to cause unease on a continent where military coups had afflicted the majority of newly independent nations, including neighbouring Uganda.

Indeed, with the dawning of the 1970s, the optimism of the first years of independence had faded, to be replaced by a mood of unease, disenchantment and division. The increasingly hostile international economic scene, and growing instability on Kenya's borders served to exacerbate domestic problems, particularly in terms of internal security and student unrest. Dangers were omnipresent. To the west, Idi Amin's bloody takeover of Uganda in 1971 and his increasingly bellicose statements regarding Kenyan territory inevitably heightened tensions. To the north the vicious Ogaden war between Ethiopia and Somalia made the north-west region of Kenya virtually ungovernable because of incursions by *shifta* (guerrillas). To the south, relations between socialist Tanzania and capitalist Kenya had deteriorated to the point where the borders were closed.

Surrounded by military or Marxist regimes, Kenya, a pro-West, moderate, free-enterprise country, found herself increasingly isolated. Continual student unrest at home emphasised the growing ideological divide between left-wing academics, many trained in Eastern Bloc countries or Dar es Salaam, then the capital of Tanzania and a breeding ground for the continent's revolutionaries, and the conservative KANU government. At the same time, OPEC's decision in 1973 to raise oil prices by a huge percentage pulled the economic rug from under Kenyatta, since all Kenya's oil has to be imported. Where before the country had enjoyed a surging 7 per cent growth rate which had paid for a massive increase in education, health and other costs, the nation's economy now came to a juddering halt. Sluggish growth led to balance-of-payments deficits which, combined with a rapidly rising population, high unemployment, famine and drought punctured the myth of Kenya's golden economy and added further fuel to the grumblings of the *wananchi*.

Inevitably, the hard realities of Kenya's stumbling progress infected the political process. At the grass-roots level KANU became so ineffectual that Kenya was dubbed the 'no party state', while at the top, feuding, corruption and nepotism became the political norm. Furthermore, Kenyatta's health was deteriorating, and as it did so his grip on government weakened; weeks would go by without a single Cabinet meeting. In this atmosphere the politics of the succession held sway. With the ruling elite desperate to maintain power within the House of Mumbi, Moi's position as Vice-President was not merely precarious, but dangerous. Indeed his constant clarion call for national unity, for an end to tribalism, for support for KANU and the President, seemed little more than window-dressing – behind the scenes he was fighting for his political life.

With an impressive array of Kikuyu and Kamba politicians ranged against Moi, there were many who despaired of his survival in office. Others, dismayed by the corruption at the top and sobered by the imminent collapse of the country into tribal chaos and war if the Kikuyu continued their untrammelled rule, realised that he was the only realistic hope of ensuring peace and unity after Kenyatta died.

His enemies employed three main methods – constitutional, political and military – to oust the Vice-President. However, he proved a good deal more difficult to dislodge than they had thought. This circle of Moi's detractors, principally Mbiyu Koinange, Dr Njoroge Mungai, Kihika Kimani, Paul Ngei, James Gichuru, Njenga Karume and Jackson Angaine, as well as senior civil servants, police and military chiefs, became known in 1976 as the 'Change the Constitution' group, its aim being to remove Vice-President Moi by altering the constitution in their favour.

While the Change the Constitution movement was the culmination of their campaign, efforts to dilute Moi's power began shortly after the assassination of Mboya with talk during 1970 of altering the constitution to allow for the position of 'executive Prime Minister' instead of executive President and so undermine Moi. However, Njonjo, the Attorney-General, moved quickly to scotch this talk, stating in May: 'There is absolutely no truth in it. This rumour must have been started by some politicians who want a constitution to suit their ambitions. But the present constitution stands as far as I know.' At the same time as Mutiso and his fellow conspirators were plotting to assassinate Kenyatta, so the Kiambu clique were planning to use their political muscle to alter the body politic in their favour. In spite of Njonjo's implicit warning, the manoeuvring continued throughout the winter, so that by the spring of 1971 he had to repeat his statement. Amidst this atmosphere of plots and counter-plots directed at Moi or the Kenyatta government, contending factions of the dominant Kikuyu attempted a reconciliation, agreeing to set up a welfare society, on the lines of the Luo Union, that would protect the interests of all the Kikuyu. To give the process due solemnity, Kenyatta agreed to chair the first meeting at Gatundu. As a result, the Gikuyu, Embu, Meru Association (GEMA) was born, a formidable organisation that in the end would boast more than 100,000 members. Very soon, however, its initial aims of unity and welfare had become channelled into stopping political leadership leaving Central Province. A number of politicians at that first meeting, among them Mwai Kibaki, Jeremiah Nyagah, G. G. Kariuki and Dr Julius Kiano, dropped out when they saw that GEMA was being hijacked by Kiambu chauvinists determined to oust Vice-President Moi. Even though GEMA activists attempted to disguise its work, there was little doubt that it was operating as a party within KANU, and enjoyed links with people of influence inside the civil service, police and military, as well as with key figures in other tribes.

Substantially financed, these activists had an ample war chest of Ksh 3 million both to promote their own aims and to muzzle or oust Moi's supporters. In 1972, for example, the man they dismissed as 'the Arab', Shariff Nassir, was arrested and detained for allegedly planting stories that Kenyatta had killed Mboya. Nassir, a stout defender of the Vice-President, and who was fighting for the post of KANU Vice-Chairman in Mombasa, was imprisoned, tightly blindfolded, in the notorious Manyani gaol, where for three days he awaited an uncertain fate. When Moi heard of Nassir's plight, he and Ronald Ngala, then the Minister of Power and Communications, went formally to Kenyatta to seek his release, telling the President that Nassir was a victim of political squabbling. Kenyatta agreed to free him, although Nassir stills carries the scars of the blindfold to this day. It later emerged that he had been detained at the behest of Koinange, who had wanted a KANU candidate more amenable to GEMA installed in the post.

Shortly before Christmas that same year Ngala, one of Moi's closest allies, died after having been in a car crash whilst he was travelling to Mombasa. While an inquest concluded that the crash had been an accident, this did not prevent questions being asked in the National Assembly about the suspicious nature of his death, the unspoken assumption being that he was murdered by the anti-Moi faction in KANU. The very fact that a tragedy involving a Moi loyalist prompted such concerns illustrates the heightened tensions and misgivings at this time.

Moi did not stand idly by as his authority was gradually eroded and his allies slowly undermined. At huge rallies in Nakuru and Elburgon he attacked a 'few troublesome MPs' who claimed to be supporting the President, yet who were trying to establish another political party in Kenya. He explained that a group was secretly attempting to assume the executive powers of both the President and the Vice-President. After firing this warning shot he refrained from naming this clique saying that if he did 'they would collapse from shock'.

In spite of Moi's broadside, the cabal of GEMA activists attempted to consolidate their political influence during the 1974 elections, surreptitiously putting up their own candidates against those known to be in Moi's camp. Surprisingly, in spite of the endorsement of GEMA, one of its leading lights, Dr Mungai, lost his parliamentary seat, as did eighty-seven other MPs. Some pro-constitution MPs, including Dr Kiano and Jeremiah Nyagah, came under pressure to fall in line with GEMA aims. Kiano recalls: 'I was accused of being Moi's man and reminded that power should remain in Central Province. But I have never regretted my decision. I went for the person not the tribe. As Kenyatta nominated Moi as Vice-President and I was loyal to Kenyatta, therefore I supported his choice.'

Here was the nub of the dilemma facing GEMA loyalists. By attacking Moi, they were also questioning the authority of the head of state, and were therefore subject to accusations of disloyalty both to KANU and to the country. In 1975, Kenyatta threatened to ban all welfare organisations, including GEMA, because of their growing competition with KANU.

At the same time, the dynamic transformation of welfare organisations into ersatz political parties was in part due to the vacuum at the heart of Kenyan political life. Since the Limuru Conference of 1966 the organs of the ruling KANU party had withered into atrophy. Elections of party officials had not been held, branches had been allowed to die, membership records and finances were in a state of utter chaos. The mass political movement which had helped deliver independence was no more. It suited Kenyatta, an instinctive autocrat, to reign over the nation by employing the administration as the instrument of his bidding. The first President, unlike his successor, preferred to rule by decree than consensus.

In April 1970, four years after the Limuru Conference, Kenyatta had agreed to set up a KANU organisation committee, chaired by Moi, to 'reorganise, reactivate and revitalise' the party, so that it could 'meet the demands of changing times and the rising expectations of *wananchi*'. Party elections were set for March 1972, but KANU proved to be in worse shape than anyone had expected.

Moi's inability to shape events was revealed when he said publicly that KANU elections could take place. Yet a few weeks later the polls were delayed, something which happened throughout the 1970s, the continual postponements frustrating MPs and public alike. Even Moi complained that people were 'tired of waiting for elections'.

Matters came to a head when Martin Shikuku accused some fellow MPs of trying 'to kill Parliament in the way that KANU has been killed'. Amidst the uproar caused by his remarks, the Deputy Speaker, J. M. Seroney, ruled that there was 'no need to substantiate the obvious'. Moi, as the Leader of Government Business, led a walk-out of loyalist MPs. 'When someone says KANU is dead, it is tantamount to saying that we all agree KANU is dead. Now if KANU is dead then I am also dead,' stated the Vice-President as the parliamentary session came to a premature end. Shortly afterwards both Shikuku and Seroney were arrested in the confines of the House, in blatant violation of parliamentary immunity, and placed in detention, where they remained until Moi became President.

Although Vice-President Moi had headed the walk-out, in fact the incident merely served to underline his own political weakness and personal vulnerability. The absence of the KANU elections which he had lobbied for; the detention of the two MPs, one a senior Kalenjin leader; the subsequent arrest of the Rift Valley MP Philomena Mutai; as well as the rumblings of discontent over Moi's perceived weakness where Rift Valley land sales were concerned; all these combined to give an impression of political impotence. On many lips was the question: If he could not protect leaders from his own region, how could he defend himself? He was Kenyatta's loyal mouthpiece and his defender in Parliament and the country at large, yet he had little influence over critical decisions; in short, as Vice-President he exercised responsibility without power. The former minister Isaac Omolo Okero of the Luo tribe, a Moi supporter, recalls: 'At that time Moi as a man was warm and receptive but with no power. He would only say: "I will mention this to Mzee." He was not part of the inner decision-making process.'

The murder of J. M. Kariuki in March 1975, a wealthy Kikuyu politician who had been a thorn in the flesh of Kenyatta's government because he spoke out against corruption, as well as advocating radical wealth and land redistribution, also highlighted Moi's political weakness. Moi, who was in charge of internal security as Minister for Home Affairs, was forced to apologise to Parliament for misleading it about Kariuki's whereabouts when news of his disappearance was announced. Initially, Moi had stated, on information given to him by the police force he headed, that Kariuki's whereabouts was unknown, when in fact a post mortem examination had already taken place in a city morgue. The fact that he could not rely upon the force he headed showed very publicly how tenuous was his position.

Moi's emotional defence of democracy and freedom – 'It is terrible, I don't know where we are heading', he said – in the debate about Kariuki's murder was given a sympathetic hearing by his fellow MPs, who recognised that he was as much in the dark about Kariuki's assassination as they were. The Vice-President told the House that he had not intentionally hidden the truth of Kariuki's disappearance. 'I love peace and I have always been advocating it and could not have hidden the truth from you if I knew it,' he said, admitting that he should have been more aware of police operations. 'Only democracy will save our nation for the benefit of present and future generations . . . Kenya has been in the past one country championing democracy, and come what may, this democracy should be upheld.'

Accusing fingers were pointed firmly in the direction of the Kiambu clique and GEMA leaders as prime suspects in Kariuki's murder. As John Keen remarked: 'The hyenas have eaten one of their own,' meaning that the Kikuyu elite had assassinated a fellow tribesman who had irritated them because of his outspokenness. Kariuki had drawn the wrath of GEMA and KANU leaders when he attacked Kenyatta's achievements since Independence, accusing the 'greedy, self-seeking elite' of monopolising the nation's wealth. 'We do not want a Kenya of ten millionaires and ten million beggars,' he had said.

If Kariuki's radical views made him a target, it is equally true that the mid-1970s were uncertain and even perilous for the loyal Vice-President. Politically and personally he was increasingly isolated and yet soldiered on, shielded by his natural stoicism and Christian faith. The atmosphere of fear and trepidation which gripped the country following the murder of Kariuki and a murderous bombing campaign in Nairobi, accompanied by a growing belief that it was only a matter of time before Moi became the next victim of the political killers. As Shariff Nassir who was detained during this period recalls:

> There was a real mood of repression in those days. You could never talk in front of Kenyatta. I remember he once called MPs together and told them: 'If you talk my bird will take you away.' After the murder of Kariuki I was very much in fear of my life. It was such a dangerous time and people didn't know how much Moi could do or how long he could last. The terror was such that you were never able to sit down with three people without knowing who was who. You were afraid it might get to Kenyatta and you would be jailed.

It was a view endorsed by the Maasai MP John Keen, at that time no friend of Moi, who now admits that:

> It seemed that Governor Renison's words that Kenyatta would be leader until darkness and death were coming true. It was an ugly atmosphere. We never knew when we were going to be picked up and thrown behind bars. It was a period of suppression. The Kikuyu dominated the police force, the provincial commissioners were like little governors, the country was gripped by fear and nobody could say anything. This was an era of political exploitation – ivory poaching, coffee smuggling and so on. The rich were getting richer and the robbers were falling out over the spoils. Moi couldn't do anything because the Kikuyu were very powerful politically, economically and administratively. He didn't stand a chance. Only his tolerance and sober attitude enabled him to win through. Many other people would have resigned a long time ago.

It would, however, be wrong to depict Moi as a lamb going to the slaughter. Not only did he enjoy the patronage of the President, albeit somewhat ambivalent patronage, but he also had the support of his friend the Attorney-General, Charles Njonjo, and of leaders of the Nyeri Kikuyu, particularly Mwai Kibaki. At the same time he was the beneficiary of the factional politics of the ruling tribe. Not only were the Nyeri Kikuyu suspicious of the Kiambu clan, but within the Kiambu clique there was considerable squabbling between Koinange and Dr Mungai, whose influence ebbed following his election defeat in 1974.

Within the vital area of the security services, Moi's patronage was patchy. He could count on the support of some uniformed police – he preferred to travel in police aircraft rather than those of the Kikuyu-dominated Kenyan Air Force – and of the tough GSU led by Ben Gethi. In some regions, however, Kikuyu police commissioners refused to give the Vice-President official escorts. By contrast, in other districts loyal police top brass regularly warned him of the threat to his life. Alphonse Mullame, then the Superintendent of Police, who regularly accompanied the Vice-President on his tours around the country, recalls that Moi was phlegmatic about the dangers he faced. 'Each night he prayed, knowing that he could be assassinated at any time,' he says.

Many politicians believed that the writing was on the wall when Moi returned from an Organisation of African Unity meeting in Kampala in 1975 and was accused of bringing guns into the country from Uganda as part of a conspiracy to oust Kenyatta. It looked as if he was about to go the same way as his predecessor, Oginga Odinga, whose troubles had begun over similar allegations. On this occasion the hand of Mbiyu Koinange was clearly evident. Rift Valley police chief James Mungai, Koinange's man in that region, conducted a vigorous search for the weapons, ordering his men to examine Moi's offices at the Nakuru Oil and Flour Mills, of which he was company Chairman.

Mungai's men also raided his home at Kabarak and searched his offices in Nairobi; they even made a late-night raid on homes and sugar-cane fields near Kisumu where it was believed Moi had dumped weapons. Although all the searches were in vain, Moi's Kalenjin supporters were outraged, and a large delegation went to see Kenyatta at State House, Nakuru, to complain about the treatment meted out to their MP. Such was their anger that Moi had to calm them down before the deputation got out of hand.

In spite of Moi's local popularity, however, the campaign of harassment continued. On at least two occasions James Mungai slapped Moi in the face in front of President Kenyatta at State House, Nakuru. 'He was not polite to the Vice-President,' is Charles Njonjo's dry recollection. Moi's motorcade was regularly stopped and searched by Mungai's men outside Nakuru as he was returning to his home or to his constituency. Mungai's men regularly camped near Moi's farmhouse at Kabarak to monitor his movements, and often placed roadblocks at night on the roads that he would be taking on his way from Nakuru. Such was the routine persecution that Moi and his supporters faced from Mungai's loutish police that Nakuru became, for them, virtually a no-go zone. 'Moi bore that humiliation very stoically. He knew it was a matter of time before he took over,' recalls G. G. Kariuki. 'Even so he was very troubled as he was holding on to his job by the skin of his teeth. Most people would not have accepted that indignity. When Moi and I discussed these people who tried to force him to resign, I urged him stick it out and only go if they sacked him.'

More worrying was the fact that Kenyatta was aware of, and even present during, several of these events, a sign that Moi only mustered ambiguous support from a President whose day-to-day activities were increasingly circumscribed by age and health. The Kiambu elite took full advantage of his incapacity, exploiting his name and regularly forging his signature on official purchasing documents as they feathered their own nests. It was as if the murder of J. M. Kariuki signalled a free-for-all as the ruling elite scrambled for their own piece of Africa. Within a matter of months the country teetered on the brink of economic and political anarchy. Land-grabbing became the norm, police-sponsored robbery was endemic, while ivory poaching and coffee smuggling, thanks to a worldwide boom in prices, reached epic proportions. It is said that at one point Lloyds of London, the renowned insurance company, refused to insure shipments of Kenyan coffee because so much of it went missing in transit. As Ben Kipkulei, a former Kenyan High Commissioner to Britain, recalls: 'The system had collapsed and the country had become a playground for a few playboys who were perceived to be protected by Kenyatta. He didn't know what they were doing but they used his name very effectively to do terrible things. If matters had continued in this way the country's economy would have collapsed within three years.'

Farms around Nakuru in the Rift Valley, already a focus of Kikuyu expansion, became particular targets for a form of state appropriation. Moi, who had bought a 1,000-acre farm at Kabarak from a Greek sisal exporter at around the time of his divorce in 1974, waged a rearguard battle to protect the homes of Europeans, Asians and Africans. In 1976, when he returned from a visit to the US President, Jimmy Carter, during which they had had talks in an attempt to resolve the fighting in the Horn of Africa, he discovered that many of his European neighbours, including Peter Barclay, the Murrays, the Llewellyns and the Nightingales (who had farmed the area since 1906), had been told that their land was to be compulsorily purchased and that a notice to that effect had appeared in the *Kenya Gazette*. The farmers were deeply suspicious, as well as resentful, of the whole exercise, since normally the government has to give a good reason when land is compulsorily acquired. On this occasion no such explanation was offered. Through the good offices of Humphrey Slade, the first Speaker of the National Assembly, these worried European farmers, who believed that Angaine, Koinange, Dr Mungai and Kenyatta's wife, Mama Ngina, were behind the pseudo-official plan, contacted Moi and Njonjo. They agreed to take the case up with the President himself.

Meanwhile Peter Barclay, Moi's immediate neighbour, an affable man who farms 3,000 acres of arable land, literally took the bull by the horns. When the Minister of Lands, Jackson Angaine, visited Barclay's well-kept farm and said that it had to be sold on Kenyatta's personal orders, the farmer called his bluff. He refused to believe Angaine, arguing that the *Gazette* notice was illegal and asking him to bring the President to his farm. As a result, one morning Kenyatta, Mama Ngina and Angaine visited Barclay's farm. The President, who had a farm at Rongai near by, sat on the verandah, sipped coffee and admired the view, before leaving with a pair of heifers which Barclay gave him as a mark of respect. During the entire visit he said not one word about the farm. Angaine, realising that his game was up, subsequently dropped the bid to take over these farms. While acknowledging his debt to Moi and Njonjo, Barclay argues: 'If you were prepared to stand up for yourself, then you could fight off these underhand attempts at acquisition. It is also fair to say that when Moi came in the land-grabbing stopped.'

While individual acts of piracy were not in themselves driving the fledgeling Kenya into the abyss of chaos, what concerned many was that the state seemed to be rotting from the head down. The land-grabbing, ivory poaching and coffee smuggling by the political elite and their police confederates represented a wholesale abuse of the system of government which ultimately endangered the survival of a fragile new nation. In what was described as a 'thorough and stinging' indictment of the Kenyatta years, Dr Arthur Eshiwani concluded from a study of tribalism under the first president that the Kikuyu had entrenched themselves so as to 'virtually eclipse and dominate the economic, political and social affairs of Kenya and push the other communities to the periphery or oblivion.' Ironically, it was the economic success enjoyed by this clique, the core of GEMA, which ultimately brought about their political failure.

For these leaders, who had earned their phenomenal wealth by 'fixing' the administrative system, made the cardinal mistake: they came to believe in their own invincibility. Largely unchallenged, they thought that they could grab power in the same way that they grabbed land. Yet the very methods which had made them so successful in securing the lion's share of the spoils of independence for themselves and their Kikuyu supporters were so transparent that many leaders from other tribes, who until then had had little time for or faith in the Vice-President, were driven into his arms.

In this atmosphere of political uncertainty and widespread corruption, the GEMA leaders finally showed their hand, revealing their ambition to change the constitution in order to evict Moi and replace him with a member of the Kiambu elite. Now that the politics of the succession were out in the open, two camps emerged, the GEMA clique, who formed the backbone of the Change the Constitution movement, and the constitutionalists, who supported Moi. As the journalist Philip Ochieng wrote in his book *The Kenyatta Succession*: 'The Njonjo-Moi-Kibaki faction was notable for its attachment to the constitutional methods of doing things, for its adherence to law and order, whereas the other faction [the Change the Constitution movement] was more notable for its will to flout all the set ways of doing things – for its lumpen tendencies.'

On the surface, the aims of the Change the Constitution movement, which gathered pace during 1976, appeared guilelessly innocent. However, cloaked in the woolly arguments of democracy, lurked the wolf of self-interest. Put simply, they wanted to maintain the hegemony of the Kiambu elite after President Kenyatta's death by altering the constitution in their favour. As Kenya's constitution stood, and still stands, if a President dies in office, the Vice-President takes over the post for ninety days until a new President is elected. This lengthy period naturally gives the President-in-waiting – that is, the Vice-President – ample opportunity to consolidate his position and nullify any opposition – hence the argument for a change. Moi's enemies asserted that the Speaker of the National Assembly – they proposed Dr Mungai for the post – should be in charge of the country while the various presidential candidates stood for election. In this way, Moi could be shoehorned out of office so that another Kikuyu leader could take Kenyatta's place.

Given the economic muscle of GEMA, the political ascendancy of the Kiambu elite, and the ease with which the constitution had been changed in the past, this manoeuvre should have been effected relatively painlessly. Yet a combination of internal bickering, political arrogance and skilful resistance ensured that their ambitions came to naught. The quiet backroom tactics which Moi had used so successfully to oust Odinga at the Limuru Conference were once again deployed. His unobtrusive style contrasted with the boastful public rallies and clumsy stratagems of the Change the Constitution group. A rambling, gloating speech by their leader, Kihika Kimani, during a huge rally at Meru in October 1976 was typical: 'If need be, we can organise a million people to go to Mzee to tell him we don't want a particular person in a particular office . . . we are a decisive group and we can change things for the benefit of this country.'

Kimani and the others missed the obvious point that in order to change the constitution they needed the support of politicians in Parliament rather than *wananchi* at noisy meetings. Even Kenyatta despaired of their crude scheming; earlier, he had told the Coast Provincial Commissioner, Eliud Mahihu: 'These people are mistaken. You do not show a cow the thong you will use for tying its neck and killing it.' In short he believed that the Change the Constitution group showed their hand too soon.

In the autumn of 1976, days before the Change the Constitution campaign began in earnest, Njenga Karume fired a warning shot when he criticised Moi in Parliament for making it difficult for MPs to enter Jogoo House in Nairobi, the Vice-President's office. Other GEMA MPs joined the fray, suggesting that Moi had instructed his staff to address him as Mzee – a title reserved for the President and father of the nation. Since Moi had a reputation as the least pretentious and unassuming of men – the fact that he didn't even have a carpet in his office, unlike his junior colleagues, had prompted wry comment in local newspapers – inevitably led shrewd commentators to conclude that there was more to these attacks than met the eye. Moi spoke openly about the double standards of those around him, concluding a speech before Parliament by saying that he did not know what was driving these hostile MPs, 'but I hope that whatever is itching them will not become an epidemic'.

Whilst endeavouring to build a head of steam against the Vice-President in the country, the Change the Constitution group, through the machinations of Dr Mungai, widened their political net by wooing Oginga Odinga to their cause. In theory, this would give the movement tribal credibility beyond the Tana River, as well as providing a charismatic counterbalance to Moi. Even though Odinga (who had been released after eighteen months' detention following representations to Kenyatta from Moi and two moderate Luo leaders) had been prevented from contesting the 1974 elections, he still exerted considerable influence in his region; the Kenya People's Union may have been dead, but its spirit lived on. Although Odinga's radical egalitarianism was diametrically opposed to the tribal elitism of the Change the Constitution group, he was enough of an opportunist to feel able to place his principles on one side. Although he never took an active public part, his right-hand man, Achieng Oneko, joined GEMA leaders at several rallies. As the moderate Luo leader Isaac Okero observes: 'He totally threw his hand in with the Change the Constitution people even though they had been the ones who had imprisoned him. It was a very Machiavellian move.'

The campaign to oust Moi hit its stride at a rally in Nakuru in September 1976 attended by numerous Cabinet ministers and MPs, who resolved to table a motion in Parliament to change the constitution. It was the first stage in a strategy aimed at holding a series of rallies all over Kenya in order to generate popular support for their constitutional amendment, which would in turn give them the mandate with which they could secure the necessary parliamentary votes. 'It was a very tense time,' recalls Shariff Nassir. The feeling was that if the Change the Constitution people had won there could have been civil war. Certainly the minority tribes would have suffered.'

The fact that the Change the Constitution plotters had given notice of their intent meant that Moi and his allies had time to organise a counter-attack. Not that he needed much warning, for Kikuyu political allies like G. G. Kariuki, who had personal contacts with both camps, regularly reported to him with details of his opponents' plans. Many observers were fooled by Moi's silence, however, mistaking this for inaction. It is one of Moi's trademarks. As his opponents have realised to their cost, when Moi goes underground he is carefully watching the political landscape and shaping his purposes accordingly. His plan, announced without fanfare, was to spike the guns of the Change the Constitutionalists in the one arena that mattered – the National Assembly. The first public counter-blast to the Change the Constitution group came early in October from Nassir, who said: 'Those calling for the amendment are day-dreaming, greedy, jealous people.' Nassir, the Maasai minister Stanley Oloitiptip, Dr Julius Kiano and others then organised ninety-eight MPs to sign a declaration condemning the proposed constitutional amendment as 'unethical, immoral, bordering on criminality and very un-African'.

In the meantime, the Attorney-General issued a ringing warning to the Change the Constitution group: 'It is a criminal offence for any person to encompass imagine, devise or intend the death or deposition of the President.' This statement, quoted directly from the Kenyan constitution, was issued by Njonjo because, he argues: 'I was the Attorney-General and I wanted to follow the constitution.' At the same time, Njonjo spoke to the President at State House, Nakuru, outlining the situation and explaining that the Change the Constitution group were saying that Kenyatta was going to die, and that this was why they wanted to amend the law to stop Moi from taking over.

Njonjo had then to fly to London on business, and even though Kenyatta agreed to end this public debate about changing the constitution when he chaired the next Cabinet meeting, the Attorney-General left the country a worried man. The truth was that he was not entirely certain that the President would stick to his word. In fact, while Njonjo was away, Kenyatta did test the political water by hearing the views of delegations from different tribes. Not only did he see the

Change the Constitution group, but he also had meetings with Luo politicians and other tribal groupings. One fascinating cameo illustrates the subtle power play at State House during this time. When a delegation of Luo politicians and members of the Luo Union arrived to pay their respects to the President, the Minister of State, Mbiyu Koinange, who orchestrated the Change the Constitution movement behind the scenes, attempted to engineer a situation where the Luo Union, who were pro-Odinga and pro-Change the Constitution, saw the President ahead of the Luo politicians, who supported Moi. The hidden agenda was that the Luo Union delegates would give the impression that constitutional change was acceptable to the Luo. As it turned out, however, Isaac Okero, the chairman of the Luo parliamentary group, saw through this ploy and resisted Koinange's attempts to influence the presidential audience in this way. His group saw the President first.

As the President took soundings, the Change the Constitution group held another meeting at Meru, a rally which proved to be their last. On the following day Kenyatta chaired a tense Cabinet meeting in State House, Nakuru, where he angrily upbraided Ngei, Angaine and others for trying to alter the constitution. As Moi sat by his side, his face clearly showing the strain, Kenyatta railed at his dissident colleagues, naming each one in turn. 'You want to change the constitution? Who told you that I am going to die?' he told them, before proceeding to give the plotters a piece of his mind. 'If I was in his shoes,' the President said, looking at Moi, 'I would feel the way that Moi is feeling now.' It was a dramatic and powerful presidential performance in support of his right-hand man, and it effectively spelled the end of the Change the Constitution movement – at least in the open. As Jeremiah Nyagah, who was present at that fateful meeting, recalls: 'Kenyatta defended Moi to the hilt and that was the end of the open war. Then the fight went underground.'

The prospect of KANU elections in April 1977, the first party elections since 1966, offered the GEMA group another avenue for the pursuit of their ambitions. Two groups vied for executive office: the supporters of the Vice-President, and the group which formed the nucleus of GEMA. While Moi was Vice-President of the government he was only one of several Vice-Presidents of the KANU party; under new rules the elections would produce only one KANU Vice-President. This gave Moi's opponents a lever with which to weaken him, for if he was unable to win the KANU post they would be able to argue that he did not command nationwide support, and so urge Kenyatta to sack him from the national vice-presidency.

Cleverly, those opposed to Moi convinced his former KADU colleague and fellow Kalenjin MP, Taitta Toweet, to stand for the KANU vice-presidency. In promoting the candidature of Toweet, their tactics were twofold: to prove to Kenyatta that another Kalenjin was more popular than the incumbent; and also, by distinguishing between the posts of Vice-President of the party and of the country, so to weaken both office holders that these Kalenjin rivals could be dispensed with in the future.

During the campaigning, Moi experienced the dilemma that faces all vice-presidents. If support for him was over enthusiastic, this might have given the impression that he was an independent centre of power and therefore a potential rival to Kenyatta. On the other hand, if he failed to canvass enough support he was in danger of losing out to Toweet and Odinga, who also declared himself a candidate. So, rather like a swan, he adopted a pose of superficial serenity while paddling hard beneath the surface. Although he continued to busy himself with state functions rather than involve himself directly in party elections, behaving with the dignity commensurate with his office, behind the scenes he ensured that his supporters campaigned hard to win over uncommitted political leaders.

As election day approached it seemed that Moi's supporters, the so-called 'Kamukunji Group', were riding a winning wave. Then, at the last minute, the Party Secretary, Robert Matano, cancelled what would have been the first KANU elections in a decade, leading to accusations that the GEMA faction, which had been in some disarray, had convinced the President to intervene. While Kenyatta's ill health was the real reason for the cancellation, the public perception remained that Moi's position was precarious, as it seemed GEMA had exercised their influence to stop him winning the election.

Indeed, the cancellation of the KANU elections coincided with the most dangerous period of his political life. The physical intimidation intensified as his tormentor-in-chief, James Mungai, doubled his efforts. Just after Matano's announcement that the KANU elections were postponed, Moi's car was stopped by Mungai's police as he drove from a meeting with Kenyatta at State House, Nakuru. He was searched, and treated with a rudeness bordering on contempt. The following day he faced similarly provocative treatment when he was stopped and delayed at a roadblock near his Kabarak home.

Continual physical harassment, endless petty personal humiliations and the political provocations severely tested Moi's mettle. The purpose behind these tactics was clear – to ease him out of office by fair means or foul. As the deaths of Pinto, Mboya, and J. M. Kariuki had proved – and as the slaughter of prominent opponents of Amin in Uganda emphasised – the higher the political profile, the greater the physical danger. Moi's enemies wanted him to realise that only by resignation could he save his skin. 'Throughout this time they were snapping at his heels, damaging him in any way they could,' recalls his friend Reuben Chesire.

Politically, he was weakened, some thought fatally, when shortly after the KANU elections were abandoned Mbiyu Koinange wrested the police portfolio, which Moi held as Minister of Home Affairs, from his grasp. It was a move seen as a deliberate bid to dilute the Vice-President's influence and reduce his status. Kenyatta's brother-in-law was now responsible for the police, the GSU and the Special Branch, leaving Moi in charge of prisons and immigration. The loss of this portfolio was a turning point, signifying to many of Moi's allies that he was in mortal danger. 'We felt that he was the next one to be murdered,' recalls G. G. Kariuki, adding: 'If it had happened, it would have been without Kenyatta's knowledge.'

At the same time, it was slowly emerging that the actions of Mungai and his men were not simply the behaviour of an arrogant policeman with well-placed political friends, but part of a sinister and coherent plot to ensure that the presidency should never leave the House of Mumbi. When Moi first got wind of these machinations he ordered an investigation into accounts that Mungai was training a special 'anti-stock theft unit.' Before he received the report, responsibility for the police was transferred to Koinange, then Minister in the office of the President.

What was abundantly clear was that Mungai's 250-strong special unit, known as the Rift Valley Operations Team or 'Ng'oroko', was acting as a private army whose ostensible purpose as a squad to hunt cattle rustlers was an elaborate smokescreen. The men were expensively well equipped with silenced Uzi submachine-guns, sophisticated self-loading rifles, mortars and explosives, including plastic explosives. In fact the Ng'oroko, which was based just outside Nakuru, was funded from government sources as well as by highly placed Kikuyu politicians, most notably Koinange. It was he who acted as the conduit between the Ng'oroko on the one hand and GEMA and the Change the Constitution movement on the other.

Indeed, the overwhelming majority of the Ng'oroko were Kiambu Kikuyu, many of whom had taken an oath to ensure that the presidency remained with their clan, and that it would not go to Kabarnet – that is, to Moi. 'There is no doubt that they wanted to eliminate Moi. I never visited Nakuru because of my fear of those people,' recalls G. G. Kariuki. As Kenyatta's health deteriorated, night meetings, held near the Lanet army barracks, became commonplace; at these the Ng'oroko and Kikuyu politicians reasserted their tribal allegiance. Such was the concern surrounding the activities of the Ng'oroko that in July 1977 Mungai was summoned to Nairobi to see Geoffrey Kariithi, then the Cabinet Secretary. He was asked why the Rift Valley Operations Team was buying such sophisticated weaponry when all the unit needed to catch cattle rustlers were a few Land Rovers. Mungai vigorously defended himself and his actions, but Kariithi remained unimpressed.

In fact, the Cabinet Secretary knew that Mungai was lying, for his own undercover intelligence operatives had discovered details of a plot, involving Mungai and the Ng'oroko, among others, to assassinate Moi and other high-ranking politicians and civil servants, including Kariithi himself, and replace them with their Kikuyu confederates. While the full details of the conspiracy were not revealed until three months after Kenyatta's death, by the Attorney-General, Njonjo, those who had been singled out for execution by the plotters had known for months about the true nature of the Ng'oroko.

In a dramatic intervention in Parliament in October 1978, Njonjo spelt out the dread purpose of the Ng'oroko – to stage a coup d'état in the wake of Kenyatta's death. Under their far-fetched plan they would murder Moi, Njonjo, Kibaki and about 300 politicians and civil servants before installing their own supporters as a new government. First of all they aimed to lure Moi and fourteen other key ministers to State House, Nakuru, on the pretext that the President was gravely ill and wished to see them before he died.

As Moi and his colleagues gathered round Kenyatta, Ng'oroko *askaris* (soldiers), armed with their silenced weapons, would gun them down, later telling the world that they had been forced into this action because the Vice-President and other ministers had killed Kenyatta as he lay on his sickbed. After they had committed this murderous act a forty-eight-hour curfew would be announced to allow the full Ng'oroko unit to go into action. During the curfew they planned to murder the remaining politicians and officials on their master list; in some cases they aimed to blow up their victims' houses or parachute into their *shambas* and assassinate them. In the aftermath of this bloody coup, a provisional government would be established.

This plot, which might have been culled from the pages of a cheap thriller, demanded split-second timing, cool cunning and a degree of tacit co-operation from the armed forces. As the Ng'oroko were seen as an ill-disciplined, if brutal, rabble, the conspiracy was dismissed as 'childish' by those insiders who knew of the true nature of the unit. At the same time, however, precautions were taken. The highly trained General Service Unit, alerted to the Ng'oroko's plotting, kept their barracks under constant surveillance, and were authorised to stop them at any cost if they attempted to put their plans into action. As Geoffrey Kariithi recalls: 'The Ng'oroko was seen as a nuisance and no more. But then again, history could have been different if Kenyatta had died in Nakuru and Koinange had been by his side.'

In fact Kenyatta spent the last few weeks of his long life in Mombasa. There was a final irony. In the days before his death, his confidant and adviser, Mbiyu Koinange, had constantly begged the President to be given leave to travel to Nairobi to attend two meetings. Late in the evening of 21 August, Kenyatta relented, much to Koinange's relief. Hours later, at 3.30 in the morning of 22 August 1978, the first President of the Republic of Kenya died of a heart attack. By then, Koinange, the man who had tried so desperately to prevent Moi from becoming President, was hundreds of miles away. While he slept, power slipped irretrievably from his grasp.

As G. G. Kariuki says: 'That's how miracles work.'

Chapter nine

The Passing Cloud

The Vice-President had spent a restless night. For some reason he was unable to sleep and at four in the morning found himself padding around his Kabarak home. Then his telephone made a faint 'ping'. For weeks it had been on the blink, sometimes ringing, sometimes not. If he had been asleep he certainly would not have heard that soft mechanical sound. When he picked up the receiver, he heard the shaky voice of the Coast Provincial Commissioner, Eliud Mahihu. Breathlessly, Mahihu told Moi 'The eyes of Kenyatta have closed,' and requested him to travel to State House in Nairobi immediately. 'Your Excellency, please keep your eyes open,' he implored him, before ringing off to call Mwai Kibaki, the Finance Minister, who was staying in Mombasa, and Geoffrey Kariithi, the head of the civil service. Minutes later, as the new President tried to absorb the news, Kariithi telephoned and urged him to make haste.

Kariithi, aware of the Ng'oroko plot to kill the new President, also knew that the longer Moi delayed the greater the chance the assassination squad would have to take matters into their own hands. Shortly after speaking to Moi, Kariithi broke the news to Mbiyu Koinange in Nairobi, leaving him literally speechless with shock. In those few minutes Moi quickly dressed and drove quietly out of Kabarak and through the virtually deserted streets of Nakuru on his way to Nairobi. He passed through one roadblock outside the Ng'oroko camp but, as he was accompanied only by his bodyguard, he was not recognised and was able to continue his journey. Arriving at his official residence in Nairobi, he found a squad of loyal GSU men waiting for him. The new President had made his escape with only minutes to spare. Within half an hour of him leaving Kabarak, Ng'oroko units had set up roadblocks on routes into and out of Nakuru. Moi is wont to say of the 'ping that saved a president': 'It was God's will that I got through.'

As dawn broke, the Ng'oroko *askaris* manning the roadblocks, realising that they had miscalculated, returned to their base. Now they came under surveillance; the GSU was ordered to round them up if they left their camp. By now events were moving at bewildering speed. Kenyatta's body was quietly taken to State House, Nairobi, while Kariithi and his colleagues tried to contact as many members of the Cabinet as possible before Moi was sworn in as the new President – at least for the ninety-day-period specified by the constitution. With the arrangements in place, the Voice of Kenya was told the tragic news. So at 12.39 a radio announcer said: 'It has been announced from State House Nairobi that His Excellency the President and Commander-in-Chief Mzee Jomo Kenyatta, father of our nation, died at 3.30am this morning in his sleep.'

The country came to a virtual halt – businesses closed, schoolchildren were sent home, and many Asians and Europeans considered their future in a potentially threatening political climate. By three in the afternoon most of the Cabinet had assembled in the Cabinet Room at State House to witness the historic swearing in ceremony, conducted by the Chief Justice, Sir James Wicks. It was on the Protestant Bible, the same that Kenyatta had used himself, that Daniel Toroitich arap Moi took the oath of allegiance and 'swore to uphold the functions of the Office of President'. As the press and photographers filed out, the country's new leader sat at the head of the polished oval table and conducted his first Cabinet meeting to discuss the funeral arrangements for the late President.

This was a time of high drama, deep sadness and anxious anticipation as the world watched to see whether Kenya could pass her sternest test as a new democracy – the peaceful transfer of power. As he now recalls: 'The main priority at that time was the unity of all Kenyans and a peaceful transition. That mattered a lot.' During the ten days in which Kenyatta's body lay in state, Kenyans behaved with exemplary dignity as they grieved the father of the nation. The new President reflected that mood when he reassured the people that he would continue in his predecessor's footsteps. 'With the help of God I will try my best to carry on with the work President Jomo Kenyatta has already started,' said Moi in his eulogy at Kenyatta's state funeral in Nairobi.

Even in his sorrow for his friend and mentor, Moi was aware of the burden he now carried and the forces ranged against him. His enemies were not idle. Charles Njonjo recalls a visit from Kenneth Matiba, then the Chairman of East African Breweries, to the Attorney-General's elegant colonial-style home on the outskirts of Nairobi on the day of Kenyatta's death. As far as Njonjo was concerned Matiba, who had worked as Moi's Permanent Secretary during the 1960s, had, with Mbiyu Koinange, Dr Njoroge Mungai and Paul Ngei, provided the bulk of the funds for the Change the Constitution group.

Njonjo remembers Matiba asking: 'Charles, don't you think you should do something? Why should we allow this man to become President?' Njonjo replied tersely: 'I have followed the constitution from the word go, and tomorrow I shall support Moi as President of this country.' Following this inconclusive discussion, Matiba went to see Kibaki, who lived near by, and the two men talked for most of the night.

Matiba, former chairman of the FORD-Asili Party, whom I interviewed in London before Njonjo made this allegation, confirmed that he spent the evening with Kibaki but that the conversation dwelt on 'the peace and tranquillity of the country'. Nor does he admit ever having supported the Change the Constitution movement, since his 'strong' belief in the democratic process prevented him from doing so. It is, however, worth mentioning that Matiba was prosecuted for oathing Kikuyu during the 1979 election. Although he was found not guilty, the former Chief Justice, Robin Hancox, believes that the verdict would have gone the other way if Matiba's defence counsel had not won a ruling that ensured that the evidence against him had to be overwhelming.

While Matiba came away empty-handed from Njonjo's home, Moi's enemies still did not think that everything had been lost. The weekend following Kenyatta's death saw a number of clandestine gatherings among Change the Constitution supporters who desperately sought a Kikuyu leader willing to take on Moi. 'Opposition to Moi went underground during the ninety-day transition period but it was still very active,' recalls G. G. Kariuki. At one point Major-General J. K. Mulinge, the head of the armed forces, was approached by 'a senior political figure' with a view to organising a coup d'état. Mulinge, quite properly, reported the matter to the authorities and the politician was picked up for questioning. Njonjo stated in Parliament that if it had not been for Mulinge's loyalty to the constitution, 'Kenya would now be under military rule.'

Njonjo is in no doubt that if the Kikuyu elite had genuinely wanted to take over the government they could have done so easily. A Kikuyu himself, he says: 'I was the Attorney-General, the Commissioner of Police was Kikuyu, the Director of Intelligence was Kikuyu, the head of the GSU was Kikuyu, the senior officers in the Army and Air Force were Kikuyu. If we had wanted to organise something different and not follow the constitution, we were in a position to do it.'

None the less the Kiambu faction could scarcely countenance the fact that Moi, the quiet, hesitant and self-effacing shadow of the father of the nation, the man from one of the smallest and most backward Kenyan tribes, had either the qualities or the support to last long as the country's second President. They referred to him dismissively as 'the passing cloud', and convinced themselves that his elevation was only temporary until a more fitting candidate took over. When a delegation of Kiambu politicians and businessmen, led by Njonjo, went to pay their respects at State House, Nairobi, a number of Change the Constitution politicians, including Mbiyu Koinange, Peter Kenyatta, Njenga Karume and others, were noticeably absent. During the meeting Njonjo took up the 'passing cloud' theme, acknowledging that there had been much talk in Central Province to the effect that Moi would not last. Njonjo went on to say that he had tried to disavow people there of these sentiments, arguing that Moi had properly succeeded Kenyatta and was there to stay.

In the first few months of his presidency Moi began to reveal the man behind the mask, to demonstrate the dogged resilience and shrewd political judgement which had been so often overlooked by those who dismissed him as a Kenyatta cipher and a political lightweight. They expected him to be unprepared, indecisive and overwhelmed by the high office he had now attained, a belief fuelled by the fact that he had no obvious agenda to pursue.

G. G. Kariuki remembers imploring him, just three days before Kenyatta's death, to start planning for the day he became President. Moi, who had scrupulously avoided talking, or even thinking, about the succession, replied that when Kenyatta died he would just get on and run the country, sustained in this simple certainty by his Christian faith and his belief in God's guidance. His eleven-year apprenticeship as Vice-President was sufficient training, giving him an unparalleled insight into the *realpolitik* and personalities of Kenya's ruling elite. At the same time, as he had shown during his days on the Legislative Council and with KADU, Moi had a clear moral and political vision, a vision inevitably eclipsed during his time as Vice-President, when he had been a loyal cheerleader for Kenyatta's policies.

A few months before Kenyatta's death, Moi gave a snapshot of his political principles in a speech at a leaders' conference, an address that indicated the direction his government would take once he became President. He told delegates:

> We all know what we want – namely that peace and stability should continue so that the prosperity of our people and the enjoyment of personal freedom can continue to thrive. But peace and stability do not drop upon a people from the heavens. Peace and stability are the result of deliberate actions by a people to make for themselves a social, economic and political system which give the people what they need most, protects their lives and property through a system of popular laws, and a system in which the national wealth is equitably accessible to the greatest majority. To perpetuate that system . . . we must accept discipline and orderliness as a means of ensuring our system and operate in a manner that mirrors a considerable degree of credibility, forthrightness, justice and understanding.

Peace and stability, discipline and order – these were the watchwords central to Moi's vision of Kenya. The new President, appreciating more than perhaps anyone the threat from disaffected forces in the country, moved quickly to snuff out any potential threat to the nation's equilibrium. After disbanding the Ngoroko unit, he made far-reaching changes in the officer cadre of the armed forces and shook up the top echelons of the police force. A number of senior police chiefs, including Police Commissioner Bernard Hinga, retired, while Assistant Commissioner James Mungai, the head of the Ngoroko unit, fled the country.

At the same time Moi was deluged with pledges of loyalty as delegation after delegation arrived at State House to affirm their allegiance to the new President. Any possibility that one of the Change the Constitution heavyweights, notably Koinange or Ngei, was about to challenge Moi for his position during the ninety-day interregnum seemed to evaporate when the entire Cabinet proclaimed its confidence in and support for the new President.

Behind the scenes, the Change the Constitution leaders made one last effort to subvert the process. As Charles Njonjo remembers: 'Koinange, Mungai and the others tried their best to undermine the system.' They campaigned in the districts for voters to either boycott or vote against the KANU election for President. Their last-ditch bid to thwart Moi failed miserably, however, and it soon became clear that the KANU nomination for the post of President of the party would be a formality. Delegates, who met on 3 October to elect Moi as the party's new President, were delighted when he announced that there would be further elections for the party's executive, elections which KANU had not held since the 1966 Limuru conference. It was the first sign of Moi's reformist and populist intent. So on 10 October Moi presented his nomination papers at the Attorney-General's chambers and four days later, before an excited crowd which thronged Uhuru Park in Nairobi, he was sworn in as the second President of the Republic of Kenya. The transition had been as smooth as it had been meticulously observed, the country moving effortlessly from the *harambee* to the Nyayo era.

While the country's new leader promised to follow in the footsteps of the late President, he implied that there would be change within that continuity. Moi pledged an open administration, vowing to stamp out corruption and overhaul the machinery of government. 'I shall undertake any necessary measures to root out indiscipline, inefficiency and corrupt practices where such undesirable activities might exist,' he stated. He was as good as his word; indeed, his first deed as acting President had been to suspend land allocations, something which won immediate public support as both *wananchi* and MPs had consistently complained that highly placed civil servants, abusing their inside knowledge, were buying land before it was released to the public. As one political observer commented: 'Moi is coming up trumps in his first weeks of presidency. He seems to be tackling issues head on, that have been talked about but shelved in the past. Here he is, talking about beating corruption, tribalism and laziness and now, dealing with the land allocations nightmares. This is all very pleasing for the people.'

There was a profound sense of relief that the transition had been effected so peacefully, as well as a sense of optimism that the repression and corruption which had tarnished the last years of Kenyatta's reign were over. As Ben Kipkulei, a Kenyan historian and former Permanent Secretary in the Ministry of Finance, recalls:

When Moi came in there was a collective sigh of relief. Even those people involved in corruption were secretly pleased as many realised that this whole process [corruption] was going to end in disaster. There was a period of national rapprochement. Everybody said thank God we have had a smooth transition, we have a God-fearing President, we have a populist President. Just as in 1963, the year of Independence, there was a feeling of national unity, of patriotism and brotherhood across the tribes.

Another Kenyan commentator observed: 'If Kenyatta was our father, Moi is like our brother. He seems much more approachable and willing to listen.' During the honeymoon period of his presidency, Moi slowly moved out of Kenyatta's shadow to stamp his own beliefs and style on the direction of the government. Examining his deeds and pronouncements during the first months of his presidency, what is remarkable is the congruity between his philosophy during his days in the Legislative Council and KADU and his time as President. Indeed, his first Jamhuri Day speech, with its emphasis on education and illiteracy, unemployment and morality, on 12 December 1978, might have been made at any time during his political career.

These Jamhuri Day directives were followed by a plethora of orders from the President as he crisscrossed the country in his efforts to meet his people. Such commands ranged from ordering a halt to a multi-million-shilling tourism complex at Diana Beach, to instructing the Ministry of Agriculture to set up a fertiliser plant at Mombasa, to ordering the Ministry of Housing to take over private beerhalls in Taita-Taveta and turn them into classrooms for adult literacy classes. Dynamic certainly, decisive undoubtedly – but, as was to be demonstrated time and again during his presidency, policy-making on the hoof often resulted in hapless civil servants picking up the pieces, only to discover that the populist rhetoric could not be made to match the reality. More often than not the result would be a series of half-baked compromises, or benign neglect as administrators quietly shelved presidential directives once Moi had moved on to pastures new.

Public disenchantment, as Kenyans began to recognise the distinction between presidential aspiration and administrative action, was slow in coming, the *wananchi* overwhelmed by an energetic President whom they saw in person rather than, as in Kenyatta's day, only heard on the *Voice of Kenya*. Just as Moi's presidential directives echoed his Legislative Council career, during which he had been a one-man suggestion box, so his frenetic nationwide tours reflected his work as a constituency MP in the Rift Valley and his days as a dynamic Vice-President. In his presidential progress he would regularly swap his official Mercedes limousine for an old Volkswagen Kombi so that he could reach the more inhospitable regions of Kenya. He travelled from sunrise to sunset, spending nights under canvas, washing from a small basin and eating under the shade of a tree. In the first year of his presidency he visited more places and received more people than had Kenyatta during his fifteen years as President.

This peripatetic president sought to bring government back to the people, opening up administrative structures so that the public felt more comfortable in bringing their grievances to the state. On occasions when individuals spoke to him about their problems it was the President, rather than local administrators, who relayed them back to Nairobi. Moi was proving himself to be a man of the people, a quality noted by the Cambridge academic John Lonsdale: 'Colonial history and then the Kenyatta presidency widened the ethnic and regional divisions, not to mention the gap between rich and poor. Moi has tried to close them – at the beginning of his rule he even tried to close the gap between wealth and poverty by a ceiling on land holdings.'

The prodigious energy and populist appeal which Moi demonstrated on the domestic front was also on display internationally. As Vice-President he had regularly represented Kenyatta abroad, for the late President hated travelling by air. It was natural that Moi should want to attend these meetings now that he had come to power; moreover, his presence at international forums injected a credibility into Kenya's foreign policy which had been lacking in the last years of Kenyatta's reign. At the same time, the fact that he could absent himself from the country so soon after his succession was graphic evidence that Kenya was a stable, orderly and mature nation. Just weeks after assuming control he visited France, chaired an Organisation of African Unity (OAU) conference in Nairobi, and mediated between Kenya's warring neighbours, Tanzania and Uganda, following the ousting of the Ugandan dictator Idi Amin.

One action in particular won him international acclaim – his dramatic gesture during his first Jamhuri Day speech in releasing the remaining twenty-six political detainees, including the MPs Martin Shikuku and J. M. Seroney, as well as the writer Ngugi wa Thiong'o. (He had earlier freed the Kalenjin MP Philomena Mutai from gaol.) In accepting the worldwide plaudits, he also expressed his irritation at attempts both by members of the Kenyan Parliament and by the respected human-rights group, Amnesty International, to force his hand and release prisoners on their terms rather than his. He went out of his way to tell Amnesty to concentrate its efforts on South Africa and Rhodesia rather than his country. For years, Kenyan officials had felt that human-rights groups were less than even-handed in their approach, condemning Kenya, which had a handful of detainees, whilst ignoring neighbouring countries like Tanzania, where at least 2,000 detainees languished in gaol at any one time.

The releasing of the detainees, while it had a happy outcome, demonstrated a characteristic of the President which diplomats, politicians and pressure groups have overlooked throughout his rule. As the head of state he reserves the right to decide when, where and how he should act. Those who lecture him in public on a course of action, even though he may privately agree with that view, find that he resists their pressure to the last. Moi, as leader of the Kenyan nation, demands the respect due to an African chief. He will not be pushed around in public, nor will he be patronised by the West. Conversely, a quiet word at State House or a little discreet lobbying elicits a far more positive response. Indeed British businessman John Ward, the indefatigable father of Julie who was murdered in 1988, concedes that it was only when he stopped confronting the Kenyan authorities through the megaphone diplomacy of the mass media that he earned the respect of those he needed to solve his daughter's murder. His new policy of cooperation and mutual regard has resulted, at the time of writing, with at least one arrest in relation to his daughter's killing.

While his release of detainees signalled a break with the previous regime, Moi was all too aware of the constraints he faced since assuming Kenyatta's mantle. His choice of the Finance Minister Mwai Kibaki, a Nyeri Kikuyu, as Vice-

President was both an acknowledgement of his political debt to his colleague and an acceptance of the political realities – namely, that the largest, most influential and well-entrenched tribe demanded a place at the heart of government. It would take several years before Moi became master in his own house.

The first Cabinet reshuffle following the 1979 general elections reflected his reluctance to disturb the hierarchy of power, as well as an awareness of the tribal equation which, in Kenya, dominates all decision-making. Besides moving a few Permanent Secretaries, the most significant casualty was 'the man who would be President', Mbiyu Koinange, who was shifted from State House to the much less influential Ministry of Natural Resources. At the same time Moi signalled a new beginning with the Luo community by elevating Dr Robert Ouko to the position of Minister of Economic Planning and Community Affairs, a post once held by Tom Mboya.

This political tinkering demonstrated that Moi had learned well the Maasai saying: 'Never kill two lions under the same tree' – that is, do not take on all your enemies at the same time. Moi gave notice of this feline strategy when in the same year he launched a crusade against corruption. 'If you know of any case of corruption, report it to the police,' he urged, knowing full well that bribery and the police were inextricably linked. While he took the moral high ground publicly, he also authorised a well-timed campaign by Charles Njonjo, who let it be known that the new President had no faith in the top hierarchy of the police. In Parliament, the Attorney-General charged that senior police officers were involved in all manner of corruption, including coffee smuggling. In quick succession a number of police chiefs resigned or retired.

In reality then, this purge of the top echelons of the police was as much to do with the rumbling conspiracy against Moi as it was with corruption. In this context, therefore, the corruption issue was used as a sprat to catch a number of large mackerel. His style in tackling his foes was very different to that of Kenyatta. Whereas Kenyatta used the bludgeon, Moi preferred the rapier, attacking with pinpoint precision rather than belabouring his antagonists. He is the master of manoeuvring opponents so that their own actions are seen to precipitate their downfall. Over the next few months numerous civil servants, army officers and the holders of other senior offices were allowed to retire with dignity rather than face the humiliation of dismissal and a possible court case. 'His overriding aim was to maintain unity, to keep the country together,' recalls a close friend. 'Neither he nor the country could afford endless corruption trials. It would have been divisive and encouraged tribalism.'

Even when the disgraced Assistant Police Commissioner James Mungai returned to Kenya in 1980 after his hasty flight, the President preached the gospel of conciliation rather than revenge. He exhorted the nation to 'bury' the Ng'oroko conspiracy. 'The time has come when we should stop talking about the Ng'oroko issue and instead preach the Nyayo philosophy of unity, love and peace', he said, referring to his oft-stated aims of following in the footsteps of the late President. Njonjo went further, announcing that Mungai would not be prosecuted. 'We regard the Ng'oroko affair as a closed chapter in our country's history,' he said. 'God was good to us. Some of us are still alive and those with any guilty conscience will carry it to their graves.'

The weeding-out process was complicated by the need to introduce a tribal balance into the top echelons of government without unduly alarming the dominant Kikuyu. Ultimately, this was proved to be an impossible task. For the first years of his presidency Moi was aware that he was a hostage to the existing tribal arithmetic both in Cabinet and in the civil service, whilst having to acknowledge the aspirations of the tribes which had been out in the cold or had supported him whilst Vice-President. Early on he seized the one political arena that had been neglected by Kenyatta – KANU. Immediately he became President he began the long process of revitalising the moribund party, an ambition which had been thwarted during Kenyatta's days. At the KANU conference in October 1979, the election of Mwai Kibaki as KANU Vice-President together with a slate of candidates virtually hand-picked by Moi to represent the eight provinces of Kenya, was the first move in establishing a loyal power base, independent of Parliament and the executive. 'The elections provided a rare spectacle of democracy at work within the ruling party,' commented the *Weekly Review*. Certainly many of the delegates believed that the long-awaited conference ushered in a new era of tolerance. At the same time, the process of electing officials in order to maintain a regional tribal balance in the KANU executive resulted in a trend whereby those elected owed their offices to accidents of geography rather than to their own suitability or competence.

It was the parliamentary elections of November 1979 that truly marked Moi's emergence as a national leader in his own right, a President making a conscious effort to stamp his own style on government. In spite of his immense popularity – candidates vied with one another in voicing their loyalty to the Nyayo philosophy – Moi was uncertain that the complexion of Parliament would reflect his aims. Before the elections he used his countrywide tours to endorse favoured candidates, donating huge sums to their harambees. These gatherings thus proved an effective method of demonstrating to the *wananchi* that their local MP was able to deliver economic benefits to their communities. At the same time the ruling party's decision in the run-up to the election to ban Odinga and other former KPU politicians from standing for election on obscure technical grounds indicated that here was a populist president not entirely confident of his political support.

In the event, he need not have been so concerned. As in previous elections, a whole raft of his political opponents – and some allies, particularly moderate Luos like Isaac Okero – fell by the wayside giving him enormous room for manoeuvre. Almost half the incumbents, as had been the case in the previous two elections, lost their seats, including Mbiyu Koinange, Jackson Angaine and Kihika Kimani, all prominent members of the Change the Constitution group. Besides the spectacular purge of local councillors, MPs and ministers, the election went down in history as being the first in independent Kenya to see a European, Philip Leakey, and an Asian, the lawyer Krishna Gautama, win parliamentary seats. Again as had been the case in earlier elections, the criteria an increasingly sophisticated electorate used to judge the performance of their MPs was not their parliamentary rhetoric but what they had delivered to their constituencies in terms of investment and harambee donations; questions of ideology or social class were largely irrelevant, especially in rural areas.

The results of the elections enabled Moi to consolidate his authority. He appointed his former private secretary, Nicholas Biwott, and G.G. Kariuki, who had masterminded the recent KANU elections, as Ministers of State while his early political mentor Moses Mudavadi, who entered Parliament in 1976, became an education minister, with two of his most stalwart supporters, Shariff Nassir and Stanley Oloitiptip, being appointed to front-bench posts.

Unlike Kenyatta, who left opponents out in the cold, Moi preferred to co-opt potential dissidents either into his government or into parastatals. Living by the motto, 'Keep your friends close but your enemies closer,' Moi was aware of the political necessity to embrace the Luo community, which had been effectively in the political wilderness since the assassination of Tom Mboya. In a drastic shake-up of the Cabinet immediately after the election, twelve new ministers moved in, with moderate Luo politicians like Robert Ouko, Matthews Ogutu and James Osogo taking significant portfolios. A number of Luo, including former members of the KPU, were promoted within the universities, the civil service and the parastatals. Moi laid the final brick in this bridge-building exercise by rehabilitating Oginga Odinga, appointing him Chairman of the Cotton Lint Marketing Board and making him a life member of KANU.

In his attempt to embrace all tribes, virtually every district in Kenya was represented by an assistant minister in the new government. Where Kenyatta had enjoyed the support of the Kikuyu as of right, Moi has never had the luxury of the backing of an influential tribe. As a result, the establishment of a tribal consensus has always been central to his political calculations. In his study of Kenyan tribalism, Dr Eshiwani concluded that during Moi's presidency no tribe, including the Kalenjin, has been allowed to dominate national life. 'The President himself has demonstrated his commitment by very well tribally balanced appointments in the public sector. No one can fairly accuse him of ushering in his Kalenjin tribe in public appointments.' While Moi had ended Kikuyu hegemony, they still enjoyed the largest single block of Cabinet seats, and not least because the new President had been careful to include Change the Constitution stalwarts like Paul Ngei and Njenga Karume, as well as Kikuyu allies.

With KANU revitalised and loyal, and with Parliament and the executive shaped more to his liking, Moi was now able to diffuse the influence of the welfare organisations, like GEMA, which posed such a potent threat to his position. The final demise of GEMA, which, along with other welfare organisations, went into 'voluntary' liquidation between July and December 1980, was a classic example of Moi's divide-and-rule strategy, as well as his desire to diminish the ethnic factor in the political process.

A dynamic President, populist policies and a chastened tribal elite – it was all too good to last. In 1980 Moi was hit by a series of crises that racked Kenya. Not only were the country's industries virtually paralysed by a huge hike in oil prices, but for the first time in a decade Kenya found herself unable to feed her people. Food queues and power failures became commonplace, leading to disenchantment and unrest. As John Lonsdale observes: 'Kenyatta was a lucky president in terms of the world economy, Moi unlucky.'

In 1979 the second oil crisis, with its attendant inflation, to which were added widespread drought and mismanagement of grain stocks, meant that Moi had to go cap in hand to the Americans and other nations to ask for aid, investment and maize supplies. As an ambitious five-year development plan fell by the wayside, he admitted: 'It is no consolation to us that most other developing countries are faced with similar problems.' During a year of travelling, he expended much energy desperately trying to shore up Kenya's ailing economy.

His initiatives in seeking international aid and organising a massive relief effort were matched only by the indolence, incompetence and corruption of the politicians and bureaucracy originally assigned to the task of feeding the nation. During Kenyatta's era the country's maize reserves had been thoughtlessly run down. Yet when the new President asked those responsible for safeguarding supplies if there would be any shortages he was assured that all was well. Even when long food queues became commonplace, his experts still contended that there was enough food to go round.

Finally, Moi decided to look for himself. He visited numerous grain stores and was appalled to find them virtually empty. Boldly, the President told the country that it faced a major food crisis, but still the various ministries did not seem prepared to acknowledge the scale or gravity of the crisis. While Moi's hectic arrangements had prevented a major crisis, what was more worrying was that whatever he said or did, particularly concerning corruption and smuggling, he enjoyed only lukewarm support from the administration, some of whom had made money out of the public's distress.

Many suspected that the shortages of food and electricity had been intentionally created in order to embarrass Moi and eventually bring down his government. It was said, for example, that farmers in Central Province were deliberately holding back their produce in order to cause trouble. Faced with such obduracy, particularly in the civil service, Moi attempted to bypass the administrative system by going direct to the *wananchi*; in one such initiative he called on members of KANU's youth wing, and others, especially those living in border regions, to set up vigilante groups to combat smuggling. That he had to resort to such desperate measures was a sign of his exasperation, his tenuous hold on the administration, and the deep well of institutionalised corruption he had inherited.

The maize crisis made him realise, however, that many of those in power merely paid lip service to his Nyayo philosophy, scorning his egalitarian approach as a sign of weakness. Rather like US President Jimmy Carter, whose administration foundered on the shoals of the Washington establishment, the Kenyan President discovered that even though he was conducting, the orchestra was trying to play a different tune.

Inevitably, comparisons were made with his predecessor, Moi's approachable and clubbable character contrasting dramatically with Kenyatta's fierce aloofness. 'When you looked into his eyes, you knew that you were in the gaze of a lion,' recalls Charles Njonjo of the first President. Eyebrows were raised at the way Njonjo, Biwott and Kariuki travelled in the presidential limousine, using it so often that it was dubbed the 'office *matatu*' (minibus). On occasion they would hitch a lift with the presidential motorcade, asking the cars to stop when they had reached their destination. At State House Njonjo's lunchtime cocktail – Moi, a teetotaller, had specifically warned civil servants against drinking – and his habit of padding around his office in his socks caused comment. The fact that Njonjo, like Moi, sported a rose in his buttonhole indicated to the new court that the Attorney-General was a man rather too familiar with the trappings of presidency. John Keen, then an Assistant Minister, recalls: 'People were asking: "Who is the President – is it Moi, Njonjo or Kariuki?" They didn't like their behaviour and thought it disrespectful.' In the early days Moi would join his Cabinet colleagues for lunch in Nairobi, dining at the Red Bull and other restaurants. His plain tastes and sober bearing, as well as his humble background, supported the view of the political elite that here was a leader of whom they could take advantage. As James Karugu, who took over from Njonjo as Attorney-General, remarks: 'In Moi's early days as President he didn't take on the robes of office. He didn't really set himself apart. People felt that it was wrong for him to be behaving in this way.'

In a country – indeed, a continent – where the strong man, the autocratic chief, is central to the tribal culture, Moi's policy of conciliation and forgiveness merely encouraged many, radicals and elitists alike, to push his patience to the limits. Philip Leakey, who was made an Assistant Minister when he first entered Parliament, observes:

Moi didn't want any tribe to feel left out, he wanted everyone to feel part of the family. He was much more skilful than Kenyatta at balancing the tribes. In the beginning he thought everyone was working for the same end, to bring about a better Kenya. It wasn't always the case. As a man Moi is incredibly self-disciplined and has sacrificed himself for the nation. He expected the same iron self-control from others. Because other people don't match his own behaviour he frequently feels let down.

The whispering campaign about the President's approachable style, the growing antagonism between Njonjo and Vice-President Mwai Kibaki, as well as talk of Kibaki's possible departure to the World Bank, added to the impression of weakness at the top. Moi caught the mood and acted, asserting himself as never before at a leaders' conference in July 1980, during which he publicly admonished the 300 politicians and senior civil servants gathered before him. He made it clear that, while he embraced the family of tribes into his government, he was the overall chief, and bluntly warned political barons that they were not indispensable. At the same time, he roundly criticised many of the leaders present for failing to support him in his struggle against corruption and for allowing personality clashes to derail his policy of Nyayoism. In one telling passage of his speech he said, alluding to the rehabilitation of former KPU activists:

I hope that no one doubts the sincerity of my commitment and efforts so far to bring about reconciliation in our nation, and to establish an open and broadly based government machinery for running our affairs. I hope that no one would say that I have not given many people a second chance to mend their ways and recognise their reponsibilities to the nation. I am now beginning to suspect that my approach, an approach which I know to be correct, is being regarded by some as lack of strength. There are those who are saying that my approach of reconciliation and tolerance is based on the consideration that without the support of the individuals concerned I would not be able to govern this country.

Moi's trenchant denunciation of the barons was not the only event to ruffle political feathers. Earlier that year there had been a fluttering in the political dovecote when Njonjo announced his decision to resign as Attorney-General and stand for Parliament at a by-election in Kikuyu. It was an issue that he had discussed with Moi and Kariuki at the Commonwealth Conference in Lusaka, Zambia, in 1979, the President agreeing to create the post of Minister of Home and Constitutional Affairs once Njonjo was elected. It was a decision – one in which he had been influenced by his friend Stanley Githunguri, the owner of the Nairobi Safari Club – which Njonjo would for ever regret.

Political hackles were raised immediately, Kibaki believing that Njonjo was eyeing his own position as Vice-President, others speculating that the Attorney-General's move into Parliament was part of a Machiavellian scheme to become President and blow the 'passing cloud' over the horizon. Such was the alarm that at a KANU delegates' conference in March 1980 discussions were dominated by the twin issues of political groupings threatening to undermine Moi's government, and alleged manoeuvrings by, among others, Njonjo and Kariuki to sideline and replace Kibaki. As Njonjo recalls: 'Obviously Kibaki was very nervous, because he thought that I was going to take over his job. But I was happy with the post which had been agreed. I did not want the post of Vice-President.' He maintains that as soon as Moi became President they had discussed the possibility of himself becoming Vice-President. During this informal discussion at State House, Nairobi, Njonjo reminded Moi that as a civil servant he himself was disbarred from holding political office. Furthermore, far from trying to undermine Kibaki, Njonjo asserts that it was he who recommended him for the post and who subsequently went to his home to inform him of the President's decision. 'From that day on Kibaki became my enemy,' he adds.

In spite of his pleas of innocence, however, surely it was the case that Njonjo, an unashamed elitist effortlessly at home in the corridors of power, harboured a secret ambition to crown his already glittering career by becoming President? When I put this question to him in the garden of his Muthaiga home, there was a deliberate, rather melodramatic pause before he answered emphatically: 'N . . . O . . . ', the morning sun glinting on gold scales-of-justice buttons of his blazer.

Whatever his motives, Njonjo's dramatic move from the legislature to the executive significantly altered his relationship with the President. As a senior civil servant he had been relatively independent, enjoying access to the levers of power without having to answer to the people. At the same time, rather like the President himself, he could appear to be above politics, whispering advice in Moi's ear with seeming impartiality. As a politician, however, his relationship with both the President and the people changed, the one subtly and the other dramatically, as he found himself suddenly more accountable to the *wananchi* and to the head of state. From being an overmighty subject who ruled supreme over his legal bailiwick, Njonjo was now one member, albeit a dominant one, of a Cabinet, a group of people whose fates were closely controlled by the President. If indeed Njonjo had harboured no ambitions to become President, it seems curiously maladroit that this consummate player should have thrown away an ace in the poker game of high politics.

The perils of submitting to the political process were demonstrated during a wide-ranging Cabinet reshuffle in early 1982. Njonjo was left only with his Constitutional Affairs department, Home Affairs going to Kibaki, who thereby lost the Finance Ministry, while Njonjo's ally, G. G. Kariuki, together with Nicholas Biwott, both criticised for overfamiliarity towards the President, were shunted out of State House into their own ministries.

While the beleaguered Kibaki frequently hit out at 'baseless' rumours that he wanted the President's job, his arch-rival Njonjo did not find the going as easy as he would have liked when he entered the political arena. In 1981 he became embroiled in an embarrassing and potentially serious trial involving his cousin Andrew Muthemba, who was accused of treason together with Dickson Muiruri. Muthemba had approached Njonjo with alarming information that there were people trying to buy arms to overthrow the government. Njonjo told him to report his story to the police. Instead, Muthemba was arrested and a trial hastily convened. While Njonjo's cousin and his co-defendant were acquitted – the court noted that the prosecution's investigations were rushed and unprofessional and that Njonjo's reputation had been unfairly impugned – the mud of disloyalty stuck. In fact, the trial had more to do with the antipathy the new Attorney-General, James Karugu, felt towards his predecessor than with the facts of the case. Shortly after the humiliating verdict Karugu resigned.

However, the significance of the treason trial lay in its timing, for it unwittingly marked a sea change in the country's social and political climate. The tolerance and patience which the President had shown both to political allies and enemies had worn thin. During the early 1980s, with the economy in a tailspin, currency smuggling rampant, a nationwide doctors' strike, insurrection in northern Kenya, a bomb detonated in the Norfolk Hotel, Nairobi, by a member of the PLO which left dozens dead and injured, tribal clashes between Luhya and Nandi in the Rift Valley, industrial unrest and student riots, it seemed that the country was lurching out of control. In the summer of 1981 John Keen, himself a former detainee, stated that as far as he was concerned the reintroduction of detention was now necessary as a deterrent measure against the civil unrest gripping the country. Keen, then a junior Security Minister in the office of the President, was doing no more than flying a kite on behalf of an exasperated President.

While at home Moi's rule seemed less like considered government than an exercise in crisis management, with policy continually made on the run, internationally the President's star was in the ascendant. The country which had been more or less sidelined on the world stage during the Kenyatta period, was now bathed in limelight as Nairobi played host to the 1981 conference of the Organisation of African Unity. The respect Moi commanded among African leaders was reflected in the record attendance at the summit. As Chairman of the OAU he tackled the continent's problems with characteristic vigour, brokering a deal – typically, after patient all-night negotiations – for a ceasefire in the conflict between Morocco and the Polisario of the western Sahara. At the same time, during his year's chairmanship, he tried to mediate between Libya and the Sudan, organised a peacekeeping force for Chad, and drummed up material and military support for Angola following the invasion by South Africa. Within days he flew to Washington to convey to President Reagan the anger felt by African countries over America's support for South Africa's apartheid regime. In an address to the General Assembly of the United Nations, he urged that there be no compromise with apartheid, which he described as an 'evil' and an 'anguish upon the conscience of civilised men'. Yet even in these matters, Moi was to be unlucky. His chairmanship of the OAU, which began so effectively, ended in disarray after the Polisario rebels were given membership of the OAU by the organisation's Secretary-General, a move which split the OAU and threatened the future of the pan-African movement.

While Moi's international diplomacy met with mixed success, his energetic commitment to conservation won him international praise; indeed, he was awarded a gold medal by the United Nations Environment Programme in recognition of his work for conservation. When he became President one of his first moves had been to create a Ministry of Environment and Natural Resources, and he had gone on to instigate a multitude of practical conservation schemes. Over the years his tree planting efforts have saved many regions, particularly the Rift Valley, from becoming vast featureless prairies. During his 1980 Madaraka Day speech he announced the setting-up of a permanent Presidential Commission to co-ordinate policies aimed at soil conservation and reafforestation. Nor was all this merely gesture politics. His willingness to roll up his sleeves to preserve Kenya's environment was vividly demonstrated in March 1982 when he led the entire Cabinet and legislature to Machakos District, where they spent the day hauling rocks to fill gabions, used to prevent soil erosion. His intervention was remarkably successful, for today the region, which had been in danger of becoming desert, now supports a healthy farming community. As Moi says: 'I don't want to go into history as the President who allowed the destruction of forests.' Since then he has continually warned his fellow countrymen about the 'erosion and destruction of natural resources on which the coming generations must depend'.

His conservation crusade – practical, energetic, communal – provides a useful insight into his values; here is a hands-on President endeavouring to save his country for present and future generations. 'We want a nation of doers not talkers,' was his rallying cry, evidence of a mind-set which indicates why, temperamentally and ideologically, he has never seen eye to eye with Kenya's intelligentsia. Even as he grappled with the nation's political elite, the President discovered that the honeymoon with Kenya's educated classes, particularly in the universities and churches, was over. The 1979 elections signalled the change as students, who only a year earlier had filled the streets in support of the new President, now protested against a decision by the KANU executive committee to bar the former Luo leader, Oginga Odinga, and other former KPU politicians from standing at the forthcoming elections. While student demonstrations were nothing new in Kenya the President's response to their calls for 'justice' was delivered more in sorrow than anger. 'What do they mean when they say they are demanding justice? Are they suggesting that there is no justice in Kenya? How many countries in Africa and around the world can say they have no political prisoners? How many countries have the freedom of expression that is part of our life?' asked an irritated Moi.

His growing frustration with the nation's young intellectuals had as much to do with the age gap as it did with ideology. Moi comes from a generation of politicians who were, of necessity, concerned with the basic practicalities of building the engine of state rather than fine-tuning it, politicians more worried about water pipes for *wananchi* than the words of Wittgenstein. By temperament and background, Moi is a man of action rather than reflection, with a robust political philosophy. 'Our nation has no time for idle and irrelevant debate,' he said during his second Jamhuri Day speech, chiding students, as he was to do regularly, for debating rather than doing.

Ironically, at the time Kenya's seats of learning were derided in East Africa as conservative and introspective, their students more concerned about 'politics of the stomach' than advancing the cause of socialism in a corner of the world where Kenya stood out as an island of capitalism in a sea of revolutionary advance. Surrounded by socialist states and revolutionary universities like Dar es Salaam, which produced the guerrilla leaders of Uganda, Mozambique and Ethiopia, the Kenyan campuses were a fertile ground for radical politics in which the Nyayo philosophy was dismissed as an irrelevant hippy mantra. Moi's thinking and actions failed to strike a chord with fashionable intellectual thought precisely because it had few points of reference with the Cold War debate between the capitalist West and Communist Eastern Bloc. The talk on campus was of the wants of the proletariat, the class struggle, and the need to end, by violence if necessary, the Westernisation of Kenya. Peace, love and unity, the driving precepts of Nyayoism, formed no part of that debate.

Paradoxically the Kenyan students who despised Western colonialism, used the language and constructs of Western protest to define and describe their uniquely African experience. How relevant, for example, was the bitter language of class struggle in a land where tribe, not class, was the mark of a man. As Dr Kiano has observed: 'We all come from humble beginnings. We are all related by blood, marriage, school ties or political ties which give us national solidarity.' In many crucial respects, Kenya's intelligentsia succumbed to a kind of intellectual colonialism, digesting wholesale Western ideas, both radical and conservative, without placing them in the context of the tribal history and cultural roots of their own nation. It is this intellectual sleight of hand which was to seduce both Western and domestic critics of Moi's regime during the debate about multi-partism and democracy in a Kenya dominated by the prerogatives of the tribe.

At the same time, campus dissent reflected the radical thread of Kenyan politics embodied by the Mau Mau, the struggle for independence, the fight inside KANU between the capitalists and collectivists, the formation of the KPU, and the demagogic socialism of J. M. Kariuki. At the heart of this ideological struggle stood Oginga Odinga, for decades the enduring symbol of Kenya's fractured past. In the first years of Moi's rule it seemed as if Odinga wanted to break with the past and make a fresh start with KANU. Moi, who had led a delegation to have him released from detention during Kenyatta's rule, was magnanimous, granting him life membership of KANU, appointing him chairman of a parastatal and using his influence to allow him to stand for a by-election in the Bondo constituency.

True to form, however, the combative Odinga displayed his unerring ability to snatch defeat from the jaws of victory. During a fundraising meeting in Mombasa in April 1981 he accused Kenyatta of having been a 'land-grabber', and then told his audience that, when he invited Odinga back into the political fold, Moi had said: 'Come Baba [father], join me and let us work together for this country.' Privately, an angry President phoned Shariff Nassir, Odinga's host, and asked him tersely why he had rolled out the red carpet for a man who had besmirched the memory of the father of the nation. Publicly, he scornfully rebuked the former Vice-President, saying that he had never referred to anyone other than Kenyatta as 'father'. 'Any other leader who thinks he qualifies to be addressed as such by me must have lost his head and sense of direction,' he said coldly. In short, Moi was deeply annoyed by Odinga's tactless remarks, especially after he himself had prepared the ground for his political rehabilitation.

Forced to resign from his chairmanship of the Cotton Seed and Lint Board, and once again out in the cold, Odinga capitalised on the government's problems – in early 1982 the Kenya shilling plummeted, civil servants' wages were withheld, and the debate on corruption gained a new intensity – to mount a series of attacks on economic and foreign policy. University lecturers, the former MP George Anyona, and a group of radical MPs, including Koigi wa Wamwere, added their dissenting voices.

In fact Odinga, with his son Raila, the politicians Anyona and Koigi wa Wamwere, a journalist, Otieno Mak'Onyango, and a university lecturer, David Mullam Ng'anga, formed part of a clandestine cabal who planned to start a new political party, the Kenya African Socialist Alliance. Working in secret, they drew up a manifesto and constitution for the party, which they intended to launch at the Norfolk Hotel in May 1982. Meetings were held in Kisumu in April to finalise the programme, but then Odinga, as he had done so often during his political career, let the cat out of the bag. During a visit to London he spoke to MPs to whom he said that he was about to start a new political party. On his return he denied that there was any need for another party as 'KANU was socialistic enough'. 'Any opposition party is immaterial now,' he announced in a press statement, a bald-faced contradiction of his underground activities. Clearly Moi was not taken in, for he expelled Odinga and Anyona from KANU.

With the political temperature at fever pitch as a result of Odinga's machinations, the distinction that Kenya had enjoyed for four years of being the only African country without political detainees came to an abrupt end. The President made it plain that his patience was at an end when he made his Madaraka Day address to the nation on 1 June 1982: 'I want to make it clear that we shall not allow a few individuals who regard themselves as revolutionaries promoting foreign ideologies to disrupt our education and training programme.' Surprisingly, Stephen Muriithi, the former Deputy Director of Intelligence, was the first to be arrested, followed by George Anyona and a number of university lecturers. In spite of these setbacks – the conspirators also discovered that one of their number had tipped off Special Branch about their meeting places – they decided to go ahead with the launch of the new party.

Hours before the new party was due to be launched, Parliament rushed through a bill amending Section 2A of the constitution, making Kenya a *de jure*, as opposed to a *de facto*, one-party state. As Raila Odinga admits: 'The political competition had outsmarted us.' The new legislation, proposed by Njonjo and seconded by Kibaki, raised serious concerns among many domestic and international observers. Since the constitution already gave the President the power to license political parties – Moi could simply have refused to register Odinga's party on the grounds that it was a threat to law and order – a number of Kenyan politicians now feel that the amendment was an overreaction. 'It was a sledgehammer to crack a nut,' observed Philip Leakey. 'We could have stopped Odinga without changing the constitution. It was the biggest mistake we ever made; politics were driven underground and it changed the course of the country's history.' Even Njonjo concedes that Odinga's party had little national support, although he also contends that the government legislated for a one-party state simply as an exercise in good housekeeping. 'People were always asking why we left this provision for another party if we are all one party where we can have criticism. At that time it was a very happy arrangement.' The President now concedes that the decision to make Kenya a *de jure* one party state is a matter of regret as it placed the country's politics in a straitjacket. However he argues that while the decision was taken on the spur of the moment the intention was to protect the country from the threat of tribalism as, since independence, every new political party has been a tribal party. This included Odinga's planned party which drew its support almost exclusively from his Luo tribe. As Moi says: 'At the time we were responding to the wishes of the people, it was a question of closing ranks with the intention of stopping tribalism. It is a regret that we made that decision, we should have allowed room for anybody to form his own party.'

There were other factors at play which had little to do with changing the constitution. During the spring and summer of 1982 several top-secret reports landed on Moi's desk claiming that there was unrest in the armed forces. With subversive pamphlets enjoying wide circulation, bomb hoaxes everyday occurrences, and rumours of an underground revolutionary group called 'December 12' common currency, Moi ordered the intelligence services to investigate further.

Late in July 1982, as he prepared to fly to Tripoli to hand over the chair of the OAU to the Libyan leader Colonel Gaddafi, he received a warning from his security chiefs: 'Don't go, there is a plot to overthrow you.'

Chapter ten

Pistols at Dawn

The shrill, anxious sound of a telephone shattered the still of early morning. Elijah Sumbeiywo, the commander of the Presidential Escort, reached out a weary arm, picked up the receiver and listened. It was three o'clock on Sunday, 1 August 1982, and what Sumbeiywo heard startled him from his stupor. He was told that the Army had staged a coup and even now rebel troops were advancing on Kabarak, the President's modest farm home several miles north-west of Nakuru. Sumbeiywo, a trim, wiry man who had known Moi since his days as a teacher at Tambach, knew his duty was to be by his President's side. As he dressed he quickly made a phone call to his brother Lazarus, then an army major stationed at Nakuru. He knew nothing about the force's involvement in the uprising and raced to join his brother at his quarters at State House, Nakuru. Together they made their way in Lazarus's tiny Peugeot 204 car to Kabarak, where they found fifty Presidential Guards in a state of armed agitation.

Sumbeiywo armed himself with two submachine-guns and strapped ammunition belts over both shoulders in the manner of a South American revolutionary. Suitably attired in his warlike garb, he went in to see his boss. He found the President, casually dressed in a blazer and grey slacks, talking on the telephone. He seemed calm, concerned to ease the tensions and fears of those milling in and out of the room.

By now it was five o'clock and it had been established that it was not the Army but elements of the Kenyan Air Force which had mutinied, putting into operation a secret plan to take over the country by securing strategic sites in Nairobi, notably Jomo Kenyatta and Wilson airports, the General Post Office and the *Voice of Kenya* radio station. It was from the latter's studios at dawn that a shaky voice announced that Moi, who had been President for just under four years, had been overthrown and his government replaced by the 'National Redemption Council'. After condemning Moi's government as 'corrupt and dictatorial', the anonymous voice on the radio announced the release of all prisoners, before bizarrely playing reggae music by Bob Marley and Jimmy Cliff.

The incongruous musical interlude did little to ease the concerns of John Keen, then an Assistant Minister at State House. Nervously pacing the floor of his home on Ngong Road in Nairobi he could hear the dull crump of heavy shellfire mixed with staccato bursts of small arms. As dawn broke the firing seemed to get louder and closer. All his worst nightmares appeared to be coming true. Just days before Keen, who was responsible for internal security, had warned the President personally about an imminent coup attempt and suggested that he cancel his proposed trip to the Organisation of African Unity meeting in Libya. Throughout the summer the capital had been plagued by bomb hoaxes, seditious literature and anonymous letters. Something was in the air, although no one was quite sure what.

Keen phoned Ben Gethi, the tough head of the feared General Service Unit, and asked him to send a Land Rover, with some troops and machine-guns, because he realised that if the coup were successful his name would be one of the first on the death list. The firefight was so intense, however, that it was too dangerous to send anyone. Keen, fearing that the rebels would soon be coming to pick him up, sent his children and wives to their farm buildings about a quarter of a mile from his house, ordering them to stay there even if they heard shooting. If he was going to die, he would go down fighting. He armed himself with a pistol and drove to Karen police station for help. The police were not interested in rallying to his cause, were reluctant even to form a roadblock. After touring the area he returned to his home, rather regretting his bravado.

Keen was not the only high-ranking politician in Nairobi to be grappling with the implications of the night's momentous events. When Philip Leakey, who lives on the edge of Nairobi National Park, heard an announcement on the hijacked *Voice of Kenya* that all MPs had to wait in their homes to be arrested, he decided to go on the run. He quickly packed a bag with a blanket and essential supplies, took his rifle out of the safe and headed for the bush.

Meanwhile, at his elegant colonial home on Naivasha Avenue in Muthaiga, Charles Njonjo had come to the same conclusion as John Keen – he was a wanted man. With his hooded eyes, inscrutable mandarin manner, and gift for the pithy putdown, the man known as 'the Duke of Kabeteshire' had plenty of enemies – notably among the Luo tribe, whose members formed the bulk of the Air Force rebels. At first light armed airmen came running down the street, clearly looking for his house. They mistook the home of a woman neighbour for his residence and fired off several rounds in its direction. Then they made off down a passage that runs alongside his home. 'I was in fear of my life,' he recalls. 'Bombs dropped from an aeroplane near my home. I was certainly a target. That's what has made me so furious, the suspicion that I had anything to do with the coup.'

It was the same fear of an air raid by rebel pilots that preyed on the mind of the President's senior bodyguard, Elijah Sumbeiywo. As they reviewed the uncertain prospect he said to the President: 'Your Excellency, can we move away from this house as it can be bombed?' Moi, who had been assured that the situation in Nairobi was coming under control thanks to the timely and courageous intervention of the army commander, General Mahamud Mohamed, needed some convincing. 'No, I'm not moving from this house. Do you think I am a coward?' he told his escort commander. 'No sir,' came the reply, 'but I think your life is in danger.' Finally Sumbeiywo took his President's arm and said: 'Let's go.'

They squeezed into his brother's Peugeot and, followed by a dozen guards in other cars, headed off into the bush, putting several miles between themselves and Kabarak. Initially the plan was to leave Moi and his guards hidden in the scrub, without vehicles, tents or other identifying supplies until the news from Nairobi became clearer. It was a time of high anxiety and strong emotion. As Sumbeiywo prepared to leave for Kabarak to renew radio contact with the security services, he told the President: 'Mzee, we are all prepared to die for you.' As a committed Christian Moi, though moved, was adamant in refusing this sacrifice. 'You have wives and children,' he told the small group, 'there is no need to throw your lives away for one man.' This exhibition of stoic courage still brings tears to Sumbeiywo's eyes as he recounts that dramatic exchange. When the escort commander returned from Kabarak an hour later he was accompanied by the Rift Valley Provincial Commissioner, Hezekiah Oyugi, who made a similar gesture of support and sacrifice, announcing: 'I will die for you, Mzee. I am not going anywhere.' Moi, then facing the possibility of death, was deeply impressed by this expression of loyalty, a gesture which would have a profound influence on the future governance of the country. The emotional temperature was raised even higher by the arrival of the head of the Presidential Press Unit, who promptly burst into tears as he hugged Moi, telling him to have courage.

With the situation in Nairobi still in a state of flux, Sumbeiywo had two plans in mind. The first was to drive to Eldoret, Kenya's fourth largest town, in the heart of Kalenjin country, and then fly Moi out of Kenya. Alternatively, they could head north-west and rally the Pokot, a fiercely loyal warrior tribe who would have fought to the bitter end to protect their Kalenjin President. After a short discussion they decided on the latter option. They had only just set out the journey when they were told on their military radio that the Army was now in control of the capital and that it was safe for the President to return to Kabarak.

During these hours of uncertainty, the President ordered several lorryloads of loyal troops to Kabimoi in order to evacuate his former wife, Lena, to a place of safety. She flatly refused to leave either her home or her country, however; instead, she invited the officers into her house telling them that she had a telephone that reached from Kabimoi to Heaven. The men went inside and removed their caps while she knelt in supplication. As she prayed for the country, for deliverance from the enemy and for her husband's protection, a soldier sitting outside listening to the radio suddenly cried out in delight. He yelled the news that Moi himself was on the radio, saying that the enemy had been defeated. Gently, the officer in charge told Lena Moi that her prayers had been answered.

The President's reassuring message had been recorded as soon as Moi arrived back at Kabarak from his hiding place in the bush. However, in spite of the urgings of Sumbeiywo and assorted military and police chiefs who had now gathered at Kabarak, Moi refused to make the short journey to State House, Nakuru, in an armoured car, insisting on going in his blue presidential Mercedes.

The convoy that barrelled out of Kabarak late on Sunday morning made an extraordinary sight, with bodyguards, submachine-guns at hand, clinging to the sides of escort cars which surrounded the presidential limousine. When they had reached the safety of the compound they radioed Nairobi, from where senior military officers advised the President to remain in Nakuru, since it was their view that the capital was still dangerous. Once again, Moi would have none of it, arguing that he should be back in the seat of government. His view prevailed yet again, and this time a convoy of fifty vehicles, including armoured personnel carriers and Land Rovers crammed with soldiers, set off on the two-hour journey to Nairobi. The crowds of hawkers, street vendors and the simply curious who stood at the roadside watched the passing procession with a kind of sombre perplexity, not knowing whether their President had been taken captive by the military. Even when Moi gave the single-finger KANU salute, they dismissed it off as a display of bravado by the deposed head of state.

When the convoy reached the outskirts of the city, gunfire could still be heard, and even though they took a circuitous route to State House the danger wasn't over. As they stormed by the Silver Springs Hotel the crackle of gunshots, aimed at the convoy, erupted from within. The Presidential Guard held their fire. Once Moi was safely installed at State House, it was many hours later before order was restored to downtown Nairobi. Indeed, the capital was gripped by anarchy as thousands of people took to the streets in an orgy of looting and vandalism. Scenes of bedlam were enacted on every street corner, dark emotions unleashed by the coup swamping every civilised instinct. Mohamed Amin, the late award-winning cameraman, remembers seeing a man who, although he had been shot in the leg by soldiers, still managed to drag a giant fridge on his back. Outside one clothes shop a policeman had taken off his raincoat before stepping inside the shattered store to try on a jacket. While he was doing so another looter stole his raincoat. During the eight hours of pandemonium, women were raped and children beaten up, while men drank themselves into alcoholic stupor.

These scenes of mayhem – around Ksh 640 million worth of damage was caused by the brief rebellion – almost as much as the 152 people, mainly civilians, who lost their lives, profoundly affected the President. For a Christian of steely self-discipline who respected the rule of law, the behaviour of his fellow Kenyans who had rampaged through the city, wrecking mainly Asian-owned businesses which it had taken lifetimes to build, vividly endorsed the Old Testament view of man as an uncontrollable sinner once unleashed from the redemptive shackles of religion and civilising society. This lust for looting and violence confirmed to the President the truth of his oft-repeated maxim: 'It has taken years to build State House, but it will take only hours to knock it down.'

That such primitive animal lusts lurked so close to the surface of Kenyan society was deeply shocking to a man who had dedicated his life to building a proud, independent nation from the wreckage of fifty years of colonial rule. Moi now watched as his Nyayo philosophy of peace, love and unity crumble in the rubbish-strewn Nairobi streets. As he says: 'Destruction can take place very easily. How to put things back is a matter which deeply concerns me.'

On the day after the abortive coup, it was a rather subdued President who silently listened to a detailed briefing about an event which was seen as a stain on Kenya's reputation for stability and common sense. Moi learned that the rebellion had been instigated by men, mainly Luo, of the Kenyan Air Force's Cadu Squadron, stationed at the Embakasi air base in Nairobi. The KAF rebels linked up with student activists from Nairobi University as well as disaffected Luo civilians in a bid to topple Moi. As the inquest continued it emerged that several of the key plotters had been involved in the failed 1971 coup in which KPU activists had been involved.

Inevitably, suspicion fell on the Luo community, and at the subsequent courts martial, which involved predominantly Luo KAF personnel, the name of Oginga Odinga was frequently mentioned as either having given cash or his blessing to the plotters. He was placed under house arrest while his son Raila, together with a number of Luo civilians, including a journalist and several lecturers, ended up in court on charges of treason. The Luo Minister of Information, Peter Oloo

Aringo, was abruptly sacked for disloyalty. It later emerged that Raila Odinga, who was to become the longest-serving detainee in Kenyan history, was linked to the coup leader, Senior Private Hezekiah Ochuka, in that he had been scheduled to write the intended Presidential speech, had established links with neighbouring countries which had promised to close their borders, and had organised a command headquarters for the rebels.

The Luo politician Bill Omamo recalls the mood in Luoland before and after the coup.

> There is no doubt that Odinga supporters organised themselves as an interim government. Before the coup a number of Odinga youth wingers left Luoland for Nairobi and said that they would return with the national flag. The irony was that one came back in a coffin which indeed was wrapped in a flag. In Luoland at that time there was an underground organisation and they knew what was being planned. Odinga and his son were definitely linked to the coup. They were so close to it that even if they didn't touch it, they felt its warmth.

At the same time, while it seemed that the rebellion had been primarily a Luo affair, there remained the suspicion that this was but the prelude to a coup organised by Kikuyu, who had been waiting for Moi to leave the country for the OAU meeting before they acted. Certainly a number of leading Kikuyu were implicated, rightly or wrongly, the inaction of Gethi's GSU and other security forces, including the police, the incompetence of the KAF Commandant, Major-General Peter Kariuki, who was eventually sentenced to four years in jail, and the slow reaction of many senior Army commanders exacerbated these suspicions.

As Moi began to consider the political implications of the rebellion, what was uppermost in his mind was that the deaths, the looting and violence of that bloody Sunday could so easily have been avoided. Notice had already been served in public about the plots against him during the treason trial of Njonjo's cousin Andrew Muthemba. The President, together with ministers like Njonjo and G. G. Kariuki (who then held the Internal Security portfolio in the office of the President), as well as the head of the armed forces, General Mulinge, were well aware of other intelligence reports specifically naming units of the KAF as centres of unrest. Indeed, at the court martial of General Kariuki it was stated that senior officers knew of the plot three weeks before the rebellion actually took place.

In addition, the head of Special Branch, James Kanyotu, had identified many of the plotters and planned to make widespread arrests the day before the coup actually took place. He proposed to act after the President had opened the Nyeri Agricultural Show on the previous Friday. On that day the President was accompanied by G. G. Kariuki, who had by then been transferred from Internal Security to the Ministry of Lands and Settlement. Although he was aware of the plot, because of his ministerial transfer he was no longer kept informed of the day-to-day security plans. As he watched a KAF flypast during the show, he wondered if all measures had been taken to weed out the plotters. 'I was feeling really jittery,' he recalls. 'I knew that something was happening but I also believed that the situation was under control.' According to Charles Njonjo, however, during the Nyeri Show the President was advised by his military commanders, including General Mulinge and Major-General Kariuki, that there was nothing to worry about. As a result of this advice the proposed round-up never took place – with tragic consequences. 'I was annoyed that the coup could have been allowed to take place when it could have so easily have been avoided,' recalls G. G. Kariuki.

The coup had a sobering effect not only on the President and his entourage, but on the whole nation. The people of Kenya had looked over the edge of the abyss, and had not liked what they had seen. All over the country there were huge demonstrations of support for Moi, and many called for the traitors to face the firing squad in public. Several of the plotters were indeed hanged, and others received lengthy gaol sentences.

Politically and personally, Moi had learned a number of hard lessons from the abortive rebellion. The conflicting advice he had received from experts taught him to trust such counsel less and listen harder to the mood of the country. He quietly reviewed the way he had been performing his duties, and admitted that because of his endeavours at home and abroad he had allowed others, notably Njonjo, Kariuki and other State House insiders, to establish a *cordon sanitaire* around him which had left many influential voices, particularly from Luoland, out in the cold. It was a stark contrast with the early days of his presidency, during which he had shown that his strength lay in his populist appeal, his empathy with the public rather than with the nation's social and intellectual elite. He had, however, been gradually corralled by those very same people, the senior civil servants and the political aristocracy, whom he so distrusted. This in turn had meant that the early momentum for reform at the grass roots had slowed, a process aggravated by the country's economic problems. In short, his populist instincts had been blunted by a self-serving political and administrative bureaucracy.

At the same time, Moi also realised that the coup had given him a renewed mandate for change, a chance to break the political and administrative shackles which had limited his room for manoeuvre since he had inherited Kenyatta's mantle. It was a process he began almost at once, particularly as regards internal security. The KAF was disbanded and then radically reorganised, a number of high-ranking army officers dismissed or demoted, five provincial commissioners weeded out, the Special Branch reorganised and the uniformed police revamped.

Politically, the days of easygoing camaraderie and collective decision-making, a reflection of his Tugen heritage, abruptly ended. A necessary distance was deliberately built up between the President and those who sought to control his thoughts and actions. Unqualified trust gave way to scepticism and suspicion. Njonjo, Kariuki and other confidants could no longer wander into State House and see the President when the mood took them. Now ministers could only meet him after making an appointment, and then only to discuss official business.

As G. G. Kariuki recalls: 'There were accusations and counter-accusations. Everyone became very suspicious. The atmosphere at State House was very wary and more controlled.' In various speeches Moi talked over the heads of the tribal leaders to the *wananchi*, warning that the 'big men' in the country were those the people should be wary of. Moi emphasised that when he became President he had retained in his government all shades of opinion from every community. Yet as he now ruefully observed, his magnaminity had not been reciprocated by his colleagues. There were many leaders who still refused to accept him as the President of Kenya, even though they claimed to be Nyayo followers.

In his drive to involve the *wananchi* he overturned his previous ruling that only life members of KANU could stand for parliamentary or local government elections. From now on, he decreed, any member of the party could stand for the National Assembly, a decision which dramatically opened up access to the levers of power. Now everyone had a chance to battle for seats, not just the rich and privileged.

His attempts to widen the base of democracy within the now official one-party state went further. Before the coup, there had been discussion within KANU to limit the number of candidates contesting individual seats. Now he announced a free-for-all – 'We shall allow even ten people to stand for a seat,' the President told one rally. When a general election was announced a year after the coup, he was as good as his word. In the past the vetting of candidates had been the most contentious issue, with scores of prospective politicians denied the chance to stand by KANU branch officials. This time it was different. At the national delegates' conference in 1983 only 4 of the 995 candidates were barred, all for sensible reasons. For the first time all former KPU supporters were given the go-ahead to stand for office. Once again, it was Moi's way of telling the nation that the power lay with the *wananchi*, not the political leaders.

The opening-up of the democratic process confounded the views of those who expected a severe crackdown following the failure of the coup. While a number of academics and civilians were held in detention, in February 1983 Moi granted Presidential clemency to hundreds of servicemen and students, a move which the *East Africa Standard* described as demonstrating his 'statesmanship, magnanimity, forgiveness and, above all, his commitment to the unity of Kenya'. At the same time he was determined to get to the root of the malaise inside the universities, with the result that he asked the former Cabinet Secretary, Geoffrey Kariithi, to head a commission to investigate the problems in the nation's higher-education system.

It was, therefore, little wonder that he was nettled when in April 1983 David Steel, a visiting British opposition politician, claimed that Kenya's government had been unsympathetic to dissent following the coup attempt. Ironically, several weeks after Steel's intervention, the President was presented with the annual Alexander Solzhenitsyn Freedom Award by the Christian Solidarity International of America for 'his stand in guaranteeing all people of Africa the right to their God-given freedoms.'

In many respects, the fallout from the coup masked the explosive political forces which had been building up before the rebellion had even been contemplated. Since he had come to power, Moi had never been master in his own house. Not only had he inherited a predominantly Kikuyu establishment in the civil service, police and judiciary, he had, in the urbane figure of Charles Mugane Njonjo, acquired an individual whose connections and standing in the international and government communities rivalled, and at some points exceeded, those of the President. His role as 'Grand Vizier' during Kenyatta's long reign had enabled him to establish a powerful machinery with which to serve his interests in the civil service, the international business community and the diplomatic corps. Njonjo was more than a man, he was a system.

The political rivalry between Njonjo and Kibaki, the Vice-President, had disguised the true power struggle between the President and the man who was now the Minister for Constitutional Affairs. It was a classic conflict, echoing the clashes between Henry VIII and Cardinal Wolsey, Bismarck and the Kaiser and, in more recent times, President Truman and General MacArthur.

The Kenyatta style of government had perfectly suited Njonjo's persona. The first President had ruled from afar, using the machinery of the civil service rather than Parliament and KANU, and thus effectively placing Njonjo in charge of day-to-day details of policy and personnel. By contrast, Moi's populist policies and hands-on approach challenged not just the style of the former administration but, more crucially, its direction. As the tide of Kenyatta's era ebbed, the differences between Moi and Njonjo, like two sandbanks, became gradually exposed.

Njonjo, with his circle of European and Asian friends and business connections, was the epitome of the right-wing, pro-Western, African elitist. In Parliament he particularly enjoyed goading Martin Shikuku and the radical group of MPs whom he had dubbed 'the Seven Bearded Sisters'. His hostility, as a Kikuyu, towards the Luo community – 'I would never shake hands with Luo people – they are prone to cholera,' he once famously said – as well as his antipathy towards the Africanisation policy, galled many of his compatriots. His contempt towards fellow Kenyans combined with his enmity towards President Julius Nyerere's socialist Tanzania and the East African Community, his friendships with South African businessmen and favouritism towards expatriates, made him the darling of the West but an object of loathing to radicals and pan-African nationalists.

In diplomatic and business circles it was routine for there to be a Njonjo and a Moi camp, viewing the two men as joint heads of state. At the British High Commission and within the influential multinational, Lonhro, for example, there were those who preferred to deal with Njonjo and others with the President. Crucially, although Njonjo was loyal to the new President, those who made up the layer of government Njonjo had created were first and foremost his men. Their loyalty to Moi was always going to come second.

While many of the nation's elite owed their positions, and thus their loyalty, to 'the Duke of Kabeteshire', Njonjo had little or no grass-roots support among ordinary Kenyans. It is no exaggeration to say that some of the dissent towards government policies among the universities, the Luo community, backbenchers and the legal profession, was in reality opposition to Njonjo. He was the uncompromising hawk in Cabinet, masterminding the moves to make Kenya a *de jure* one-party state, a change which alienated Odinga and other Luo radicals. At the same time, he was vociferous in defence of the government's decision in 1982 to restore detention after a four-year break.

It became clearer as the months went by that Njonjo's vision of Kenya was not shared by the President. Moi was and is a man of the people who shares a genuine fellow feeling for, and sympathy with, the needs and aspirations of the rural community; the small farmer, the *jua kali* (literally, 'hot sun') worker, the country teacher, the weaker tribes. Personally and politically he has little time for or patience with the urban elite, while his emphasis on reconciliation and forgiveness contrasted with Njonjo's confrontational style. At the same time, as his chairmanship of the OAU had amply demonstrated, he was a leader who placed high emphasis on a dynamic foreign policy. Though his conservative instincts and mission background made him fiercely pro-West and anti-Communist, he was and is first and foremost pro-African, emphasising again and again that the problems in his country and his continent had to be solved from within, not from without. Moi put his country and region first; for his part, often Njonjo seemed more of a black colonialist than a nationalist.

In essence, Charles Njonjo represented a stumbling block if Moi were ever to be recognised as an effective head of state both at home and abroad. A parting of the ways became inevitable. It was to be a painful process. Just as he used attacks on corruption in the police force to weed out those senior uniformed officers he suspected of plotting against him, so Moi used the smokescreen of the coup to mount a series of attacks on Njonjo. First came his talk of 'the big men' who wanted to grab power, then both cabinet and assistant ministers charged that there were disloyal elements in Cabinet who aimed to bring down the government. In May 1983 Moi himself sent shock waves through the nation when he spoke of foreign countries grooming an unnamed person to take over the presidency of the country. He made it clear that that person was not his Vice-President, Mwai Kibaki.

The hunt was on to find the traitor. Njonjo's enemies in Parliament and elsewhere fell to the task with glee. Moi had chosen a shrewd moment at which to launch this oblique attack on his overweening minister. Uncharacteristically, Njonjo had been involved in several political scrapes: the treason trial of his cousin Andrew Muthemba; his alleged involvement with the attempted coup in the Seychelles Islands in 1981 which sought to restore his friend James Mancham to the presidency; the disgrace of his appointee as Attorney-General, Joseph Kamere, who was found to have received corrupt loans from the Bank of Baroda. Already on the defensive, this chorus of accusation placed Njonjo firmly on the back foot.

Even before he was denounced in Parliament, in June, as the traitor by the Minister for Tourism and Wildlife, Elijah Mwangale, Njonjo knew that the end was in sight. When the hue and cry first arose in May he was in London on business, among other things collecting suits for Moi from the tailor they shared, Tobias of Savile Row. He went to see Bethwell Kiplagat, then the Kenyan High Commissioner, to convey a message to the President that he had nothing to do with foreign governments. Despite his refutation, however, Moi insisted that he return to Nairobi immediately. When Njonjo arrived at State House with the President's suits, he realised that the atmosphere was poisoned. 'I would go to State House and Moi would rush out straight past me,' recalls Njonjo. 'When I tried to see him, he was not available. I'm an old hand at this game and I knew that something was afoot.'

Days later, a debate in Parliament was initiated, during which Njonjo was named as the traitor and Martin Shikuku, his arch-enemy, dramatically revealed details of a bank account held by the Minister for Constitutional Affairs to maintain funds for the last election. What was not mentioned was that the

President and Vice-President were joint signatories to the election fund account. It was clear to Njonjo that his enemies had convinced the President that he had in some way been involved with the coup. 'I was very sad,' recalls Njonjo, who is particularly critical of the role of Simeon Nyachae, then a Chief Secretary, in his downfall.

> I said to myself: 'Here is a man [Moi] whom I've worked with and helped and done everything for. I've been loyal to him. He hasn't called me to ask me about this accusation. He accepted their word.' I felt betrayed by Moi. He had believed everything he had been told by Nyachae, that I had something to do with the coup and was trying to undermine the government.

On 26 June the government announced an inquiry, headed by Justice Cecil Miller, to investigate Njonjo's alleged treasonous behaviour. This examined everything from Njonjo's links to the coup plotters, the importation of hunting rifles by Indonesian business friends, his involvement with the Andrew Muthemba treason case, his South African connections, his opposition to the OAU, his passports, and even the payment of excess baggage fees on overseas flights. During the eight-month inquiry there were even allegations that he had been involved with Tom Mboya's murder. At no stage, however, was the issue of the bank account raised, following an agreement between Njonjo's lawyers and State House. As the inquiry wound its weary way, picking over the bones of Njonjo's public life, it was apparent to shrewd observers of the Kenyan scene that the judiciary was being used to resolve a political problem.

Nor was it a political issue alone, for it also marked a wounding personal rift between two men who had a great affection and respect for one another. The entire episode placed an immense strain on both the President and his former friend and ally. Just as they shared the same tailor, they also shared the same doctor, the Chicago-born heart specialist Dr David Silverstein, who was the only man who saw the two men privately during the inquiry. Over the years Silverstein has come to know both men very well; indeed, their first public appearance together after the inquiry was at his fiftieth birthday party in August 1994. Of their visits to him at the time of the inquiry he recalls:

> One would come in the morning, the other in the afternoon. It was a very stressful time for both men. As devout Christians they both prayed that the commission's conclusions would go their way. Both have a true fondness for one another but I think that Njonjo would have to admit that Moi is the better poker player. He respects him for that even though he would never say so publicly.

In fact, the whole Njonjo inquiry was an acid test of Moi's Presidential style in dealing with a powerful politician who had become a direct threat to his authority. The fate of J. M. Kariuki, Tom Mboya and Pio Pinto showed how Kenyatta and his allies resolved the issue of overmighty subjects. As Dr Silverstein observes: 'In most of Africa this kind of power play between two strong men normally ends up with one or the other being killed. Njonjo was taken out of power and never spent a day in gaol.' This is an assessment endorsed by Philip Leakey, who sees the episode as the defining moment of Moi's presidency:

> Njonjo was a potential threat to his leadership and so had to be removed. This is why I've always admired Moi because anyone else would have killed those who oppose him. He has been brilliant, outmanoeuvring his political opponents without having to shed blood. That's why it is so wrong to attack him for being some kind of dictator or bloodthirsty autocrat.

As it turned out, the commission found that all the allegations against Njonjo except the crucial one of treason had been proved. Their findings were made public on Jamhuri Day in 1984 by the President himself, who used the occasion to pardon his former friend, citing his age and past service to the country as reasons for clemency.

Following Njonjo's fall, Moi took the opportunity to purge KANU and the government of his erstwhile friend's placemen and supporters. By the end of 1984 virtually all those in the civil service and police who owed their posts to Njonjo had been retired, while in September 1984 the KANU executive expelled the former Attorney-General and a number of his supporters, including G. G. Kariuki, Stanley Oloitiptip and Joseph Kamotho.

The fall of Njonjo sent out a powerful signal about Moi's style of government both at home and abroad, enabling the President to conduct a vigorous exercise in fence-mending. There was a distinct thaw in relations in the whole of the East African region as emissaries from Somalia, Tanzania, Uganda and other countries travelled to Nairobi to test the political temperature. After years of mutual suspicion, Tanzania and Kenya agreed to the reopening of their joint border, which had been closed since 1977 following the collapse of the East African Community – a collapse which had caused Njonjo to drink five celebratory glasses of champagne. When President Nyerere of Tanzania played host to President Moi and Uganda's President Obote at an historic meeting in Arusha in November 1983 which saw the signing by the three Presidents of the agreement to wind up the assets held by the now defunct community, it seemed to mark the beginning of a new era.

At home, the removal of Njonjo cooled the political temperature as Moi moved to embrace traditional opponents. He met with a number of leaders, both inside and outside politics, who would have been outcasts at State House during the Njonjo period, and he also wooed the Luo community by releasing Oginga Odinga and others from detention. At the same time, he elevated other Luo politicians to key positions in the government and or in parastatals.

Perhaps the most obvious sign of a new political dawn was the astonishing turnaround in relations between the government and Nairobi University, a campus which had been closed eighteen times during its short history, and a number of whose students languished in jail because of their involvement with the coup. As soon as the university reopened following the coup, Moi extended a personal olive branch, asking student leaders to State House for tea, visiting them at their sports grounds and even inviting their representatives on presidential visits abroad. (On other occasions he donated steers to be slaughtered for student parties.) At the height of this honeymoon period students regularly lined the university to cheer the President when he passed.

It all seemed too good to last, this mood of conciliation and compromise showing the President at his best, a man prepared to forgive past transgressions in the hope of a brighter tomorrow. Almost inevitably, it proved to be a false dawn, the lull before the coming storm.

Chapter eleven
Man in a Hurry

It was every bodyguard's nightmare. All day long the President had been driving through the countryside around Eldoret, racing from one remote estate to another before heading off on foot into the bush. Often the thick screen of trees and scrub obscured him from view as Moi, deep in conversation with the Indian architect Harbans Singh, pushed his way through thorny thickets and clinging vegetation. Moi, however, had other things on his mind than personal security – he was considering the options on offer for the site of Kenya's newest university. Finally the President made his choice. In the midst of a wattle tree plantation near the small market town of Kesses, in the heart of Uasin Gishu in the Rift Valley, he decided on the site and designs for Kenya's grandest seat of learning, Moi University.

Within months, the trees and scrub had given way to dozens of elegant red-tiled buildings built in a neo-classical Palladian style. The campus, with its halls of residence, lecture rooms, a model village for estate workers and a magnificent tree-lined avenue which leads to the graceful Senate House, is a testimony to the President's resourcefulness, drive and ambition. As Michael Blundell once observed: 'This decision alone shows imagination, a concept of long-term planning, and a desire to lift the human spirit above the whirls of dust, the waving grassy plains, the innumerable trials and tribulations of the peasant scene in Africa, which seems to me to augur well for the future of Kenya.'

This ambitious project, which was launched in July 1984, says much about Moi's character. He is a man in a hurry, impelled by a gnawing fear that Kenya's creaking infrastructure, particularly in education, can never keep up with the demands of the country's rising population and aspirations. As he himself says: 'We must run or else we shall be overrun by problems. We should be doers and not talkers.' The way he cajoled 3,000 acres of land for Moi University from the Lonhro chairman, Tiny Rowland, set about raising other funds through *harambees* whilst haggling with builders about costs and architects about deadlines, is typical of his driven nature, a man in an endless race against time.

Unsurprisingly, education has been a particular passion, not only because of his original career as a teacher but as an engine of progress. When, in 1983, the '8.4.4' system of education was decided upon – eight years in primary school followed by four in secondary and four at university – he organised the new regime with almost wartime zeal, personally organising committees of academics to write the relevant textbooks, as well numerous harambees to raise money to build extra classrooms. His enthusiastic embrace of the system demonstrated a growing national confidence, a willingness to forgo the British scheme of classical and academic education in favour of a more practical and technical system of greater suitability to Kenya's needs.

The same qualities he demonstrated in the field of education also came to the fore when, in 1984, the country was assailed by drought and famine, the biggest single natural calamity to befall Kenya since 1888. The emergency highlighted Moi's energetic traits, a man at his best when dealing with practical matters affecting his fellow Kenyans. He set up a ministerial committee to oversee relief supplies of maize, powdered milk and other foodstuffs, liaised with other international and domestic relief agencies, and ensured that food from the ports reached the stricken regions. It was a triumph of efficient organisation in a continent routinely criticised for ineptitude and corruption. The Cambridge academic John Lonsdale observed: 'Moi took the crisis very seriously indeed and made sure that no Kenyan starved. It remains one of the very considerable virtues of his government.' It is a view amplified by Michael Blundell, a former Minister of Agriculture during the days of the Legislative Council: 'Whereas in Ethiopia many thousands of people died, the Kenya government, without overseas aid other than the provision of essential food supplies, moved thousands of tons of maize and wheat from the port of Kilindini to the famine areas with little fuss, minimal corruption and great efficiency.'

Besides the President's energy, the way he dealt with the crisis demonstrated another facet of his character, notably a fierce pride in his nation's ability to manage its own affairs without outside interference. Moi is a dignified man: as the chief, the father to the nation, he finds it demeaning if his country is forced to hold out the begging bowl. For that same reason he resents outside intrusion and interference, in what he considers to be domestic issues, in a new nation striving manfully to forge its own identity from a chequered colonial past. He believes that the ideologies of Karl Marx and Adam Smith, fashioned in the cooler climes and industrial structures of the northern hemisphere have little resonance in the Kenyan context. The challenge as he sees it is to have the faith and boldness to seek African solutions to African problems.

This pride and confidence in his country and continent is apparent in his architectural tastes. Moi University, with its red tiled roofs, large rooms, grand entrances, and Palladian columns, exudes an air of solidity and assurance. Prominent and authoritative in scale and execution, the overall effect of his buildings is a sense of strength and permanence although Singh's architectural signature is at times too urban and unimaginative for rural settings. Harbans Singh remarks of Moi:

> He has very strong ideas and demands buildings that will last for fifty years without maintenance as he believes that in the future people will be too lazy to look after them. He likes great big rooms and often says: 'Let's make this

so big that if a thief comes in he will get so scared, he will run away.' The President dismisses small, congested buildings as chicken shacks.

The truth is that the university, the colleges, schools, Nyayo hospital wards and churches which Moi has had a hand in building bear the imprint of a man with a clear vision of his country's future. They are far more indicative of the man's character – and of far greater practical use – than the rather half-hearted Nyayo monuments scattered around the country.

Moi's architectural vision reflects his personal belief in encouraging self-confidence based not just on what Kenyans have achieved, but on what they can achieve. Indeed, the very permanence of the structures shows his fellow Kenyans that this is a mature, self-assured nation with an independent future, an important statement in a world where the African is routinely depicted as a second-class citizen. This secure architectural style contrasts with that of the colonial era, during which buildings were designed to overawe and subdue the native, or with the transient, rather dreary manner of architecture during Kenyatta's era.

While there are many Moi-inspired buildings around Kenya – the most prolific period was during the mid-1980s – there has never been a grand master plan. In keeping with the character of the President, many decisions to build in local communities are quite spontaneous. One afternoon in November 1985, for example, the President stopped off in Kamukunji in Nairobi, not just drawn by the incessant hammering and clatter of the metalworkers but also as a gesture of solidarity with the *jua kali* workers. He promised sheds to shade them as they worked, a highly symbolic act for an industrial sector so long neglected by even his own government. Two weeks later he was back to organise a Christmas party for the workers. He returned on four other occasions to make sure that the siting of the sheds, the installation of water and electricity and the title deeds which came with these modest constructions were all being properly dealt with. Indeed, the success of the once disregarded *jua kali* sector was highlighted in the 1986 Sessional Paper on the country's economic future, which viewed the business as a major avenue for creating jobs cheaply and effectively.

Herein lies another key to Moi's political philosophy. These sporadic acts of personal paternalistic intervention have meshed into an ad hoc policy which echoes his creed of Nyayoism. The Nyayo buses (although that business is now in receivership), tea zones and hospital wards originated after he had witnessed the problems experienced by ordinary Kenyans as he toured the country.

So the creation of Nyayo wards began after the President, seeing the delay in the building of an out-patient ward at the Rift Valley Provincial General Hospital, personally intervened and pushed the construction forward with funds raised from harambees rather than central government. Similar programmes have been repeated endlessly throughout his presidency. In the spring of 1995, for example, he visited a dispensary near Eldama Ravine in his native Baringo District and was so horrified by the filth and squalor he saw that he vowed to build a new hospital. A harambee was organised, donations were made, and work commenced; within six months, in October, the President returned to open a brand-new country hospital.

Again, the introduction of the Nyayo buses in October 1986 came about as a direct result of Moi seeing the endless queues of Nairobi commuters, particularly schoolchildren, jostling for places on the few buses or on the notorious *matatu* minibuses. Here, however, there was a political dimension; rather like the gun lobby in America, the *matatu* owners and their powerful political allies had regularly defied the government's plans to introduce improved safety legislation. As a result he promised to establish a government-run bus service to rival that of Kenya Bus Services and the *matatu* trade. Two years later there were some 250 buses, funded by overseas aid, ready to ply for trade on the streets of the capital.

Another apparent success story was the introduction in the late 1980s of the Nyayo tea zones, government-run tea-growing areas established on the edges of forests. The thinking was that these zones would protect the forests from destruction by local people, preserve the environment, stop soil erosion, earn much-needed foreign currency and create jobs. By the end of the 1980s there were zones in fifteen districts, administered by the Nyayo Tea Development Corporation, a parastatal which Moi had founded in 1987.

Unfortunately, as with a number of the President's well-intentioned ideas, the reality did not match the dream. These narrow strips of tea skirting the forests created problems with grazing, interfered with the local tribesmen's traditional way of life and, most important, undercut the prices of local tea farmers, who burnt their tea crops in protest at the government-sponsored newcomer. It was a similar story at the Nyayo Bus Corporation, which foundered on the rocks of nepotism, vandalism, corruption, and inefficiency. By 1995 it had amassed debts running into millions of shillings, and the company went into liquidation.

The difficulties inherent in the President's impulsive, if well-meaning, efforts to push the nation forward were to a considerable extent symbolised by the Nyayo car. In 1986 he challenged the University of Nairobi to design and produce a car using indigenous skills and labour, once again revealing his determination to demonstrate that Kenya was a thrusting and sophisticated nation, and at the same time to generate commitment to the new country. The project was launched in 1990 amidst much fanfare but, after the production of just three cars, it fizzled out – at a cost to the Kenyan taxpayer of millions of shillings.

Nothing has illustrated better the gap between aspiration and reality than the harambee system. During the first few years of Moi's presidency he took it to heights only dreamed of during Kenyatta's days, with 14,028 projects, more than double those of the previous decade. Ironically, the successful invigoration of this self-help movement was the cause of its undoing. Under the fund-raising scheme, once the local people had raised enough to pay the capital costs of, say, a school, the government undertook to pay the day-to-day costs of teachers' salaries, maintenance and so on. Unfortunately, there was simply not enough money to go round, with the result that a number of projects remained half-finished or underfunded. The government's 1986 Sessional Paper on the economy acknowledged the problem and suggested that donor governments, who were reluctant to pay recurrent costs, should fund the original project, enabling the harambee contributions to be invested and used for day-to-day expenditure. It seemed that while Kenya's President could run, sadly for him the economy of his country, the eighteenth poorest in the world, could only walk.

The failure of a number of his pet schemes proved to Moi that, in a country where the population had grown fourfold since he had entered politics, he could not do everything himself. In an increasingly complex and sophisticated society the politics of symbolism have to work hand-in-hand with coherent government policy. What is striking, however, is the dovetailing of Moi's day-to-day experiences with government strategy. The integration of the *jua kali* system into long-term national planning following Moi's personal recognition of their contribution to the economy is a case in point.

What was also apparent to the President as he toured the country was the striking inequality between regions, particularly in education. His attendance at harambees drove home the disparity, as his former Cabinet Secretary, Professor Philip Mbithi, explained: 'It was heartbreaking at times – you would attend a harambee where you might give the majority of the money and the local community would only come up with a small amount, giving their chickens and so on. In another area, a vast amount of money was given so therefore the cycle of deprivation and poverty was continued.' In order to break that cycle, Moi practised what is now known as the politics of positive discrimination, attempting to create a greater equality of opportunity so that every tribe, every community, might have the chance to play a role in society by improving its position.

This policy was a recognition too that in a capitalist society, which by definition exacerbates inequalities, it is the government's role to modify the workings of the free market. There is a particular Kenyan dimension. The success, both politically and economically, of the most populous tribe, the Kikuyu, has meant that it has secured the lion's share of the nation's largesse. Moi has attempted the ticklish task of helping other tribes without alienating the Kikuyu – with mixed success.

Education has been the primary battleground. Since Independence, children had been chosen for secondary school and university on a first-past-the-post system. While this attracted the brightest youngsters it made no allowances for under-resourced communities, particularly in the rural areas. This unhealthy state of affairs was discovered by chance during a presidential visit to Machakos Girls' High School. While the local community was from the Kamba tribe, the girls who went on to university came from Central Province or Nairobi, something which created an unpleasant climate of tribal suspicion and unrest. On further investigation, it was found that this tribal imbalance was echoed around the country, a discovery that inspired the introduction of the '85-per-cent' policy, which made it a requirement that that percentage of any local community should attend higher education.

Again, a study by Nairobi University found that potential students from more backward regions were failing to meet the basic entrance qualifications because of local underfunding. As a result Moi approved a scheme to weight the entrance requirements so as to give due acknowlegement to local conditions. It was a policy that bore some fruit. While the numbers involved were insignificant, those who did benefit soon performed as well as their contemporaries from well-resourced regions once they had joined the university system.

The energy Moi funnelled into education was part of a wider vision, a belief that a more equitable education system would break down tribal resentments and thus promote a more homogeneous society. It is a conviction that runs like a golden thread throughout his life, an acknowledgement that tribalism lies very close to the surface of society and that only by making everyone feel part of this new country called Kenya will a peaceful, harmonious and prosperous society ever develop. Just as he tried to curb traditional tribal practices – he banned female circumcision, for example – he also urged tribespeople to accept mixed tribal businesses, encouraged inter-tribal marriages and suggested the building of a national school in each district to break down tribal barriers. As ever, he set the pace, donating 500 acres of his farm at Kabarak to build Moi High School, a model establishment which draws pupils from all the tribes of Kenya. He visits the school on most weekends, regularly attending the church in the grounds. There have been others, too, notably Sacho High School and Moi Educational Centre, Nairobi. As he himself has observed: 'As a teacher I regard these model schools as my special laboratories for experiments in education and youth transformation. They are for the illumination of the nation.'

Just as Moi's energy and hands-on style were a marked departure from the Kenyatta era, so his attempts to address the imbalance in Kenyan society, to give everyone a chance to contribute to the nation's future, marked a significant and fundamental shift in policy away from that of his predecessor. What is clear is that since Independence there have been three economic phases: the tribal economics of the Kenyatta period, under which the ruling tribe savoured the sweetest milk; political economics, which characterised the period of Moi's rule until multi-partyism; and free-market economics, which have dominated Kenya since 1992.

Political economics, which reached its high point during the mid-1980s, was Moi's attempt to overlay on to a centralised, tribally lopsided capitalist society policies which in the long term would have evened out these imbalances. Essentially it was a trade-off between keeping the nation's social fabric intact and allowing its economic productivity to fall. So just as Moi chose the Cabinet and the KANU executive on the basis of geography as well as talent, so he promoted policies which owed as much to their social as to their economic dimension. In the police, the armed forces, the universities, the civil service and the parastatals, social and tribal arithmetic was as much a factor in recruitment as proficiency. None the less the Kikuyu continued to dominate.

Nowhere was this policy switch from tribal to political economics more apparent than in the adoption in 1983 of a policy known as the 'District Focus Strategy for Rural Development'. By contrast with the centralisation of the Kenyatta years, Moi attempted to diffuse power from Nairobi and so involve the grass roots in decisions affecting their districts. The civic empowerment of the *wananchi*, building from the bottom rather than imposing from the top, was mirrored in the revitalisation of KANU, and owed much to the populist beliefs which Moi had formed during his days in the long-defunct KADU. While District Focus was not majimboism by another name – these local committees had no revenue-raising powers, for example – the scheme did embody the KADU idea of giving authority to the regions, and placed great emphasis and responsibility on the districts in planning and implementing development. It was not only a recognition of the importance of the rural community, Moi's natural constituency, in the affairs of state, but also an acknowledgement of the limits of central government. As Dr Eshiwani argues in his study of Kenyan tribalism, the rural focus strategy is 'objective and fair' and superior to that under Kenyatta where top civil servants, invariably Kikuyu, exerted tribal bias. 'It deserves every support because it seeks to bring the ultimate integration of the people of Kenya into one nation. It deserves support because it is the guarantee of peace.'

Nowhere is the gap between tribal and political economics better demonstrated than in the contentious subject of corruption. Moi's attempts to redistribute resources fairly has, according to a Nairobi academic, Professor Henry Mwanzi, made Kenya 'less corrupt, less tribal than it was under Kenyatta'. Indeed, long before the donor community raised their concerns about corrupt state corporations, the parastatals, in the late 1980s Moi had attempted to implement the conclusions of a committee on public affairs which reported in 1983 that state participation had been carried too far, citing reckless investments in schemes like the notorious Kisumu molasses plant. As a result the State Corporations Act of 1986 clipped the wings of these bloated companies, forcing closer inspection and audit of their operations and finances in an attempt to end nepotism and corruption. An exasperated President even announced the appointment of women to head twenty parastatals because he believed that they were more honest than men.

There was, however, a high political price to be paid. Inevitably, the fall-out from this policy of redistribution resulted in vociferous complaints and accusations that Moi had merely switched resources from Central Province to the Rift Valley, from the Kikuyu to his own tribe, the Kalenjin. When he tackled the overblown parastatals, Kikuyu businessmen who had prospered by their privileged access to state resources during the Kenyatta era felt threatened. Others in Central Province looked back to the 'golden era' under Kenyatta when the economy had flourished, forgetting the natural and international calamities which blew the nation off course during the 1980s, particularly the increases in the price of oil and the drought.

This widespread belief that the Kikuyu have lost out under Moi was a significant if not central contribution to the social upheaval of the 1990s that preceded multi-partyism. Yet this almost universal perception does not bear close scrutiny. A highly confidential study of the tribal makeup of the executive officers of the civil service, carried out by the Cabinet Office in 1996 on the orders of the then Cabinet Secretary, Professor Philip Mbithi, proved conclusively that even after eighteen years of Moi's rule, the Kikuyu, now – who comprise a fifth of the country's population and now oppose the ruling party, KANU – still dominate the civil service. For example, of the 309 government economists, around a third were Kikuyu while only one in twenty were Kalenjin. Of the 321 agricultural officers, 187 – well over half – were Kikuyu, while only 38 were from Moi's region. Again, in the field of engineering, the Kikuyu, who comprise just a fifth of the Kenyan population, occupied more than half the jobs, while other areas of the civil service yielded similar figures. As Professor Mbithi, who commissioned the top-secret survey for the Cabinet, acknowledged: 'It is quite clear from these statistics that there has been no deliberate purge of any community since the President came to power.'

While this report gives the lie to the oft repeated claim that Moi has culled the Kikuyu from high government office in order to elevate his own Kalenjin tribe, the findings further underline Moi's determination to build a homogeneous society, embracing all tribes and all regions. As has been seen, the reform of KANU, taking power away from the cliques and cabals and broadening the electoral base, was matched by the return to grass roots administration, a revitalisation of the harambee movement and an attempt to spread evenly the fruits of independence among all tribes, especially in education and jobs.

Naturally there was a political imperative. Ever since he had assumed power, Moi had always been aware that the ruling elite, in business, government and the military, had never truly accepted his authority. He led a political army in which the officer corps marched reluctantly behind him, often confounding his orders and compromising his ideals. This hesitation was made manifest in the multi-party era, for those who left KANU then to form their own parties were leaders, notably from the 1970s Change the Constitution movement and the radical left, who had always quietly nursed a resentment towards Moi's rule. For his part, Moi's continual and vigorous appeal to the masses over the heads of an untrustworthy political elite was as much practical politics as personal idealism, his popularity his main weapon in consolidating and maintaining his authority.

Perhaps the high-water mark of his populist regime was reached in the mid-1980s. By then he had made peace with the universities; revived KANU as a mass movement once more; peaceably humbled an overmighty subject, Charles Njonjo; instilled discipline into the Cabinet and civil service with a new code of conduct; expanded the harambee system; reshaped many organs of state on more equitable lines; and overcome a series of natural disasters, notably the 1984 famine. Kenya, long lauded as an island of sanity and stability in a continent racked by wars and ravaged by disease and hunger, demonstrated a civic maturity, political dynamism and renewed sense of nationhood which boded well for the future.

The crowning achievement of this era was the 1986 Sessional Paper, *Economic Management for New Growth*, written by the Economics Minister, Bob Ouko, which superseded Tom Mboya's famous 1965 document. It was a sobering yet lucid manifesto, acknowledging the twin threats to stability of population growth and unemployment, whilst anticipating many of the policy solutions, notably the need for privatisation and a recognition of the limits of state intervention, which the donor community identified during the 1990s. The British Prime Minister, Margaret Thatcher, caught the mood during a whirlwind tour of the country in 1988, a tour sealed by the donation of a library to Moi University, Eldoret. At the end of a momentous visit she described Kenya under Moi as 'an impressive country, impressively run politically, with great stability, great wisdom and always with the long term effect in view.'

Moi's growing international stature was enhanced not only by his domestic policies but by the vigour he brought to the nation's foreign strategy, particularly with regard to securing peace and stability along Kenya's borders. In 1985 his offer of a second amnesty to *shifta* bandits in North-Eastern Province and the promotion of a Somali, Maalim Mohamed, to his Cabinet finally healed this long-running and bloody sore on the nation's frontier. At the same time he went out of his way to normalise relations with Somalia, an oppressive military regime led by the treacherous Siad Barre, whilst maintaining an equally even-handed approach towards Ethiopia, then on the brink of war with Somalia.

With Kenya's northern and eastern borders more settled and a new under-standing reached with Tanzania, he was able to devote much time and energy to brokering, in Nairobi, a peace deal between the warring parties in Uganda. His efforts were a triumph of patience and pragmatism in the face of truculent and often rude behaviour by Yoweri Museveni, leader of the National Resistance Movement, and General Tito Okello, head of the Uganda National Liberation Army. Agreement was reached only after Moi, exasperated by three months of shilly-shallying, gave the two opponents an ultimatum – sign or go home and fight. This gave the talks a fresh impetus. In the last days of negotiation during December 1985, he chaired marathon meetings which sometimes lasted as long as fourteen hours. The final day was probably the longest and toughest, the three leaders emerging late in the evening to announce that a peace accord had been reached. As the sober American newspaper, the *Christian Science Monitor*, commented, the peace agreement, described as a 'worthy achievement', boosted Moi's prestige internationally.

While there was some talk about the possible nomination of the President for a Nobel Peace Prize, the truth was that his actions over Kenya's neighbours were motivated by hard-headed realities. Open and peaceful borders equalled trade and greater prosperity for the region, especially as Uganda and Tanzania were Kenya's major export markets. At the same time, Moi's foreign-policy initiatives were not wholly driven by national self-interest, but also by his belief that Africans should resolve their own problems; they were, too, and at the risk of sounding pious, imbued with his solid Christian faith.

This moral dimension came to the fore during the late 1980s when Kenya was drawn into brokering a peace agreement between the warring Frelimo and Renamo factions in Mozambique. As it happened, however, Moi became involved quite by chance. An American Christian with contacts with both parties in Mozambique contacted Bethwell Kiplagat, then Permanent Secretary at the Ministry of Foreign Affairs. The American stranger explained that the fighting between Frelimo and Renamo had gone on for more than a decade, that there was no solution in sight and that, of all the countries in the region, only Kenya, with no interests with any of the warring parties, could act as honest broker. Kiplagat was unconvinced. He recalls: 'We had no interest at all in Mozambique. Our trade was zero, we didn't speak the same language, it wasn't in our sphere of interests. We had nothing to gain and everything to lose by getting involved.'

He gave Moi a negative briefing about his meeting, but found to his surprise that the President was prepared to take a risk. As Kiplagat recalls: 'From that moment, I knew that I had the mandate to get started on the job. Once Moi undertook that job, he never let go, he stuck to it. He gave me full backing to conduct negotiations behind the scenes. I would report back to him and he would give me advice and guidance.'

It proved a tortuous road until, the final peace agreement was signed in Rome. By then Kenya had been accused of supplying troops to one side or another, and Lonhro boss Tiny Rowland, who had fallen out badly with Kiplagat when he tried to muscle in on the peace process, had used his newspapers, including the London

President Moi pictured in front of a 2,000-year-old tree in Jerusalem during his first holiday in more than 10 years. He has always had a special affection for Israel because it is the cradle of Christianity and also because his Kalenjin tribe are said to have descended from the lost Jewish tribes of antiquity.

The President, who trained as a teacher and became one of the first African headmasters, has always recognised that it is only through education that Kenya will become the homogeneous society of his dreams.

One of his first acts on becoming President was to donate 500 acres of his farm at Kabarak for a school that enrols pupils from every tribe.

Above: A keen footballer in his youth, the President was known as 'Wheelbarrow' because of his wide arcing tackles that took both the man and the ball.

Below left and right: In a light-hearted mood, the President tries out a bicycle and his hand at the guitar. As a youngster he sang in a church choir and even now will occasionally break into a gospel song at a public rally.

Above: Moi helping a local Nandi family to harvest corncobs. Throughout his presidency he has always been more comfortable with the rural majority than the urban elite.

Below: The President at Sunday worship at the Kabarak church he helped to build. A committed Christian, his regular appearances at church are such a feature of Kenyan life that when, in February 1995, he failed to attend church service there was widespread panic in the country.

Above: Moi with his ivory and gold rungu, a ceremonial symbol of authority, at the 1985 KANU Delegates' Conference. Like Kenyatta and his fly-whisk, Moi is rarely seen without the rungu.

Below: President Moi queues behind the candidate he supports during the KANU grass-roots nomination at Kabarnet.

Right: President Moi sits on a traditional stool after being made a Mijikenda elder in Mombasa in 1996.

President Moi casts his vote
on 29 December 1997 at
Tandui Primary School in
Baringo Central Constituency.

Observer, to criticise Moi's government. As Kiplagat recalls: 'We became involved because of the President's commitment to peace. We endured an awful lot of flak for nothing, but Moi never gave up. There is a Christian dimension to his approach; he felt that these people, particularly the children, had suffered and needed peace.'

Again, it was his Christian sense of duty that took Moi to Iran in 1989 on a secret mission to try to secure the release of Terry Waite, the Archbishop of Canterbury's envoy to the Lebanon, who was being held hostage by Islamic militants with strong links to the Iranian government in Tehran. His attempts at mediation failed, however, as did a similar appeal in March 1996 for the life of Ken Saro-Wiwa, the Nigerian poet, scholar and leader of the Ogoni nationalists, who, with others, had been sentenced to death by the Nigerian military regime. His was the last throw of the dice after entreaties by Nelson Mandela, the South African President, and a number of Western nations, including Britain and America, had fallen on deaf ears. At very short notice a state visit to Nigeria was organised, talks were held, and the Nigerian President assured Moi that he would exercise clemency. For a time it looked as though he had pulled off a major diplomatic coup. Then, in the face of international indignation, the Nigerians went ahead with the planned executions. Moi was so angered by this volte-face that at the 1996 Commonwealth Conference held in New Zealand he was one of the first to support a motion suspending Nigeria from the Commonwealth.

It was at this same conference that observers began routinely to refer to Moi in the same breath as the leaders of the ruthless Nigerian junta and other bloody African tyrants like the 'Emperor' Bokassa of Central African Republic and Idi Amin of Uganda. The man who had been given a special United Nations award for outstanding achievement in 1989 was now described as an 'odious monster' and a 'corrupt dictator', his very surname an epithet for avaricious, dishonest and authoritarian rule. It was a Jekyll-into-Hyde transformation which revealed rather more about changing attitudes in the West, than it did about the character of the man.

PART III
New World, New Order

Chapter twelve

The Strange Death of Bob Ouko

One event more than any other has fixed Moi in the eyes of the world as an unyielding dictator with blood on his hands. This was the bizarre and so far unsolved murder, in February 1991, of his much loved and respected Foreign Minister, Dr Robert Ouko, which caused rioting in the country and horror throughout the developed world. His murder was the culmination of a series of disasters, some self-inflicted, which beset his government and ultimately stained Moi's reputation.

Even at the moment of his greatest triumph, the signing of the Ugandan peace accord in December 1985, Moi's sorrows have come not as single spies, but in battalions. The constitutional changes in KANU in the mid-1980s, namely the issue of queue-voting and the disciplinary committee, were classic examples of the elements which contributed to his misfortune. It exposed the canker inside State House, the complacency of KANU, the growing resentment towards Moi amongst the Kikuyu and, following the murder of his Foreign Minister, Dr Bob Ouko, amongst the Luo tribe, as well. All this tested Moi's gift for finding the face-saving compromise and his willingness to take tough decisions.

One of the political hallmarks of his rule was his rejuvenation and expansion of the ruling party, KANU, throughout the 1980s, in order to make a democratic system inherited wholesale from the colonialists more sensitive to the needs and demands of a Kenyan electorate. Through massive recruitment drives the President transformed the moribund party of the Kenyatta era into a formidable political force. His secret was to transfer power from a closed cabal of local politicians back to the party rank and file. Thus political issues which had been settled by civil servants during Kenyatta's day, were once again solved by a national political body which enjoyed a popular mandate from the *wananchi*.

One of the most significant and welcome reforms was the formation, early in 1986, of a disciplinary committee within KANU to ajudicate on vexatious confrontations between rival politicians. In the past a group of party officials would decide the fate of troublesome politicians, often without bothering to listen to the evidence. The replacement of these kangaroo courts by an impartial body was a significant step in the direction of grass-roots democracy.

Yet within twenty-one months Moi had dissolved the disciplinary committee, even though two of his most trusted lieutenants, Nicholas Biwott, the Minister for Energy, and Shariff Nassir, were key members. Once again it became clear that those the President had trusted had abused their power, turning an institution designed to instil discipline into an organ of fear. Many of the committee, far from behaving as neutral judges, used their powers to settle scores with their political rivals. High-handed, petty and vindictive, the KANU disciplinary committee vividly exposed the arrogance that walks hand in hand with untrammelled power. It became the vogue for politicians to call for the suspension from KANU of their political opponents for the simplest of disagreements, a practice which brought KANU into a head-on clash with Parliament, since in the *de jure* one-party state suspension from KANU automatically meant suspension from the National Assembly. More importantly, it effectively ostracised a number of conservative and hitherto loyal KANU leaders from the political club, building up an explosive well of resentment and frustration. 'KANU was like a pressure cooker without a safety valve,' recalls one party loyalist.

Moi's second major reform, the introduction of queue-voting for the 1988 general election, ensured that this simmering stew of opposition boiled over. The President's original intention had been simple. His thinking behind the introduction of queue-voting, under which KANU members queued behind their chosen candidates at the selection stage, was that the system was transparent, cost-effective and fair, a practical alternative to the secret ballot which, in his experience, was prone to rigging. At the same time, queue-voting also boasted a distinctly African history, being used at *barazas*, within the agricultural co-operatives and, during the colonial period, for elections to African Native Councils and other local bodies. It enjoyed a creditable history in Uganda, Nigeria, Swaziland and Zimbabwe. As the President now concedes: "Queue voting was popular, it was a distinctly African solution to African problems. Unfortunately some officials, district commissioners and so on, those who were trusted, twisted their own people."

His directive to employ queue-voting in the 1988 local and parliamentary elections met with widespread opposition, however, particularly from the Church and the legal profession. When the National Council of Churches of Kenya (NCCK) announced that it would not participate in elections based on the queue-voting system, it caused the biggest schism between Church and State since the issue of circumcision during the 1920s. As the debate sharpened, the hostility of the political establishment towards the Church caused unease both at home and abroad. Bishop Alexander Kipsang Muge attracted attention from Anglican leaders worldwide, including the Archbishop of Canterbury, when he declared; 'I shall not protest against the violation of human rights in South Africa if I am not allowed to protest the violation of human rights in my own country.' Archbishop Manasses Kuria described the new voting system as 'unChristian, undemocratic and embarrassing.' Such was the sour pitch of the debate that the Anglican church magazine *Beyond* was proscribed. Significantly, however, the NCCK leadership, despite their misgivings about queue-voting, did express their continued faith in the one-party system.

As the issue threatened to get out of hand, Moi compromised, agreeing before the 1988 elections that religious leaders, certain cadres of civil servants and members of the armed forces would be exempt from queueing and would instead vote 'by proxy'. The fact that this ruling was not implemented by the time elections were held created a gap of trust between the President and the intelligentsia, who felt disenfranchised by the new system. Yet first reports of the queue-voting procedure were favourable. Official foreign observers of the elections were impressed with the orderly and peaceful way in which some 2 million KANU members decided on the candidates who would go on to the next stage, during which all the electorate voted by secret ballot, demonstrating a powerful commitment to the democratic way of life.

The idea may have been well-intentioned, but the practice was a charade. When the results of the secret ballot were announced, there was uproar as numerous candidates claimed that their results had been rigged, those in Nyanza Province were particularly incensed. A former minister, Bill Omamo, the MP for Bondo, stormed out of the count, claiming that the civil servants in charge of it had indulged in a blatant fix. He was not the only one. The finger of suspicion pointed at one man – the State House Permanent Secretary for Provincial Administration, Hezekiah Oyugi.

Since the dramatic moment at Kabarak in August 1982 when he had offered to lay down his life for his President, Oyugi's rise had been as rapid as it had been contentious. He came from a humble background in South Nyanza, his father working as a houseboy for the wealthy Indian traders Somaia family, in Kisumu, a lifelong link which was to prove highly lucrative for Oyugi. Having joined the civil service, he quickly rose through the ranks so that at the time of the 1982 coup he was the Provincial Commissioner for the Rift Valley, one of the most powerful regional positions in the land. Hard-working, shrewd and immensely ambitious, once he had earned the President's confidence he never looked back. He was promoted to State House where he was in charge of internal security and the provincial administration – the latter being the selfsame department in charge of ensuring fair play at the ballot box.

Quickly, quietly and skilfully, he built his own empire, using his position to secure lucrative arms contracts for his friend and business partner, Ketan Somaia. Oyugi's ambitions did not stop at lining his pockets, however – he craved power. During his tenure at State House, Oyugi effectively dismantled the Special Branch, creating his own intelligence service which shadowed the work of the official security forces; he even organised for Somaia to conduct intelligence snoops on his own Asian community. Moreover, just as he shaped the security forces as a personal fiefdom, so he controlled the civil administration of the provinces with an iron rule. He was held in such thrall that when he telephoned a district commissioner in a far-flung corner of the country, the hapless official would more often than not stand to attention and salute when he heard Oyugi's voice.

By the mid-1980s, Oyugi was one of the most influential men in Kenya, his authority overshadowing that of the head of the civil service, Joseph Leting. He feared only two men, Simeon Nyachae, the Chief Secretary before Leting, and Nicholas Biwott, the Minister of Energy. When Nyachae retired to pursue a political career, Oyugi and Biwott were suspected of masterminding moves preventing him from standing for Parliament. For his part, Nyachae, the man who had helped engineer Njonjo's downfall, was now made to enjoy a taste of his own medicine. With his departure, only Biwott was left as Oyugi's rival for the President's ear, an influence which provoked mutual suspicion and loathing between the two men.

Biwott and Oyugi had different approaches to dealing with the President. While the former, like Nyachae, would tell the President the realities of any given political situation whatever Moi's mood, Oyugi, had the ability to engage and hold the President's attention, laughing and joking all the while, as he put a word in here, a comment there, any of which might make or break a career. When Oyugi was with the President, the rest of the staff at State House knew that they were on 'Nyanza time'; any plans to leave at the usual time of five o'clock would be forgotten when Oyugi held court, for he would often chat with the President until late into the evening. As one of Oyugi's former confidants recalls: 'He had an uncanny hold over the President – he instinctively knew all the right psychological buttons to push. Even though he was always laughing, that was a mask because all the time he was calculating, trying to use every situation to his advantage.' Warnings to Moi from his allies that Oyugi was a dangerous character simply fell on deaf ears. If Oyugi was prepared to die for him, that was proof positive of his loyalty. Even when a delegation of senior military and police chiefs spoke to the President about the duplicity of Oyugi, they were sent packing.

Oyugi ruthlessly used his influence to secure favour for his Luo tribe, guests at a New Year's Eve party at State House in Nakuru still remember his behaviour as he surveyed the throng, barely able to contain his glee at the number of Luo guests, all his friends and allies, who filled the room. As he surveyed the scene, seated like a miniature emperor surrounded by admirers, he said; 'Do you know what power is? This is power. We Luos are now in control.' Then he laughed like a clown.

Ambition seeped from every pore. By the late 1980s, just as he wielded untrammelled authority over the civil service and security services, so he wanted to extend his influence into the political arena. He nursed one dream as though it were a favourite child: 'One day I am going to be President,' he would boast to confidants. 'He wanted to take over, that's why he behaved as he did,' recalls one of Oyugi's circle. He was canny enough, however, to play the waiting game, aiming first to be the undisputed leader of the Luo and then to be made the first ever Luo Vice-President of the Moi era.

The elections under the newly adopted queue-voting system were the first stage in the consolidation of his position and power, enabling him to place his own supporters as candidates in Nyanza Province whilst ensuring, by rigging the vote, that his potential enemies lost their seats. As Bill Omamo, who lost his own seat to a relatively unknown candidate, Dr Gilbert Oluoch, recalls: 'Oyugi participated in the rigging of the election which has left such a bitter taste in the mouths of many Kenyans. The election was supposed to be transparent, but in the end it quickly became translucent and even opaque as a democratic process. I blame Oyugi for this.'

Oyugi's actions exposed the crucial flaw in the workings of queue-voting, since so much depended on the integrity of the civil servants running the ballot. And Oyugi controlled the civil servants. Even so, while he might have secured his own coterie of supporters in Parliament, he created a rump of disgruntled, powerful and angry KANU loyalists in Luoland and Central Province, most notably Charles Rubia, Masinde Muliro and Ken Matiba.

Just as significantly, with Oginga Odinga no longer as dominating a figure in

Luo politics as he had been, the man who posed the greatest threat to Oyugi's short-term goal of tribal leadership was the Industry Minister, Bob Ouko, an internationally respected diplomat, a brilliant orator, and the architect of the ground-breaking 1986 Sessional Paper. However, even though his political star was rising, Ouko was seen by himself and others inside State House more as a civil servant than a future political leader. As the elections approached, Ouko, a man prone to self-doubt and pessimism, was not even confident of holding on to his seat in Kisumu. Oyugi saw his chance, intending to oust his potential rival by rigging the result in the forthcoming election.

Fatally, however, he hesitated when he saw the way the wind was blowing inside State House. He knew that President Moi had asked Ouko once more to take on the post of Foreign Minister when the election campaign was over. Ouko, who suffered from high blood pressure, was reluctant to resume such a draining and hectic position again. He only relented when Moi promised to campaign in his constituency to help smooth the path of his re-election. It was not an offer to be taken lightly. Since the coup, Moi had deliberately stood above the fray at election time, so that he would be able to see the true popularity of his ministers. In the event, as a result of Moi's intervention, Oyugi left Ouko largely to his own devices during the campaign and the voting, although the latter did claim afterwards that some rigging had taken place.

Eighteen months later Bob Ouko was dead, an unresolved murder that has stained Moi's presidency and his government to this day, providing a continually embarrassing backdrop to the domestic unrest and international pressure which preceded the reintroduction of multi-party politics in 1991. As with the murders of Tom Mboya, Pio Pinto and J. M. Kariuki, the finger of suspicion pointed directly at State House.

Months before he was killed, Ouko's almost routine paranoia as well as his highly developed sense of the dramatic had become a standing joke in the Foreign Ministry. He was always claiming that somebody or some government was out to kill him – one month it would be the Libyans, the next the CIA. 'No one took any notice because he was that kind of guy, disorganised, highly intellectual and a great womaniser,' recalls one of his colleagues, Philip Leakey. In January 1990 the Foreign Minister joined the President and other Cabinet colleagues on a trip to Washington, the highlight of which was a prayer breakfast with US President George Bush, a number of Congressmen and other leading lights of American politics.

Human-rights violations in Kenya dominated the public side of the visit, a factor which later prompted the London *Sunday Times* and other newspapers to allege that the President ordered Ouko's killing because his Foreign Minister enjoyed higher prestige in America than did the head of state, and had as a result blamed Ouko for organising such an embarrassing visit. Certainly Moi was irritated; his frustration was, however, directed not at Ouko but at the American media, as well as the incompetence of an expensive American public-relations company the Kenyan government had hired to improve its image – an experience which has made him very wary of employing, ever again, the dark arts of the spin doctor.

Personally, the President was delighted with the way Ouko defended his government's record on human rights not only in America but also during a flying visit to Norway in February, where he spoke with such panache and aplomb that the recording of the press conference he held was repeated several times on Kenyan television and radio – with Moi's enthusiastic blessing. On his way from Norway Ouko rejoined the President in London for a brief visit before flying on to Kenya. The two men met for breakfast in the presence of several others, including Sally Kosgei, then the Kenyan High Commissioner to London. Ouko had spent a few hours sightseeing and, having been impressed by the number of statues of famous men dotted around the capital, had suggested to the President that it would be fitting if a similar monument to their head of state were to be built in Nairobi. Moi's reply was briskly jocular: 'Haven't you read what it says in the Bible, Bob? You should never worship false gods.' (At the time a row was raging in Nairobi about the new *Kenya Times* building, a 60-storey skyscraper due to be built adjacent to Uhuru Park, and the giant statue of the President scheduled to be erected in front of it. Indeed, it was only after Moi had made this riposte to Ouko that he was apprised of plans for his statue – an illustration of how the filtering process inside State House so often kept awkward or controversial issues away from the head of state.) In any event, it was a happy and relaxed group that returned to Nairobi, Ouko basking in his President's appreciation of a job well done.

During what turned out to be the penultimate weekend he spent alive, 3–4 February 1990, Ouko had a meeting with Hezekiah Oyugi at the latter's Nairobi home and afterwards with his solicitor, who noted that the Foreign Minister was distracted and worried. His last meeting ever with the President was at State House on the following Monday, where he joined Bethwell Kiplagat and the newly appointed Canadian High Commissioner, Mrs Andreychuk. As Kiplagat recalls: 'It was a cordial meeting, we all walked out smiling.' In fact, Ouko stayed chatting with the President for a few moments longer, and as they parted Moi clasped both the Foreign Minister's hands in an emotional gesture of thanks for the work Ouko had done on Kenya's behalf, readily acceding to his request for a few days off so that he could go home to Kisumu. It was the last time the President saw him alive.

Ouko spent the following week at his home, cancelling a press conference in Nairobi but giving a speech to the Rotary Club in the Imperial Hotel in Kisumu. During the subsequent inquiry into his murder, conducted by Superintendent John Troon of Scotland Yard, it was discovered that Oyugi had been booked into a nearby hotel in Kisumu by an Asian friend and was seen at a post office near Ouko's home very early on the day that Ouko disappeared.

On the last full day of his life, Monday, 12 February, the Foreign Minister's behaviour was odd. He dismissed his bodyguards from his home outside Kisumu and then sent his wife, Christabel, on the 300-mile journey to Nairobi in his official Mercedes car, leaving him without transport to get to the airport to fly back to Nairobi. All the evidence suggests that he had a secret rendezvous planned with people he already knew. Between two and three in the early hours of Tuesday morning his maid, Selina Aoko, heard a loud bang and saw a white Peugeot pick-up, similar to those used by the Kenyan Special Branch, drive away. Three days later, on the morning of Friday, 16 February, his body was found on a tree-covered hill called Got Alila, a little under four miles from his Koru home.

He had been shot through the head, and his body then set on fire. All around the corpse were personal effects; his own .38 revolver with one spent cartridge case in the cylinder, his walking stick, a sword, a jerrycan, and a plastic bag containing folded clothes and money.

The alarm was only raised the following day, Tuesday, when he failed to meet his bodyguard at Kisumu airport as planned. When the President and his entourage, who were at State Lodge, Nyeri, were informed that Ouko had missed a flight to the Gambia where he was scheduled to represent Moi at that country's twenty-fifth Independence Day celebrations, at first no one was unduly concerned. It has since emerged, however, that throughout the Monday night, Oyugi hovered over the telephone switchboard in State Lodge monitoring all calls so that he could censor any news before it reached the ears of the President. On the Tuesday, as concern about Ouko's whereabouts mounted, Oyugi seemed to be behaving in a manner that was disturbed, sullen and reserved, a far cry from the bombastic and ebullient man everyone knew. Indeed, during the journey to State House, Nakuru, Oyugi told, amongst others, Abraham Kiptanui, then the Comptroller of State House: 'If Ouko is dead I will join politics.' It seemed to Kiptanui a strange remark, especially as there were then no real fears as to Ouko's safety.

As the hours passed the President became increasingly agitated. By now he was alarmed not just by Ouko's disappearance, but also by the suspected poisoning of his recently appointed Vice-President, Professor George Saitoti, who had been taken ill in Nairobi at the same time as the hue and cry was raised over Ouko's disappearance – indeed, he would later link the two events as having been the work of the same people. The President ordered the navy commander to organise diving in Lake Victoria as part of the search for Ouko, and overruled Oyugi's counsel that they should maintain an official policy of silence with regard to the missing Foreign Minister. The *Voice of Kenya* announced the news of his disappearance; then, on 16 February, after his body had been discovered and identified, the President spoke to the nation in a radio broadcast of his 'profound sorrow' at the death of Dr Ouko. He vowed to leave no stone unturned in the search for the truth about the murder of Ouko, whom he described as a 'loyal and dedicated friend' and the 'best Foreign Minister the country has had'.

With the country shaken by the news, parallels were rapidly drawn with the deaths of other prominent politicians. The perplexing difference was that Ouko, unlike Mboya, Pinto and Kariuki, had had no apparent enemies either at local or national level. In the immediate aftermath of his murder, however, demonstrating students in Nairobi and Kisumu denounced Oyugi and ridiculed the initial clumsy statement issued by the government, which had implied that Ouko had committed suicide, a theory that Oyugi promoted consistently inside State House. It was noticeable, too, that at Ouko's funeral Oyugi kept very close to the President, almost as though he were using him as a shield in case of trouble. 'He was extremely nervous throughout, especially when the crowd started shouting his name,' recalls a member of the presidential party.

With speculation about Ouko's killers at fever pitch, Moi saw the British High Commissioner, Sir John Johnson, and asked for help from Scotland Yard, who responded by immediately flying over a pathologist and a team of detectives led by

Superintendent John Troon. As he and his men interviewed witnesses and other interested parties they found their inquiries hampered by Oyugi's plain-clothed police, who shadowed their every move, making life as difficult as possible for them. Intriguingly, Troon and his team were met in Nairobi by the then Nakuru District Commissioner, Jonah Anguka, a close ally of Oyugi, and driven directly to Kisumu. This irregular behaviour raised the suspicions of the Rift Valley Provincial Commissioner, Yusuf Haji, who asked Oyugi why the local DC had not accompanied the Scotland Yard detectives as protocol decreed. At the time he received a dusty answer, but with hindsight Haji concedes it could have been done to keep Troon away from those who did not enjoy Oyugi's favour. Troon himself recalls that the Kenyan police were obsessed by the suicide theory, in spite of overwhelming evidence refuting that notion. On one occasion Ouko's sister, Dorothy, was telephoned by Nyanza Provincial Commissioner Julius Kobia and ordered to tell Troon that her brother had committed suicide. She refused. Then Kobia put pressure on Troon himself, making veiled threats to the British detective, telling him 'You watch your back, you're getting too close. If you are not careful, something is going to happen to you.'

As the weeks passed, Troon focused on deals relating to the notorious Kisumu molasses plant, a multi-million-dollar government-funded white elephant. He discovered that Ouko and Nicholas Biwott were at odds over which company should be favoured to run the plant, the latter favouring a Canadian company, while Ouko preferred an Italian consortium. It was this consortium, backed by the Swiss-based BAK Industries, which, during his investigation, sent Troon a detailed dossier of documents outlining corruption in high places, and particularly focusing on Biwott and Oyugi.

At the same time, Troon believed that Ouko had been asked by the President to conduct a secret investigation into corruption inside the government, a probe which allegedly revealed the widespread underhand activities of Biwott and Oyugi. One possible motive for murder, as far as Troon was concerned, was that Ouko had been worried about the implications of the corruption report and had feared for his personal safety. In fact Troon was misled over this issue. The President, who had ordered several inquiries into corruption during the 1980s and has since set up an anti-corruption unit, never asked Ouko to compile any such report. It is one of many red-herrings in this complex affair.

It has since emerged that there was a delicate personal dimension to this tangled case. What Troon failed to discover was that Dr Ouko, a well-known womaniser, had been enjoying a friendship with Oyugi's third and favourite wife, Betty. The couple had had problems in conceiving children, so much so that Oyugi had sent Betty to a Harley Street clinic for tests; even after this, however, they discovered that they were unable to have children, much to Oyugi's distress. His reaction when he discovered that his wife was close to Ouko can only be guessed at.

In September 1990, at the end of his 110-day inquiry, Troon handed over his weighty 150-page report to the Attorney-General, Matthew Muli, fully expecting the immediate arrests of his two principal suspects, Nicholas Biwott and Hezekiah Oyugi. Instead, the government set up a judicial inquiry chaired by Mr Justice Evans Gicheru. At that time the President took no action because the man who briefed him on the conclusions of Troon's report was one of the main suspects, Hezekiah Oyugi. He poured cold water on much of Troon's evidence, sometimes emphasising the suicide theory, sometimes the possible involvement of his principal rival at State House, Nicholas Biwott. 'Oyugi thoroughly doctored the report,' recalls the former Cabinet Secretary, Professor Philip Mbithi. 'It took a long time before the President discovered the full extent of Oyugi's treachery.'

Oyugi even tried to direct the inquiry's conclusions, regularly entertaining the commission judges at his home, on at least one occasion slaughtering a goat in their honour. It was only after the commission had been sitting for a year that Troon was called back from Britain to give his evidence. For the first time the two principal suspects were named in public. By now, though, the full extent of Oyugi's duplicity was beginning to be appreciated by the President, and these suspicions were confirmed when James Kanyotu, the head of the Special Branch, bugged the hotel rooms of the three judges. Transcripts of their conversations showed that Oyugi was attempting to direct the commission to find Biwott guilty.

The fact that the commission had lost sight of its original brief by admitting all kinds of wild and often malicious conjecture lay behind the President's decision, in November 1991, to bring its deliberations to an end. At the same time, now aware of the true nature of Troon's evidence, he ordered the arrest of Oyugi, Biwott, the former Nakuru District Commissioner Jonah Anguka, the Nyanza Provincial Commissioner Julius Kobia and others.

All those arrested on the day the commission was dissolved were released without charge, with the exception of Oyugi, Biwott and Anguka. Then, after two weeks in police custody, amidst a considerable outcry, Biwott and Oyugi were freed. Anguka was later charged with Ouko's murder but was acquitted after two trials. As Professor Mbithi, who was with the President daily during this time, recalled: 'We wanted some blood, we wanted heads to roll. The government was hurting. If it was possible to have a hanging, we would have had a hanging. We wanted blood and the President was nearly crying about this whole business. He knew that keeping them in prison would have saved his government from attack but there wasn't the evidence.' None the less, Biwott, Oyugi and Kobia were later sacked. Oyugi, who from then on suffered total ostracism by his former colleagues, died a year later in London of motor neurone disease. There is a sense among those who knew Oyugi that the distressing manner in which he died was God's retribution for Ouko's death. As one who knew Oyugi well says: 'Ouko's death was a Luo affair. Every tribe in Kenya knows that.'

The Ouko episode, which remains unresolved, was personally and politically painful for the President. Not only did he lose a close friend, he also lost a valuable political ally, a highly competent, unambitious and loyal minister. The stories that he had in some way been involved in Ouko's murder merely added insult to injury. 'How could I kill my minister who was so trusted?' he has said. It is an issue he has raised in Cabinet, spelling out his Christian creed to his fellow ministers, as well as his loathing for bloodshed.

The Ouko affair also closed a chapter in Moi's presidency. To a far greater extent than after the coup, he no longer put his full trust in those around him, his relationships with fellow politicians and government officials becoming more distant and professional. Again, Mbithi observes: 'Moi gets very suspicious easily after the Oyugi situation. Even if you love the President and want to serve him you get close to him and then see him withdraw because he no longer trusts anyone.' It is an observation echoed by several in the President's circle.

Besides the personal toll, the Ouko affair exacted and continues to exact a high political price. Not only did it alienate a substantial tranche of Luo supporters from the KANU government, the investigation and commission of inquiry were an open wound on the body politic at a time of mounting opposition both at home and abroad. There was a certain symbolic timing in the fact that the arrests of Oyugi and Biwott in November 1991 were followed within days by an announcement by the World Bank and the IMF at a meeting of donor nations in Paris that foreign aid to Kenya would be frozen until the economy was liberalised and a more democratic and answerable system of government implemented. Five days later, on 3 December, the single-party state was abolished and a new era of multi-partyism dawned.

Chapter thirteen

High Noon

Like an ageing gunslinger in a Western movie, the United States Ambassador to Kenya, Smith Hempstone, moseyed into town in the winter of 1989. Tough-talking, hard-drinking, chain-smoking, the former-journalist-turned-diplomat soon made it known that he had one man in his sights – the town sheriff, President Daniel T. arap Moi. 'I intend to get rid of Moi,' he privately told the British High Commissioner, Sir John Johnson. Lauded by the opposition, loathed by the government, Hempstone arrived at a turbulent moment, indeed, a turning point, in Kenyan history. Certainly he was an unlikely revolutionary. Once a right-wing columnist for the *Washington Times*, he had supported the bombing of Cambodia, thought the Vietnam War a noble conflict, and had enthusiastically backed the notorious Contra rebels in Nicaragua. Confrontational in manner, truculent in speech, unconventional in behaviour, he acted more like an Ernest Hemingway, to whom he bore a passing resemblance, than an earnest emissary. To many, he was the quintessential wrong man in the wrong place at the wrong time, for others he was the saviour of Kenya, the one man who inspired a cowed opposition to rise up against the Moi government. 'When he came on the scene it was the equivalent of throwing petrol on a fire,' recalls American businessman Bromley Keables Smith.

Not only did Moi, a non-smoking teetotaller, find Hempstone's manners offensive – the Ambassador often blew smoke in the face of Kenyan officials, and would arrive at State House dishevelled and smelling of drink – he was especially irritated by the fact that Hempstone broke all the rules of diplomacy by saying in public what should only have been discussed in private. 'It was not what he was saying that Moi found insulting, but the way he said it,' recalls Keables Smith. 'It was disrespectful, arrogant and deliberately provocative.' In fact, the speech that fuelled the growing conflagration seemed innocuous enough. In an address to the Rotary Club of Nairobi in May 1990 Hempstone said that in future United States economic assistance would only go to nations that 'nourish democratic institutions, defend human rights, and practise multi-party politics'.

It came at a time when the President and his country had been under sustained and critical attack, both at home and abroad, for the erosion of the judicial process, particularly the ending of life tenure for judges; human rights violations, particularly where political dissidents were concerned; and the abuse of the democratic system, especially the decision to incorporate queue-voting into the workings of the electoral system. Hempstone's remarks were the latest in a series of events which had produced a bewildering transformation in Kenya's image. No longer seen by the West as an oasis of security and success in a desert of despair and deprivation, the country was in 1991 routinely portrayed as a nightmare land of repression, state-sponsored torture and corruption. The brooding master of ceremonies in this chamber of horrors was the implacable, malevolent and dictatorial presence of President Daniel T. arap Moi.

While the demonisation of Moi says as much about Western attitudes towards Africa than it does about the character of the President, crucially the metamorphosis from saint to sinner occurred at a time when domestic disenchantment, particularly among the dominant Kikuyu elite, was mounting as the world witnessed the wholesale washing away of monolithic dictatorships by the spread of two words, *perestroika* and *glasnost*. The tearing-down of the Berlin Wall and the eventual collapse of Communism in Russia and Eastern Europe transformed utterly the West's approach to Africa.

During the Cold War, Western policy had been to bolster 'client states' with aid linked to arms in order to stop the barbarians at the gate, turn back the advance of the Red Horde. For decades this realpolitik had meant turning a blind eye to those pro-Western African leaders who served their own interests rather than those of their countries.

The demise of the bipolar world led to its being replaced by the so-called 'New World Order', under which America would lead the free world in a moral crusade to secure peace, democracy and free trade. By one of the ironies of history the new order faced its sternest test in the Gulf War of 1991, in which the American President, George Bush, steered a coalition of Western, and some Middle Eastern, countries in a campaign to free oil-rich Kuwait, a country ruled by an oppressive, venal family oligarchy, from the clutches of Iraqi forces under their equally tyrannical leader, Saddam Hussein.

The realities of economic self-interest underpinning the bogus morality of the New World Order were not lost on Kenyan leaders as they listened to the pious tones of Smith Hempstone and other diplomats. Indeed, when Philip Leakey, then an assistant minister in Foreign Affairs, and Professor George Saitoti, then the Finance Minister, visited Washington to see the US Secretary of State, James Baker, during the late 1980s, they were given a true insight into the nature of the New World Order. As Leakey was leaving Baker's office, the avuncular Texan put his arm round him and said: 'Let me tell you about the New World Order – we give the orders.'

For the New World Order was based on a crucial self-delusion, the belief that the economic victory over Communism had also confirmed the moral ascendancy of America and her allies. Flowing from the triumph of the free market, with its current emphasis on privatisation and deregulation, was a corresponding tone of moral triumphalism, expressed by the vigorous imposition on developing countries of the West's civic culture of multi-party democracy and self-image of high public virtue. Such moral absolutes do not, however, seem to apply to oil-rich Gulf states or, for that matter, to the Order's own governments. Indeed, the only thing consistent about Western policy towards Africa has been its awful hypocrisy. As the South African President Nelson Mandela said during a visit to Nairobi at the height of the multi-party debate: 'What have the whites anywhere to teach us about democracy when they executed those who asked for democracy during the colonial period?'

The New World Order is simply exploitation by another name, the application of Western might and superiority concealed behind the moral figleaf of democracy and freedom. So just as the missionaries who came to Kenya never once considered the existing culture of the tribes they tried to 'civilise', so the West has embarked on another bout of colonialism, imposing its governmental structures on people and leaders about whom they know little and care even less.

Kenya's strategic and economic insignificance combined with its dependency on donor aid have ensured that it is perfectly suited to the aggressive paternalism of the New World Order. As a result, purely domestic Kenyan issues have assumed an international dimension, a dimension which accelerated change but also created economic calamity and tribal divisions which are still to be healed. It could be argued that Western agencies actively fostered civil dissent, encouraged tribal unrest, attempted to oust the head of state and then, when the country was on its knees economically and politically, washed their hands financially, leaving a bewildered government to pick up the pieces.

While Western observers like to blame Moi and his KANU party for the tribal clashes that followed the introduction of multi-partyism in 1992, historians may well judge that the interference of the West in the development of democracy in Kenya has left much blood on the hands of the white man. The comment of Rudyard Kipling, Britain's greatest imperial writer, made at the beginning of the century, that the exercise of power without responsibility has been the prerogative of the harlot throughout the ages, serves as a fitting epitaph to the West's behaviour in Kenya and elsewhere as we reach the end of the millennium.

Beautifully dovetailing with the revised political imperatives of the New World Order is the fundamental racism that informs the dealings of the liberal West with the Third World. While Kenya is no longer a colony it is still, as is the rest of Africa, colonised intellectually, culturally, economically and socially by the West whose architecture of power is that of white dominion and black submission. The narcissistic representation in Western culture of the white man in Africa, be it as explorer, coloniser or missionary, is matched only by the stereotyping of the African as mindless savage, evil witch doctor, nascent rapist, docile slave, educated fool.

This lexicon of cultural repression, a legacy of several hundred years of Western expansion and hegemony, has been given a new twist, since independence swept the African states, with the caricature of 'the Big Man'; the greedy, cruel and selfish leader whose acts of debauchery and irrational exploitation of his own people are modified only by the intervention of the West. This convention, drawing on the rich culture of racism and the actual behaviour of certain African leaders, notably Siad Barre of Somalia and Mobutu Sese Seko of the former Zaire, has confirmed to the West once more the nobility of its civilising mission in the 'Dark Continent'. The soldiers, settlers and missionaries of the Edwardian era have been replaced by the diplomats, journalists and aid workers whose actions and conclusions are routinely based on their preconceived ideas of Africa and African leaders. Indeed, it could be argued that the West's relationship with Africa today is a greater triumph of image over reality than at any time this century; America's tragi-comic invasion of Somalia in 1992 is a case in point. So the morality of the New World Order, the belief in the rightness of the West, is reinforced by a cultural heritage of the white man as the fount of all wisdom, justice and knowledge – white man as godlike figures who left behind a veritable Garden of Eden at independence which Africans turned rotten to the core once they had gained control.

Caught in the middle of this myth-based analysis was President Moi, whose stolid demeanour, awkward speech and, it was assumed, ruthless behaviour perfectly fitted him to play the 'Big Man' of the West's cliché. As this scenario was played out, far from being a gunslinger, Smith Hempstone was seen as the virtuous sheriff who had vowed to rid a frightened town of a gang of desperadoes led by Daniel arap Moi. In this modern-day morality play, the Western diplomats, journalists and aid workers unwittingly supported and complemented this thesis of good and evil, democracy versus authoritarianism, corruption versus duty. It was a spectacle which found its most vivid expression in the mid-1990s with the conflict between a black man, President Moi, and a white man, Dr Richard Leakey, the former Director of the Kenya Wildlife Service.

The ultimate irony of this morality play is that the reputation and image of Moi and his country have suffered so considerably precisely because there is in Kenya a vibrant and vocal civic society and articulate intelligentsia, many of whom have been educated in Europe and America. As a result, the white man's analysis of life in Kenya has been encouraged because it struck a domestic resonance, an echo which is not found in Uganda, Somalia and other African countries. Thus the very diversity and relative freedom enjoyed by Kenyans was the key which persuaded the West to try to unlock the door of democracy. It was the confluence of internal dissent (in which self-interest often masquerades as high idealism) with the consequences of the New World Order which threatened to overwhelm and destroy the Moi government, in the process sending the country lurching to the brink of a wholly unnecessary civil war.

What was so galling for the President, a man sensitive to public criticism from the West, was what he considered to be the hypocrisy and unfairness of the treatment meted out both to himself and to his country by the West. It substantially contributed to his growing disillusion with the West and all its works, and his retreat into the rhetoric of African nationalism; 'The dignity of Kenya is not for sale,' he says defiantly.

At the same time, Moi was angered by the way in which the West automatically assumed that those in Kenya who were against his government occupied, as of right, the moral and political high ground. A favourite saying of his is that you can never know what is going on in an African's mind – in other words, that while an African may do one thing in public, he will do quite another in private. Thus the pro-democracy movement that sprang up in Kenya after the fall of the Berlin Wall was as much a vehicle for Kikuyu dissatisfaction and dissent as it was concerned with constitutional reform, while those who sought political asylum abroad were often criminals posing as fleeing freedom fighters. At one point the frustration felt by Moi, and by many other Kenyans, spilled over into a number of heavy-handed decisions, notably the severing of diplomatic relations with Norway for its defence of Kenyan dissidents, the expulsion of journalist Christopher Walker of *The Times*, and even attacks on the uneven reporting of his beloved BBC. When Margaret Thatcher visited the country in 1988 Moi deliberately decided that he would not complain about his country's treatment or moan about its human-rights image. Instead, he simply let the people speak for him and for Kenya, taking her on a gruelling tour of the Rift Valley. At one point Mrs Thatcher, looking at a sea of cheering, smiling faces, turned to her husband Denis and observed: 'There is no way this country is a dictatorship.'

Ultimately, the 'Big Man' theory of African politics, in which the national leader behaves as an absolute monarch with total control over every facet of his nation's activities, is deceptive in the context of Moi's presidency. As with his crusade against corruption, land-grabbing, KANU in-fighting, smuggling and famine relief, throughout his presidency Moi has been a 'political fireman', intervening only as a last resort to damp down problems ignited by others, be they friend or foe. Moreover, much of his rule has been spent grappling with a political, intellectual and business elite, mainly Kikuyu, whose resentment of the 'passing cloud' has manifested itself in mute civil disobedience, anything from ignoring his orders to sabotaging his policies. It is this tribal undertone in Kenyan society which Western observers ignored during the months preceding the introduction of multi-party politics.

Ironically, the debate about multi-partyism began in earnest as Moi and Bob Ouko, were preparing for the ill-fated visit to Washington in January 1990. Various Kenyan churchmen, notably the Reverend Timothy Njoya, as well as lawyers, discussed the wave of change sweeping both Africa and the Eastern Bloc, arguing that the tide of history was turning in favour of wider democracy in their country. It was a debate Moi entered early on, nailing his own colours to the mast: as far as he was concerned multi-partyism was unsuitable for Africa 'at the moment'. He feared that it would breed tribal alliances in which political parties would express tribal sentiments rather than genuine public opinion. 'Starting multi-party systems will definitely trigger chaotic situations which would be difficult to reverse,' he said during talks with the President of the International Red Cross. Yet while he emphasised the issue of tribalism, he did not rule out the introduction of multi-party politics at some unspecified date in the future. Opening the 1990 parliamentary session, he said in his speech:

Kenyans are not opposed to the multi-party system because of ideological reasons or design by those in leadership to impose their will on the people. What we have said is that until our society has become cohesive enough so that tribalism is of no significance in the economic and political activities of the nation, the strategy of a mass based, democratic and accountable one-party system is best.

Kenyan history seemed to be on his side, as tribes who formed opposition groups have effectively cut their regions off from government largesse. In the first year of the Kenyatta government regions such as the Coast and Rift Valley which supported the opposition KADU party were left in the economic wilderness. It was a similar story with Paul Ngei's Kamba opposition party, the African People's Party, and with the Luo-based Kenya People's Union (KPU), started by Oginga Odinga in 1966; indeed, the Luo tribe were to remain out in the political cold until Moi took power twelve years later.

Furthermore, even as Moi was outlining his thoughts on multi-partyism in the early 1990s, he was also speaking against a rising tide of tribal unrest, particularly in Central Province. As has been said, the Kikuyu elite had never accepted the man they derided as 'the Tugen herdsboy' and as Moi consolidated his position, there was much grumbling in Central Province at what some saw as an intolerable decline of the tribe's influence in business and government.

The ousting of Kikuyu chauvinists such as Mbiyu Koinange was followed by the political demise of Charles Njonjo, and then that of the Nyeri leader, the former Vice-President Mwai Kibaki. His political fortunes fell inexorably from 1986 with the collapse of a large number of Kikuyu-dominated banks and other financial institutions which he had initiated. At the same time his behaviour as Vice-President, more often than not failing to sing in tune with the President, signalled his lukewarm support for the Moi government. His replacement by a fellow Kikuyu, Josephat Karanja, who had been Kenya's first High Commissioner in London, a political greenhorn with a diffused urban constituency, did little to quell Kikuyu fears that the chances of there being another President from the House of Mumbi were diminishing.

This simmering resentment was further fuelled by Moi's redistributive policies in the mid-1980s. The revolutionary District Focus Scheme, the introduction of the '85-per-cent quota system' in education and to give all tribes a fair chance of attaining secondary schooling, a code of practice ensuring government jobs and services like health and housing were spread around the tribal regions confirmed Central Province in its 'laager mentality', a belief that Moi's tribe, the Kalenjin, were winning out at the expense of the Kikuyu. While the statistics did not bear out this contention – the Kikuyu still dominated the government, the parastatals, the civil service and the banks – Kikuyu nationalism enjoyed a vigorous resurgence.

The disaffection which bubbled to the surface was mirrored by developments underground. It did not escape anyone's notice that most people convicted of belonging to Mwakenya, an illegal militant movement founded in the mid-1980s and pledged to the violent overthrow of the Moi government, were from Central Province, as also were the most prominent and vocal political exiles. The widespread oathing within the Kikuyu-dominated Mwakenya, its links with the 1982 coup and the Change the Constitution movement, the distribution of seditious literature and a campaign of civil disturbance culminating in the derailment of a train in Nyanza Province led many to believe that the dissident group was in the van of a fresh attempt to oust the President. Just as worrying, however, was the fact that, from 1986 onwards, as relations with Museveni's Uganda rapidly deteriorated, the neighbouring president began to provide safe passage for Kenyan agitators, some of whom were sent to Libya – no friend of capitalist Kenya – for terrorist training. Indeed, a number of Libyan diplomats were expelled from Nairobi in April 1987 for spying. Moi, well aware of the failure of his security forces to prevent the 1982 coup attempt in spite of fore-warning, was determined that the actions of Mwakenya would not lead to bloodshed and loss.

The vigorous police crackdown on Mwakenya, which seemed justified when the former Nakuru MP Koigi wa Wamwere, leader of the self-styled Kenya Patriotic Front, was arrested in Nairobi in 1990 with a cache of arms and grenades, brought in its train a series of complaints about human rights abuses. Allegations that dissident suspects in custody had been tortured, and the arrests of lawyers associated with Mwakenya, raised concerns among Western diplomats and human-rights groups. It would be disingenuous to pretend that the Kenyan police, whose history is that of a paramilitary colonial force with no tradition of public service, are innocent of random brutality or routine harassment. There have been numerous well-documented cases of beatings, and sometimes deaths, in police custody. All too often the Kenyan police use the violent Route One method of extracting information rather than adopting the more painstaking approach of interviewing suspects and witnesses and collecting evidence. Lack of time, resources and training, as well as the poor quality of some recruits, are much to blame; so too is a culture of insularity within the police in which the public are viewed as enemies rather than citizens to be protected.

In the wake of the Mwakenya affair he took a robust attitude towards the police in an attempt to end the circumstances which were beginning to give Kenya a bad name abroad. His release of all but three detainees in early 1988, the prosecution of a number of police officers and the transfer and retirement of others signalled his intention to return to the detention-free atmosphere of the first four years of his presidency, and to attempt to break down the cultural suspicion between the people and the police force, which all too often acted as a law unto itself.

While international observers focused on human-rights issues, politically astute Kenyans saw the developing situation simply as history repeating itself. Tribalism was in the air. The upsurge of Kikuyu nationalism – that combina-tion of militant radicalism and conservative chauvinism which can be traced back through the tangle of the years to the Mau Mau movement, the loyalist Kikuyu elite during the Emergency, the early days of KANU and the Change the Constitution movement – dominated the domestic scene. At the same time, the radical strand, epitomised by the history of the Odinga family, of Luo nationalism, which had been diffused following the demise of the KPU, now enjoyed a resurgence following the collapse of European Communism and the renewed interest of the West in political reform in developing countries.

At the same time, this worrying revival of Kikuyu and Luo tribal nationalism ignited memories among the smaller tribes of the brand of ethnic domination which had followed Independence. Leaders of the Maasai, the Kalenjin and the Coast tribes talked of a return to majimboism as a political counterweight to the arguments for multi-partyism. The so-called KANU 'hawks', men like Nicholas Biwott, the Coast leader Shariff Nassir and the Maasai leader William ole Ntimama, organised meetings in the Rift Valley, taking the political scene by storm with a series of aggressive measures for dealing with critics of the government, such as banning advocates of multi-partyism from entering their regions. At a meeting in Narok attended by thirteen Cabinet ministers, including the Vice-President, Professor George Saitoti, there were calls for Moi to be made President for life, a resolution the President himself quickly rejected. Kikuyu chauvinism, Luo radicalism, small-tribe insularity; the faces might have changed, but the issues were remarkably similar to those aired during the jostling for power in the run-up to Independence.

As in the early 1960s, tribalism was the potent sub-text that lay behind the calls for multi-partyism, majimboism and other constitutional changes. This time, however, the international dimension was rather different. Whereas in 1961 an anxious colonial government had done everything in its power to hobble the dominant Kikuyu tribe, by developing the majimbo constitution, this time the prerogatives of the New World Order placed a premium on those who ostensibly favoured multi-partyism, no matter what Kenya's earlier history. They seemed to ignore the tribal dimension underlying the pro-democracy movement where the two-fingered salute for multi-partyism was both a signal of Kikuyu tribal loyalties as well as concern about widening democracy.

In the spring of 1990, while Kenyans still mourned the murdered Robert Ouko, the river of domestic ethnicity met the tributary of the New World Order when two conservative Kikuyu politicians from Murang'a, Charles Rubia and Ken Matiba, became the first senior national figures to voice their support for a multi-party state. Ignored by the international media, but central to their case, were demands which echoed Kikuyu disenchantment with the government, notably an end to tribal favouritism in the public service, the failure to promote experienced personnel, invariably Kikuyu, in parastatals, and reform of the 8.4.4 education system. It was no coincidence that their press conference in May 1990 at the New Stanley Hotel in Nairobi came just a week after the United States Ambassador, Smith Hempstone, had chosen to hold forth on the multi-party debate, his convictions reflecting in part the view of the US Congress, which now linked the continuance of aid to democratic reforms. At the same time, the fact that Rubia and Matiba had been at the KANU conference in 1982 which had endorsed the creation of a one-party state did not go unnoticed.

While Moi drummed up support for political reform within the existing framework of the one-party state, Matiba and Rubia moved to broaden the tribal base of their campaign, enlisting the support of Oginga Odinga in a series of closed-door meetings. The political temperature reached boiling point in July 1990 when the two Kikuyu politicians applied for a licence to convene a rally at Kamukunji in Nairobi. Not only did the government refuse their request, but Rubia, Matiba and Raila Odinga were placed in detention a few days before the date of the intended rally, 7 July. On that fateful day, known as 'Saba Saba' ('Seven Seven'), bloody riots broke out in Nairobi and Central Province, protesters flashing the two-finger salute in support of multi-partyism.

The Saba Saba day riots and the subsequent crackdown made international headlines, *The Times* of London attacking Moi's 'savagery towards dissent' and describing the conciliatory attitude of the British government towards him as a 'disgrace'. In Nairobi the American Embassy publicly protested about the bloodshed, and gave sanctuary to the dissident lawyer Gibson Kamau Kuria. While the West portrayed the debate as pro-democracy versus an authoritarian regime, domestically the crucial discussion revolved around the need to reform rather than replace the one-party state.

The impact of queue-voting, the arbitrary and unfair workings of the KANU disciplinary committee, the violent behaviour of KANU youth wingers, and the fact that even KANU supporters had little outlet for dissent were the most pressing grievances. In response, Moi set up a commission, headed by his Vice-President George Saitoti, with a mandate to tour the country, test public opinion and make recommendations to a party conference. His findings were that the people wanted reform of the discredited queue-voting system and other constitutional failings, but wished to retain the one-party state. It was at this conference, held at Kasarani in December 1990, that Moi demonstrated his political courage and his flexibility by going against the wishes of the vast majority of the party delegates to suggest that KANU scrap the controversial queue-voting system, drop expulsion as a means of maintaining party discipline, and abolish the unpopular '70-per-cent rule', under which those candidates who secured 70 per cent of the vote at the nomination stage were automatically elected to Parliament. He acknowledged: 'The party and this country stand to gain nothing, indeed we shall all lose a great deal, by any attempt to subvert the wishes of the people.'

The fact that the President was in a tiny minority of KANU moderates who originally endorsed the Saitoti proposals demonstrated the difficulty of trying to hold the ring in Kenyan politics. Whilst he had to contend with the KANU hawks who wanted to maintain the status quo, he also had to recognise the changed political realities of the New World Order. With pressure from Western governments – particularly America, which cut off military aid following the Saba Saba Day riots – intensifying; with other African countries, including Niger, Congo and Mali, succumbing to calls for multi-partyism; and with growing clamour at home, especially among the church and legal profession, for a multi-party polity, Moi caught between a rock and a hard place. The result was that the KANU reforms, instituted at the Kasarani conference, not only failed to stem the tide of protest, they also alienated many hard-line KANU loyalists.

As 1991 dawned, it seemed that the KANU reforms had done little to lower the political temperature. Oginga Odinga announced the formation of the National Democratic Party, later teaming up with other politicians, including the former legislators Martin Shikuku and Masinde Muliro, to launch the Forum for the Restoration of Democracy (FORD). Their organisation gained greater momentum following the release from detention of Rubia, Matiba and Raila Odinga in the spring of 1991. Matiba, who suffered a stroke whilst in jail, flew to London for treatment.

Their efforts were complemented by those of radical churchmen, lawyers, non-government organisations (NGOs) and Western diplomats, so that the political scene became reminiscent of Poland during the days of Solidarity. Overseas politicians would make a courtesy call on the government, only to go on to see dissident leaders for substantive discussions. The result invariably favoured the dissidents, as Richard Dowden, a Western newspaper correspondent, noted: 'In contrast to Mr Moi, the multi-party movement has maintained dignified and sophisticated language and has learnt the new phrases of Western aid donors.' At the same time, the diplomatic community, led by the American Ambassador, encouraged opposition activists, hosting functions in their honour and even, it was suspected, helping to fund their movement through the work of non-government organisations.

The President found the tactic of foreign governments deliberately giving aid and succour to a tribally based opposition as destabilising as it was insulting. In a pointed speech at the opening of the first East Africa-America Trade Expo, he made clear that Kenya had sovereignty over her own destiny and would not be dictated to by foreigners.

> Today we hear voices urging us to follow other paths. We are being asked to risk that which we have so painstakingly built in order to live up to some generalised prescriptions of political behaviour. And we are threatened that unless we do as we are told, we risk losing friends and their financial aid. Let me say emphatically that we do not fear taking risks on behalf of our people . . . We are not tied to the past. We are a pragmatic people.

Behind the scenes, the personal antipathy between the President and the US Ambassador did little to soothe the situation. During one stormy meeting at State House Hempstone bellowed at the President: 'You can't run this country like your personal fiefdom,' to which Moi shouted back: 'This is not your country, Mr Ambassador.' Hempstone's rude and insensitive behaviour, as well as his public posturing, exasperated Moi, a man not known for displays of temper, beyond endurance. Many in Moi's circle contend that if the ambassador had played less to the gallery and behaved more like a conventional diplomat he would have achieved his aims more effectively, and without souring the relationship between the two governments. As Bethwell Kiplagat, who in fact enjoyed good relations with Hempstone, recalls: 'I often told him that you can say what you like inside State House but outside be more circumspect.'

When FORD staged an opposition motorcade in November 1991 – a procession which, almost inevitably, started from the American Embassy – the subsequent arrest of a number of leaders resulted in further domestic and international furore. The German government issued a strong public protest, Denmark threatened to cut off all aid, and even the British government said that it was 'very concerned to hear of the arrests'. At the same time, the British Foreign Secretary, Douglas Hurd, in marked contrast to other diplomats, made it clear that Britain wanted to talk *to* Kenya, not *at* her. Domestically, however, KANU doves were beginning to recognise the changed political realities. The former Vice-President Josephat Karanja, John Keen, Peter Aringo, and the former

Cabinet Secretary, Simeon Nyachae, were among the leading voices who now began to admit that the ruling party should acknowledge the existence of a formidable opposition to the *de jure* one-party state in the country.

The KANU reforms, the setting-up of a commission to investigate the 8.4.4 education system, the restoration of the tenure of the judiciary, moves to privatise parastatals, a vigorous Cabinet reshuffle which saw the demise of a number of KANU hawks, as well as a tough new Prevention of Corruption Act all seemed to be too little, too late. By the end of 1991, it looked as though the country's political fabric was unravelling. With tribal clashes in Western Kenya, the aborted commission of inquiry into Bob Ouko's murder, international concern about democracy and corruption, the freezing of aid by the donor communities, KANU chauvinism and a raucous opposition – in the face of all this, Moi's belief in orderly and disciplined political progress seemed to be in tatters. 'We must plan our future on our own, and implement the necessary changes in a manner that does not disrupt the tempo and direction of our national development,' he said at a rally on Moi Day in October 1991, words that were to sound distinctly hollow just a few weeks later.

With the tumult raging all around, the President quietly reviewed the seething domestic scene. Professor Philip Mbithi, who first joined him as Cabinet Secretary at the height of the storm in November 1991, recalls:

When I came into the government, I came into the middle of a whirlwind. The opposition was going full blast, the American Embassy were hiding people in the basement; that's when I started watching how Moi thinks. When there is a crisis, Moi remains very calm. He won't shout, he won't cut you short, he will listen. Sometimes we dread it when things are quiet, because he becomes very difficult. In a crisis, he's very courageous – he'll listen and make decisions. When President Moi is thinking about something, we usually sit down and drink tea and talk. In fact what he is really doing is thinking and he was thinking about changing the constitution.

The President, who is of a generation of Africans who prefer to watch situations brew before making final decisions, made up his mind during a visit up-country that same November. As he toured Kakamega District he watched, as he had hundreds of times before, a group of schoolchildren singing and dancing. Yet while he observed this colourful scene his mind was on other topics. At the end of the day he telephoned Mbithi and asked him to organise a special KANU delegates' conference to discuss the abolition of Clause 2A of the constitution, the legal paragraph which made Kenya a *de jure* one-party state. Moi told his Cabinet Secretary: 'These children, I cannot guarantee their future. I cannot guarantee their lives away from fire and fighting. We have to do something.'

When the conference gathered at Kasarani in December 1991, it seemed that it was to be a rerun of the previous year. The overwhelming majority of delegates were against reform, many speakers advancing the now familiar argument that the country was not ready for political pluralism, and would be torn apart by tribal animosities if other parties were permitted. The President, whose priority was "the unity of Kenyans", went to the conference with an open mind, prepared to listen to all the arguments. At the executive meeting before the conference proper, Moi, as is his practice, remained silent, listening as the other office-holders gave their views. The former Vice-President, Mwai Kibaki, was particularly persuasive, arguing that to end the one-party state would be to kill the country, akin to cutting a fig tree with a razor blade.

At the executive meeting, as the tension mounted, the President, in his summing-up, appealed to his fellow leaders 'like my sons' to recognise the changed political realities which now existed in Kenya, and accordingly to alter the constitution to allow other national parties to compete with KANU. It was an argument he amplified when he spoke to the 3,600 delegates at the conference, telling them: 'It is prudent that we allow those in our country who want to form their own parties to do so. But these parties must not be tribally based, but must be national.' At the same time, he emphasised that KANU was committed to peaceful and fair elections. The move towards multi-partyism was irreversible, he said, but 'human life must be spared. We must avoid personal differences and other self-serving actions which might cause chaos.'

It was, by any standards, a gamble, a high-risk strategy in the face of a unified and vociferous opposition basking in the approval of the West and composed almost exclusively of members of the two most vigorous and powerful tribes, the Luo and Kikuyu. Even Moi's supporters viewed his volte-face as tantamount to writing a political suicide note on behalf of KANU. For the last eighteen months, however, the KANU government had been on the back foot, the Ouko affair, the Gulf War and the Western donors having damaged its credibility both morally and economically. In one move Moi had recaptured the political initiative, setting the agenda for the future political make-up of Kenya.

There was, though, little joy in this victory. He felt indignation and bewilderment at his treatment at the hands of the West – 'I have always felt that I was fighting for democracy,' he told colleagues. 'Why have the West abandoned us now?' – coupled with a sense of gloom, even of foreboding, about the future of the nation. To President Moi and his supporters, it seemed that Kenya was about to be crucified upon the high altar of the New World Order.

Chapter fourteen

Stop This Nonsense

President Moi's worst nightmare seemed to have come true. 'Stop this nonsense, get people over there to stop this nonsense now,' he shouted down the telephone from his hotel suite in Vienna. Moi was furious, angrier than his doctor, the American David Silverstein, had ever seen him in all the years he had known him. The cause of his wrath was news, that autumn of 1991, that clashes between tribes living in the Rift Valley, notably the Kalenjin, Kikuyu, Luhya and

Luo, were sweeping the region, leaving scores dead and injured and thousands homeless. As he barked orders to officials at State House, Nairobi, Moi could see all he had worked for during his entire political life unravelling before his eyes. From his days in the Legislative Council, when he had arbitrated on potentially violent disputes between antagonistic tribes, through his time as Vice-President, during which he had provoked the ire of fellow Kalenjin by facilitating the influx of Kikuyu into the Rift Valley, to his days as President, when he had brought the Luo back into the political fold, Moi has always maintained a steadfast vision of a homogeneous Kenya, a vision matched only by his dread of tribalism. 'I am a nationalist, not a tribalist,' he says, and virtually every speech he has made throughout his career is peppered with references to the need for unity, the need to work for Kenya.

As it happened, it was no accident that the clashes, which came and went like a vicious flash flood, coincided with the angry debate about multi-partyism. Just as the political uncertainties surrounding the Lancaster House talks during the 1960s heightened tribal tensions, so the angry rhetoric and inflammatory language of the new politics of opposition had served to draw people back to their tribal groupings. Moi's warnings, dismissed as political posturing, that Kenyan society was not cohesive enough for multi-party politics were coming true with a vengeance. The inter-tribal fighting polarised Kenyan society as never before, bringing the country to within an ace of civil war. Neighbour fought with neighbour, brother-in-law against brother-in-law. The violence left an indelible stain on the country, the government and the President. By the time the dust had settled, one pervasive and pernicious image remained – that Moi, as the Kalenjin leader, had ordered his warriors to clear the Kikuyu from the Rift Valley as a means of proving his thesis that multi-party politics were unworkable in Kenya. The phrase 'state-sponsored ethnic cleansing' was adopted as the shorthand explanation for the troubles by Western journalists and human-rights groups, eager to sell the Rift Valley story in the same context as the horrors perpetrated by the Serbs and Bosnians in the former Yugoslavia. It also became common currency to cite Moi's former minister, Nicholas Biwott, as controlling a private army of 3,000 Kalenjin warriors who, having been trained by the dreaded Romanian Securitate secret police, had been smuggled into Kikuyu areas in government lorries so as to spread panic, murder and mayhem.

Although this has now become the accepted image, was the reality so very different? Picking a way through the thickets and pitfalls of gossip, hearsay and innuendo is never easy in Kenya, a country which thrives on rumour and where too much is taken at face value. As Yusuf Haji, then the Rift Valley Provincial Commissioner, says: 'I have spoken to hundreds of people, elders, chiefs and victims, and I still don't know where the truth lies.' Yet even if that truth remains hidden, it is worth pruning away some of the creeping ivy of mis-conception in order to gain a clearer view, particularly of the role played by the President.

Ostensibly, the clashes began in October 1991 at Metetei farm in Nandi with a simple, if violent, land dispute which left one Kalenjin dead. The violence quickly spread to Uasin Gishu and Trans-Nzoia Districts. After a lull there was a flare-up in Sondu, where a number of Kalenjin traders were chased into a river by

Luo, and the fighting then swept through Molo, a Kikuyu stronghold and centre of opposition politics in the Rift Valley. It quickly became clear that there was a degree of political organisation and planning to some of the later conflicts. A common denominator was that the Kalenjin, either from the Nandi, Kipsigis or Elgeyo tribes, were involved in every dispute, leading to the inevitable conclusion that Moi's people were behind the clashes.

At the same time there were complaints that both the police and the local administration were showing partiality towards the Kalenjin, either by turning a blind eye to their violence or by actively assisting them. Opposition politicians argued that the seeds of violence had been sown shortly before the introduction of multi-partyism in December 1991, when senior KANU politicians in the Rift Valley had held a series of rallies throughout that autumn to promote majimboism. During these meetings, attended by such notables as Nicholas Biwott and William ole Ntimama, the Maasai leader and a senior KANU minister, it was argued that 'non-native' residents of Kenya's largest administrative province would be expelled to their home districts if political pluralism were adopted. The debate, which was both sterile and short-lived, was ended by President Moi, who chastised leaders for promoting tribal sentiments. None the less, not long afterwards the first of the violence erupted in the Rift Valley, the finger of suspicion pointing firmly at Kalenjin leaders.

So far, this is a sweet story of Kalenjin chauvinism, government connivance and KANU dirty politics, a tale of a desperate President clinging to power by fair means or foul. Yet, as any detective mounting an investigation would ask, what was the motive behind the violence, and who had most to gain from it? It was immediately clear that the chief beneficiary was the opposition Forum for the Restoration of Democracy party. The violence left the government discredited, the Kalenjin isolated from every other tribe, whilst those tribes wavering between KANU and the opposition, notably the Luhya, moved towards FORD. During the course of 1992, however, vicious infighting in the new opposition caused a major split in FORD, as the age-old tensions between Luo and Kikuyu were exposed. The Kikuyu leader Ken Matiba formed FORD-Asili (*asili* meaning 'original'), drawing support almost exclusively from Central Province, while Oginga Odinga's FORD-Kenya was centred on Luoland. The anti-KANU forces were further fragmented when Mwai Kibaki, Moi's first Vice-President, founded the Democratic Party, largely made up of Nyeri Kikuyu. As a result of the violence KANU leaders estimated that the party lost 200,000 Luhya voters, thousands of moderate Luo supporters, more than half the Kisii vote, while the clashes also ensured that the Kikuyu embraced opposition leaders like Ken Matiba who returned from London to a tumultuous welcome.

Since Moi and KANU had embarked on a high-risk strategy by abandoning the single-party system, their only hope lay in wooing tribes into KANU's orbit. In terms of the party's bid to regain political control, however, to have fomented the tribal clashes would have been the political tactics of the madhouse. This is a point made by G. G. Kariuki, a former Kikuyu-nominated MP, who argues:

> Could Moi have won the support of the Kalenjin, the Luo, the Luhya, Kisii and others by having the Kalenjin fight with each individual tribe? Who

of those tribes is then going to vote for him? The answer is no. The clashes were exploitation by cheap inexperienced politicians – and, speaking as a Kikuyu politician, I would say that Kikuyu have blood on their hands. The Kikuyu-Kalenjin war was being forced by jubilant opposition politicians.

Significantly, the longest-lasting and most brutal clashes took place in Molo, Londiani and Burnt Forest, where the Kikuyu predominated. As several seasoned Rift Valley politicians have observed, as a simple matter of common sense, if the Kalenjin had indeed orchestrated the violence they would have started by driving out other tribes in areas where they enjoyed a numerical superiority. This didn't happen. In Baringo, Moi's own constituency, for example, there was no violence even though Eldama Ravine, in the heart of the district, has a substantial Kikuyu population. Just as significantly, Moi's clan, the Tugen, remained aloof from the numerous tribal conflicts that swept through the Rift Valley before and after the December 1992 general election.

In Molo, the epicentre of the fighting, evidence from independent witnesses – that is to say, people from neither of the warring tribes – shows that the origins of the violence were by no means one-sided. The night before the first of the clashes, which started in the district in March 1992, Philip Leakey was driving through Molo on his way to Nairobi after attending a forestry conference. He remembers seeing truckloads of Kikuyu from outside the area being brought into the town centre. 'There were lots of gangs lounging around, it was obvious that the opposition were out to cause trouble. It was very tense,' he says. In fact, tension had been growing following the murder of a member of the Dorobo tribe, a forest-dwelling clan who mainly work as labourers for Kikuyu smallholders. They had come under pressure from their Kikuyu bosses to join the opposition parties. When they refused, one Dorobo was slashed to death with a panga (a broad bush knife; machete) – a favourite weapon of the Kikuyu. Another *mzungu*, Yorkshireman Arthur Garbutt, who has lived in Molo for thirty-eight years and has a Kikuyu wife, has another perspective.

> The violence came out of the blue. It took everyone by surprise. I lost eight good friends, two Kalenjin and six Kikuyu, people I've known since they were children. I remember giving two Kalenjin boys a lift in my pick-up. When we got near to Molo town, we were stopped by Kikuyus manning a roadblock. The two boys jumped out and started running. The Kikuyu chased them, one was murdered and one escaped. Then I was stopped at a second roadblock and told that I had to take Kikuyu warriors to the scene of the fight that was in the forest. The Kikuyu were armed with pangas and blowpipes, but the Kalenjin were in the forest, armed with bows and arrows. As they could shoot from a distance it meant that the Kikuyu sustained more casualties.

Certainly there is clear evidence that the reign of terror that swept through Molo was planned. Once again, as in the pre-Independence days of KANU and KADU, oathing among Kikuyu became widespread, supplies were stored in secret caches in readiness, and at least one Kikuyu activist was arrested for making petrol bombs and spears, and for sharpening pangas. Inevitably, versions vary as to whether these measures were taken in self-defence rather than for offence. What is indisputable is that the greatest number of refugees were Kikuyu, while Kalenjin predominated among those arrested and gaoled for crimes associated with the clashes. The truth is that although as many Kalenjin as Kikuyu were made homeless in the fighting, most went to their kith and kin in the Rift Valley rather than stay in church or government refuges, which meant that many Kalenjin victims were not officially registered as refugees. To escape the fighting, thousands of Kalenjin fled through the forest to camp in places like Bomet and Sambret, but their plight failed to make headlines. Again, the disparity in arrests between the tribes is partially explained by police and administration officers by cultural differences. The Kalenjin are said to be more guileless and open than their Kikuyu enemy, whose tradition of secrecy and oathing, a distinctly Kikuyu characteristic, makes them less amenable to exposing their compatriots to arrest.

Just as at ground level the picture is not black and white – Kalenjin aggressors, Kikuyu victims – so the notion of a top-level government conspiracy to oust the Kikuyu from the Rift Valley does not bear close examination. A constant complaint from victims of the fighting was the partiality of the police, media and local administration towards one tribe or other, usually the Kalenjin, something which is undoubtedly true. The West likes to think that the civil services and police forces of its own nations are even-handed. This is not so in Kenya, however, where a tribal colouring has always affected decision-making. This bias was exacerbated when the country adopted the multi-party system, so that today the nation's administration is polarised and politicised as never before. For example, a civil servant active in the opposition can sabotage government policy in a variety of subtle ways, using methods ranging from a go-slow through the ineffectual implementation of orders to actually engineering situations that will embarrass the administration. This debilitating disloyalty is an unhealthy spin-off from multi-partyism, a creeping tribalism that gnaws at the heart of government. By the same token, civil servants loyal to KANU are often accused of discriminating against opposition politicians and regions hostile to the government.

During the clashes, confusion, insubordination and attempts to shift the blame gripped elements of the police and the local administration. Both had been taken completely by surprise by the ferocity and extent of the fighting, utterly unprepared for, and wholly unable to deal with, the civil disturbances. Some police chiefs displayed a lack of nerve in trying to quell the riots, preferring to try to draw the army into restoring law and order. The disarray at the top was reflected on the ground when uniformed police officers refused to follow orders from district commissioners; indeed, on at least two occasions they threatened to shoot district commissioners rather than arrest or open fire on rioters.

At the same time, district commissioners, area chiefs and other functionaries let their own tribal sympathies cloud their judgement, often sending misleading or downright false reports to the Provincial Commissioner and thence to State House. This was a problem only resolved when the Provincial Commissioner, Yusuf Haaji, brought in 750 administration police and 15 district officers from other regions. From that time the clashes subsided, ceasing almost completely when Molo and other affected districts were declared 'closed' areas in September

1993 and visitors, many of whom were believed to have provoked the violence, were barred. Haji recalls: 'I felt that the existing administration officers were not doing their job. I was depending on information from these people, who were either Kalenjin or Kikuyu, and some were not impartial. There were two types, those who were anti the system, that is opposition sympathisers, and others who were partisan because their tribes were involved.'

In tandem with the paralysis and prejudice amongst grass-roots administrators and police, the emasculation of the Special Branch during the tenure of Hezekiah Oyugi as an internal security Permanent Secretary meant that, during this critical period, the government lacked accurate intelligence from its eyes and ears in the field. As one security chief concedes: 'Oyugi had turned the security forces into his own unit. Because of his actions the traditional work of the security forces was neglected. It meant that there was no planning and no monitoring of potential flashpoints by our personnel.' Since high-quality intelligence reports often provide the basis for government decisions, the lack of accurate information and realistic assessments, combined with the tribal bias displayed by a number of Rift Valley administrators and police, meant that State House was effectively working in the dark. Since that time, it has been a matter of policy to assign intelligence personnel to potential trouble spots in order to give an early warning of trouble.

Critically, the explosive situation in the Rift Valley was further inflamed in late 1992 by heightened political tensions in the run-up to the first multi-party elections. For local and provincial administrators and police trying to calm a volatile region – numerous peace meetings were convened between district officers and tribal elders – the violent political rhetoric served to drive tribal communities even further apart. Neither Opposition nor KANU politicians covered themselves in glory as peacemakers, most preferring to sit on their hands as the violence escalated. Indeed, the fears of KANU MPs that the Kalenjin could lose the presidency if KANU lost the elections infected every action. Several KANU MPs publicly exulted in the fact that the clashes proved their assertion that multi-partyism would breed tribalism.

As the months progressed, claim was met by counter-claim, each becoming more and more outlandish. FORD-Kenya chairman Oginga Odinga declared in mid-1992 that secret armies were training in the Maasai Mara, a gibe refuted by the government, which took journalists on a fact-finding mission to the populous tourist region. Others said that the Vice-President, George Saitoti, who has a home in Molo, was harbouring Kalenjin warriors on his *shamba*. On closer inspection they turned out to be refugees from the fighting. When these rumours and anonymous leaflets were tracked down they were often found to have originated with the Opposition. In Central Province, for instance, Kikuyu were urged to arm themselves after fifty Kikuyu children and ten teachers had allegedly been butchered by Kalenjin warriors. This baseless charge, sparked by a FORD-Asili activist, was just one of a series of examples served up in a dry but detailed government statement in May 1992 analysing the extent to which the opposition had provoked tribal unrest in various regions.

These charges of opposition collusion in the unrest served as a counterpoint to the oft-repeated assertion that a private army of Kalenjin warriors, backed by the government, was causing mayhem throughout the Rift Valley. This claim gained greater credence in September 1993 when a parliamentary committee chaired by Kennedy Kiliku published its report into the clashes. In the 238-page document, which was heavily criticised for relying on circumstantial or hearsay evidence, politicians, the police, the administration and the media were attacked. The centrepiece of the report, however, was the series of allegations surrounding Nicholas Biwott's private army of Kalenjin warriors. Central to this contention was the evidence given by one Valentine Kodipo, the star opposition witness, who claimed to have been a member of a Kalenjin warrior army since 1981; indeed, he went so far as to detail the scale of bounty Biwott and other leading Kalenjin were prepared to pay for killing, wounding and burning huts. How these 3,000 warriors stayed hidden, and were fed, watered and transported, on the open rolling prairie of the Maasai Mara which, as a game reserve, is a tourist attraction infested with more eager eyes and cameras than anywhere else in Kenya, remained a mystery, as did the activities of the army since 1981.

Two years later, in 1995, Kodipo resurfaced, this time in connection with the case of Julie Ward, the British girl found murdered in the Maasai Mara in 1988. He told the girl's father, John Ward – who has spent years, and a fortune with it, in seeking his daughter's killers – a lurid, almost pornographic tale of how she was killed, her murder allegedly aided and abetted by three powerful Kalenjin personalities, Nicholas Biwott, Jonathan Moi, the President's eldest son, and Noah arap Too, then the head of the CID. Ward, indefatigable in his search for justice, spent months and many millions of shillings checking out Kodipo's story. His conclusion is that the very believable convicted burglar, mugger and impersonator was a skilful con man. He says: 'Kodipo was a stooge put up by the Opposition to embarrass the government. I regard him less as a witness and more as a suspect for my daughter's death. I am certain that the guy is a phoney and may be mentally deranged.' Kodipo, who went into self-imposed exile, is now living in Denmark as a guest of the Danish government, where he was for a time an out-patient at a psychiatric clinic. Indeed, at the time of writing, a senior member of the Kenya Wildlife Service, Simon Makallah, faces trial for Julie's murder.

Unreliable witnesses, groundless or malicious accusations, media bias, administrative incompetence in the rural districts, police indiscipline or partiality – these were some of the ingredients that went into the violent cocktail of the tribal clashes. What then of the role of President Moi? According to popular myth, he was the master puppeteer of tribal conflict, the principal architect of 'state-sponsored ethnic cleansing' in which 800 people died, around 56,000 families lost their homes, and property worth an estimated Ksh 210 million was destroyed. Was his behaviour, both in private and in public, past and present, consistent with a Kalenjin chauvinist seizing the chance to rid the Rift Valley of the Kikuyu and other interlopers? In order to give a considered verdict it is necessary to look at his response to the crisis in three key areas: the judicial, the administrative and the political.

During his tenure as President, Moi has been criticised by the judiciary for advocating the resolution of disputes within KANU, regarding land and over affairs in state universities, without automatic recourse to the courts. His faith in the traditional methods of arbitration, by families, clans or councils of elders, is matched by a proper and punctilious distancing of his office from the functions of the judiciary. During the period of the tribal clashes, however, he made an exception, instructing his then Cabinet Secretary, Philip Mbithi, to protest that a large number of those arrested for involvement in the violence had been granted bail. In defence of the judiciary, the Chief Justice, Robin Hancox, pointed out that of the 258 prisoners remanded in custody only 10 had been given bail. This went at least some way towards placating the President, whose constant inquiry throughout this trying time was aimed at discovering who was behind the mayhem and killing. Without labouring the point, since the majority of those in custody were Kalenjin, Moi's actions hardly constituted favouritism towards his own people.

He took a similar hard line with the local administration, constantly urging them to crack down on the perpetrators of violence and, in September 1993, giving police the go-ahead to shoot those involved in riots or the burning of property. Aware of the favouritism shown by civil servants, he publicly warned administrators that they faced 'dire consequences' if they displayed bias in their handling of the situation. Yusuf Haji recalls:

> Most of the time he was telling us to stop the nonsense that was going on. Every time something happened he would be on the telephone, often very agitated. He would be asking why the fighting hadn't been stopped and what the police were doing about it, why people weren't being arrested and who was behind the trouble. He was very annoyed and wanted answers.

The decision to make Molo and other areas closed security zones was taken personally by the President as a final attempt to end the violence once and for all. The delay in implementing a number of these tough measures was in part the result of distorted reports or lack of good-quality intelligence received by State House. In concert with the hard line Moi took against agitators, of whatever tribe, were his persistent attempts to lower the political temperature and to reconcile warring factions. He showed a degree of leadership under fire which contrasted starkly with the utterances of politicians, both within his own party and the opposition, which merely heightened tensions. The President's visits, throughout the period of the clashes, to Molo, Sondu, Londiani and other affected districts were not without personal risk, but he refused to be deflected from his mission by nervous security chiefs. As his Cabinet Secretary at the time, Philip Mbithi, recalls: 'Imagine what the security men felt when he decided to see for himself what the trouble was about. At Sondu it was like a Western movie. The Luo were at the top of the hill, the Kalenjin at the bottom and Moi was in the middle. Eventually, they came down and he single-handedly cured the disease by talking to the elders.'

Besides visiting affected areas, Moi personally hosted a number of meetings to resolve the conflict; in August 1992 he received a 4,000-strong delegation from Molo with the aim of ending the hostilities, while in Bungoma District in September he brought together 200 elders, from all ethnic groups, who agreed in his presence to end the clashes. Again in May 1993, for example, he chaired a series of low-profile meetings of Kikuyu, Maasai and Kalenjin leaders at his Kabarak home to examine the origins of the conflict, as well as to work out a way of resettling those Kikuyus displaced by the fighting. These talks were a prelude to formal meetings that same year between Kalenjin and Kikuyu leaders, also aimed at resolving the clashes. As a sign of the souring of Kenyan politics, a number of politicians criticised the fact that the meetings had even taken place at all.

The period of the tribal clashes was a painful one for the President. As a man who saw himself as the leader not just of his own tribe but of all Kenyan clans and ethnic groupings, Moi was both deeply hurt and personally affected by the bloodshed and fighting. Not only was the violence a bitter confirmation of his fears about the introduction of multi-partyism, but at a stroke it washed away his efforts, over so many years, to build a unified society free of tribal conflicts. He says: "I don't know how a sane person could blame me when I am the one opposed to tribalism to this day. Others started the fighting and left me to heal the wounds. Sometimes I get very angry about it."

When he became President his 'One-Nation' vision found its fullest expression. A feature of his rule has been to embrace all tribes and clans within government, whether in the Cabinet, the higher echelons of the civil service, the diplomatic corps, the parastatal sector or the KANU executive. This principle of inclusion, of admitting minority tribes into the system of government, has come at a price. Often it has been sustained at the expense of quality, placing those of moderate abilities in positions of prominence for reasons simply of geographical or tribal significance. He has been prepared to sacrifice dynamism for the sake of unity, economic efficiency for political peace, short-term popularity for long-term stability. When he tours the countryside, speaking to *wananchi* at his frequent roadside stops, his message reinforces this vision. His talk is of conserving trees for future generations, of setting aside tribal differences for the sake of Kenya's children, of working for the nation rather than the tribe. Virtually his every public utterance hammers home these issues – often to the point of tedium.

Just as the loss of life in the Rift Valley offended his Christian sensibilities, so his sorrow and anger were tinged with disappointment at his own KANU supporters, indignation at opposition machinations to fuel the fighting, and downright exasperation with the developed world because, as ever, the West sided with anyone but the legitimate government of Kenya. He was critical of Kalenjin politicians who had failed to show any leadership or initiative in resolving the fighting, leaving him to pick up the pieces. It distressed him, and still does, that he had to defend the Kalenjin from accusations that they had masterminded the clashes, a justification that should have been made by Rift Valley leaders. As he says: 'It wasn't my job. It is my job to represent the whole of Kenya, not just one tribe.' (He demonstrated this impartiality yet again in 1994 when he chastised Kalenjin leaders for once again raising the majimbo debate). At the same time, he felt an impotent fury that the West bent over backwards to support the opposition, swallowing wholesale their argument that KANU had orchestrated the fighting. 'The pain was phenomenal on Mzee's part,' recalls Professor Mbithi. 'He knew what was going on but couldn't convince anyone, especially the [world's] press.'

In many respects, the clashes marked the end of Moi's long-time love affair with the West, and particularly with America and Britain. For most of his life he had admired these two countries for their mature political systems, their tolerance, their civilised and democratic way of life. Even when it was unfashionable for an African leader to do so, his support for the West and hostility towards Communism were unswerving. On issues ranging from the backing of the boycott of the 1980 Moscow Olympics to military pacts with Britain and the US, allowing their forces access to training facilities and to the Indian Ocean port of Mombasa, Moi had proved himself a steadfast ally, even at a time when much of Africa espoused socialist values. He believed, rather guilelessly, that the two Western nations would appreciate that here was a man who paid more than lip service to Western values; and at the same time believed that they would apply their notions of fair play and even-handedness in their judgement of Kenya's progress as a newly independent country. Once again, he had made the fatal mistake of trusting too much for too long.

Gradually it dawned on him that the West was primarily interested in Kenya for economic exploitation, and had little sympathy for her history or her problems, merely seeking to impose their own political and economic systems in a manner that was often insensitive, patronising and arrogant. Most of all, behind the diplomatic courtesies, Western politicians and journalists believed that Moi was a corrupt tyrant whose words and deeds were not to be trusted and whose departure would automatically benefit Kenya. At the same time, Moi did not improve his position by failing to grasp the need, in the modern age, to woo Western diplomats and journalists, as the Ugandan President, Yoweri Museveni, had done so successfully.

The tribal clashes underscored his growing disillusion with the West. Ignored when he warned that multi-party democracy could provoke tribal conflict, he was then damned for his predictions, his foresight taken as evidence of culpability in organising the violence. This classic example of political sophistry neatly let the West which had pushed so hard for the introduction of multi-party democracy off the hook of moral responsibility for the violence which followed in its train.

Of course, it might all have been a good deal worse. For the 1990s in Kenya have been characterised by two revolutions, political and economic, which few countries have ever managed without catastrophic social consequences. Multi-party democracy has been introduced in tandem with the liberalisation of the Kenyan economy – the opening up of markets, the abolition of tariffs and the privatisation of numerous parastatals. Under the liberal free-market imperatives of the New World Order, Kenya, in common with other African countries, has been forced to submit to an experiment in social engineering as risky as it is potentially damaging. While wider democratisation and economic liberalisation have dramatically changed the social landscape of Kenya, the pace of this change has been dictated as much by the World Bank, the IMF and the international donor community as by the country's sovereign government. At meetings in Paris with the donor nations, Kenyan ministers have protested, usually in vain, that the government was elected by people in their country, not in Paris.

It is worth noting, as Kenya grapples with this transition, that it is a rare country that has managed industrialisation and democratisation at the same time. Britain industrialised when she was ruled by an aristocratic oligarchy, America when she was a slave society, while, more recently, the much-lauded 'tiger economies' of the

Far East are mainly characterised by authoritarian or repressive regimes. The so-called 'Thatcher revolution' in Britain during the 1980s which liberalised the economy was only effected after considerable rioting and widespread social unrest, caused by the mass unemployment attendant upon that liberalisation.

Yet President Moi has attempted to struggle with this incredible social and economic upheaval in one of the poorest countries of the world. In addition to the day-to-day problems of running an impoverished nation, he faced the extra burden of 500,000 refugees fleeing from fighting in Somalia, a severe drought that has left huge swaths of the country teetering on the brink of starvation, the economically devastating effects of the Gulf War, rampant inflation, spiralling interest rates and, of probably the greatest long-term significance, a turbulent domestic political scene.

As Moi feared, the political alignment following the multi-party election of December 1992 was on tribal rather than ideological grounds. The split among the opposition parties enabled KANU to win with 36 per cent of the vote, a result which left Moi shorn of some of his most experienced ministers and MPs, many of whom lost their seats. FORD-Asili and FORD-Kenya were the two main opposition parties, with Kibaki's Democratic Party bringing up the rear. The first parliament of the multi-party era was a classic example of the phenomenon of ethnic politics, with party leaders attracting votes from their own tribes. Thus Oginga Odinga's FORD-Kenya won the vote of the Luo, Mwai Kibaki's Democratic Party the support of the Nyeri Kikuyu, while FORD-Asili, the party led by the Kikuyu businessman Ken Matiba, was composed of MPs from only three tribes, Kikuyu, Luhya and Kamba. The vote for KANU only served to illustrate the fact that its victory in the polls was due to a tacit alliance by the smaller tribes against the country's two largest, the Luo and Kikuyu. The days of KANU and KADU had returned once again, although the KANU of 1992 now resembled the tribal composition of KADU of 1961. As British journalist Richard Dowden observed: 'The tribal factor Moi predicted would dominate a multi-party democracy has indeed formed the basis of the new parties . . . ethnicity, region and tribe are the main issue in the election.' The Kenyan perspective was given by Hilary Ng'weno, the veteran editor of the *Weekly Review*, who commented: 'It is pointless if not dangerous to continue deluding ourselves that ours is not a nation driven primarily by crude ethnic political forces . . . Foreign donors should resist the temptation to play God in Kenya's politics.'

While the Western nations did not assume such an obviously omnipotent role, their presence in the theatrical gods was conspicuous as they watched the Kenyan political dramatis personae strut the stage. This presence dramatically coloured the behaviour and attitudes of Kenyan politicians, particularly those in the opposition. Emboldened by the support of many diplomats, particularly the American Ambassador, Smith Hempstone, the language and rhetoric of the first parliament of the multi-party era was more vituperative, while theatrical postures were struck not for domestic but for international consumption.

While the multi-party parliament has invigorated Moi politically, given him a challenge after the torpor of the last days of the one-party state, it has made Kenya much more difficult to govern at a critical and dangerous time in her history. In the short term the impact of multi-partyism, the influence of the West and

STOP THIS NONSENSE **185**

the political generation gap has been to destabilise the normal processes of government and weaken the sovereign authority of the nation's leader. The belief that there is a 'shadow government' based in Paris, London or Washington which monitors the activities of the KANU administration inevitably unsettles the political process. For example, Ken Matiba, the wealthy leader of FORD-Asili, spends a substantial six-figure (sterling) sum on the services of a British company, Westminster Strategy, to lobby MPs, newspaper editors and other influential people in Britain about the alleged iniquities of the KANU government. Similarly, Dr Richard Leakey, now a senior player in the Safina political party, uses his international authority as a conservationist to talk down Kenya and thus influence donor attitudes. His brother Philip, however, a former assistant minister, has little time for this approach, remarking: 'My brother is a moral traitor to this country. When you go to a foreign government to elicit support it's the equivalent to declaring war on your own country. This behaviour is unpatriotic and yet my brother and others like Ken Matiba expect the government to tolerate this disloyalty. Many people find it deeply offensive.'

Moi, endlessly exasperated by the way his country is portrayed abroad, is most concerned about the way the irresponsible lobbying of foreign powers by the opposition elite affects ordinary Kenyans. He says:

> Leaders must come to grips with the simple reality that their utterances and activities are hurting our economy, particularly the welfare of the ordinary Kenyan. Calls for aid cuts by donors have resulted in stalled development projects meant to benefit the ordinary *wananchi*, such as the construction of hospitals, roads, water supply and various women's group projects.

In the longer term, the effects of this strategy of bypassing the government of the day, for whatever reason, and appealing to the donor community will have a pernicious effect on Kenya's political future. During the 1990s the 'begging-bowl mentality', that culture of dependency which characterised many African governments during the Cold War, has been replaced by a kind of intellectual addiction to the West, an automatic deference to Western values and authority, particularly among opposition leaders. While this is still an effective strategy of protest, using international agencies as allies, this has developed into supine political genuflection, every public gesture and utterance made with half an eye towards pleasing or placating the international community rather than the domestic constituency. This 'creeping colonialism' inevitably delays the day when Kenyans will be able to work out specifically Kenyan solutions, based on their unique circumstances, culture and history, to the challenges facing the nation. More worryingly, there is now a whole generation of urban, Eurocentric elitist politicians, such as the Kikuyu lawyer Paul Muite, who seem to have little time for or understanding of Kenya's rural majority. Instead, they look to Europe and America for their political and cultural direction, rather than attempt to develop a sustainable African polity.

For Moi, whose formative years were lived out under colonial rule, this political neo-colonialism is demeaning, a tacit assumption that African values and culture are second-class. 'We threw out colonialism so that we can be independent,' he says. 'Why do you people want to become *wazungu* [white people]?' It was a theme he developed during a visit to Nandi in 1997: 'Some of the Opposition leaders are youths who cannot offer tangible leadership other than following foreigners like parrots without assessing the pros and cons to suit their motherland. Our destiny seems to be to dance to the tune we do not always know, without looking back to consider our own lives and economic development in the continent.'

This tendency to look to the West for approval has been accompanied by a harder edge to decent standards of political behaviour, typified by the rejection of any spirit of national reconciliation in favour of the politics of boycott, confrontation and ultimatum. The inability to distinguish between Moi's position as both leader of a political party and head of state is a manifestation of this clash between the older and younger generations, and one which has offended many Kenyans. Thus it is noticeable that Moi singled out Mwai Kibaki and Oginga Odinga as elder statesmen who never demeaned the office of President, in sharp contrast to the younger politicians. Indeed, before his death in January 1994, Odinga was criticised by young officials of his party for endorsing a policy of co-operation with the KANU government, rather than one of confrontation. Unmoved, the FORD-Kenya leader even made a passionate appeal to the donor community for it to resume aid, arguing that he was convinced that Moi believed in 'transparency' and accountability in public affairs. In the event, international aid to Kenya was resumed in 1993.

If the ending of consensus politics, the increased suspicion and hostility between tribes, the uncertainty and instability which inevitably accompanies the approach to multi-party elections and the politicisation of the civil service and other public institutions, are unwelcome and damaging consequences of the multi-party era, the vigour and rigour of political debate, as well as greater freedom of expression and tolerance of criticism have helped usher in a period where the executive can no longer hide behind bland statements mouthed by party hacks. The scrutiny of political decisions, particularly the focus on corruption among the elite and abuse of executive power, have been welcomed both domestically and internationally. It is open to question, for example, if the Goldenberg scandal, in which senior banking and government figures syphoned off billions of shillings in a bogus diamond-and-gold-export scam, would have been pursued so thoroughly in the one-party era.

The Goldenberg affair, the biggest financial scandal in Kenya's history, symbolised the cancer at the heart of government and confirmed the fears of donor nations that the country's elite were out of control, lining their pockets at the expense of the public. Founded in 1990 by Kamlesh Pattni, a young Kenyan Asian from a family of goldsmiths, Goldenberg International was ostensibly set up to handle gold and jewellery exports, along the way receiving billions of shillings from the Central Bank of Kenya by way of export compensation, because of exchange rate differences, and at preferential rates not enjoyed by other exporters. The scheme, similar to one operated in Burundi, was supposed to bring in much-needed foreign exchange at a time when the Kenyan economy was suffering because of the political uncertainty surrounding multi-partyism. Moi, who gave his approval for the government to become involved, saw the plan as an unexpected, indeed vital, windfall for the country. However, a few corrupt politicians, Central Bank executives and officials from other ministries saw the scheme as a way of getting very rich very quickly through bribes. 'The original concept was fantastic and perfectly legal,' argues Philip Leakey. 'There was no need to break the law, but a few people got greedy.' In the end the promised precious metal turned out to be fools' gold, for Goldenberg never undertook such exports, but received huge financial compensation of billions of shillings for its fictitious transactions. The breathtaking audacity of the scam, the alleged involvement of senior bank and political figures, seemed to prove everything the opposition and the donor countries had been saying about corruption at the heart of the Kenyan government. However the key issue is whether the scandal should be regarded as a one-off criminal conspiracy by well-placed crooks which could have happened anywhere or an affair that symbolises the deficient checks and balances at the centre of government. As far as the World Bank, the IMF and donor countries are concerned they err to the latter view, hence their continued insistence on 'transparency and good governance' as a condition for loans. The President's circle see Goldenberg more as a criminal aberration, and argue that Moi's vigour in pursuing wrongdoers through the courts shows his personal determination to curb corruption. As the President says: "The matter is now in court and there is nothing I want to hide. It is a criminal matter which unfortunately has been politicised."

Indeed a businessman who had the misfortune to be with the President on the morning that he found out about the scandal remembers his reaction vividly. 'I have never seen Mzee in such a foul mood,' he recalls. 'When I asked him what was wrong he handed me a letter that Wilfred Koinange, [then the Permanent Secretary at the Treasury] had written transferring money from the Central Bank, money that had already vanished. The money had been used to pay commissions.' In 1991 Moi discovered the extent of the fraud about three months after the money had gone missing – at the same time as his new Minister of Finance, the youthful Musalia Mudavadi (the son of his political mentor, Moses), was trying to make sense of the scandal. For his part Mudavadi, who had been in the post for only three months, told friends: 'I was mad, really angry about what was going on.'

Following a tense ninety-minute briefing about the extent of the scam, the President immediately removed Eric Kotut, the Governor of the Central Bank, the Treasury Permanent Secretary, Wilfred Koinange, and other executives. A number of those dismissed, including Eric Kotut and Koinange, faced criminal proceedings. He ordered his new Finance Minister to hand over all the relevant papers to the Auditor-General, and commanded the new Governor of the Central Bank, Micah Cheserem, to claw back the purloined funds, actions which included seizing the Pattni-owned five-star Grand Regency Hotel in downtown Nairobi. The young Governor, whose integrity and reforming zeal have subsequently earned him plaudits even from the donor community, recalls: 'The President told me to use every means to recover the cash and so far we have recovered a substantial sum. I must say he has given me every support.'

There was to be a similar reaction in December 1996 when the President learned of a massive tax swindle involving the import of cars at Mombasa. His Cabinet Secretary at the time, Philip Mbithi, recalls: 'He called me into his room at 7.20 in the morning and was untouchable he was so angry. He asked how far had it gone and was all the more upset because the man who then ran the port, Simon Mkalla, was one of his blue-eyed boys, a man he trusted.' Moi swiftly removed Mkalla and replaced him with Robert Breneissan, a former managing director of Portland Cement in Kenya. Mkalla's dismissal provoked riots among his Coast tribe, the Mijikenda, who felt their integrity was being insulted – a demonstration of the tribal sensitivity which is attached to high-profile public positions, and of the potential political consequences of removing powerful local barons. At the time of writing, Mkalla and nineteen other port and customs officials are facing trial for fraud.

The President, who has since set up an anti-corruption agency, has cracked down hard on abuse of public office and on favouritism – even when it involves his own family. When he discovered that his son, Major Philip Moi, was lobbying government officials over various business schemes in which he was involved, the President sent a memo to all government departments ordering them not to deal with him. For good measure, he gave his son a dressing down for abusing the position he owed to the family name. Yet in spite of the efforts of Moi, and others, corruption in high and low places remains a cancer eating at the core of government, threatening international investment, deterring foreign aid, undermining consumer confidence and demoralising the public. Moi himself is far from being blind to this, as he has said: 'No single government in the world can claim to be perfect in its operations. We too have had our share of management shortcomings such as corruption, theft, lack of teamwork, favouritism and laxity.'

For Moi, the personal consequences of the scandals which have afflicted his government have caused him to make a far-reaching reassessment of his political priorities. He has become more briskly businesslike and professional in his political relations, a transition demonstrated by the replacement of the Old Guard with well-educated younger technocrats in key positions, men like Micah Cheserem, Musalia Mudavadi, and the Education Minister, Stephen Musyoka. It is a question of balance, of preserving the best of the one-party system whilst working within the revised economic and political priorities of multi-partyism and the New World Order. Thus, while he has not shirked from adopting the prescriptions of donor countries in liberalising the economy, he has also at times dug his heels in when the economic pill has been too bitter to swallow.

Yet more often than not Moi has taken the medicine prescribed for his country, adopting reforms, or adapting them in order to cushion the blow for the nation's poor. He is now being praised in some quarters for the way in which he has managed to liberalise many aspects of the economy, slim down the civil service and sell off a number of parastatals. Describing Kenya's performance as 'spectacular', the managing director of the IMF, Michel Camdessus, commented at the end of a visit to the country in May 1996: 'I leave Kenya with a high degree of optimism. I see the reforms initiated by the government as a new start for Kenya.' It is a view echoed by Tony Groag who, as former managing director of Standard Chartered Bank in Kenya, has witnessed the painful reform process at first hand. He says: 'Given the existing socio-economic hardships, Moi has taken great practical risks in moving Kenya into the twenty-first century. In years to come his stance from 1993 to 1995 will be seen as the father of the industrial development of the country.'

In the end, however, the quality which characterised Moi's relations with the donor governments, the IMF and the World Bank has been trust – or rather, the absence of trust and respect. In the most difficult period of transition following the multi-party elections the Kenyan government was endlessly lectured by donor governments on the need for transparency and accountability, the President being treated like an errant schoolboy rather than partner. A witness to this, the former Foreign Minister, Stephen Kalonzo Musyoka, observed: 'He is deeply resentful of the way he is pushed into a corner and made to seem as though he is being brought to heel. He often says: 'I cannot fight the West but I have the right to be heard. I have the right to be treated with courtesy and respect because I am the leader of my people.'

Chapter fifteen

The President and the Showman

He received the call, as so many had before him, on the one o'clock *Voice of Kenya* news bulletin. The appointment of the famed anthropologist Dr Richard Leakey as the overall head of Kenya's crisis-torn wildlife service sent shock waves through the conservation world, helped save the elephant in Kenya and initiated a relationship between the President and the man described as the 'great showman' that illustrated the gulf between the West and Africa.

As a case study, the Leakey affair illustrated the ill-disguised racism and colonial arrogance of the international media as well as the issues of trust and betrayal which lie at the heart of Moi's public and private associations. The Leakeys are one of Kenya's best-known settler families; Richard's parents, Louis and Mary Leakey, achieving international acclaim for their work on the African origins of man. They were and are seen as honorary Kikuyu: Louis Leakey's study of the anthropology of the tribe remains a standard text; Kenyatta's friend, Mbiyu Koinange, was best man at their wedding; while the father of the former Attorney-General, Charles Njonjo, was their houseboy. Richard has continued their work, during the 1970s and 1980s combining his role as Director of Kenya's National Museums with important research into man's beginnings.

It was during his time as Museums Director that Richard Leakey first came into contact with Moi, when the former's political mentor, Njonjo, asked the President to intercede after Leakey, whose reputation for dynamism is matched only by his reputation for arrogance, had been accused of racism and discrimination by Luo academics, notably the renowned scholar Professor Bethuel Ogot. While the President saved Leakey's job, such is the antipathy felt towards him in some quarters that two former colleagues have seen fit to publish a book in Kenya entitled: *Richard Leakey: Master of Deceit.*

Leakey's next major contact with Moi came in 1984 when he, Dr David Western, now the Director of the Kenya Wildlife Service, (KWS) and the conservationist Daphne Sheldrick formed a deputation to lobby the President about the crisis facing the rhinoceros in Kenya, which had been poached almost to extinction. As a result, Moi agreed to establish a rhino reserve, which ultimately ensured that the population of these animals not only stabilised but multiplied. The crisis in the conservation of the nation's wildlife did not end with the saving of the rhino, however. By the late 1980s widespread poaching, much of it undertaken by corrupt wildlife officers or by heavily armed *shifta* gangs, the decimation of elephant herds, and rock-bottom morale amongst wildlife workers could no longer be ignored.

As a result of lobbying, the President sacked the then Wildlife Director and replaced him with the internationally respected conservationist Perez Olindo. His brief was to stop poaching, establish a code of practice for the wildlife service, and implement the international ban on the ivory trade. Crucially, the Department of Wildlife Conservation, which was then part of the Ministry of Tourism, was to be renamed the Kenya Wildlife Service (KWS) and made an independent parastatal with its own board of trustees. But while the policy, which was to prove extremely successful during the Leakey era, was now in place, what was absent was the political will to enact them. Without the proper funding or the support of his immediate political masters, Olindo found himself fighting a losing battle. When he sacked forty of the most corrupt wildlife officers he faced threats on his life, while his loyal officers, equipped with elderly bolt-action Lee-Enfield rifles, suffered heavy casualties when they took on gangs of poachers armed with modern automatic weapons. A series of political blunders, particularly his attempt to take over the Maasai Mara from the local council, combined with the shocking news that Somali poachers had killed the last five white rhinos in Kenya, effectively sealed Olindo's fate. In 1989 he was replaced.

The mess inside the wildlife service seemed to symbolise the atrophy inside the KANU government, its activities typified by policy drift and lethargy unless the President personally intervened. It was clear that the only way to save the elephant and other endangered species was to give Olindo's successor as head of the Wildlife Service direct access to the head of state. The policies were in place, and even the funding for a revamped service had been arranged thanks to successful lobbying of the World Bank and the donor community by Dr David Western (the present Director of KWS) and Perez Olindo. All that was needed was the right man.

In 1988 Dr Leakey made headlines over his blistering attack on the Kenyan Minister of Tourism, George Muhoho, for his inactivity in stamping out poaching. For his pains, Leakey was accused of having a 'cheeky white mentality'. It was therefore with a surprise bordering on astonishment that, a few months later in April 1989, Leakey heard over the radio that he had been appointed Director of the Department of Wildlife Conservation, later more famous as the Kenya Wildlife Service. In truth, his name had been in the frame for some time. His brother Philip, then an assistant minister, was one of several influential people, including the British High Commissioner, Sir John Johnson, who had asked the President to look favourably on the charismatic, if confrontational, palaeontologist.

The appointment was a leap of faith on the President's part. He had always been rather wary of Richard Leakey, seeing the National Museums Director as a troublemaker, and overly dictatorial in his manner. On more than one occasion he had considered sacking him because of his high-handed actions, particularly with regard to his staffing policies. At the same time, Richard was seen as an honorary Kikuyu, unlike his brothers Philip and Jonathan (a snake farmer in Baringo), who were looked on as honorary Kalenjin. What was more, Richard was also viewed as a protégé and supporter of Moi's rival, Charles Njonjo. In addition he had no tribal following so Moi's government, reeling from the clamour for change that preceded multi-partyism, gained no domestic political advantage by the appointment of a white man, whatever his international renown. Moi had much to lose and, apparently, little to gain by placing this rather volatile Njonjo supporter in charge of a high-profile parastatal with a multi-million dollar budget and a small independent armed force of game wardens to boot. As a further demonstration of his trust Moi gave Leakey access to the presidential hot line – a telephone system giving the select few direct contact with him – and, rather more important, his complete political support. As David Western observes: 'That direct access to Moi was critical to his success. Leakey could not have accomplished what he did in that short space of time without the direct backing of the President.'

Before he took up his appointment, his brother Philip gave Leakey a few words of advice culled from his years inside the KANU government. He recalls: 'I told him that he had to build up trust with the old man, not to do things without telling him as the President does not like surprises.' In the beginning the relationship was a roaring success. Leakey's ringing phrase, 'The only good poacher is a dead poacher,' reverberated around the world, the international community watching with approval as he revitalised the ranger service, improved its morale, training and weaponry, and virtually stopped poaching in its tracks. The zenith of this collaboration between the president and the palaeontologist came when Moi publicly set fire to millions of dollars' worth of ivory, rhino horn and animal skins in a dramatic ceremony in Nairobi National Park. It was a powerful gesture to the world that Kenya was serious about conservation and her commitment to the international ban on ivory sales. At a time when Moi was under fire, nationally and internationally, over the need for political reform and for alleged human-rights abuses, the success in conservation brought a welcome breathing space. In Moi's eyes, Leakey, in refreshing contrast to many KANU ministers, had proved himself to be a man who came to him with solutions rather than problems.

Difficulties were not long in coming, however, most of them stemming from Leakey's personality, his wildlife policies and his political judgement. The rot set in in the early 1990s when the Kenya Wildlife Service, having effectively stamped out poaching, changed direction, from being a quasi-military structure to a body which now had to consult with, and was answerable to, the community on matters of conservation. While the main priority had been to stop poaching, Leakey's autocratic personality was entirely suited to a centralised, command-driven organisation that rode roughshod over dissent. But for a man who brooked no opposition, he was ill at ease in the world of consultation and compromise, when he had to work hand in hand with county councillors, politicians and landowners to establish long-term programmes that recognised the requirements of local people alongside the conservation of wildlife, particularly elephants. It was not long before Leakey was accused of putting the needs of the elephant before those of people. As the elephant population rose, increasing numbers of Kenyans were killed by rogue animals, while complaints about crop damage rose dramatically. At one point elephants were causing nearly half the animal-related deaths in the country – a fact which was hidden from the international community and the president.

Leakey's proposals to fence in the national parks, at an estimated cost of 100 million US dollars, alarmed conservationists, while his fight with Maasai politicians, notably William ole Ntimama, to turn the Maasai Mara from a game reserve run by the local council into a national park administered by the KWS, proved his political limitations. Nor did his brusque personal style endear him to those he had to win and woo. During one heated exchange at Jomo Kenyatta airport, for example, Leakey threatened to go to the President and have him sack Ntimama. The Maasai leader told him to go ahead but, knowing that Leakey had the presidential ear, he truly believed that his days were numbered. In practice, however, Leakey proved to be less sure-footed as an ersatz politician than as a hunter of poachers. Rather than convincing the Maasai that it was in their best interests to allow the KWS some input in the running of the Maasai Mara, he went directly to the President and persuaded him to issue a directive allowing him to take control of Kenya's most famous wildlife reserve. Such was the howl of protest from the Maasai that within forty-eight hours Moi was forced to back down, an embarrassing volte-face which caused him to look rather more sceptically at the policies of his impetuous KWS Director.

His successor, David Western, observes that while Leakey gained tremendous international credibility for the way he ended poaching, he was in too much of a hurry to bother to win over the hearts and minds of local communities. Western says: 'You cannot do that by fear, it requires sitting down, especially with the Maasai, and spending a great deal of time debating and discussing to win trust and respect. He didn't want to do that and it was unreasonable of him to go to the President to get a directive. He misled the President in this respect.'

Emboldened by his initial success, notably against the poachers, Leakey began to consult the President less and less, and at the same time, according to his critics, failed to build a relationship of mutual respect between the KWS and the various local leaders and councils. Moi was shocked when he learned that during the 1992 elections Dr Leakey, a senior government official and a KANU life member, was helping to raise funds for Mwai Kibaki's Democratic Party, and encouraging his staff to stand as candidates for that party. As his brother Philip observes:

> That was the beginning of the end. He didn't endear himself to many people, tried to bully and browbeat and behaved like a spoilt brat. So when

he lost the support of the President his enemies ganged up on him. He showed no loyalty to the man who had supported him. That was inexcusable, especially as he was responsible for the wildlife of this country. If he was concerned about wildlife he should have been correct in the relations with people he worked for, the people who trusted him.

There was a further dramatic twist to the story. In 1993 as pressure on Leakey began to mount, a plane he was piloting crashed, resulting in such severe injury that both his legs had to be amputated. Conspiracy theorists now had a field day, claiming that the aircraft had been sabotaged by his political enemies. Indeed, a BBC TV documentary about Leakey, screened in Britain 1996, deliberately juxtaposed a comment from Ntimama to the effect that Leakey's career was like an exploding firework, alongside pictures of his crashed plane, so that it looked as though the Maasai leader was exulting in his opponent's misfortune. Even the television critic of *The Times* baulked at this biased editorialising.

Ironically, it was Moi's gesture of concern about Leakey's health that emphasised the growing gulf between them. By the 1990s Charles Njonjo had effected a personal, if not a political, reconciliation between himself and the President. They speak often on the telephone, and Moi occasionally visits Njonjo's Muthaiga home for afternoon tea. The former Attorney-General, who saw Leakey while he was recuperating in hospital, would often ring the President to ask him to remember Leakey in his evening prayers. When Moi visited the KWS Director in hospital he mentioned that he was praying for his recovery, to which Leakey, an avowed atheist, sharply replied: 'Don't bother.' It was an ungracious gesture, and one which offended the President deeply.

In spite of Leakey's misfortune, the political pressure on him mounted, with the result that in January 1994 he resigned in indignation, saying that the relentless attacks from ministers had become too much to bear. 'I have given the best part of my life serving my country and I recently gave my legs too. I have no wish to give my life at this stage and the stress and pain of being vilified by senior politicians and others is more than I think is good for my health,' he said in his resignation statement. It was a short-lived departure, however, for the President, recognising Leakey's undoubted talents, told him to 'stop his nonsense' and return to work – albeit with his wings clipped. He was told that in future he would have to refer all his decisions to the KWS board of trustees; must work more effectively with local communities in conservation work; and must give urgent attention to the recommendations of an investigation into the operations of the KWS, particularly with regard to weapons procurement. The one-man band now had to learn to play with others. Politically, the President was once again taking a huge gamble with Leakey; since Independence, no senior government official or minister had ever resigned, still less been reinstated.

Within a few months Leakey resigned again, on the principled grounds that there were dark forces within the Kenyan elite which were preventing him doing his job. Shortly afterwards he became one of the founder members, who include Koigi wa Wamwere and Paul Muite, of the political party Safina, whose platform is the fight against corruption, the restoration of the health and education systems, and the bringing of justice and freedom to all Kenyans. Dr Leakey presented himself as a man of modest ambition interested merely in helping the country he loves.

The reality, however, is rather different. In April 1995 Leakey arranged to meet the President at State House, Nairobi, for a morning consultation. As the head of state was pouring tea, Leakey delivered his ultimatum: he was considering forming his own political party, and would only desist from that course if he was made head of the civil service. As he listened to this rather transparent form of blackmail, Moi was flabbergasted. Nevertheless, while he may have been seething inside, as a true Kalenjin he did not let his anger show – after all, it was not the first time he had seen low ambition masquerading as high principle. Although the answer he gave Leakey was ambivalent, the archaeologist took this as a rebuttal and subsequently called a press conference to announce the formation of the new political party.

In actual fact, Leakey had been closer to the prize than he could have imagined. Moi had become increasingly disenchanted with his then Cabinet Secretary, Professor Philip Mbithi. A year later he saw the chance to move him, offering Mbithi, a Kamba leader, the post of Secretary-General of the newly revitalised Commission for East African Co-operation. When he refused, as Moi knew he would, it gave the President the opportunity to sack him without alienating the vital Kamba constituency. Such are the labyrinthine subtleties of tribal politics in Kenya, skills which Moi has in abundance. Indeed, several State House insiders believe that Leakey would have achieved his ambition if he had allowed the President the leeway to appoint him at a time of his own choosing. In short, his impatience was his downfall. As Leakey's brother Philip observes: 'Richard's problem is that he has never been able to read Moi as a person. He's grown up in the country but he has a very Western attitude. As a result, he's a misfit. Richard is for Richard and not for anyone else and that's no good for a leader.'

His younger brother's views were very much in the minority, however. Dr Leakey's decision to go into politics – and thus possibly become the country's first white President – sent the media, particularly the Western press, into paroxysms of pleasure. There were at least two laudatory prime-time TV documentaries about the wildlife warrior, and countless profiles in which he was universally portrayed as the principled saviour of a country mired in corruption with a dictatorial leader who had surrounded himself with politicians bankrupt of ideas but rich in bank balances.

As an example of racial stereotyping it is a classic. At no point in this welter of media coverage were the grievances of the Maasai, landowners or other communities affected by Leakey's high-handed policies seriously addressed, nor was Moi given any credit for the trust and support he had given the man whose image he had helped to create, and whose fame he had helped to establish. There was little or no attempt by the Western media to critically examine Dr Leakey's track record, such was the Gadarene rush to deify his life. Even diplomats at the British High Commission in Nairobi felt that Dr Leakey's career had been viewed by the media through 'rose-tinted' spectacles.

At the same time, however, the President did little to help his own cause. His anger at what he considered to be Leakey's treachery spilled over into abuse, amongst other things linking Leakey to the Italian Mafia and the Ku-Klux-Klan, and dubbing him an atheist and colonialist. Even when members of his Cabinet sent notes pleading with the President to calm down, Moi continued his assaults. Such was the concern of the settler community at the President's fury that they sent a delegation, led, ironically enough, by Leakey's brother Philip, to pledge their loyalty to Kenya. While domestically Moi was one of many voices attacking Leakey and Safina, internationally his complaints left him open to ridicule. Raila Odinga, who dismisses Leakey as a creation of the media and Safina as an elitist party composed of Kikuyu aristocrats, believes that Moi overreacted because he knew of Leakey's ability to influence the donor nations, the settler community and the British government.

These considerations were given scant regard when Leakey and several other Safina activists travelled to a Nakuru courthouse to visit a Safina founder member held in the cells there, the former KANU MP Koigi wa Wamwere, who was facing serious arms charges which, if he were convicted, carried a possible death sentence. As Leakey left the court he was set upon by a gang of thugs who whipped him and some bystanders, including the elderly father of a British journalist. In a second incident later the same day a British journalist, the redoubtable Louise Tonbridge, and several Kenyan correspondents were beaten outside Nakuru prison. The attacks, clearly planned by political activists, provoked international outrage, with the inevitable deluge of criticism pouring down on the President's head. It seemed clear that the violence of Moi's verbal assaults upon his one-time ally had spilled over into this shameful physical attack, condoned, even if it was not organised, by State House.

For his part, Moi believed that the attack was the work of over-zealous KANU youth wingers. In fact, it appears that Leakey and the others were victims of Nakuru's notoriously violent political scene. In terms of the realities of Kenyan politics Safina activists made the classic mistake of announcing their visit to Nakuru in advance, thus giving their adversaries time to organise a robust welcome committee. As one senior British diplomat observed: 'It seems that Safina were trying to engineer a confrontation, and they succeeded.'

At that time there were three main political factions in Nakuru, one of them led by a former opposition politician who had recently rejoined KANU, and who was therefore anxious to ingratiate himself with State House. Moreover, political hostility towards Leakey and his associates was at its height. While the international community expressed its revulsion at the beatings, it is worth noting that there was a degree of satisfaction amongst Kenyans, particularly the Kikuyu, who had suffered the brunt of the Emergency, at the spectacle of white people receiving a taste of the medicine they had dished out with impunity during the colonial era – echoes, perhaps of the President's observation about not knowing what is going on in the back of an African's mind.

The unpleasant incident reinforced internationally the sense that Kenya was, in the words of one Western commentator, 'a repellent neo-fascist regime'. So when Richard Leakey spoke about possible threats to his life he was taken at his word. 'The government might bump me off,' he said in more than one press interview. 'I might get beaten up or my car set on fire and be unable to get out, or be shot. But the threat of death in Kenya's opposition is real.'

The West lapped up this image of a repressive African government, failing to see that in Kenya things are never quite as they seem to Western eyes. In spite of his furious disagreement with Moi, Dr Leakey, now an MP for the Safina Party, is still an occasional visitor to State House, Nairobi, where he meets senior officials for informal discussions. Naturally, therefore, Moi's entourage were surprised when they read that he considered his life to be in danger. He was promptly offered a military bodyguard, and one, moreover, from any tribe of his choosing. Given Leakey's well-publicised concerns, State House functionaries were doubly bewildered when he declined the offer. However, when he was questioned further about the true nature of the death threats, he admitted that they had little basis in fact. As for his reasons for making these exaggerated claims, the great showman simply shrugged and said: 'That's politics, man.' His brother Philip remarks: 'If he was going to be killed it would be by the opposition in order to discredit the government. Moi has absolutely nothing to gain if anything happened to Richard.'

The Leakey affair is a further example of how, during the last decade President Moi has been driven to adopting postures that do little to burnish his images as the leader of his people and of the East African region. A litany of incidents: the murder of Bob Ouko, the tribal clashes, the Goldenberg scandal, Safina, disputes with the donor nations and with the opposition, have confirmed Moi, in the minds of many in Kenya and the West, as an intolerant and oppressive dictator.

As his relations with Leakey demonstrate, however, in Kenya appearances are deceptive. Behind the stern visage is a politician who has survived because of his flexibility, pragmatism and willingness to compromise and to take risks, a supple and subtle mind beneath the halting speech and the old-fashioned manner of the African leader.

The rebirth of regional co-operation, impelled by the necessities of realpolitik, coincides with Moi's estrangement from the West and his retreat into the rhetoric that argues that Africans should work towards a polity suitable to their own needs and history. His belief that Kenyans must solve their own problems, work out their own destiny in terms, specifically, of their special heritage, is balanced by a recognition that not all the ills that afflict Africa can be laid at the door of the continent's former colonial masters. 'Africans are to blame for the mess we are in now,' he says, referring explicitly to the fighting in Zaire during 1997. 'It is Africans themselves who are causing chaos under the cover of democracy.'

Moi's political philosophy is a question of balance; of acknowledging that Kenyan society is moving from a tribal to a Western-orientated culture, while recognising the need to preserve the best of the old and incorporate it into modern Kenya. At the same time, he believes that Kenyans should understand that Westminster and Washington do not have all the solutions to the nation's problems, and feels strongly that the West should respect his country's sovereignty and appreciate the efforts Kenya has made towards adjusting to a modern economic and political climate.

As Moi says: 'We have made mistakes, but we have done our best for our country. What more can you ask?'

Chapter sixteen

A Question of Succession

For days Nairobi was consumed by a subdued panic as gossip begat rumour, which in turn prompted dire supposition. Whispers whistled round the streets. Then the word made its way to the countryside: Moi had had a stroke, Moi was dying, Moi was dead. Who would take over? Children were taken out of school, workers left their offices early, townsfolk hurried back to their tribal regions, housewives stocked up with provisions, businessmen made hasty airline bookings. The country feared the worst when the sonorous phrase: 'President Daniel arap Moi today . . . ' was missing from the *Voice of Kenya* radio bulletins, and the President failed to appear at Sunday church service. Opposition politicians and clergy called for a government statement, while KANU ministers condemned the doom-laden chatter, saying that it would consume those who had created it. To no avail, for as the silence about the President's health became increasingly ominous, so Kenya was gripped by a palpable anxiety and fear reminiscent of the days following the death of Kenyatta and during the 1982 coup.

A surprise stroll in the spring sunshine stopped the speculation stone dead. President Moi was mobbed by relieved crowds as he jauntily walked through the streets of Nairobi, from his offices at Harambee House to the National Assembly, making light of the rumours about his health. 'Do I look like I'm dying,' he joked. The incident, in February 1995, illustrates much about modern Kenya, the President's style and personality, the country's political culture and, probably most important, the issue that hangs unspoken in the air, the question of the succession.

That a wildfire rumour can grip the nation so quickly indicates the uncertainty and nervousness that underlies the body politic, and graphically illustrates how precarious – and precious – is the stability of this recently independent nation. This fundamental ambivalence about the future of Kenya manifests itself in numerous ways, from the members of the Asian and settler communities and of the Kenyan elite having bank accounts outside the country, to the willingness of Kenyans, and others, to believe the most far-fetched nonsense masquerading as fact. There is a desire to believe the worst precisely because Kenyans always fear the worst. Only in Kenya, for example, could an Opposition leader like Ken Matiba get away with announcing, in a radio broadcast for the Voice of America, that Moi was dying of AIDS – and be believed.

The President's sudden 'disappearance' also gives an insight into his personality and political thinking. He was actually suffering from Achilles tendonitis in his left ankle, which made walking difficult. As a proud man, he refused to give in to this minor ailment and ignored his doctor's advice to rest. Finally his personal physician, David Silverstein, convinced him that a short period of inactivity was the only cure and fitted a small plastic cast to Moi's ankle to make sure he rested the damaged foot. The President, just as he dislikes wearing glasses in public, was unwilling to show the world that he was anything other than fit and virile, and therefore decided to stay out of the limelight while his ankle healed. As Dr Silverstein remarks: 'It's very much in keeping with the African idea of the whole man, the total man.'

At the same time, Moi used this period of convalesence to see how the political wind was blowing, to watch who would panic, who would come out for him, who against. As he said to aides: 'You don't strike when the first rat comes out of hole, he is there to look out for rest. You bide your time and when they all come out then you strike.' While Moi watched and waited, government spokesmen did little to quell speculation, a characteristic passivity that is both frustrating and infuriating for diplomats and journalists alike. A touch of personal vanity, a dash of political patience and guile, a trademark official silence; this was the heady brew which left Kenyans intoxicated with fearful hearsay, a sign that beneath the surface sophistication of Nairobi is a nation whose sense of togetherness is rather less than skin deep.

It reveals, too, the overarching place of the President in the nation's consciousness. He is at once a father figure and a symbol of unity, stability and continuity in a brittle, indeed fledgeling, political framework which edgily exists in a turbulent continent. The prospect of Moi's departure from the national stage graphically demonstrated to Kenyans the void that would be left, and the awesome task of filling his shoes.

That one 'disappearance' in February 1995 raised in many minds the question of succession, and of whether, as in 1978, that transition could be achieved smoothly and peacefully. *Après* Moi, *le déluge* is a fear close to the surface of Kenyan life. A flight of capital, a departure of the Asian community, the collapse of the tourist industry, civil disturbance, the crumbling of Kenya into anarchy; this is the nightmare scenario, discussed in hushed voices by experienced Africa-watchers, if the President fails to ensure an orderly and peaceful transition when he retires in 2002, the date of the next presidential election. It is a problem that continually exercises the President's mind, for it is no exaggeration to say that he holds Kenya's future in his hands. He is acutely aware that the judgement of history will be calculated as much from the state of the nation he leaves behind as the accomplishments of his rule. Just as he regards peace and stability as the greatest achievements of his presidency, so he sees that he has an overriding responsibility in the final years of his rule to ensure that his successor inherits a nation at peace with itself, the rancour and tribal divison things of the past. As he said during the 1997 Jamhuri Day celebrations: 'I would like to leave a permanent legacy in Kenya's history, a legacy of one strong and united Kenya, you, the people of Kenya will cherish.'

It is a sentiment shared by Moi's staunchest critics, including Raila Odinga who said: 'It is in the gift of the President to bequeath a peaceful transition in a democratic country. It would be appreciated for generations to come.'

This is not, however, simply an issue of choosing the appropriate candidate. In a complex and volatile multi-party democracy, it is a question of ensuring that the political climate smiles on a smooth succession. Following the 1997 elections the President is constitutionally bound to stand down in 2002. By then he will be seventy-eight, and feels, taking former American President Ronald Reagan as an example, that it will be an appropriate time to bow out of public life. Even so, he knows that there is much work to be done. 'We are passing from an old to a new culture,' he says, recognising that the urbanisation and industrialisation of the country is inevitably reshaping the political and social landscape. In a nation where the values of the silicon chip and the Stone Age co-exist, the obstacles cannot be overemphasised. Just as Moi's life straddles the passing of a tribal culture, the rise and fall of colonialism and the passage of a new nation-state into the rigours of independence, so the final period of his presidency is perhaps the most important of all. He must ensure the transition from the last vestiges of colonialism, one-party democracy and a command economy, to a multi-party, flexible, free-market society that enjoys freedom of speech and of association, as well as democratic pluralism, within a secure and orderly nation. He himself defined both the problem and the solution during the 1997 Madaraka Day speech:

> My vision for the future is for a calmer and more confident Kenya where endless confrontation no longer dominates the domestic agenda. I want to see a nation where political differences do not mean personal antagonism. I want to see a nation which can hold its head up proudly as the nucleus of a new dynamic economic region. Above all, I want to see a nation that is free to concentrate her energies on progress and development. Only in this way shall we be able to harness our energies and confront out single greatest challenge, the challenge of poverty.

A cornerstone of change is a radical overhaul of the constitution, to cut away the last vestiges of the colonial era and the one-party state so that Kenya's transition to multi-party politics is complete. It was the President himself who set the constitutional hare running when he announced in his 1995 New Year message that the country's constitution would be reviewed, a move welcomed at home and abroad. It was the first public indication of Moi's personal long-term thinking, a recognition that the country's constitutional framework must be altered to incorporate the changed political realities of the multi-party era.

In tandem with his promise to review the constitution, Moi attempted to lower the political temperature. He encouraged the language of conciliation and com- promise rather than, as had been a trademark of several Opposition leaders, making outlandish demands and engineering confrontations. When he returned from Israel in 1996 – where he had gone for a cataract operation, at the same time taking his first holiday in forty years, something itself indicative of a slight thawing in his approach to life – he held out an olive branch to opposition leaders, inviting the then FORD-Kenya national chairman and official Leader of the Opposition, Michael Wamalwa, the national chairman of the Democratic Party, Mwai Kibaki, and the then FORD-Asili Secretary General, Martin Shikuku, to State House, Nairobi, for talks on national issues.

The meeting in the spring of 1996 signalled something of a political sea change, an attempt by the President to end the sour politics of conflict and suspicion which, in his eyes, have diverted into argument and bitterness, energy that should have been directed into nation building. As he said during a visit to Central Province, where he tried to heal the breach between the ruling party and the Kikuyu: 'My stand is that we cannot fight the many problems we are facing without unity.' At the same time as making placatory noises to the Kikuyu – describing the first President's son, Uhuru Kenyatta as 'a man of vision' – Moi travelled to Narok to chastise the chauvinistic Maasai leader William ole Ntimama, ordering him to 'preach peace amongst all ethnic communities'. Such actions are part of a continuing process, Moi's attempts to dilute the damaging political and cultural consequences of tribalism whilst promoting a more homogeneous society. Again, when meetings, known as the Gema-Kamatusa talks, aimed at reconciling the warring tribes in the Rift Valley broke down, Moi initiated a series of private gatherings involving major political figures in order to kick start the peace process. At the same time as wooing the Kikuyu, he chastised regional administrators and police for breaking up opposition rallies, a frequent complaint since the country had reverted to multi-party politics. He even intervened to order the reinstatement of a headmaster removed by the education authorities after he had accepted building materials for his school from his local Opposition MP.

Initially, with an opposition more interested in internecine warfare than constructive discussions, it seemed that Moi could control both the pace and direction of constitutional debate, arguing strongly that any constitutional reforms should come after the 1997 elections when the political temperature had cooled. Certainly, in the opinion of many Kenyan political commentators, the splintered opposition had signally failed to invigorate the political scene intellectually. All too often theatrical, rather than practical, democracy has been offered to the Kenyan people. As a leader in the *East African Standard* in early 1996 observed tartly:

> No thinking African would wish to return to the authoritarian single-party rule of the past. But it would be dishonest to pretend that our new democracies have lived up to their expectations. This is largely because Opposition parties have failed to grasp the essence of their role which puts national and party loyalty ahead of personal ambition and which offers a truly alternative platform . . .

The *Sunday Nation* was even blunter: 'There are no new ideas for the development of Kenya's politics from this tired lot. They should pack their bags and go into deserved and in some cases, early retirement. Now.'

The issue which managed to unite and enthuse an ethnically divided and largely discredited opposition was the fall of President Mobutu Sese Seko of Zaire in May 1997, and his replacement by Laurent Kabila, an event dubbed the 'second liberation' by some Kenyan opposition politicians. To many, the demise of Mobutu and the rise of younger so-called 'New African' leaders like Yoweri Museveni of Uganda left Moi looking politically vulnerable, a presidential dinosaur whom history had passed by. As *The Economist* observed: 'After 19 years in power Moi is seen as one of the last of a dying breed of African Big Men – rulers from a one-party era for whom fear, corruption and manipulation of ethnic differences are seen as acceptable tools of governing.'

The prevailing belief in the West that Moi's end would be hastened by

Mobutu's fall, as well as his reluctance to implement a radical overhaul of the constitution until after the 1997 elections, rejuvenated the domestic political scene as an alliance of lawyers, international human-rights groups such as Amnesty International, and churchmen joined with the opposition to demand reform of the constitution in the months before the election. For Kenya it was a case of history repeating itself for, as with the reluctant embrace of a multi-party state in 1991, the flames of domestic discontent were once again fanned by global winds of change,

Some leaders of the opposition alliance, particularly Kikuyu politicians linked to GEMA, now used the language of civil disobedience and armed insurrection in their belated adoption of the cause of constitutional change. In deliberate shows of defiance opposition rallies were held without applying for licences, as required by Kenyan law. One gathering in Nairobi at the end of May degenerated into an orgy of looting of shops and stoning of motorists. This new tactic gained inter-national attention after violent scenes in the National Assembly during which opposition politicians engaged in fist fights, and vigorously heckled the then Finance Minister, Musalia Mudavadi, to prevent him delivering his budget speech. At the same time as this fracas, *The Times* reflected the feeling of shock and disgust, arguing that 'Moi's brutality will be the ruin of Kenya. If confirmation were required that President Moi would rather destroy the last vestiges of public trust in authority than give way to legitimate calls for constitutional reform, then that is provided by this latest demonstration of his contempt for law as well as for life.' Britain, the United States, Japan and a number of European Union countries condemned the excessive use of force, twenty-two countries urging the President to introduce constitutional reforms before the election.

In one of the most violent weeks in Kenya's recent political history, students rioted the following day, reacting to rumours, later found to be false, that four students had died in the riots earlier in May. Moi ordered the closure of Nairobi University, specifically directing that the feared GSU should be kept away. His directive was ignored, the police and GSU using strong-arm tactics to clear the campus, once again provoking international protest.

Days later the President who, during the disturbance, had been immersed in hosting the Inter-Governmental Authority on Development (IGAD) Head of State summit on the conflicts in Sudan and Somalia, invited church and opposition leaders to State House, Nairobi, to discuss ways of calming the situation in Kenya. Following these soundings the KANU National Executive announced that it would recommend the publishing of a bill during the current parliament to establish a commission to review the constitution. It further recommended that a number of laws, many dating back to the colonial period, be repealed or amended. At a stroke the wind was taken out of the opposition sails. Safina leader Richard Leakey now a nominated MP, reflected the views of many moderates when he said: 'If this is what we have been asking for and they have agreed to it, then I cannot criticise . . . a sincere offer.' Others were less impressed, calling for a nationwide strike in protest because they had not been consulted about the proposed constitutional changes.

The way Moi manoeuvred the country away from further civil strife was typical both of his political strengths and weaknesses. First of all, as is characteristic of his age set, he allowed the issue, in this case constitutional reform, to brew to a crisis before taking control. At the same time he showed a flexibility and willingness to compromise which is so often overlooked by his critics as well as an insistence that any constitutional reform be discussed and initiated through the National Assembly, again illustrating his long-standing belief in following proper democratic procedure. He told MPs that their authority was being questioned by outside civic bodies and warned them that the moment they allowed unelected groups to talk about the constitution they were surrendering their responsibilities as leaders and politicians. The resulting reforms, agreed by the Inter-Parties Parliamentary Group (IPPG), which brought KANU and opposition MPs together for the first time, considerably cooled the temperature before the crucial 1997 elections. As MPs thrashed out numerous constitutional amendments to give the opposition a 'level playing field', the spectre of tribal violence once more reared its head. Armed gangs on the coast attacked a police station as well as residents, mainly Kikuyu and Luo, whom their leaders considered to be up-country intruders. While the fighting badly damaged the tourist industry and image abroad, there was a realisation that, unlike 1992, the looting, mayhem and murder was localised with no wider national ramifications. The President described the fighting as 'senseless', blaming politicians from all parties for stirring up trouble. A subsequent public inquiry heard how a local witchdoctor had inflamed passions, promising gullible youths that bullets would not hurt them when they raided a police station in search of weapons.

The rancorous debate about the constitution throws into sharp relief the wider issue of the prospect of violent civil unrest as an integral and inevitable consequence of further democratisation in an ethnically polarised society. It is a question that continually exercises Moi; balancing the demands for an extension of individual freedoms and wider democracy against the practicalities of ensuring peace and stability in a nation where tribe, not ideology, is the dominant focus. While aid agencies and diplomats accept, with a kind of disengaged insouciance, the fact that, historically, violence is the necessary handmaiden of genuine democratisation, it is a consequence that the President will never tolerate for his people. It is for this reason that he argues that the democratic march of Kenyans must be accompanied by a more homogeneous and less polarised society. In short, the price of freedom must be measured against the likelihood of social breakdown and widespread violence.

Yet the overwhelming majority of commentators and diplomats simply recite the mantra of multi-partyism and economic liberalisation, whilst ignoring the specific domestic consequences of the gigantic impact these twin revolutions, political and economic, have had on the body politic. While multi-partyism has made the Kenyan political scene more open and less authoritarian, the new era of democracy has merely recast historic problems in a different form. Thus the spectre of tribalism which runs like a river through Kenyan history has been reshaped and institutionalised into the various political parties. So the Democratic Party and FORD-Asili are almost entirely drawn from Kikuyu tribes, whilst the National Development Party enjoys support from the Luo community. Only KANU can boast national support, and then only because of an alliance of the smaller Kenyan tribes against the two dominant ones. As the *Financial Times* correspondent Michela Wrong, a consistent critic of the Kenyan President, admitted recently: 'Moi's argument was that Kenya as a multi-tribal society was not suited to multi-party democracy as it would merely exacerbate ethnic tensions . . . Four years on the argument is not looking quite as spurious as it once did.'

While Moi, consistently suspected of longing for the restoration of the one-party system, has absolutely no intention of returning to the old days, he is acutely aware of the immense drawbacks of the new system. Multi-partyism is an engine for social, economic and political instability in a country where, as Moi's 'disappearing act' in February 1995 graphically illustrated, insecurity and insurrection are just a heartbeat away. While the choppy political scene deters overseas investment, the most pernicious side effect of the new political era, as far as Moi is concerned, is tribal polarisation, an ethnic division that was made violently manifest in the tribal clashes of the early 1990s. Communities are now even more suspicious of one another, rumour and counter-rumour are the norm, while energy which might be spent on practical projects such as housing developments and water supplies is dissipated in politics. In a country as poor as Kenya, Moi argues – as did Kenyatta and Mboya – that the draining of economic and political energy into partisan infighting is a luxury the nation can ill afford. The 1997 budget, for example, set aside Ksh 2.3 billion for the electoral process, as opposed to Ksh 690 million for drought aid and Ksh 250 million for the school milk programme. As the Kenyan scholar John K. Mburu observed: 'Democracy is highly expensive for regimes that are extremely poor. They are now forced to cough up resources with which to try to maintain at least a semblance of order among perennially suspicious tribes.'

On a day-to-day basis tribalism affects the workings of the police, the civil service and other state institutions – although the military is largely a tribally integrated force – to the detriment of the nation. In particular the rapid politicisation of the civil service since the introduction of multi-partyism in 1992 is a matter which greatly vexes the President. He often cites the examples of France and Italy as countries which have enjoyed stability thanks to an impartial civil service despite having endless changes of government. He says: 'In Kenya we have a civil service based on tribal lines which further divides the country. This is a problem that no one in the West wants to deal with let alone provide a solution for.' The partisan behaviour of the local administration during the Rift Valley clashes is a classic example of this, but there are other inevitable by-products which have a deleterious practical effect on Kenya's social and economic fabric. During an election year the administration goes into a state of paralysis, as a result of pro-opposition civil servants working to undermine the system or those loyal to the administration who, fearing for their jobs and prospects, focus their attention on their private businesses. This administrative deadness is matched only by those squeezing personal advantage out of a government they fear will change after the polls. Until the country enjoys long-term stability these effects will be felt every five years no matter what party is in power.

Yet following the IPPG agreement the omens for the 1997 election seemed to be set fair and in many aspects the election demonstrated significant advances in the maturity of the democratic process. Not only did the security forces remain above the fray, but the civil service, for so long the handmaidens of the ruling party, stayed largely neutral, Provincial and District Commissioners strenuously and publicly warning their staff, including chiefs and sub-chiefs, to stay out of politics.

At the same time a well-publicised lunch attended by wealthy businessmen to raise funds for KANU's election campaign signified that the commercial community were prepared to take over the financial vacuum once occupied by government. As a result, unlike the 1992 election, the Kenya shilling remained stable throughout the campaign once investors saw that the outgoing government were prepared to play within the IPPG rules. As millionaire Kikuyu businessman Chris Kirubi observed: 'The private sector has belatedly come to realise that we must participate in the running of the nation rather than standing aloof.'

It was the President himself who set the tone and style of the campaign. From the start he urged that there should be no repetition of the rancour and violence of the previous five years. For the first time he faced a rival in his Baringo Central constituency, a man, rather appropriately, whose local nickname is 'He who dares lightning.' While some KANU supporters were outraged by what they considered an insult to the President, Moi deliberately preached tolerance, shaking hands with his opponent and his supporters in his Kabarnet heartland.

It was a move which had a profound effect, every one of the scores of KANU candidates I spoke to at State House mentioning the need for a peaceful election and citing Moi's example as one to follow. His speech during the Jamhuri Day celebrations continued the theme, arguing that the elections would be a test of the country's 'maturity and integrity,' pleading with candidates and voters to show 'tolerance, peace, discipline and responsibility.' It was, as expected, a forlorn hope. During the two-week campaign there were several deaths, numerous injuries in clashes between rival parties as well as accusations of vote buying and rigging. These incidents, though regrettable, are entirely consistent with the tribal rough and tumble of Kenyan politics since independence and did not remotely resemble the disorder and insurrection of 1992.

Yet an election which could have been hailed as a triumph for common sense was soured by the chaotic and incompetent way the poll was conducted by the Electoral Commission. Missing ballot papers, endless recounts and voting extended over several days because of administrative cock-ups cast a pall over the procedure. Even so the majority of the 28,000 observers were satisfied that many of the problems were due to inexperience rather than vote tampering. Indeed given the flooding, washed out roads, the mammoth and complex task of organising three separate polls for presidential, parliamentary and local elections without a central electoral register or the clerical assistance of the administration, it was surprising that there were not more problems.

None the less the European Union believed that the General Election had fallen short of 'normal democratic standards' although the overwhelming majority of observers accepted that the poll did reflect the people's will. Initially Presidential losers Mwai Kibaki, Raila Odinga and Charity Ngilu called for a re-run of the ballot, though within days Kibaki was left isolated as other political parties acknowledged that Moi had won an election, though flawed and chaotic, by polling more votes. President Moi had substantially increased his support since 1992, polling 2,490,000 votes or 40.4 per cent of the electorate. Indeed he was the only presidential candidate to enjoy support across the whole country rather than his tribal region, making significant inroads into Nairobi, Western and Eastern Province.

Only Central Province, the heart of Kikuyu country, remained immune to his message of national unity, revealing the fundamental fault lines in Kenyan society. At heart the elections were a rerun of the previous poll with the tribal factor dominating voting patterns. That the Kikuyu, universally seen as the best educated, most sophisticated and progressive tribe, voted almost exclusively on tribal lines for their man, Democratic party leader Mwai Kibaki, shows how far Kenya has to travel before it achieves Moi's dream of becoming a homogeneous society. It was a source of disappointment to the President that, in spite of all his efforts in the previous five years to woo the so called Kikuyu elite and the *wananchi*, he only managed to gain five per cent of the vote in Central Province, a region where 90 per cent chose Kibaki.

Even Kenyatta's son, Uhuru, who stood for KANU, was trounced. It is one of the ironies of Kenyan politics that Moi had always considered Kibaki, a man of moderation, as his natural successor and was deeply hurt when he left KANU on Christmas Day 1991 to form his own party. As one State House observer says, 'He feels that Kibaki could have been President if he had been patient as he has similar policies to Moi. He is a solid politician who is not tribalistic unlike Ken Matiba.'

So it was a buoyant but thoughtful President who took the oath of office in Uhuru Park in January 1998 before a watching crowd who included the Presidents of Tanzania and Uganda. For not only was there the tribal dimension to consider, at the same time the clear message from the electorate was that they wanted change within continuity. While Moi's personal vote was higher, KANU lost a number of seats, including a fistful of ministers and long-serving MPs. Even the local power barons found it difficult to maintain control of their regions, a sign that 'big family' politics may have had their day. The most notable casualty was Vice-President Professor George Saitoti who, while preserving his own seat, suffered the humiliating setback of losing a seat in his Kajiado District to the Opposition.

In his presidential acceptance speech, Moi made it clear that he had listened to the voice of the people, promising to be more sensitive to the needs of the *wananchi*. While he pledged to fight corruption, rebuild the economy and reform the health and education services, his mind was focused on the legacy of peace and stability which he wants to leave behind.

He realised, perhaps even more clearly, that, as the voting in Central Province demonstrated, the tribal equation is as insoluble as ever. Even when Kenya becomes a more industrialised and urban society in the next century, tribal self-interest will almost certainly dominate voting patterns, making each election as predictable as the last. It makes a mockery of the whole notion of democracy, exposing the idea, promoted by the West, that multi-partyism was the constitutional panacea for the country's ills. Indeed all multi-partyism has achieved is to worsen the condition. As one State House official said: 'The President now feels that the need for constitutional reform is more urgent than ever.'

The first signal of his thinking was in post-election cabinet when Moi deliberately left vacant the post of Vice-President. While the move undercut George Saitoti's presidential ambitions, it signified that Moi envisages a more radical overhaul of the constitution than has been hitherto imagined. A dilution of presidential powers, the possibility of a Prime Minister, a first and second Vice-President and majimboism, the devolution of authority to the regions, are all on the agenda. Indeed these issues were discussed openly within Moi's circle at State House months before it became a life and death issue in the summer of 1997. As the President says: 'I want to see a united not a factional country. I want to make sure that Kenyans have an opportunity to choose somebody who will carry the majority of Kenyans and enable Kenya to move forward into the future. I would like the constitutional review to move forward realistically. It is my constant regret that some Kenyans are not seeing the future of the country in the right perspective, I'm working hard to remedy that. Quite simply I want to see the majority of Kenyans happy.'

There is now the conviction that Moi will be the last Kenyan President to enjoy virtually unlimited authority. In short the constitutional debate in the next five years will be much more than the rather sterile discussion of who will be Moi's successor. It should be a broader argument about the very structure of government predicated on the provocative assertion that if the *wananchi* and the elite vote routinely for tribal self-interest then they should have their wish, with each region being granted a greater degree of autonomy. At the same time any dilution of power in the centre will provide a series of checks and balances to prevent one-man rule. It may be one of the ironies of Kenyan history that a majimbo constitution, which was so derided as a colonial tool to divide and rule Kenyans in the 1960s, is the foundation for her future stability.

As a result, before Moi can retire to his farm, spend more time with his grandchildren and, as he says, spend time preaching, he will have to orchestrate a political reform as difficult as any in his long career.

In many respects the fact that he is attempting to grapple with Kenya's underlying problems head-on and has presided over a momentous, if stormy, democratic and economic transition which has demanded courage, flexibility, patience and vision, gives the lie to the widespread belief that he is an obdurate dictator. So often his pragmatism has been interpreted by the West as untrustworthiness, his iron self-discipline as authoritarianism, and his Old Testament morality as antediluvian. At heart, the values and criteria by which he makes his policy and his personal judgements contrast with those of his critics, particularly Westerners, and so crucially determine the way he is judged.

He is a man more sinned against than sinning but even so, he has doggedly attempted, albeit without much success or sympathy internationally, to state the case for Kenya, to seek for the best of the nation's heritage and culture to be respected, preserved and absorbed into the body politic in the face of a tidal wave of Western values. The ultimate irony is that the new younger generation of African presidents who are lauded for introducing African solutions to African problems are singing from the hymn sheet Moi has been using for the last decade.

Perhaps his greatest, and his least understood, achievement has been his ability to hold the political ring in a volatile and intrinsically unstable society. It is his proudest boast that he has managed to keep the country intact in spite of a fragile climate, an uncertain economy, troubled borders, an ethnically divided society, and insensitive, often bullying, foreign interference. His failings have been those typical of his tribal age set; to trust too much and for too long, and to allow problems to brew to a crisis before they are resolved. For more than forty years President Daniel Toroitich arap Moi has had a shining vision of Kenya, Kenya as a homogeneous nation of all tribes and all races. It is an idea he has pursued steadfastly, from his days in the Legislative Council, to his time as Vice-President and then as President. As Kenya approaches a new millennium it is his dearest wish that the peace and unity he craves will continue with his successor.

Chronology

1890: Anglo-German Treaty gives interior of what were to become Kenya and Uganda over to Britain and Tanganyika to Germany. Start of Nandi wars of resistance which continue until early 1900s.

1905: Kenya named the East Africa Protectorate.

1907: Legislative Council composed of white settlers is set up.

1920: East Africa Protectorate becomes the colony of Kenya. Protectorate now a 10-mile coastal strip administered by Sultan of Zanzibar.

1922: African nationalist Harry Thuku, founder of the Young Kikuyu Association, arrested; at least 23 shot dead in mêlée outside Nairobi police station where he is held. Winston Churchill says that 'Highlands of East Africa' – Kenya's White Highlands – for whites only.

1924 (September): Daniel Toroitich arap Moi, later to be the second President of Kenya, is born at Kurieng'wo in Sacho Location in the Baringo North District of the Rift Valley.

1929: Jomo Kenyatta (originally named Kamau wa Ngengi) travels to England to make representations about Kikuyu grievances, and to study.

1938: Kenyatta's magnum opus, *Facing Mount Kenya*, is published.

1944: Eliud Mathu becomes the first African to be nominated a member of the Legislative Council. Kenya African Study Union formed (the word 'Study' is dropped from title the following year).

1946: Kenyatta returns from England and becomes KAU President.

1952 (October): Government declares State of Emergency as Mau Mau activity increases. Kenyatta and five others arrested.

1954: Lyttelton Plan brings non-Europeans into Kenya's government for first time. Operation Anvil mounted against Mau Mau in Nairobi resulting in 27,000 arrests.

1955 (October): Daniel T. arap Moi nominated to the Legislative Council representing the Rift Valley.

1957: Elections for eight African members of the Legislative Council are held for the first time.

1958: Lennox-Boyd constitution boycotted by African leaders.

1959: Hola camp scandal, which drastically changes British Government's attitude to its Kenya colony.

1960: Kenya African National Union (KANU) and Kenya African Democratic Union (KADU) are formed; Moi chairman of KADU. First Lancaster House Conference held to discuss future constitutional composition of Kenya.

1961: KANU secure majority of votes in first ever general election involving majority of Africans. Kenyatta and companions released from detention. Kenyatta becomes President of KANU.

1962: Second Lancaster House Conference, during which KADU party advocates introduction of *majimbo* or regional type of government.

1963: General elections on full franchise. KANU form government with

Kenyatta as Prime Minister. He gives Kenya the national motto 'Harambee' – 'Pull together'. Third Lancaster House Conference. December 12: Kenya becomes a free independent country.

1964: Attempted mutiny at Lanet. KADU joins government and Kenya becomes a one-party state and a republic. Moi given portfolio of Minister of Home Affairs in new government. Oginga Odinga becomes Kenya's first Vice-President.

1965: Pio Gama Pinto assassinated. Tom Mboya launches Sessional Paper No 10, the blueprint for Kenya's African socialism. Moi heads Famine Relief Committee.

1966: KANU conference at Limuru ousts Vice-President Oginga Odinga. Moi elected Vice-President for the Rift Valley. Odinga forms Kenya People's Union; 'Little General Election' held.

1967: Daniel T. arap Moi is appointed Vice-President of Kenya.

1968: Kenyatta appoints Kitili Mwendwa as first African Chief Justice.

1969: Tom Mboya murdered. In Kisumu 9 people killed when Presidential Guard opens fire on stone-throwing crowd. Oginga Odinga detained. General elections held.

1970: Widespread oathing among Kikuyu politicians.

1971: Conspiracy to overthrow government is thwarted.

1974: General elections see half of Kenya's MPs lose their seats.

1975: Bomb blast at Nairobi bus terminal kills 27 people. Nakuru MP J. M. Kariuki murdered.

1976: Cabinet meeting condemns the 'Change the Constitution' movement which is trying to prevent Moi becoming President.

1977: Long-awaited KANU elections are postponed because of Kenyatta's ill health.

1978 (August): Kenyatta dies in his sleep and Moi is sworn in as Kenya's second President vowing to follow in Mzee's footsteps. Mwai Kibaki appointed Vice-President. All detainees released.

1979: Moi chairs OAU meeting in Nairobi. In general election, nearly half the incumbents lose their seats. Oginga Odinga appointed Chairman of the Cotton Lint and Seed Marketing Board.

1980: Attorney-General Charles Njonjo resigns post and becomes Minister for Home and Constitutional Affairs after a by-election. Bomb explosion at Norfolk Hotel, Nairobi, leaves 20 dead.

1982: Attempted air force coup is crushed. Kenya becomes *de jure* one-party state.

1983: Inquiry into affairs of Charles Njonjo. General election sees 5 ministers and 12 assistant ministers lose seats.

1984: Kenya suffering from famine. Njonjo pardoned by President Moi.

1985: Warring factions in Uganda sign peace accord after Moi brokers talks.

1986: Crackdown on Mwakenya dissidents. Nyayo buses launched. International concern over human-rights violations.

1987: KANU disciplinary committee dissolved by President Moi. Border clashes with Uganda.

1988: British Prime Minister Margaret Thatcher visits Kenya. General election under much-criticised system of queue-voting. Kenyans reject 70 MPs including three ministers. Allegations of widespread rigging. Church declares support for secret ballot. Security of tenure of judges is removed.

1989: Charles Rubia and Ken Matiba expelled from KANU. Richard Leakey becomes new Director of what became Kenya Wildlife Service. Vice-President Dr Karanja resigns; Professor George Saitoti replaces him. Raila Odinga released from detention. Moi torches 12 tons of ivory at Nairobi National Park.

1990: Foreign Minister Dr Robert Ouko murdered; Scotland Yard detectives investigate. Matiba and Rubia call for end of single party. Both men detained. International criticism increases, and Kenya cuts ties with Norway. Special KANU Delegates' Conference agrees to end queue-voting, among other electoral changes.

1991: Rubia and Matiba released from detention. Odinga and others launch Forum for the Restoration of Democracy (FORD) party. IMF and World Bank curtail aid until economy is liberalised and more democratic government implemented. Moi proposes the scrapping of Section 2a of the Constitution, ending a decade of single-party rule. Ethnic violence breaks out in Rift Valley.

1992: Democratic Party launched by Mwai Kibaki, and numerous KANU ministers join FORD. FORD splits into FORD-Asili, led by Ken Matiba, and FORD-Kenya, registered by Oginga Odinga. Kenyans vote in first multi-party elections with eight presidential candidates.

1993: KANU, led by President Moi, wins multi-party election. Koigi wa Wamwere arrested. Liberalisation of economy continues.

1994: Richard Leakey resigns as Director of Kenya Wildlife Service. Death of Oginga Odinga. FORD-Kenya Chairman Wamalwa Kijana becomes Leader of Opposition. East African Community resurrected.

1995: IMF blocks loans over Goldenberg scandal. Richard Leakey and others start the Safina political party. Moi promises constitutional review.

1996: Kenya Airways privatised. President Moi travels to Israel for cataract operation. Controversy over presidential jet.

1997: Opposition unite over need for constitutional reform before general elections. Clashes at coast.

1997: General Elections. Moi wins again.

1998: Bomb explodes outside American Embassy, Nairobi. Muslim extremists suspected. Constitutional review undertaken. Inquiry held into tribal clashes.

Select Bibliography

Books

Anderson, Dick, *We Felt Like Grasshoppers: The Story of the Africa Inland Mission*, Crossway, 1994

Arnold, Guy, *Kenyatta and the Politics of Kenya*, Dent, 1974

Bailey, Jim, *Kenya, The National Epic*, Kenway Publications, 1993

Bennett, George, *Kenya: A Political History*, Oxford University Press, 1963

Bennett, George and Rosberg, Carl G., *The Kenyatta Election 1960–1961*, Oxford University Press, 1961

Bienen, Henry, *Kenya: The Politics of Participation and Control*, Princeton University Press, 1974

Blundell, Michael, *A Love Affair With the Sun: A Memoir of Seventy Years in Kenya*, Kenway Publications, 1994

Bogonko, Sorobea N., *Kenya 1945–1963: A Study in African National Movements*, Kenya Literature Bureau, 1980

Bushan, Kul, *Kenya Factbook 1990–1996*

Fish, Burnette and Gerald, *The Kalenjin Heritage*, African Gospel Church, 1995

Fox, James, *White Mischief*, Cape, 1982

Fukuyama, Francis, *Trust*, Penguin, 1996

Harden, Blaine, *Dispatches From a Fragile Continent*, HarperCollins, 1990

Hermet, Guy, Rose, Richard and Rouquise, Alain (eds), *Elections Without Choice*, Macmillan, 1978

Hetherington, Penelope, *British Paternalism and Africa 1920–1940*, Frank Cass, 1978

Himbara, David, *Kenyan Capitalists, the State and Development*, East African Educational Publishers, 1994

Karimi, Joseph and Ochieng, Philip, *The Kenyatta Succession*, Transafrica, 1980

Kenyatta, Jomo, *Facing Mount Kenya*, Nairobi, East African Educational Publishers, 1982

King, Kenneth, *Jua Kali Kenya: Change and Development in an Informal Economy 1970–95*, East African Educational Publishers, 1996

Kipkorir, B. E. (ed.), *Imperialism and Collaboration in Colonial Kenya*, Kenya Literature Bureau, 1980

Leys, Colin, *Underdevelopment in Kenya: The Political Economy of Neo-Colonialism 1964–1971*, University of California Press, 1975

Matson, A. T., *Nandi Resistance to British Rule 1890–1906*, East African Publishing House, 1972

Mboya, Tom, *Freedom and After*, East African Educational Publishers, 1963

Moi, Daniel T. arap, *Kenya African Nationalism: Nyayo Philosophy and Principles*, Macmillan, 1986

Moi: Mindful of Others, Presidential Press Unit

Moi: What Has He Done, Presidential Press Unit, 1992

Mwanzi, Henry A., *A History of the Kipsigis*, East African Literature Bureau, 1977

Ng'weno, Hilary, *The Day Kenyatta Died*, Longman, 1978

Ochieng, William Robert (ed.), *A Modern History of Kenya 1895–1980*, Evans Brothers, 1989

Odinga, Oginga, *Not Yet Uhuru: An Autobiography*, Heinemann, 1967

Okondo, P. H., *A Commentary on the Constitution of Kenya*, Phoenix, 1995

Royle, Trevor, *Winds of Change: The End of Empire in Africa*, John Murray, 1997

Shepherd, Robert, *Iain Macleod*, Hutchinson, 1994

Snell, G. S., *Nandi Customary Law*, Kenya Literature Bureau, 1954

Swainson, Nicola, *The Development of Corporate Capitalism in Kenya 1918–1977*, Heinemann, 1980

Throup, David, *The Political Economy of Kenya*, M. G. Schatzberg (ed.), 1987

Wepman, Dennis, *Kenyatta* (World Leaders Past and Present series), Burke Publishing, 1988

Widner, Jennifer, *The Rise of the Party State in Kenya from Harambee to Nyayo*, University of California Press, 1992

Documents, reports, pamphlets, etc.

Nailing Lies, Ministry of Foreign Affairs and International Co-operation, December 1991

Kenya Human Rights Commission Report 1995

The Way It Is: Government Response to Kenya Human Rights Commission Report 1996

The Presidential, Parliamentary and Civic Elections in Kenya, 29th December 1992, Report of the Commonwealth Observer Group, Commonwealth Secretariat, 1993

Select Committee report on the disappearance and murder of J. M. Kariuki, 1975

Report of the Judicial Inquiry into allegations involving Charles Mugane Njonjo, November 1984

Kenya Legislative Council Reports, 1955–60

Hansard, volumes from 1957–97

Sessional Paper No 10, 1965, *African Socialism and Its Application to Planning in Kenya*, Nairobi, Government Printer

Sessional Paper No 1, 1986, *Economic Management for Renewed Growth*, Nairobi, Government Printer

Lonsdale, John, *Political Culture of Kenya* (occasional paper), 1992

Baringo District Annual Reports, 1924–61

Nandi District Annual Reports, 1933, 1938–44

Kipulei, Ben, *Migration of Tugen Tribes*, archives of the University of Nairobi

Kenya, Amnesty International report, 1995

Kenya: Old Habits Die Hard, Human Rights Watch/Africa report, July 1995

Papers of former Chief Justice A. R. W. Hancox, EGH, CBE

Index

African Inland Mission 9, 10, 14, 27, 30, 32, 33–7, 39–40, 43–4
African-Elected Members' Organisation (AEMO) 60–67
Angaine, Jackson 95, 103, 108–9, 112, 123
Anguka, Jonah 162
Aringo, Peter Oloo 136–7, 172

Baring, Sir Evelyn 48, 53, 63–4
Barnett, Paul 9, 34, 41, 43–4, 47, 62
Biwott, Nicholas 7, 18, 124–5, 128, 154, 156–7, 161–3 170, 175, 180
  allegations of involvement in tribal clashes 175, 180
  and the Ouko murder 161–3
Blundell, Michael 7, 18, 67–8, 73, 79, 97, 144–5
Bomett, Eric 49, 73, 86–8, 92, 98
Bomett, Helena see Moi, Helena
Bomett, Reuben 43, 47
Bryson, Stuart 34–5, 37–9
Bultut, Joel 41, 51–3, 59, 62, 73

car import swindle 187–8
'Change the Constitution' movement 103, 109–12, 114, 117–19, 123, 151, 169
Chelimo, James 30, 35, 51–2
Chelimo, Rebecca 30–1, 35–6
Chemirmir, Paul 4, 12, 41, 43–4, 55
Cheserem, Micah 187–8
Chesire, Elizabeth 36–7, 44
Chesire, Isaiah 37, 44
Chesire, Reuben 13, 44, 50, 94–5, 113
circumcision 10, 14, 39–40, 149
Communism 5, 15, 86–7, 99, 165

Democratic Party 176, 184, 199, 202

East African Community 17, 143
Eshiwani, Dr Arthur 109, 124, 150

FORD-Asili Party 117, 176, 179, 184–5, 199, 202
FORD-Kenya Party 176, 179, 184, 199
Forum for the Restoration of Democracy (FORD) Party 171–2, 176
  see also FORD-Asili; FORD-Kenya
Francklin, Bernard 24–6, 32

Gethi, Ben 107, 134

Gichuru, James 69–70, 73–4, 90, 103
Gikuyu, Embu, Meru Association (GEMA) 103–4, 106, 109–14, 124, 201
Goldenberg bank scandal 20, 186–7

Haji, Yusuf 161, 175, 178–9, 181
Hancox, Robin 16, 117, 181
harambee system 92–3, 147
Hempstone, Smith 163–4, 170, 172, 184

Imperial British East Africa Company 24, 29
International Monetary Fund (IMF) 8, 163, 183, 187–9

Johnson, Sir John 160, 163, 191

Kabarak 3, 13
Kabarnet 34, 44, 51–2
Kabartonjo 30, 32–5, 37, 62
Kabila, Laurent 17, 200
Kabimoi 9, 63, 83
Kaggia, Bildad 48, 81
Kalenjin people 1, 4, 11, 16, 27–31, 39–40, 49, 84, 93–6, 124, 150, 176–82
  see also Tugen people
Kalenjin Poliical Alliance (KPA) 70
Kamba people 28, 184, 194
Kanyotu, James 137, 162
Karanja, Josephat 168, 172
Kariithi, Geoffrey 115–16, 139
Kariuki, G.G. 95, 99, 103, 107, 111, 113–15, 117–18, 124–6, 128, 137–8, 143, 176–7
Kariuki, J.M. 130
  murder of 15, 72, 100–1, 105–6, 108
Karugu, James 126, 128
Karume, Njenga 90–1, 103, 110, 118, 124
Keen, John 55, 71, 87, 93, 106, 126, 128, 133, 172
Kenya
  elections 23, 81–2, 100, 104, 123–4, 129, 155–7, 177, 179, 184, 200–1, 203–5
  aborted 1982 coup 19, 132–9
  constitutional reforms 132, 199-202, 205–6
  corruption in 6–8, 105, 122, 150–1, 161, 164, 173, 186–8, 205

coup plot, 1977 114–15
drought and famine, 1984 145
economy 21, 102, 124–5, 183, 188–9
education system 58, 144, 148, 168,
173
human-rights issues 15–16, 121, 155,
167, 169
independence movement 46–7, 56–7,
64–5, 67–9, 82
land issues 95–6, 108–9
State of Emergency (1952) 48, 50,
53–4, 61, 66
student protests 129–30
tribal clashes 173–83, 203
tribalism in 7–8, 21, 93–4, 96–7,
99–102, 109, 124, 149–50, 167–70,
176–7, 184, 186, 200, 203, 205
wildlife concerns 190–4
Kenya Africa Union (KAU) 46, 48, 70,
78, 81
Kenya African Democratic Union
(KADU) 66, 71–86, 88
Kenya African National Union (KANU)
21, 66, 70–9, 81–6, 88–9, 97–100,
102–6, 112–13, 123–4, 131, 139, 143,
150, 154–5, 171–4, 179, 184–6,
201–2, 204–5
Kenya African Socialist Alliance 131–2
Kenya Independence Movement (KIM)
66, 69–71
Kenya National Party (KNP) 66, 69, 71
Kenya People's Union (KPU) 89, 98,
100–1, 139
Kenya Wildlife Service 20, 190–3
Kenyatta, Jomo 7–9, 11, 20, 46, 48–9,
63–5, 71–95, 99–110, 112, 114–15
Kenyatta, Mama Ngina 63, 108
Kenyatta, Peter 118
Kenyatta, Uhuru 200, 205
Kiano, Dr Julius 65–6, 68–70, 72, 76, 79,
85, 103–4, 111, 130
Kibaki, Mwai 92, 103, 114–5, 121–2,
126–8, 132, 140, 168, 174, 176, 184,
186, 192, 199, 204
Kikuyu people 7–9, 21, 28, 49, 66, 72, 81,
89, 90–1, 93–100, 101, 103, 106–7,
114, 117, 123, 137, 148–50, 154,
168–9, 175–9, 181–2, 184, 195, 200,
202, 205
Kimani, Dixon Kihika 94, 103, 110, 123
Kimathi, Dedan 48, 53
Kipkulei, Ben 108, 119–20
Kiplagat, Bethwell 18, 20, 141, 152, 159,
172
Kipsigis people 28, 80
Kodhek, Argwings 46, 56, 70

Kodipo, Valentine 180
Koinange, Mbiyu 82, 90, 92, 100, 103–4,
107, 112–19, 123, 168, 189
Kosgei, Sally 159
Kubai, Fred 48, 86

Lancaster House Conferences 65–8,
78–80, 82–3
Land Freedom Army 80–1
Leakey, Dr Richard 166, 185, 189–96,
201
Leakey, Philip 4, 123, 126, 132, 134, 143,
158, 164, 177, 185, 187, 194–26
Legislative Council 51–7, 59–68, 71, 73–4
see also African-Elected Members'
Organisation
Lennox-Boyd, Alan 61–2, 64–5
Lonsdale, John 48, 120–1, 124
Luhya people 842 176, 184
Luo people 28, 82, 89, 96, 98, 100, 112,
124, 136–7, 140, 143, 154, 157, 162,
169–70, 176, 181, 184, 202

Maasai people 27–9, 93, 170, 192
Macleod, Iain 46, 67–9, 75
Mahihu, Eliud 110, 115
majimboism 21, 77, 80, 82–4, 170–1, 206
Mate, Bernard 60, 69, 76
Mathenge, Isaiah 91, 100–1
Mathu, Eliud 54, 57
Matiba, Kenneth 90, 117, 157, 170–1,
176, 184–5, 197
Mau Mau 15, 28, 48–54, 75
Maudling, Reginald 78, 80
Mbithi, Philip 18, 148, 150, 162, 173,
181–2, 187–8, 194
Mboya, Tom 56, 61–2, 66–74, 79, 83,
86–9, 91, 98
murder of 15, 72, 98–100
Mkalla, Simon 7, 188
Mohamed, General Mahamud 134
Moi University 144–5
Moi, Daniel Toroitich arap
aborted 1982 coup against 19, 132–9
and majimboism 84
and Richard Leakey 190–6
and the Goldenberg scandal 186–7
and tribal clashes 180–3
as Vice-President 90–3, 95–6, 107–8,
111–13
arguments for a one-party state 21–2,
65–6
belief in education 14, 58, 144–5
burning ivory 191
business interests 13, 55, 94–5
childhood 26, 30–1, 33–43

children 9–10, 47
Christian upbringing and beliefs 14–15, 37–41, 44, 49
concern for the environment 14, 58–9, 129
concern in regional conflicts 17
concerns about corruption 122, 188, 205
disillusionment with the West 166–7, 182–3
divorce 9
entry into politics 52–3
family history 26–7, 30–1
ill health rumours 197–8
marriage 47
plot to murder 114–15
political (Nyayo) philosophy 5, 9, 13–15, 61, 65–6, 118–19, 146, 196
problems with Oginga Odinga 130–1
relationship with donor governments 188–9
relationship with Smith Hempstone 172
steps against poaching 190–1
sworn in as President 116, 119
teaching experience 38, 43–5, 47, 50, 52
views on tribalism 148–9, 203
vision for future 199, 206
Moi, Gideon 10
Moi, Helena (Lena) 9, 43, 47, 135
Moi, Jonathan 10, 47, 180
Moi, Philip 10, 188
Molo 80, 96, 176–9
Mudavadi, Moses 51–2, 55, 59, 124
Mudavadi, Musalia 187–8, 201
Muite, Paul 185, 193
Muli, Matthew 161
Mulinge, J.K. 117, 138
Muliro, Masinde 60, 65, 68–72, 74–6, 78, 82, 84–5, 157, 171
multi-partyism 8, 22–3, 163–74, 182–6, 189, 191, 198–203, 205
Mungai, Dr Njoroge 82, 90, 100, 103, 107–8, 110, 117
Mungai, James 15, 100–1, 107, 113–14, 119, 122
Murgor, William 79–80, 93
Museveni, Yoweri 5, 17, 152, 183
Muthemba, Andrew 128, 137, 141
Mwakenya 168–9
Mwendwa, Kitili 97, 101

Nairobi
  rioting in 135–6
  State House 2–3

Nakuru 96, 108, 114, 195
  State House 3
Nandi people 27–8, 49, 94–6
Nassir, Shariff 103–4, 106, 111, 131, 154
New Kenya Party 67, 69, 73, 75
'New World Order' 5, 8, 164–7, 183, 188
Ngala, Ronald 54, 61, 67–9, 72, 74–6, 80–1, 83–6, 91–2, 104
Ngei, Paul 48, 81, 91, 103, 112, 117, 119, 124
Ngilu, Charity 204
Ng'oroko 114–16, 122
Njonjo, Charles 19–20, 36, 82, 85, 91, 99, 103, 107, 111, 114, 117–19, 122, 125–8, 132, 134, 137–8, 140–3, 168, 189, 191
Njuguna, Danny 75
Nkrumah, Kwame 60, 78
Ntimama, William ole 170, 176, 192–3, 200
Nyachae, Simeon 142, 156, 173
Nyagah, Jeremiah 50, 68, 76, 85, 90, 103–4, 112
Nyayo bus scheme 146–7
Nyayo car project 147
Nyayo tea zones 147

oathing 75, 99, 101, 114, 177–8
Odinga, Jaramogi Oginga 37, 60–1, 63, 65–70, 73–4, 76, 83, 85–9, 98, 100, 110, 113, 123–4, 129–32, 136–7, 143, 170–1, 176, 179, 184, 186
Odinga, Raila 131–2, 136, 170–1, 198, 204
Oguda, Lawrence 60, 66
Okero, Isaac Omolo 105, 111–2, 123
Olindo, Perez 190
Oloitiptip, Stanley 111, 124, 143
Omamo, Bill 137, 156–7
Oneko, Achieng 48, 111
Operation Anvil 53
Organisation of African Unity (OAU) 17, 107, 121, 128–9, 133
Ouko, Robert 122, 124, 151, 158–63
  1986 Sessional Paper 151
  murder of 15, 19, 154, 158–63, 173
Oyugi, Hezekiah 135, 156–63, 179
  and the Ouko murder 159–63

Pattni, Kamlesh 186–7
Pinto, Pio 86
  murder of 15, 72, 87
poaching 108, 192–4
Pokot people 14, 27–8, 58, 135
Prevention of Corruption Act 173

queue-voting 51, 154–7, 171

Renison, Sir Patrick 71, 73
Reynolds, Reg 37, 39, 42
Rift Valley Operations Team see
    Ng'oroko
Rubia, Charles 157, 170–1

Saba Saba day riots 171
Safina Party 185, 193, 195–6, 201
Saitoti, George 160, 164, 170–1, 179,
    205–6
Seroney, Jean Marie (J.M.) 34, 42, 80,
    84–5, 93, 96, 105, 121
Sese Seko, Mobutu 17, 166, 200
Shikuku, Martin 15, 105, 121, 140–1,
    171, 199
Silverstein, Dr David 4, 15, 19, 142–3,
    174, 197–8
Singh, Harbans 144–6
smuggling 108, 122
Somaia, Ketan 156
Sondu 175, 181
Sumbeiywo, Elijah 133–5

Tambach 44–7, 50
Tameno, John ole 51, 59–60
Tarus, Gedion 38–42, 59–60
Tenai, Michael Kiptanui 16
Thatcher, Margaret 151, 167
Thuku, Harry 26, 46
Timboiwo 50–1, 55
Tipis, Justus ole 59–60, 70, 80, 83
Too, Noah arap 180
Toweet, Taitta 70–1, 74–5, 84, 95, 101,
    113
Troon, John 159, 161–2
Tugen people 1, 10, 25–30, 32, 49, 81
    see also Kalenjin

Wako, Amos 13
Wamwere, Koigi wa 131, 169, 193, 195
Ward, John 121, 180
Ward, Julie
    murder of 180
Western nations, influence of 22–3, 130,
    163–8, 184–6, 189
Western, Dr David 20, 192
World Bank 8, 22, 163, 183, 187, 189